INSCRIPTION AND MODERNITY

INSCRIPTION AND MODERNITY

From Wordsworth to Mandelstam

John MacKay

INDIANA UNIVERSITY PRESS

Bloomington and Indianapolis

This book was published with the assistance of the
Frederick W. Hilles Publication Fund of Yale University.

This book is a publication of

Indiana University Press
601 North Morton Street
Bloomington, IN 47404-3797 USA

http://iupress.indiana.edu

Telephone orders 800-842-6796
Fax orders 812-855-7931
Orders by e-mail iuporder@indiana.edu

The paper used in this publication meets the minimum requirements of American National Standard for Information Sciences—Permanence of Paper for Printed Library Materials, ANSI Z39.48-1984.

Manufactured in the United States of America

Library of Congress Cataloging-in-Publication Data

MacKay, John.
Inscription and modernity : from Wordsworth to Mandelstam / John MacKay.
p. cm.
Includes bibliographical references and index.
ISBN 0-253-34749-1 (cloth : alk. paper) 1. European poetry—20th century—History and criticism. 2. European poetry—19th century—History and criticism. 3. Lyric poetry—History and criticism. 4. Inscriptions. I. Title.
PN1271.M33 2006
809.1′034—dc22

2006005253

1 2 3 4 5 11 10 09 08 07 06

To my family, my friends, my teachers

And to Moira

Contents

Acknowledgments

This book followed a lengthy, complicated, and ultimately very rewarding path to publication. Accompanying me the entire way, and in every way, were my parents, Jack and Betty MacKay, my sister and brother, Pam and Peter, and their families. They are the most supportive and loving people in the world.

I started thinking about literature in high school, under the inspiring tutelage of Richard Knutson. Later I was fortunate to have the chance to study with a host of wonderful instructors in the English department at the University of British Columbia; and still later, with other excellent teachers, in Moscow, Heidelberg, Freiburg, Berlin, and Aix-en-Provence.

My early work on the manuscript was written under the direction of Geoffrey H. Hartman and Tomas Venclova. Tomas introduced me to the wonders of Russian poetry; Geoffrey's thinking on poetry and culture informs every line of this book. My work was materially abetted by generous grants from the Woodrow Wilson Foundation, the German Academic Exchange Service (DAAD), Yale College, and the Whitney Humanities Center.

One could not ask for a more intellectually stimulating and supportive environment than the one at Yale, and my work on this book was enriched by contacts with teachers and students in (at least) four fabulous Yale humanities departments. I offer the heartiest thanks to all my friends in Comparative Literature, English, and Film Studies for all the conversations over the years. To my incomparable colleagues, past and present, in the Department of Slavic Languages and Literatures—Vladimir Alexandrov, Harvey Goldblatt, Katerina Clark, Hilary Fink, Tomas Venclova, Kate Holland, Vladimir Golstein, Ilya Kliger, Robert Greenberg, Irina Dolgova, Constantine Muravnik, Julia Titus, Slobodan Novak, Karen von Kunes, Rita Lipson, Nike Agman, Carole McNish, Helen Stopkoski, and all our graduate and undergraduate students past and present—thanks for the support, the fellowship, and the fun.

To the many readers—some anonymous, some not—who contributed so much to my reworking of the manuscript, my sincerest thanks. Special thanks to Michael Holquist, Benjamin Harshav, David Quint, Karla Oeler, Elizabeth Papazian, James Morgan, Alex Woloch, Dan Friedman, and Fredric Jameson. A very special thanks to Paul Fry, whose wonderfully attentive reading had an especially animating and enriching effect on the final product. And my gratitude to Michael Lundell for his expert editorial assistance, and to Rita Bernhard for her superb copyediting.

Over the years I have had the good fortune to be involved with two of the most exciting extra-departmental intellectual settings at Yale. Thanks to all my former colleagues at the *Yale Journal of Criticism*—Laura Wexler, Sarah Winter, Maurice Wallace, Laura Frost, Elizabeth Dillon, Joanna Spiro, Jenny Davidson, Michael Trask, Ian Baucom, Amy Hungerford, and Peter Brooks—and past and present ones in the Working Group in Marxism and Cultural Theory at the Whitney Humanities Center—especially Michael Denning, Hazel Carby, Sumanth Gopinath, Michael Cohen, and Donald Brown—for their warmth, brilliance, and good humor. To Nigel Alderman, who bridged both groups, and from whom I have learned so much, very special thanks for the friendship, wit, and solidarity.

Thanks as well to Dudley Andrew, Michael Kerbel, Paul Bushkovitch, Laura Engelstein, Gloria Monti, Michael Thurston, Jared Stark, Masha Salazkina, Barrett Watten, Monika and Peter Greenleaf, Jeffrey Sammons, Manana Sikic, Heinrich von Staden, Alan Trachtenberg, Shoshana Felman, Sarah Wolf, Robert Bird and Farida, Katie Trumpener and Richard Maxwell, Amy Chazkel and Ala Alryyes, Kathryn Lachman and her family, Laurie Chreitzberg, Mark Moorman, David Ravvin and Sara Levine and family, Michele Hayden, Henry Pickford, Irit Pöschmann, Lennie Douglass, Bea Cavaliere, Mary Jane Stevens, Angelika Schriever, Larry and Shelley Shapiro and family, Anya Petanova and family, and, last but not least, Victor and Irina Golubchikov (and Liuda and Lyosha!). Special thanks to Raúl and Anamaría Fradinger and family, y todos los amigos en Argentina.

While preparing this manuscript, I might have starved to death, mentally and physically, without Debarati Sanyal. Caren Litherland, friend of friends and reader of readers, was there from the beginning. And to Charlie Musser, for everything, I raise a glass high.

Finally, to Moira, for all her love, support, wisdom, and patience: "Renaceré yo viento, / y aún te amaré mujer a ti." What would I do without you?

INSCRIPTION AND MODERNITY

Introduction: Inscription and Modernity

Stranger, if you passing meet me and desire to speak to me,
  why
Should you not speak to me?
And why should I not speak to you?

—Walt Whitman, "To You" (one of the "Inscriptions" at the beginning of *Leaves of Grass*)

Inscription, Description

This book on lyric poetry does not have as its focus or central method a number of the (important and entirely legitimate) questions and approaches commonly applied to lyric. It does not concern itself primarily with lyric subjectivity, biography, or the theme of "the poet" as such (although the relation of individual poets to historical setting gets considerable attention). It is not a philological or prosody-based study (although it does dwell on the later vicissitudes of a single, thoroughly traditional poetic mode, about which more in a moment); nor does it read poems primarily in terms of their particular formal patternings and unfoldings of rhyme, line, sound, and image (although none of these go neglected). It is not an empirically oriented historical or sociological survey, and takes a relatively immanent stance vis-à-vis its lyric objects; nonetheless, both factual detail and broader historical frameworks play vital roles in its readings. It does not focus exclusively on the problematic of lyric language, although theoretical and social issues pertaining to language are often touched upon; nor, finally, is it an intertextual exploration, although frequent use is made of the tools of intertextual analysis.

Instead, the book carries out a speculative investigation into how, in some corners of a few of the national traditions of European lyric (namely, the English, Russian, German, and French) from roughly 1750 to 1945, a specific if highly flexible lyric form both shapes and enables responses to and reflection upon the changing historical horizon—conventionally termed "modernity"—in which the poets lived and worked. This would seem a broad temporal and geographical range indeed, and the stakes of such an investigation need to be brought into clear view; thus this introduction is devoted to an exposition of my guiding terms—"lyric form" and "historical horizon"—and of the conceptual/methodological links between them.

The lyric form in question is what I call (for convenience) the "inscriptive mode," comprising a cluster of lyric types—in particular, the locodescriptive meditation and the monumental epitaph, but also less immediately classifiable kinds of lyric—that share ancient epigrammatic poetry as a generic subtext. By epigram—or inscription, for the terms are originally synonymous—I always mean to suggest both a literary norm and (as scholarship tells us) the ritual and quite physical practice out of which that norm emerged: specifically, sepulchral and other commemorative kinds of place-marking, such as burial markers along the road, votive sites, memorial carvings, and the like. As James Hutton argued (in one of his vast studies of the European reception of the Greek Anthology, our main source for the oldest epigrams), the memorializing function persisted in the more "literary" (as opposed to instrumentally ritual) epigrams, alongside sublimated allusions to the primal physicality and situatedness of inscription itself; he states that the early epigram is best described "simply as a brief elegy."[1]

In an important 1965 essay that serves here as my conceptual starting point, Geoffrey H. Hartman argued that a major strain within modern (at its origins, pre-Romantic/Romantic) lyric can be seen as emerging out of this epigrammatic poetry that itself issued from the Greek Anthology and was carried on through countless Alexandrian, Roman, and neo-Latin imitators into the European vernaculars right into the eighteenth century and beyond.[2] The emergence in question was a dialectical one, involving a subtle but radical innovation wrought upon the very shape of the epigram as it had been normalized during the Renaissance and earlier. We still tend to think of the epigrammatic poem as a pithy, lapidary verse capped by a strong final conceit or "point"; indeed, the vast majority of epigrams (whether sepulchral, amatory, satiric, or of some other type) offer just these snappy kinds of closure. Here is a translation of a Russian example, a satiric epitaph exhibiting an entirely typical speed of disclosure and condensation, sting, and symmetry-within-inversion:

> A nobleman he was
> And a noble's life he kept:
> Mornings he slept, ate and drank;
> Nights he drank, ate and slept.[3]

There were thousands of European poems like this (although not necessarily about noblemen), and their tradition obviously continues into the present.

Yet the researches of Hutton, Richard Reitzenstein, and others indicate that early Greek epigrammatic norms allowed not only for a multiplicity of subject matters but also for relatively open forms, in contrast to the later Latin and Latin-derived epigrams that tended to put greater stress (on the insistence of authorities like Martial and Julius Caesar Scaliger) upon wit and pointed finish.[4] This inscription, "On a Grove of Laurel," included in the Anthology and attributed to Anyte, the reputed founder of the pastoral epigram, gives some sense, I think, of what Hutton had in mind by the earlier "openness"; it can also be used to identify some of the key general features of the inscription-lyric:

> Whoe'er thou art, recline beneath the shade
> By never fading leaves of laurel made;
> And here awhile thy thirst securely slake
> With the pure beverage of the crystal lake:
> So shall your languid limbs, by toil opprest,
> And summer's burning heat, find needful rest,
> And renovation from the balmy power
> That stirs and breathes within this verdant bower.[5]

The poem opens with an apostrophe, or what I will call here an "appellation": a written imitation of voice, and specifically of the call (often with an imperative inflection) to some person, a *Viator,* (passerby), *passant,* or *proezzhii*—a seemingly generalized human figure ("whoe'er"), though surely assumed to be literate—who might not otherwise attend to the inscription. Anyte's inscription also makes subdued use of the "genius loci" topos—in which the voice of some "spirit of the place" (here, the "balmy power") either informs or directly "performs" the appellation—which Hartman has shown to persist, in attenuated or displaced form, in inscriptive lyrics of the late eighteenth century and beyond.[6] For my purposes, appellation as a poetic function is important in its outward directedness, its performance of an appeal to something heterogeneous to the inscription itself; through appellative gestures, the poem's mode of address and unfolding points (within the constraints of the convention) to sociality and connection.

Anyte's poem is also an invitation, and what it offers above all is a picture or icon, in this case of a highly conventional "pleasance" or *locus amoenus*. On this level, the poem is what I term a "projection": here, of a simple and temporary haven (to be enjoyed "awhile") that sets out a certain ideal disposition of the normally recalcitrant and indifferent realities of earth, sky, body, and natural growth. Even if the poem does not provoke us to "envision" ourselves resting our overexerted limbs, I would argue that it traces out or projects the space for just such an imaginative insertion. One might object that the clichéd quality of the "pleasance" topos should dissuade us from seeing it as bearing any referential intention, as anything other than the rhetorical device it is. Yet this conventionality can be granted, I suggest, without denying that, within its historical horizon, Anyte's trope still bears the trace of the particularity of the votive marker—located on who knows what bygone roadside—together with some reference to its contours and (to us, perhaps not fully recognizable) renovating effects.

It should be noted parenthetically that similar "iconic" conventions have long existed alongside and fused with efforts poetically to represent specific places (especially in the traditions of topographical poetry that go back at least to Ausonius's *Mosella* (371 C.E.).[7] But as M. H. Abrams and others have shown, the latter part of the eighteenth century saw the conventionality of the older topoi ever more frequently absorbed and transformed into verse that purports to describe (and incorporate response to) particular, "unique" localities; titles like "Inscription for a Seat by a Roadside, Half Way up a Steep Hill, Facing the South" (Wordsworth, 1796–97) are terse in comparison with many others of the period wherein the place is named and time of composition indicated with ponderous exactitude.[8] The familiar "locodescriptive" meditations that emerge from this localizing turn (including such important lyrics as Wordsworth's "Tintern Abbey" (1798),[9] Baratynskii's "Desolation" ("Zapustenie," about the poet's father and family estate [1834]), and even Hugo's great meditation on the Arc de Triomphe (1837) involve a complex interweave of extended description of place with the poet's responses, affective and intellectual, to that place.[10] "Localization" at once enlivens the verse with concrete detail and helps to turn quotidian (or regional, or [very often] national) spaces into objects of extended contemplation without necessitating recourse to the brittle allegorical machinery of the older *paysage moralisé*. The putative specificity of the place described also corresponds to a specific engagement of the poet with the place and its description, turning it into an occasion for subjective reflection, interpretation, recollection, and imaginative projection, for tracing out seams between public and private kinds of space.

At the same time, the Romantic-era locodescriptions often open with the conventional appellative or "animating gestures"[11] of inscription—"If from the public way you turn your steps" (Wordsworth's "Michael" [1800], l. 1) naturalizes the older "stay, traveler!"—thereby borrowing, overtly or surreptitiously, from the dignity (or the putative archaic energies) of Greek epigram. Topos, meditation, and attempts to represent place precisely and "realistically" are all thus co-present in the Romantic and post-Romantic inscriptive mode, and a preservation of the tension between these impulses—alternatively universalizing, localizing, personalizing—is vital if the poems are to be read dialectically.[12] In his discussion of locodescription in Wordsworth, Alan Liu draws a useful distinction between the "picturesque" as a relatively rigid conventional framing and laying out of descriptive details and the "locodescriptive moment" proper, which always introduces a sense of instability, motion, or incipient narrative into the apparent stasis of place-description. It is this kind of inscription of motion or desire into a scene—in Anyte, indicated by little more than the imperative tense of the verbs "recline" and "slake," and a promise ("so shall . . .")—that I mean by the term "projection."[13]

A related though ultimately very different feature is the indexical posture of Anyte's verse: the longed-for respite, we are told, can happen "*here,*" within "*this* verdant bower." I call this very common aspect of inscription its "corporeal" disposition, by which I mean its acknowledgment, tacit or not, of some (immensely mediated) material substrate on which it depends. Corporeality is a vital distinguishing feature of the inscriptive mode (Hartman defines inscription as "any verse conscious of the place on which it [is] written"),[14] and I will say much more about it in the pages that follow. Suffice it to note for the moment that Anyte's themes of rest, of bodily rejuvenation, unite here with the indexical "here" and "this" to intimate a space of respite not only from physical but perhaps from mental labor as well: a kind of connectedness of body and place that might draw the "toiler" out of language and its alienated exertions toward the physical "here" as such.

Finally (and to reconnect with the theme of appellation), the poem closes with a reference to divinity—a *legitimating* reference to the superhuman "balmy power" of laurel, beloved of Apollo—that lifts the otherwise insignificant scene of the poem into contact with the sources of all significance. Anyte, while keeping her inscription open to description and development, manages a pithy finish as well, one that closes a circle between the physical place and its metaphysical, ideal validation (a "point" the translator makes through the rhyme "power-bower"). We see here the capacity of the "genius loci" myth both to imply audience and to suggest foundations: it functions *appellatively* to issue (in Hartman's words) a "call from a monument in the landscape or from the landscape itself," and as *legitimation* to make the poet "feel he is on significant ground."[15]

Of these four features constitutive of the inscriptive mode—appellation (the "call" for attention), projection (the articulation of space within language), corporeality (the effort of language to gesture outside itself), and legitimation—it is the last that becomes especially problematic as the epigrammatic tradition moves into the eighteenth century and beyond, and especially important for the readings I will perform here. Epigrammatic closure depends upon some kind of legitimating machinery in order to take place confidently and effectively: some sense of order, of what is worthy and (as in our Russian example) what is not; a horizon of propriety that enables the point to be put in its place.

The problem of "finding the point," and the anxiety (or exhilaration) at its absence, has been related both to a reemergence of the earlier, relatively un-pointed Greek inscription in the late eighteenth century and to new forces (economic, social, cultural) that began to unsettle old orders of all kinds. In his study of French epigram, Hutton noted a sharp improvement in the reputation of the Greek Anthology in France around 1750, and suggested that,

> as the social forces that had upheld French Classicism began to be undermined, a feeling of uncertainty too may have suggested a return to something not unlike the imitation of the ancients that had preceded the [French] Classical period.[16]

Hutton does not specify the "social forces" he has in mind, but the rise of skeptical and anticlerical philosophies, waning absolutist power, decreasing peasant docility, and a concomitant burgeoning of commerce are surely among the relevant factors.[17] The new Hellenic turn culminated first in "the extravagant cult of the [individualist] Plutarchan hero both before and after the Revolution," and more consequently in André Chénier's turn to the Anthology in an effort to shake off "classical" (and aristocratic) convention in pursuit of models for what he termed (independently of Friedrich Schiller) "the naïve."[18] Within the English framework, Hartman identified Mark Akenside's inscriptions of the 1750s and 1760s, with their brevity, "relative freedom from point" and "freedom from obtrusive personification," as important precursors to the more extended and supple Romantic inscriptive lyrics.[19] At the same time, a certain melancholy, "secularized" skepticism about the older inscriptive machinery is betrayed by Akenside in his last inscription when he inverts "the pattern in which the genius loci calls to the stranger," instead invoking "in his lonely anxiety for inspiration . . . the absent Muses":

> From what loved haunt
> Shall I expect you?[20]

A key word for thinking about the modern inscription is certainly "loss": loss of metaphysical certainty, loss of legitimacy, but also loss of prior limitations and prescriptions. What I will argue is that, from the late eighteenth century on, important value structures underpinning earlier epigram—social, religious, philosophical, and others—fall into question, with a concomitant and perceptible intensification of anxiety in the verse (Hartman writes that "Akenside's sense of alienation is nothing as sharp as that of the Romantics").[21] This leads in turn, and inevitably, to attempts to fill the void or to *resist* its being filled by some undesirable content: this, whether through a search for alternative sources of legitimacy or apologetic reassertion of the old or by some radical evasion of power, "balmy" or otherwise. This last option, it should be noted, would seem to be unavailable, inasmuch as it would deny the inscription any grounding for its (appellative) voice, and condemn it to a kind of radical isolation. It is this fear—the fear of a lack of audience—that leads the poets to try on different "genii," to find different rationales of appeal to "passersby" who, within modernity, run past ever more swiftly and along ever more unpredictable trajectories. The poets, of course, are passersby themselves; the relationship of the poet to the "favorite spot" can only be *"perverse,"* although it also must be made "vital" (but how?) in order to succeed.[22]

Intersection and Unevenness

The field in which this success will or will not happen I have already termed "modernity"; it will prove useful now to turn, in a rather more focused way, not to the whole question of modernity but to the way I propose to use the concept as a historicizing frame for understanding perceptible changes in the inscriptive mode over time.

My sense of modernity as a period-category derives directly from the "conjunctural" definition provided by the historian Perry Anderson in his well-known review of Marshall Berman's seminal book *All That Is Solid Melts into Air.*[23] Writing broadly of twentieth-century European modernism as an epoch stretching roughly from 1890 to the end of World War II,[24] Anderson offers three coordinates of change and reaction: the hardening of academicism in the arts, the appearance of new technologies, and what he calls "the imaginative proximity of social revolution."[25] Plotted together as points of a triangle, these coordinates demarcate a complex field of potentialities and allegiances within which modernist artists variously defined their practice: Futurist or Scythian, neo-Classic or Dada, fascist or communist.

Anderson's periodizing heuristic facilitates a more open kind of historicization of artworks—more open, that is, than methods linking moments in poems to specific biographical anecdotes, to "events," or to contemporary discursive practices. (Although these are undoubtedly valuable approaches, and later I return more pointedly to the question of how my own manner differs from them.) It will be evident, however, that I modify Anderson's scheme in three varyingly significant ways. First, I tend to emphasize, perhaps even more strongly than he does, that each "point" on the triangle is in fact split into unevenly developed, powerfully interacting factions. Thus, throughout the modern period, peasant, aristocratic, "academic," and "mass-cultural" streams coexist in ever varying ratios; "advanced" technology purrs alongside horse-drawn carriages and one-bottomed plows; and massive revolutionary movements occupy a single social space with both "old regime" and bourgeois elements. This is only a matter of emphasis, however, and I subscribe to the account Anderson gives of the efficacy of the imaginative "force field" of modernity, studded as it is by unevenness, and therefore with possibility:

> [T]he persistence of the "*anciens régimes,*" and the academicism concomitant with them, provided a critical range of cultural values *against which* insurgent forms of art could measure themselves, but also *in terms of which* they could partly articulate themselves. Without the common adversary of official academicism, the wide span of new aesthetic practices have little or no unity: their tension with the established or consecrated canons in front of them is constitutive of their definition as such. [. . .] At the same time, for a different kind of "modernist" sensibility, the energies and attractions of a new machine age were a powerful imaginative stimulus: one reflected, patently enough, in Parisian cubism, Italian futurism or Russian constructivism. The condition of this interest, however, was the abstraction of techniques and artifacts from the social relations of production that were generating them. [. . .] Finally, the haze of social revolution drifting across the horizon of this epoch gave it much of its apocalyptic light for those currents of modernism most unremittingly and violently radical in their rejection of the social order as a whole[.] European modernism [. . .] arose at the intersection between a semi-aristocratic ruling order, a semi-industrialized capitalist economy, and a semi-emergent, or -insurgent, labor movement.[26]

Second, I place greater stress on the consideration of a very broad fourth category: that of modernization itself (particularly mass production, education, transport, and media), with its twin movements of wide-ranging dissemination (or what some ideologies call "democratization") of cultural and other resources, and the simultaneous standardizing or leveling of local idiosyncrasies. There is an implicit question being asked through the entire period about the eventual absoluteness and ubiquity of modernization, about the extent to which it could or could not coexist with, or even generate, other "non-modern" (sometimes "rebarbarized") modes of existence.[27] (Historians, of course, have repeatedly demonstrated how ideologies of "development" can exacerbate, rather than eradicate, uneven development.)[28] What is finally at issue here is the capacity of modernization for absorption, transformation, and destruction, in the course of giving modernity its "content"; it is an issue lying transversely across all three "points" but not quite coinciding with any one of them.[29]

My third alteration is more consequential, for I follow Marshall Berman in extending the "modern" period considerably further into the past than Anderson does. Indeed, it seems legitimate to locate the emergence of modernity as longue durée at least as far back as the days of Genoese and Dutch mercantile capitalism, following the developmental model provided by Giovanni Arrighi in *The Long Twentieth Century.*[30] A study like Arrighi's, which traces out the large dynamics by and within which the modern "world" was fashioned, is no doubt an ideal conceptual starting point on which to base a truly materialist "world/comparative literature."[31] That, however, is *another* periodization, and another project. Lacking erudition enough, and time, for such an enterprise, I discuss a briefer modernity (a late "phase," if you will), a period centering roughly around three revolutionary moments—this, partially because of the convenient punctuality of these upheavals relative to more gradually emerging "events" in the scientific and cultural fields. As far as inscriptive lyric poetry is concerned, I will argue that the roots of some later writing designated as modernist are to be found in the Romantic (and pre-Romantic) period, a time quite clearly characterized by its own triangulation of revolutionary political, technological, and cultural forces.

Thus, for the purposes of this book, the beginnings of the modern will be centered, conventionally enough, on 1789, with the surrounding industrial, scientific, and social-economic developments vitally implicated (and informed by an awareness of crucial earlier foundational modernizations, like the one initiated by Peter I in Russia). The second phase (the focus of chapter 2) finds its axis around the events of 1830, 1848, 1871, but including in its horizon such central events as the rise of modern urban culture and the "emancipation" on a colossal scale of bondsmen in both the Old and New Worlds. The last phase (to which chapters 3 and 4 are devoted) is centered on the period stretching roughly from 1905 through the defining political event of the twentieth century, the 1917 Russian Revolution, along with the various and cataclysmic effects of that upheaval.

These phases, in my treatment, act as horizons for the poetic imagination rather than as clusters of discrete events to be correlated with moments in poems; thus the empirical historical field, although by no means ignored, is not the main object of my attention here. Nor by any means are all the poets addressed here assumed to be political radicals of whatever stripe: modernity is neither more nor less than the unstable space in which these authors live, and, as such, conditions their language and their sense of audience, indelibly etching a social background into the most apparently hermetic work.[32] Rather, some of the specific poetic achievements of figures like Shelley, Lamartine, and Mandelstam are read in terms of the changing horizon of modernity, both as it is symptomatically registered in the poetry—in its anxieties over legitimation and audience—and as the poetry articulates some active response to those changes. As literary history, the present book on the inscriptive mode is in part the beginning of an argument for regarding poetic writing from "Romanticism" through "(twentieth-century) Modernism proper" as stages of a single long modern period in poetry, straddled by "pre-" and (more problematically) "post-modern" modalities that remain to be pinpointed and defined.

Before doing that, however, the sheer length of the period under consideration, and the range of literatures treated (English, French, German, Russian), no doubt require some additional justification. Certainly, my periodization and choice of texts is not only a construction but is constrained and limited by my linguistic abilities, historical knowledge, and many other factors (such as "taste," no doubt). What I present is nothing like a full-scale survey of inscriptive poetry across 150–200 years and in four languages but rather a series of cross-sections taken at salient historical moments, and which help to reveal something about how this history shapes the ancient inscription, on the levels of both form and content, as it passes through times and places very different from the time and place in which it presumably originated. These times and places all differ from one another as well, which is why I try to keep in mind local-national historical (and literary historical) specificities as vital mediating factors, even as a common (if diversely manifested) modernity is postulated as a shared horizon.

In *The Political Unconscious,* Fredric Jameson very usefully distinguishes between three general approaches to the historicization of texts, differing from one another in terms of the time range and the degree of empirical (historical) specificity proper to them.[33] The first horizon, termed the *political,* reads the text as a response to a relatively punctual historical moment, situation, or conjuncture—in Jameson's terms, as "symbolic act." (An example might be Jameson's own allegorical reading of Spielberg's film *Jaws* as an imaginary "resolution" of a very real and conflictual social process—the rapid encroachment of techno-bureaucratic corporate power upon local economies—occurring during the crisis decade of the 1970s in the U.S.)[34] The second level is the *social,* and treats texts as precipitating out of larger class-inflected discursive units (called "ideologemes") that structure thought and practice over a longer haul; classically ideologematic would be our familiar categories of "globalization," "terrorism," or (to take an example from the French Revolutionary period and after) "liberté, fraternité, égalité."[35] The third horizon is the *historical* proper, in which reading embeds the text not into political conflicts that unfold over a short duration (as with the "symbolic act") but rather into the much more stable and slowly changing social and economic formations or "modes of production"—feudal, patriarchal, aristocratic, capitalist, artisanal, and so on, with all their various possible internal stages and nuances—whose co-present and conflicting pressures make themselves felt on the most durable literary forms, up to and including the emergence or disappearance of those forms:

> Every social formation of historically existing society has in fact consisted in the overlay and structural coexistence of several modes of production all at once, including vestiges and survivals of older modes of production, now as anticipatory tendencies which are potentially inconsistent with the existing system but have not yet generated an autonomous space of their own. . . . The triumphant moment in which a new *systemic dominant* gains ascendancy is therefore only the diachronic manifestation of a constant struggle over the perpetuation and reproduction of its dominance.[36]

Reading within this third horizon, in which the text is construed as "a field of force in which the dynamics of sign systems of several distinct modes of production can be registered and apprehended,"[37] involves attending to what Jameson calls the "ideology of form," and it is on this level that my readings here of the inscriptive mode are carried out. How else, indeed, to chart the vicissitudes of an ancient form like this one but across a relatively longue dureé and as a palimpsest of various systemic forces?

The forces I will be mentioning range from the deracinations wrought by enclosure in England to the effects of skeptical and scientific thought (in struggle with putatively unenlightened modes of apprehending the world) to the perseverance of peasant ways to Stalinist "socialist construction."

And owing in part to this range, I would not want to name the "dominant" force with any term more specific than "modernization." At the same time, however (and to move slowly back to poetry proper), it seems necessary to specify, if only in a sketchy and preliminary way, the corresponding *subdominant* or driving preoccupation characteristic of cultural production itself within the period. This subdominant, which has to be distinguished from any ubiquitous norm or set of formal features, I would identify (following many others) as *aesthetic education:* the notion, first articulated clearly in Schiller's time, that in an age of modernization, "art is supposed to become effective in place of religion as the unifying power, because it is understood to be a 'form of communication' that enters into the intersubjective relationships between people."[38] For Schiller (as is well known), art was to achieve this communicative function, on the one hand, by dint of reconstituting, if only at moments, the union of thought and sensual experience—a unity that supposedly characterized the work experiences of preindustrial artisanal laborers, for example—that modernization had divided into incommensurable fragments. At the same time, this new unification was not to carry with it the same kind of coercive necessity that was increasingly typical of the way both the rationalized world of abstract social order and the explosive proliferation of new material things and stimuli were imposing themselves upon human consciousness. Because art participates equally in both the formal and material "modes of legislation,"[39] it can house a third mode ("play") in which the combining of various forms and contents happens (in artworks and in the imagination) unconstrained by either hubristic thought or by blind material contingency—thus providing a kind of space for developing the subjective habits necessary for a person living within modernity: that is, for someone at once *free* and *citizen.*[40]

I rehearse all this, on the one hand, because, as Jacques Rancière has recently shown, Schiller's "originary scene" of aesthetic education can be read as having set the terms for a hugely various set of trajectories for modern art—from the historicized configuration of artworks within museum and survey course settings to political or "totalitarian" *Gesamtkunstwerke* to the apparently implacable separatism of much "modernism"—that can nonetheless converge toward some notion of aesthetic education.[41] As far as inscriptive poetry goes, Schiller's postulate not only offers a broad schema for thinking about the historical predicament faced by poetry (and other art) but also suggests something about how the resources of the inscriptive mode, and especially its (formal) projections and (material) corporealizations, might be mustered educatively, to draw a community into its circuit. Thus I will be concerned here with the way in which the four central features of the inscriptive mode are used and work together to attempt some kind of attachment of poem to audience and, by extension, to the social as such.[42] (Indeed, if one could name a hidden "ideologeme" under investigation here, it would probably have to be the pseudo-notion of "the People," as read through poetic form.)

It needs to be added that, all their efforts at self-contained or immanent projection of community notwithstanding, the poems we will analyze make frequent recourse—perhaps inevitable recourse—to sources of legitimacy actually available within modernity, including powerful residues from earlier social formations. Appellation, to be heard, requires some kind of legitimating backup, be it Apollo, a national spirit (or imperative), an ethical scruple, a collective project, or what have you; and poets, themselves situated in some way, put these ideologies to use in fashioning their own. What Hartman calls the (regrettable) "moralizing strain" in the Romantic inscription will be taken here as a basic part, however sublimated or displaced, of modern inscriptive poetry generally, as one of the ways the inscription tries to inscribe itself into the social.[43] (Indeed, my earlier suggestion of a "void" at the center of the modern inscription is misleading to the extent that it suggests that structure and value vanish rather than proliferate unimaginably within modernity.) At the same time, the terrifying (or liberating) possibility of a total retraction of any "pointing power," of the inscriptive surface as malleable even unto blankness, is permanent and should be taken as a constant hypothetical backdrop to the readings I will perform.

As a consequence, we will be paying attention to the enormously subtle didacticism of inscriptive poetry, even (or especially) in poems that might seem to have no didactic moment. There is a reason why "modernity" is the great period of *manifesta,* poetic and otherwise. At base is an uncertainty about audience but also often a hope, born of uncertainty, that that audience might in some way be shaped by poetry, or be interested in being shaped by it, and in shaping it in turn:

> [T]he Poems in these volumes will be found distinguished at least by one mark of difference, that each of them has a worthy purpose. Not that I mean to say, that I always began to write with a distinct purpose formally conceived; but I believe that my habits of meditation have so formed my feelings, as that my descriptions of such objects as strongly excite those feelings, will be found to carry along with them a purpose. [. . .] For our continued influxes of feeling are modified and directed by our thoughts, which are indeed the representatives of all our past feelings; and, as by contemplating the relation of these general representatives to each other we discover what is really important to men, so, by the repetition and

> continuance of this act, our feelings will be connected with important subjects, till at length, if we be originally possessed of much sensibility, such habits of mind will be produced, that, by obeying blindly and mechanically the impulses of those habits, we shall describe objects, and utter sentiments, of such a nature and in such connection with each other, that the understanding of the being to whom we address ourselves, if he be in a healthful state of association, must necessarily be in some degree enlightened, and his affections ameliorated.[44]

"What is really important to man" is Wordsworth's term here for legitimation, and it remains something to be discovered (rather than assumed), and then somehow communicated. The discovery, however, is possible for Wordsworth, and in this passage he lays out (in familiar "associationist" language) how the "important subjects" are to be distilled out of the "continued influxes of feeling"—an apparently Schillerian process of "relating" sensation and thought, the province here of the poet— and how these subjects might then find representational form in descriptions and utterances. While this contemplative relating seems a more or less spontaneous matter (given the right endowment of "sensibility," of course), the passage from distillation to representation is clearly enabled by a kind of discipline: "repetition and continuance" of the trajectory of contemplation, reinforced by further obedience, now blind and mechanical, of "impulses" that have already, indeed, become "habits." As habit or "general representative," these discoveries pass more readily into representation where, at the moment of address, they are communicated with the force of an imperative ("he . . . must necessarily be in some degree enlightened"). Without any exploitation of "triviality and meanness," "false refinement," "arbitrary innovation," or "extraordinary incident,"[45] Wordsworth proposes to discover a new, ameliorative basis for sociality grounded in a discipline of contemplation and purification. His faith, that the poet's "creative process" will lead to something sharable, is grounded in the idea that there are others like him (i.e., in "healthful states of association"), and, by extension, that those others, too, are undergoing the same processes of relating, distillation, and discipline; for them, his poetic descriptions and utterances might have a special role to play.

Aesthetic education as outlined here implies the existence and reproduction of a community, almost a kind of quasi-professional group ranged against other forces explicitly seen by Wordsworth as bad products of social change,[46] and as offering an alternative kind of aesthetic education that the poet can read only as a reduction of the mind to "savage torpor." To offset these forces a kind of counterviolence is required: a discipline of thinking, feeling, remembering, writing, and reading whose basic validation is offered by the poet, the discoverer of really "important things." Yet, in the end (and for all that he emphasizes discrimination and selection), Wordsworth does presume that the discoveries of poets and poetic readers will have something like universal validity. Despite the need for repetition, the process of distillation has an end, and its product will prove accessible to all who pass by; aesthetic distinction is about distinguishing "gross and violent" from healthful writing, not between (as earlier) vulgar and polite souls.[47] (At the same time, the poet's associationism and desire to enact a "worthy purpose" blurs the line between soul and text—a blurring necessary to any regime of aesthetic education.)

These are the kinds of aspirations—I could have selected from many other prefaces and *manifesta*—that I have in mind when I speak of the ideology of aesthetic education as a cultural subdominant within modernity, one that in many ways persists. In relation to my larger historical frame, however, I will contend here that the "ameliorative" (or otherwise transformative) hopes placed upon aesthetic education, always under profound stress, suffered an epochal setback in Europe during the period Eric Hobsbawm terms the "Age of Catastrophe" (roughly, 1914 to 1945).[48] After the murderous disappointments of those years—the world wars, Stalinism, the Holocaust—notions of the generally "human" (on which inscriptive poetry had often depended in order to fashion some sort of appellation) were compromised beyond renovation. Meanwhile, modernizing technological, state, and economic forces established, in the midst of modernity's seeming "flux," new value structures of great solidity and penetration, buttressed in no small way by culture itself. In this newly saturated environment, there could no longer be any question of the chances of poetry adopting a significant, independent, socially constructive role.[49] Some residual promise of aesthetic education as such did survive, of course, but largely in either dispersed "underground" or (conversely, and much more ubiquitously) academicized forms.

Very schematically, this is the complex post-1945 situation which I call here "postmodern"; it acts unevenly to terminate the main period I deal with, although not epigram and inscription as such—obviously. Rather, the change pertains to those *conditions* of anxious openness under which the modern, "unpointed" inscriptive mode emerged.[50] At the same time (and not wanting to engage in the deeply tedious practice of assigning punctual beginnings and ends to "poetic modernity"), in my readings I try to suggest anticipations of postmodernity within modern inscriptive lyric, and residues of the earlier moment in the later.

A Work Which Is Not Here

Immense nausée des affiches
[Immense nausea of posters].
—Baudelaire, "Mon coeur mis a nu" ["My heart laid bare"]

How does all this help us to read poems? I will return at the end of this introduction to the larger question of how "modernity" helps us read "the inscriptive mode," and vice versa. For the moment, however, it is no doubt heuristically necessary to find specific types of inscriptive poetry that in some way express the broad historical conjunctures framing our discussion. Operating very much in the hypothetical mode, I will now give examples of poems, calibrated around three types of inscriptive marking (the epitaph, the modern inscription proper, and the commercial sign) that roughly correspond to the shifts in consciousness and sense of agency I am associating with the modern, pre-modern, and postmodern. The modern inscriptive mode is best seen, I will argue, as unevenly and uneasily lodged between two contrary fields of possibility. These are the pre-Enlightenment world, structured by relatively stable religious and class categories, and the postmodern, in which the malleability and fertile precariousness that characterized the earlier, modern moment have hardened (relatively) into new orders. Again, I regard these phases as rather messily overlapping and interacting, largely because the historical processes shaping them rarely find neat startups or terminations. The phases are not, for all that, entirely indistinguishable from one another.

Epitaph

First, to illustrate briefly the pre-modern moment, consider this conventionally *epitaphic* poem by Ben Jonson, engraved on a tablet in the Sonning Church, Berkshire, and commemorating a child (Elizabeth Chute) who died on May 18, 1627:

What Beautie would have lovely stilde,
What manners prettie, Nature milde,
What wonder perfect, all were fil'd,
Upon record in this blest child.
  And, till the comming of the Soule
  To fetch the flesh, we keepe the Rowle.[51]

The poem is touching, relatively typical of the form, and usefully reflective on its own function. Terse, deictic ("*this* blest child"), the verse stands there, armed with dogma, like a taciturn guardian—but of what? The inscription does not tell a story but rather tells of what might have been a story; the poem is the engraved and sealed "Rowle" of the latent life or "Soule," the potentialities "all [...] fil'd / Upon record in this blest child." Here we distantly sense the affinity of the epitaph for charms and amulets and life-giving utterances, with words that have a more-than-memorial, *magical* function—although the "unrolling" of this record has to wait upon the trumpets of apocalypse, to be sure, and no amount of poetizing can speed *that* up. Yet the poem's "point" and closure are meant to assure that writing (a practice directly alluded to in the end words "stilde," "fil'd," "Rowle") will indeed be able to contain and archive the lost and precious content ("child," "milde," "Soule").

The words themselves are said to have the quality of latency or (better) prematurity, like a perpetual preparation for testimony. They provide less an account of the dead girl's qualities—which remain, after all, hypothetical and abstract (beauty, manners, mildness)—than an affirmation and protection of them, a protection verging on concealment.[52] The paradoxical argument for the blessing imparted by (especially *early*) death—that a life unlived is a life that remains pure—is familiar from the epitaph tradition, and appears in Jonson's famous lyrics on the deaths of his first son and (here) daughter:

> At sixe moneths end, shee parted hence
> With safetie of her innocence [....] (p. 11)

The verse also has a truly lapidary physicality that seems almost to call for some kind of stony inscriptive surface. The first four lines as a group are given an unusual, rocklike solidity through the strong end rhymes, the steady repetitions of the "What," the lapidary caesuras and the internal rhymes or near rhymes (Beautie/lovely/prettie; blest/fetch/flesh). Corporeality finds precise and moving expression here on the level of signification as well, in so far as the poem banishes all quality from the blest child's "flesh," opening a space of "*what would have been*" between the child as *living* and the child as *thing*.[53]

Yet the routes outward from the predicament of mortality are all too clearly delimited here: the height at which mortality can be viewed is the Christian God's (unattainable) height, and no other mode of contemplating the dead is or could be entertained. It is precisely this sense of the suspension of the older epitaphic inscription within a solution of religious (or other) certainty that distinguishes it from the later, more exposed inscription that began to appear in the late eighteenth century.[54] With the closure (or at least serious obstruction) of the religious pathway for the "Soule" within the modern period, other anxieties, and therefore possibilities, emerge, especially with regard to the poet's sense of his or her own auditorium.

Inscription

Thus the kind of "place-marking" most important here will be the *inscription* pure and simple, withdrawn from the sphere of value that gives the traditional epitaph and Latin-derived epigrams their meaning. Inscription borrows, of course, on the attention-grabbing rhetorical function of the epitaph—the call to stop and heed—while abjuring, not unproblematically, the divine authority standing behind the older, more properly epitaphic declaration.[55]

As I have already mentioned, Wordsworth's "Michael: A Pastoral Poem" (1800), while certainly a narrative poem of moderate length, announces its structural rootedness in inscription through its opening address, complete with place-name, to a "passerby":

> If from the public way you turn your steps
> Up the tumultuous brook of Green-head Ghyll. . . .[56]

Again, it is the inscription's centering function that is crucial: the familiar "Halt, Traveller!" gathers together the writer, the wished-for reader, and the commemorated object into a circuit. By disseminating a story—"Go, Traveller!"—it creates (ideally) a protective atmosphere of attention and memory:

> Nor should I have made mention of this Dell
> But for one object which you might pass by,
> Might see and notice not. Beside the brook
> Appears a straggling heap of unhewn stones!
> And to that simple object appertains
> A story—unenriched with strange events,
> Yet not unfit, I deem, for the fireside,
> Or for the summer shade. (ll. 14–21)

Tacitly, the inscription announces (through its very "call") that it cannot generate this atmosphere by itself; it is constitutionally incomplete, and depends upon whole and living bodies for fulfillment. Indeed, expanding on Yuri Lotman's speculations on the "romantic fragment," we might go on to say that the inscription presents itself as a fragment in order to *request,* tacitly, a community of interest, centered on the palpable traces that make up the place. The fragmentary quality of the inscription implies, that is, some additional apparatus of attention and transmission.[57] (By analogy, readers would then become, in a very Mandelstamian metaphor, an extension of the *stone* on which, classically, the original is inscribed—though much less malleable and more unpredictable, to be sure.)

But who, if anyone, is summoned by the inscription's call? The secular inscription faces an enormous, unpredictable openness of response, ranging (in its unhappy variants) from total neglect to (far less likely) an overwhelming, suffocating clatter. (Of course, poets can produce clatter as well, in the absence of a sounding board; it seems harder, however, to abjure the appeal of "extraordinary incident," to write of the lowly *as* lowly, to refuse all idolatry. How can what is ignored, idiosyncratic, marginal, or downtrodden command interest without attributing to it some kind of latent, apocalyptic power, or without setting up some kind of quasi-religious ritual around it?) Much inscriptive poetry registers an awareness of this risk, and incorporates it as proviso, as defense or sense of preparation.

Although the appellation is initially the occasion for locodescription (of the "hidden valley" in its "utter solitude" [ll. 8, 13]), it leads us quietly to a single object that acts as the intermediary between the projected place (still existent, from what the poet tells us) and the much fuller narrative projection of the vanished life of Michael's family in the valley.[58] That powerful narrative—of the frugality and hard work of the shepherd Michael and his "Helpmate," of the belated birth of their much-loved son, Luke, and Luke's upbringing, of Michael's unexpected financial distress (the consequence of being bond "in surety" to a nephew assailed by "unforeseen misfortunes" [l. 213]), Michael's difficult decision to send Luke to work with a "kinsman" in the city, and of Luke's eventual fall into dissipation and self-exile—has long been absorbed into that circuit of response we know as the English canon. With not atypical frankness, Wordsworth is quite explicit about his "target audience" for this appellation:

> It was the first
> Of those domestic tales that spake to me
> Of Shepherds, dwellers in the valleys, men
> Whom I already loved;—not verily
> For their own sakes, but for the fields and hills
> Where was their occupation and abode.
> And hence this Tale, while I was yet a Boy
> Careless of books, yet having felt the power
> Of Nature, by the gentle agency
> Of natural objects, led me on to feel
> For passions that were not my own, and think

(At random and imperfectly indeed)
On man, the heart of man, and human life.
Therefore, although it be a history
Homely and rude, I will relate the same
For the delight of a few natural hearts;
And, with yet fonder feeling, for the sake
Of youthful Poets, who among these hills
Will be my second self when I am gone. (ll. 21–39)

As David Simpson has argued, Wordsworth places the actual shepherd world inhabited by Michael and his like definitively in the past.[59] Although "natural hearts" is appropriately vague, one cannot but feel that shepherds (whose "occupation and abode" *was* [not *is*] in the "fields and hills") are not among those being appealed to here, and certainly not shepherds as men suffering from the concrete problems—financial insecurity, indebtedness, and the threat of losing property, livelihood, and family—endured to the fullest extent by Michael. While those problems, as Simpson and others have shown, were probably part of Wordsworth's own present, the poet, confident in his ability to represent the moral essence of "passions not his own" and convinced of their importance, opts for the posterity of aesthetic education rather than for a more local audience (or alliance).

This said, we notice immediately a strange conjuncture, for the poet places *himself* in the past just as he does Michael: he is writing for those "youthful Poets who among these hills / Will be my second self when I am gone." The conjuncture has a more important and reflexive layer, for the poet's hero similarly situates Luke *retrospectively* when he asks his son to inaugurate their "covenant" (l. 414) in a primitive inscriptive act:

Lay now the corner-stone,
As I requested; and hereafter, Luke,
When thou art gone away, should evil men
Be thy companions, think of me, my Son,
And of this moment. . . . (ll. 403–407)

"Going away" is a spatial figure, and though the losses it connotes are thoroughly temporal, we would do well for the moment to stick to the primary or "literal" meaning of separation and de-unification. For Michael, separation from Luke means not only the certain loss of support but also the possible loss of posterity and property;[60] for Luke, separation would seem to imply not only a sudden absence of domestic security but also the solid, legitimating context of family and home. Wordsworth, it would seem at first glance, occupies a position analogous to Michael's, inasmuch as he also depends on his poetic progeny in order to have a future; meanwhile, that progeny ("natural hearts," "youthful Poets") would (Luke-like) seem to require something of the older poet's legacy of natural "power" processed through sympathetic meditation—particularly at a moment when that nature is undergoing "great changes" (l. 478)—in order to claim the title of poet for themselves. The loss, in both cases what we might call a loss of *immediacy,* is felt to be inevitable despite being distantly perceived as the consequence of historical change; thus the attempt to find some sort of compensatory structure seems equally necessary.

In both cases, that compensatory structure is an inscription, and at the heart of the poem is the question of why one inscription (Michael's) did not work, and why the other ("Michael" itself) should not also fail. Michael's stone, laid by his son Luke's "own hands," is intended as a familial *omphalos,* connecting past, present, and future generations. In this way, the theme of the social ambition of inscription is announced but displaced onto Michael's hopes for his and his son's "work," just as Luke is about to leave for the city:

> ". . . amid all fear
> And all temptation, Luke, I pray that thou
> May'st bear in mind the life thy Fathers lived,
> Who, being innocent, did for that cause
> Bestir them in good deeds. Now, fare thee well—
> When thou return'st, thou in this place wilt see
> A work which is not here: a covenant
> 'Twill be between us; but, whatever fate
> Befal thee, I shall love thee to the last,
> And bear thy memory with me to the grave." (ll. 408–17)

There is both anxiety and defiance in Michael's act here. By attempting to link Luke's growth (in the urban setting) to his earlier lifeworld, he also refuses any pure subsumption of rural ways into modernizing innovations. At the same time, despite his illiteracy, Michael senses the limitations of the country:

> "If here [Luke] stay,
> What can be done? Where every one is poor,
> What can be gained?" (ll. 253–55)

And in assuring Luke that his experiences have been in no way limited by the shepherd's life ("in us the old and young / Have played together, nor with me didst thou / Lack any pleasure which a boy can know" [ll. 354–55]), Michael movingly (because helplessly) conjures up the opposite possibility that Luke might not, indeed, be satisfied with his existing "bonds." Yet Michael would that Luke bore in mind both "the life [his] Fathers lived" (l. 410) and the strenuous efforts taken to disentail previously "burthened" land (l. 374).

Michael tries to forge these fragile "links of love" (l. 401) through a modified act of covenanting. His very improvisation of a ritual, his *poem* I suggest, is designed to lift the burden of forgetfulness, override the dreaded discontinuity. The "principle of repetition," which James Chandler has identified as central to Wordsworth's political/poetic worldview, also involves (here at any rate) a sort of community-sustaining innovation, for all the archaic appearance of stone laying.[61] Michael-the-poet lets his son go but not without projecting a vision of some newly forged connection that would resist the reductions of either rural stasis or urban alienation, and without depending on religious rhetoric.[62] Unable to contend with the "dissolute" energies of the city or Luke's weakness of character (or both), his inscription fails to sustain that connection to Luke and, by extension, to sustain the family and property. It fails, clearly enough, because it is too localized, and is so in two respects: it is a physically isolated gesture (made in an "utter solitude") and has as its addressee a single, all-too-fallible human. As an inscription, the stone laying lacks a more broadly sharable articulation—the latter is what the poet provides us with—although its physical, hyper-localized specificity has other potential advantages we will need to consider more closely in a moment.

It is obvious, I think, that Wordsworth's "pastoral poem," which captures and unfurls Michael's hidden tale for a few (but how many?) natural hearts, by articulating Michael's inscription, effectively de-localizes and *publicizes* it, thus enabling that posterity—in the realm of feeling, thought, and memory, not property—that had eluded the shepherd. The problem with this solution is that of the detachment that goes along with any such articulation. Like Luke (and unlike Michael), Wordsworth's inscription has to make its way at large—to the city, in the marketplace—in order to succeed as an inscription. As such, it risks losing touch with "natural objects," with the legitimating sources of the inscriptive tale itself, and thus falls into a kind of "dissolution" amid the "deluges of idle and extravagant stories in verse."[63] Or else the inscription might simply not be heard and left in isolation "beyond the seas." This is a very real and complex anxiety, and it is betrayed by the slight awkwardness or implausibility of Wordsworth's hope that the coterie of "youthful Poets" will somehow remain "*among these hills*" when he is gone: the target of aesthetic education is subtly re-localized but still distinguished from the "dwellers in the valleys" themselves. Another, middle inscriptive possibility—the possibility of a different way of building the sheepfold, going beyond Luke and calling upon other valley folk in common predicaments—is neither entertained nor, indeed, even intimated.

What *is* implied, however, is another, perhaps more radical (if apparently nonsocial) reaction to the fear that the poem's appellations will either be ignored or neutered. Michael's own failed inscription, lacking even writing (but not private significance), calls attention to the mode's material ground with unusual force; the difference between the shepherd's act and a mere "straggling heap of unhewn stones" is, again, the poem itself. It is important, I think, to read both the peculiar, flat repetition of the sentence about Michael's "bodily frame" ("His bodily frame had been from youth to age / Of an unusual strength": both ll. 43–44 and 454–55) and the account of his communion with natural things in the wake of the disaster, in this light:[64]

> There is a comfort in the strength of love;
> 'Twill make a thing endurable, which else
> Would overset the brain, or break the heart:
> I have conversed with more than one who well
> Remember the old Man, and what he was
> Years after he had heard this heavy news.
> His bodily frame had been from youth to age
> Of an unusual strength. Among the rocks
> He went, and still looked up to sun and cloud,
> And listened to the wind . . . (ll. 448–57)

What persists through the poem is "bodily frame," from youth to age but presumably beyond both as well: a state beyond signification (and beyond inscriptive projections) is indexed, wherein we might find ourselves

> alone
> With a few sheep, and rocks and stones, and kites
> That overhead are sailing in the sky. (ll. 10–12)

At such moments and by way of such repetitions Wordsworth manages, by stressing the *indexical* force of descriptive language, to make us feel the thinness of signification with all its anxious fragility—thin, that is, in relation to the world beyond signification, the gesture toward which becomes an especially complex part of the experience of reading the poem.

Although mediated by genre and narrative, the poem manages to point to an extra-linguistic world lying outside the plans laid by Michael and Wordsworth alike. That this *corporeal* impulse frames the poem in a pronounced way beginning and end, and that it informs the response of those who really did sustain a memory of Michael—they "Remember the old Man, and *what* he was" (my emphasis)—suggests that the sturdiest basis for community and posterity emerging out of poetic inscription might rest on this radical appeal to a common materiality, what Paul Fry calls our "mineral community."[65] Certainly, this kind of stony "common ground" or corporeality might be thought to persevere even through "great changes" of all kinds, although for this very reason the kind of "community" it intimates is quite strictly unrepresentable. At the same time, what I call here corporeality is haunted (as an inscriptive strategy) by the possibility that poetry's traces and sounds remain as isolated as the most personal aesthetic project, and can intimate nothing whatsoever about some common world of things-in-themselves.[66]

Part of the power of "Michael" lies in the fact that these two modes of social appeal—the projection-narration of Michael's life story, which lets us know passions not our own, and the more muted corporealizing gestures—coexist but never fully conjoin as a pure fusion of the intelligible and the sensible. The failure of Michael's inscription means that he cannot actually claim any coherence or accord between his plans and the place where he hopes to realize those plans; we sense a vast gap between his physically near-autochthonous relation to his locality and everything he hopes to achieve there.[67] The closure of that gap, of course, would yield up a utopia, a space of concord between material inertia and formative ambition.[68] The Schillerian requirement of permanent play with various *Formen* and *Stoffen* certainly does not prohibit the fashioning of just such representations, strictly ideological in function, within a creative horizon governed by notions of aesthetic education.[69] Part of my job here is to show that the inscriptive mode, with its peculiar ability to link *genius* and *locus,* descriptive/narrative projection and corporeal localization, has a distinctive power to perform the central ideological task of at once naturalizing thought *and* rendering natural being somehow "conceptual" and "human."

Within the realm of ideologemes, the category of the *nation-state* has been called upon perhaps more often than any other to perform the work of uniting projective aspirations with the "natural world." Indeed, the nation-state is perhaps uniquely able to facilitate the imaginative fusion of a system of nomination, order, and modernization (the state) with a specific tradition, space, or even "soil" (the nation), and to articulate this fused space as capacious, although not without limits. The national horizon appears at first glance to be effectively absent from "Michael": when Luke goes "beyond the seas," he seems definitively beyond England (and empire) as well, and the poem as a whole seems silently to posit a place of respite from the turmoil raging through the nation (and beyond). And yet, without too much effort, we can re-signify the "corporealization" of Michael, his blending with the sun, clouds, and wind of rural England, as his near mythic conversion into "another Father Thames, an ancestral figure, virtually prophetic, the genius of the place."[70] On this reading, Michael becomes the mechanism by which the impulse toward a legitimate, serious, "high" poetry is at once reconciled both with (English) everyday life and with the agenda of aesthetic education: he is of this place, attractive and unforbidding; his story can lead us to contemplate "the heart of man, and human Life"; and this place and this story are poetic, inspirited, like comparable places and stories from the past. This national theme, a constant backdrop to Wordsworth's writing, early and late, takes on many forms and plays a vital role in some of the poems I examine here.

It should be added parenthetically that, in its role as ideological resolution, the nation-state contains inherent and drastic instabilities. Even nominally democratic nations (as Susan Buck-Morss and others have pointed out) are unable on a democratic basis to achieve two central aims: *democratically,* they can determine neither their own human constituency—given that they must always already possess a constituency in order to project decisions of any kind—nor the geographical extent of the polity's jurisdiction. The democratic integrity of the polity depends upon the forceful replacement/reconfiguration of some "external" element.[71] Accordingly, the goal of the national inscription as ideological instrument will be to eliminate these contradictions, to project a space where nation and state fully and primordially cohere. In "Michael," as we have seen, this coherence is never realized; the poem substitutes its own localized but entirely aesthetic project for Michael's, but, in so doing, betrays, in any case, the process of substitution, which remains at the level of desire (of the poet for "a few natural hearts").

Within an older leftist political tradition, the way out of this unhappy ideologematic jam bore the name of "world revolution": a (relatively) punctual unification of humans into a single self-conscious and empowered identity (as thinking laborers) that would at the same time finally enable them to determine their own (local) destinies.[72] In such a situation inscriptive verse would change utterly (like everything else), and in ways difficult to imagine. Yet the idea of world revolution, normally associated with Marxism, in fact finds potent anticipations in the Romantics. In Wordsworth's famous response to the French Revolution, we can read something like the inscriptive situation of "Michael," suddenly unburdened of all the old physical limitations, local and personal fixation, and wracking doubt:

> —Oh! Times,
> In which the meager, stale, forbidding ways
> Of custom, law, and statute, took at once
> The attraction of a country in romance!
> When Reason seemed the most to assert her rights,

When most intent on making of herself
A prime Enchantress—to assist the work,
Which then was going forward in her name!
Not favoured spots alone, but the whole earth,
The beauty wore of promise, that which sets
(As at some moment might not be unfelt
Among the bowers of paradise itself)
The budding rose above the rose full blown.
. . . .
Now was it that both found, the meek and lofty
Did both find, helpers to their heart's desires,
And stuff at hand, plastic as they could wish;
Were called upon to exercise their skill,
Not in Utopia, subterranean fields,
Or some secreted island, Heaven knows where!
But in the very world, which is the world
Of all of us,—the place where in the end
We find our happiness, or not at all![73]

Not "in Utopia," but utopian: a world where inscriptive writing would be unnecessary, perhaps because everyone "meek and lofty" would be shaping his or her *own* community, with stuff and helpers at hand. Doubtless, Wordsworth still needs to mobilize the old categories of "romance" (Reason as "prime Enchantress," the "bowers of paradise") to express this inexpressible novelty. Is it because we know even more than Wordsworth did about the problems revolutions have in escaping "custom, law and statute"—in fulfilling their "promise"—that these lines feel almost elegiac today? Whatever the case may be, the disappearance of the "world-revolutionary" ideologeme from the political imagination is one of the surest hallmarks of our specifically *postmodern* moment.[74]

Signage

In order now to imagine what an inscriptive poetry on the far side (i.e., *our* side) of the modern might be like, it will prove useful to move on from inscriptions to a wholly different kind of "place-marking" oppressively common within much contemporary space, namely, commercial signage.[75] It has to be admitted right away that a poetry based on signage (as opposed to epitaph or inscription) would seem unlikely, and it is best to regard my reflections here as a kind of thought experiment rather than literary analysis in the usual sense—although I will soon offer an "example" of the kind of poetry I hypothesize about.

It appears, certainly, that the commercial sign as such differs fundamentally from the inscription as we have discussed it. The transparency, even volatility of a sign bearing the legend "IBM" or "First Union Bank" is such that consciousness, will, and appetite can have no prolonged relationship to it—unless, of course, one wants to buy the company. At the same time, *corporate* signage stands in for so much activity, such a vast network of lives and labor, that, by occluding that activity under a proper name, it provides no entry into the structure it announces.[76] There is a danger, therefore, that any "meditation" on it would emerge as pure projection, a kind of hallucination of space, rather than (if this distinction holds) an imagining of it.

Obviously, the sign text usually neither provokes nor requires meditation on the past, if only because it points to no particular past—even if limited to verbal tense: "shee *parted* hence"—and to no strictly human fate, whether individual or collective.[77] Instead, the sign represents organizations and enterprises—comprised of humans, to be sure, and therefore susceptible to story—and serves to ease the functioning of the enterprise by ensuring its recognition. The inscription for its part always seems to point to some past event, whereas the label or "sign" concerns the distinction of its bearer alone, and enables its use. Storefront signs are like letters on a typewriter keyboard or buttons on an electronic grid; they allow us to do certain tasks more easily, to go certain places, to obtain certain things.[78] They precisely do *not* effect the same waylaying of the wandering observer, the same (to paraphrase Roman Jakobson) "impeding of perception"[79] to which inscriptions aspire.

Of course, one might argue that epitaphs like Jonson's are not entirely stubborn or occluding; they, too, invite us beyond their textual surface into memories and imaginings. The difference would seem to lie in the fact that nothing, or very little, which is palpable or saleable lies behind the epitaph, thereby throwing us back upon the text rather than onward toward an acquisition or an activity. The desires declared by epitaphs—desires for resurrection, immortality—cannot be gratified except by God and, perhaps, in some deeply mediated sense, by epitaph itself.

(Coming at the question from the other side: imagine crowds of people visiting a graveyard with the attitude of shoppers; some Gogolian salesman there, trafficking in the dead; and the epitaph as a stony label, a "For Sale" sign attached to "John Smith, 1820–1895." There is a trend [Californian, of course] of equipping headstones with tape machines that play recordings of the voice of the deceased to visitors. Does it not come as a surprise that a consumable "result"—the very voice of the dead—can be so easily provided and enjoyed at the gravesite? Recall, too, the explosive mix of horror and utopianism in the Frankenstein myth, where we see the potential appropriation of the corpse itself by reason, and vice versa.)

Under the neon glare of signage, consider now the German poet Rolf Dieter Brinkmann's frenetic "Hymne auf einen italienischen Platz" ("Hymn to an Italian square" [1972–73]), written (or perhaps *transcribed*) in Rome's Piazza Bologna during the poet's Italian sojourn:[80]

O Piazza Bologna in Rom! Banca Nazionale Del
Lavoro und Banco Di Santo Spirito, Pizza Mozzarella
Barbiere, Gomma Sport! Gipsi Boutique und Willi,
Tavola Calda, Esso Servizio, Fiat, Ginnastica,

Estetica, Yoga, Sauna! O Bar Tabacci und Gelati,
breite Hintern in Levi's Jeans, Brüste oder Titten,
alles fest, eingeklemmt, Pasticceria, Marcelleria!
O kleine Standlichter, Vini, Oli, Per Via Aerea,

Eldora Steak, Tecnotica Caruso! O Profumeria
Estivi, Chiuso Per Ferie Agosto, o Lidia Di Firenze,
Lady Wool! Cinestop! Grüner Bus! O Linie 62 und 6, das
Kleingeld! O Avanti grün! O wo? P.T. und Tee Fredo,

Visita Da Medico Ocultista, Lenti A Contatto!
O Auto Famose! Ritz Cräcker, Nuota Con Noi, o Grazie!
Tutte Nude! O Domenica, Abfälle, Plastiktüten, rosa!
Vacanze Carissime, o Nautica! Haut, Rücken, Schenkel

gebräunt, o Ölfleck, Ragazzi, Autovox, Kies! Und Oxford,
Neon, Il Gatto Di Brooklyn Aspirante Detective, Melone!
Mauern! Mösen! Knoblauch! Geriebener Parmigiano!
O dunkler
Minimarket Di Frutta, Instituto Pirandello, Inglese

Shenker, Rolläden! O gelbbrauner Hund! Um die Ecke
Banca Commerziale Italia, Flöhe, Luftdruckbremsen, BP
Coupons, Zoom! O Eva Moderna, Medaglioni, Tramezzini,
Bollati! Aperto! Locali Provvisori! Balkone, o Schatten

mit Öl, Blätter, Trasferita! O Ente Communale Di
Consumo, an der Wand! O eisern geschlossene Bar Ferranzi!
O Straßenstille! Guerlain, Hundeköttel, Germain Montail!
O Bar Fascista Riservata Permanente, Piano! O Soldaten,

Operette, Revolver gegen Hüften! O Super Pensione!
O Tiergestalt! O Farmacia Bologna, kaputte Hausecke,
Senso Unico! O Scusi! O Casa Bella! O Ultimo Tango
Pomodoro! O Sciopero! O Lire! O Scheiß!

O Piazza Bologna in Rome! Banca Nazionale Del
Lavoro and Banco Di Santo Spirito, Pizza Mozzarella
Barbiere, Gomma Sport! Gipsi Boutique and Willi,
Tavola Calda, Esso Servizio, Fiat, Ginnastica,

Estetica, Yoga, Sauna! O Bar Tabacci und Gelati,
wide rear-ends in Levi's Jeans, breasts or tits,
everything firm, clamped in, Pasticceria, Marcelleria!
O little sidelights, Vini, Oli, Per Via Aerea,

Eldora Steak, Tecnotica Caruso! O Profumeria
Estivi, Chiuso Per Ferie Agosto, o Lidia Di Firenze,
Lady Wool! Cinestop! Green Bus! O lines 62 and 6, small
change! O Avanti green! O where? P.T. and Tee Fredo,

Visita Da Medico Ocultista, Lenti A Contatto!
O Auto Famose! Ritz crackers, Nuota Con Noi, o Grace!
Tutte Nude! O Domenica, trash, plastic bags, pink!
Vacanze Carissime, o Nautica! Skin, back, tanned

thighs, o spot of oil, Ragazzi, Autovox, gravel! And
Oxford,
Neon, Il Gatto Di Brooklyn Aspirante Detective, melons!
Walls! Cunts! Garlic! Grated Parmigiano!
O dim
Minimarket Di Frutta, Istituto Pirandello, Inglese

Shenker, shutters! O yellowbrown dog! Around the corner
Banca Commerziale Italia, fleas, air brakes, BP
Coupons, Zoom! O Eva Moderna, Medaglioni, Tramezzini,
Bollati! Aperto! Locali Provvisori! Balconies, o shadows

with oil, leaves, Trasferita! O Ente Communale Di
Consumo, on the wall! O strictly-closed Bar Ferranzi!
O quiet on the streets! Guerlain, dogturd,
Germain Montail!
O Bar Fascista Riservata Permanente, Piano! O soldiers,

Operette, revolvers against the hips! O Super Pensione!
O shape of beast! O Farmacia Bologna, wrecked corners
of houses,
Senso Unico! O Scusi! O Casa Bella! O Ultimo Tango
Pomodoro! O Sciopero! O Lire! O shit!

Hymns generally seek to justify what they praise, whether that object is God's saving goodness and wisdom or nature's or mankind's or the poet's own. But, in fact, this post-hymn is situated rather than justified;[81] a compulsive cataloguing, the poem apparently discloses nothing about its motivations, implies no centered subjectivity. Even the "situation" is unclear or multiple. A reader with little or no Italian (like myself) can still discern that much of the observed "data" here is comprised of signs—of banks, boutiques, bars, restaurants—and labels. Some of them have traveled so widely in the world of commodities that neither Italian nor German nor any knowledge of the Piazza Bologna (or any other place) is necessary for their comprehension: "Esso," "Fiat," "Levi's Jeans," "Ritz Cräcker." The hymn suggests a palimpsest of differing orientations toward the "Platz"—the disposition of locals, of those who work in the saunas and bars, of tourists, of German tourists, of people watching TV in Iceland or Indonesia who might see identical bits of text flash before their eyes—while remaining indifferent to all of them. The reader is simply within these texts, rather than inscriptively drawn to them.[82] (But do the more "descriptive" sections in German also become mere "bits of text," or do they release a specific genius loci, bewildered no doubt, into the scene?)

Yet it is something of a paradox that this de-localization, effected through signage, coexists with the most fanatic recording of precise details from *this* scene and *this* moment, and with the performance of that recording. Indeed, we might say that this poem, by reporting almost exclusively the textual features of the Piazza, achieves something approaching a kind of pure mimesis or immediacy of representation; because the place is treated as a kind of lexicon, the poem can quite literally *cite,* rather than describe, the scene. (It is odd, even absurd, to think of a "postmodern" or "textualizing" aesthetic as one of immediacy, yet this might be one weird consequence of the erasure of any ontological difference between the representing "medium" and the referent. Here the old topos of the "world-as-book" finds its realization—except that the "book" is the Yellow Pages.)

The breathless, exclamatory speed of movement from one detail to another also seems to emulate a rush of stimuli or impressions; and with this kinetic collage technique, Brinkmann was, of course, extending some of the "phantasmagoric" poetic experiments of an earlier phase of drastic modernization, particularly those of Rimbaud (whom he studied intensively) and perhaps also of Jules Laforgue (in the "white prose" of the "Grande Complainte de la Ville de Paris") to a still greater, well-nigh schizophrenic level of "impersonality."[83] Certainly no lingering over the grave here: taken as a whole, the poem resembles a homogeneous series of rapid breaks, borrowing on an "interruptive" technique that Brinkmann was fond of:

Ich blicke hoch
und sehe

Have fun take a Coke

am Himmel aufgespritzt

auf einem silbrigen Grund, denn
jetzt ist es Sommer

(p. 43)

I look up
and see

Have fun take a Coke

sprayed across the sky,

on a silvery ground, for now
it is summer

But whose speed is it? The position and agency of the poet are hard to fix here. On one side, the hymn as a whole seems a drastically private utterance; we sense an observing eye wandering *flâneur*-like over the scene, willfully selecting among details and designations ("Brüste oder Titten" ["breasts or tits"]?), and (as poet) carefully modulating the rhythm of his presentation. But, on the other, the poem appears largely to be an automatic jotting down of names, including, perhaps, numerous errors of transcription; even the Italian language itself seems partially chosen for its very euphony (especially as apprehended by the Germanic ear). There is no analysis of subjectivity, no memories, no story, no project; and the compulsive, noisy listing makes us suspect a controlled or perhaps mindless, rather than an independent, voice. It is this obsessiveness that leads us to read the poem as something other than a mere burlesque (although it is that, too). But do we assign the obsessiveness to the poet or to the unknown source of all the signs?

There is something strangely layered and double about the very use of locutions like "O Bar Tabacci und Gelati." One of poetry's most overt indications of "voice," the apostrophic "O," is used to frame not a spontaneous outpouring but aggressively quoted pieces of print; we imagine the voice gradually growing rather hoarse. What happens to signage when it is written into a poem, and especially one like Brinkmann's, where the dialectic of four-line shape and enjambed enthusiasm consciously recalls visionary, odic traditions (Klopstock)? Does the poem become a string of labels, or can it incorporate them into more typically "lyric" structures of feeling? The "O" recalls both archaic modes of praise and (in keeping with the conventions of apostrophe) the call to an absent person, god, or power ("O Justice!"). It also signals an unmediated cry of pain or joy: "O, could I loose all father now," writes Jonson in the most moving of his epitaphs.[84]

If we think of the "O" as an effort to surround and invest and mark the signscape with a certain declamatory energy, we might go further and imagine the flashes of exclamation as a heap of fragmentary elegies. Each one is then pushed aside before any memory or response has had a chance to develop; the "O" becomes less an enclosure of tribute and commemoration than a hole into which everything falls. I noted earlier that aesthetic education requires a "blurring of soul and text," by which I mean, in part, the belief that texts affect persons, make a difference to their constitution. Brinkmann's poem clearly participates in some different regime of art, inasmuch as it shows sign after sign plummeting into the same pool of residue-less indifference, after being consumed by apostrophe.

One phrase, however, is distinguished by its unique use of the interrogative: "O wo?" ("O where?"), located near the end of the third stanza. It might be explained naturalistically: a partial transcription of a random statement like "O wo[hin] fährt der grüne Bus" ("O where is the green bus going?") or something like that. Yet I am inclined instead to see it as a genuine piece of lyric garbage, so to speak. After all, the question of "where" something is, the pained inquiry into the location of the missing or lost person, is perhaps the elegiac question par excellence. One especially recalls those cries of "where?" announcing the cruxes of so many Hölderlin poems:

> Weh mir, wo nehm ich, wenn
> Es Winter ist, die Blumen, und wo
> Den Sonnenschein,
> Und Schatten der Erde?[85]
> ("Hälfte des Lebens," pp. 134–35)

> Ah, where will I find
> Flowers, come winter,
> And where the sunshine
> And shade of the earth?[86]
> ("Half of Life," p. 47)

> Wo,
> Wo aber wohnt ihr, liebe Verwandten,
> Daß wir das Bündnis wiederbegehn
> Und der teuern Ahnen gedenken?
> ("Die Wanderung," p. 145)

> But where can I find you, dear kinsmen,
> That we might recelebrate the vows
> And honor the memory of our ancestors?
> ("The Migration," p. 63)

Brinkmann's is a ruined, truncated "wo," without predicate or development. It is just another "citation" of sorts, perhaps a kind of accident.

Yet the quality of interrogation, as distinct from the exclamatory product offerings that surround it—the "where?" points, without closure, toward a lack—momentarily trips up our advance through the forest of signs.

To be sure, "corporeal" obstructions do not entirely vanish from Brinkmann's description: "garlic," "dogturd," and the like. And yet their presence is largely ironic, for their naturally pungent associations are all "clamped in," singular, and end up "going with the flow" of everything else. For its part, signage seems to involve a compaction of visual and verbal modalities (think of the "Golden Arches"), never a reduction to the purely phenomenal and non-semantic. We might find a kind of (illusory) release from reification, however, in the very hyper-saturated, well-nigh "digital" texture of the poem, which invites us, in the absence of development, to plunge in anywhere and read in any order. In this respect, Brinkmann's use of the apostrophic "O" provides unexpected confirmation of Jonathan Culler's superb account of apostrophe as a device for converting what might seem like temporal/historical order into pure discursive order:

> One might identify, for example, as instances of the triumph of the apostrophic, poems which, in a very common move, substitute a fictional, non-temporal opposition for a temporal one, substitute a temporality of discourse for a referential temporality. In lyrics of this kind a temporal problem is posed: something once present has been lost or attenuated; this loss can be narrated but the temporal sequence is irreversible, like time itself. Apostrophes displace this irreversible structure by removing the opposition between presence and absence from empirical time and locating it in a discursive time.[87]

It is no small irony that a device as old-fashioned as apostrophe—although apostrophe itself, of course, knows nothing of age!—could be deployed in a manner so revelatory of postmodern spatio-temporality, and so hard to distinguish, indeed, from sheer textuality. For (to recover the historical conjuncture) by Brinkmann's time, and with the overcoming of unevenness on all levels (technological, political, cultural), the difference between local and global space is obliterated; what may once have had specific, local weight is utterly dissolved within a solution of constant change and exchange.

At the same time, it would be wrong to deny the traces here not of a "subject" as such but of tokens of subjectivity in the older sense. The vocalizing "O" resonates like a background hum through all the essentially random exchanges: a residue of the human, now without any meaning but also without apparent limit. Meanwhile, that Brinkmann transcribes the Piazza as he saw it "then and there" gives the whole thing the quality of a home video *avant le mot,* like an arrangement of private observations but devoid, to be sure, of even the slightest intimacy. This peculiar duality of technologized flux alongside static voice, drastic de-individuation and homely tourist documentary cheek by jowl, resonates with what David Simpson has written about the uneasy coexistence of technological and nontechnological (or "literary-centered") postmodernisms. The latter valorizes subjective testimony over more impersonal discourses, anecdote over argumentation, and situated knowledge over "grand theory," whereas the former (not Simpson's main focus) is all about the way technology can unleash new possibilities and free us from our subjective limitations.[88] And, as we will see, modern inscriptive poetry contains anticipations of both these orientations.[89] For the moment, let it be said that neither ideology seems especially anxious about its respective valorizations; each appears to proclaim that forms have been found which satisfy the need for authenticity (anecdote) and for liberating development (technology, but surely the market above all), and that, within all the variety, something like consensus can be assumed. (Does that fact provide the occasion for Brinkmann to cry "O Scheiß!" at the end of his ludicrous poem?)

Absent Centers

And so, to complete the "point" introduced at the start of this introduction, in this book I will show how poets writing in the inscriptive mode use the generic resources of inscription to generate legitimacies that might both justify their writing and attract an audience of "passersby," and this during a historical phase within which the identity of audiences was a matter of anxious yet fertile doubt. (Again, I should stress that this is not a reception study per se but rather a study of the desire for reception, and of the shapes which that desire can take in poetic form.) Virtually of necessity, this doubt also provokes a reflection on audience, and on the poem's historical situation, within the writing itself; thus the inscriptions have to be read as at once symptomatic and diagnostic of modernity, never as mere effects of history. The conditional resolutions of doubt, the attempts to discover new legitimizing *genii*—the absent centers of the modern inscriptive mode—are the poems themselves, issuing their appellations in an age of aesthetic education and at a time when other, non-aesthetic kinds of legitimacy (economic, scientific, national-state, and so on) are gaining authority apace.

Finally, I should emphasize that no claim for the exclusive or singular importance of inscription relative to other lyric modes (like song or confessional lyric, for instance) is being made here. Those other modes and genres have their own histories and sets of salient features, even while (as will become evident) all of them overlap and interact in various ways as well, both among themselves and with non-lyric kinds of writing. More important, I hope to show that if inscriptive poetry often becomes reflexive and theory-like in its reflections on its own possibility, inscription also helps us to understand something about criticism and theory more narrowly considered. The idea might be pursued that much "purposeless" modern art (especially of the supposedly nonrepresentational variety) partakes of the inscriptive mode inasmuch as all its accompanying *manifesta,* explanatory essays, and commentary—criticism and aesthetic education themselves, if the analogy is ambitiously extended—act either as a continual and sustaining evaluation and revaluation of art, or perhaps as an immense epitaph to a meaningfulness and immediacy that art has presumably lost. This metaphor has the benefit, at the very least, of complicating more common descriptions of commentary as "parasitic" or "curatorial"; objects of criticism might instead be seen as contingent nodes of attention within a much wider circuit of response and storytelling (in Walter Benjamin's sense).

The book consists of a set of readings, snapshots of poems within the landscape of modernity, interlaid with theoretical reflections that work to situate the poetry within that larger historical/conceptual framework. The first chapter ("Lifeless Things: Being and Structure in Romantic Inscription") discusses the central precondition of early modern lyric—the separation of being from any particular structures of being, and the emergence of "nature" as a crucial ideologeme—in light of the political, cultural/linguistic, and technological scientific upheavals of the Enlightenment and Romantic periods. Opening with an extended reading of Clare's "The Pettichaps Nest" and Shelley's "Mont Blanc," and focusing on the very different anxieties expressed in both poems about the loss of traditional structures of meaning, I show how both poets attempt to imagine how undistorted forms of communication might be discovered or fashioned. The chapter moves on to an exploration of the same issues in German Romantic and post-Romantic poetic theory (in Hegel, Schleiermacher, and Hans Blumenberg), where conceptions of poetry alternate between assertions of the radical, even meaningless and purely physical particularity of poetic utterances, and the insistence that those same utterances project novel kinds of knowledge and sensibility. Later in the chapter I focus on the political implications of the monumental inscription, and show how that most official of poetic modes (read through one of Mikhail Lomonosov's inscriptions to Peter the Great) generates its "corporeal other" in the form of the anti-monument poem (Shelley's "Ozymandias"). The chapter closes with an examination of two great Romantic locodescriptions (Wordsworth's "Mark the concentred hazels" and Hölderlin's "Der Winkel von Hardt") as positing (or denying) a possible "harmonizing" of human sensibilities with mute Nature as a way of overcoming, apparently without imposing any new metaphysical schemes, the gap between natural being and structures of consciousness.

Questions of changing modes of subjectivity within the city and the work of Baudelaire, Lamartine, and the worker-poet Charles Poncy occupy the center of chapter 2 ("Empty and Full: Poetry, Self, and Society in Lamartine, Baudelaire, and Poncy"). Relying and critically elaborating on Benjamin's diagnosis of nineteenth-century Paris, I discuss the receding of historical consciousness from social and artistic practice, the emergence of new, working-class subjectivities and their consequences for lyric production. Far too often Baudelaire's work, important though it is, is taken as the unique exemplar of early modernity within poetry; I demonstrate how damagingly reductive this view is by juxtaposing Baudelaire with some very un-Baudelairean contemporaries in order to map out a more diverse force field of varying options within this crucial period, and their implications for later writing. In his city locodescriptions, Baudelaire attempts to separate lyric experience from any kind of social effectivity—presaging later hermetic modernisms—while at the same time revealing the mechanism of that separation; the aristocratic Lamartine depicts the city as a cognitive disaster and projects a kind of administered pastoral as an alternative, thus also forecasting certain aspects of conservative-modernist social ideals; for his part, the worker-poet Poncy gropes toward the articulation of a creative laboring collectivity that would overcome the separation between the world of physical labor and the sphere of aesthetic experience—thereby powerfully prefiguring the kinds of proletarian poetry that would emerge in the revolutionary period of 1871–1917, and beyond.

The last two chapters focus on Russian writing and argue that the question of broad cultural change (rather than shifts in consciousness as such) becomes the central preoccupation for poets as the early twentieth century "Age of Extremes" unfolds. Chapter 3 ("Kernels of the Acropolis: Poetry and Modernization in Blok, Kliuev, and Khlebnikov") begins by examining the anxious response to the new cultural possibilities generated by modernity in Aleksandr Blok's post-Baudelairean city lyrics, and the way that Baudelaire's preoccupations with subjectivity take on a more explicitly social character at a time when older aristocratic and "intelligentsia" norms are undergoing profound modifications. I show how Blok's poetic imagination (as expressed in poems like

"The Stranger") veers between visions of emergent cultures so radically new as to be unreadable and apocalyptic fantasies of purely physical, culturally purgative violence. The rapidly changing peasantry and working classes are central to Blok's anxieties and indeed to the entire period in Russia, provoking widespread discussion about the shape that a new mass culture would take. In light of these concerns, the rest of the chapter focuses on the constructive responses of the peasant-poet Nikolai Kliuev and the Futurist Velimir Khlebnikov to the question of a future cultural literacy. In a discussion of the politics of poetic language in Russia, I show how Kliuev in his inscriptions wishes to maintain the material presence of the peasantry within mainstream culture through both a decadent fetishizing of peasant dialect words and an insistence on those words' right to linguistic coexistence. Khlebnikov, on the other hand, attempts to annihilate "vocabulary" itself by excavating very basic linguistic units and then redeploying them in forms both comprehensible and resistant to any determination by standardizing authorities: "mute graphic marks" become the inscriptive field for the creation of an infinitely flexible interpretive agora of readers.

The final chapter ("Unkind Weight: Mandelstam, History, and Catastrophe") addresses the theory and poetry (in roughly equal proportions) of Osip Mandelstam, who gives us an explicit, wide-ranging meditation on both the community-building aspirations of poetic modernity and (especially in his "Verses about the Unknown Soldier," to which the concluding section is devoted) the radical narrowing of utopian possibility through the work of modernization itself. I show how Mandelstam's entire work is suspended between the desire for the creation of a humanized world through the agency of poetic language and the fear of cultural impoverishment through the conversion of older cultural artifacts into historical residues. Mandelstam's concerns lead him to rely heavily on notions of "latency" and the idea of the possible circulation of "dead" material culture back into the world of living discourse. Many of these ideas, I argue, extend the concerns of those Romantic and pre-Romantic authors (particularly Schiller) who sought to build a modern human culture around the free agency of the aesthetic. By career's end, however—that is, by the time of the Great Terror, and on the eve of World War II—Mandelstam envisions an emergent culture where the difference between the meaningful and the residual is entirely determined by the administrated society: this is the burden of the anti-monumental inscription "Verses about the Unknown Solder," which explicitly shows Hegelian "Spirit" arriving at a different and far grimmer terminus than the Romantics would have anticipated.

A brief coda to the chapter (with a reading of Elizabeth Bishop's "The Monument") reflects on the possibility of imagining a socially transformative lyric poetry under "postmodern" conditions, and on the question of whether the idea of creativity itself has suffered a definitive humiliation in the wake of the disappointments of the twentieth century and the (commercial or statist) bureaucratization of culture.

— 1 —

Lifeless Things

Being and Structure in Romantic Inscription

> The primacy of the ontological, in the Romantic period, has something to do, surely, with the drawing back of the curtains of tradition and the customary, of the sacred and its conventions, of what seemed to derive a meaning from other spaces than those of human praxis and construction. Now, for a brief period, something like a "window" of the ontological, Being in all its meaninglessness and calm persistence becomes visible, like the ocean floor or the bottom of a lake, before bourgeois conventionality and a whole new system of artificial "values" come to obscure it again.
>
> —Fredric Jameson, "Ontology and Utopia"

> Their churches contain no visual representations of God, so that everyone's left free to imagine Him in whatever shape he chooses, according to which religion he thinks is best.
>
> —Thomas More, *Utopia*

Open to the Day

It seems safe to say that epitaphic inscriptions offer tributes—sometimes, ironic tributes—to whomever or whatever they commemorate. The famously death-obsessed Samuel Johnson, after quickly bracketing the possibility of satiric epitaph in his "Essay on Epitaphs," defines epitaph as simply *"an Inscription engraven on a Tomb in Honour of the Person deceased."*[1] And surely we can still accept this definition as functionally valid for panegyrists (whoever they might be) of our own day: their poems are occasions for the enunciation of discovered, publicly acknowledged (and presumably not just monetary) worth.

In this chapter I use Johnson's definition as a starting point for an inquiry into the late-eighteenth- to early-nineteenth-century

("Romantic") inscriptive mode, and also subject the definition to historicizing inquiry. What happens, I want to ask, when the traditional bases of "honor"—or the idea of honor itself—fall into dishonor, or at least into question; what happens when the panegyrist comes to hesitate about which (human) attributes are worthy of tribute? This kind of falling and hesitation is what beset European culture across the "revolutionary arch"[2] linking Johnson's 1740 essay to Wordsworth's better-known "Essay upon Epitaphs" (1810), and we can briefly contrast the two discussions as a way to bring into focus a central shift in consciousness occurring over that seventy-year span: a relativizing of values, and a concomitant and continual reevaluation of the category of nature and its relation to the social.

For Johnson, the motivation for epitaph is fundamentally ethical and educative—or, as we might say today, ideological. Epitaphs are required not only to preserve the memory of a deceased person but also to preserve and make known something of that person's exemplary worth, so that others may be incited "to the Imitation of their Excellencies" (p. 511):

> Nature and Reason have dictated to every Nation, that to preserve good Actions from Oblivion, is both the Interest and the Duty of Mankind; and therefore we find no People acquainted with the Use of Letters that omitted to grace the Tombs of their Heroes and wise Men with panegyrical Inscriptions. (p. 510)

Importantly, "Heroes and wise Men" are hardly the only or even the main recipients of epitaphic honor, for "every Man may expect to be recorded in an Epitaph" (p. 510). Indeed, "the best Subject for EPITAPHS is private Virtue." The great ones of truly major virtue—Johnson mentions a person who has "delivered his Country from Oppression, or freed the World from Ignorance and Errour"—will never find many emulators, whereas those who through the more prosaic strengths of "Firmness of Heart and Steadfastness of Resolution" may well prove able, through the mediation of epitaph, to "animate Multitudes" (all from p. 515). The foremost task of the epitaph writer thus becomes "drawing the Character of the Deceased" (p. 515) in order that the valued kernel might be vividly delineated for appreciation, veneration, emulation.

Wordsworth apparently never read Johnson's "Essay on Epitaphs," but he finds occasion in his own postrevolutionary "Essay upon Epitaphs" to attack another of Johnson's affirmations (from *Lives of the English Poets*) of the link between epitaph and the worth of the deceased. On this later occasion, Johnson reached a distinctly less democratic conclusion:

> The difficulty in writing epitaphs is to give a particular and appropriate praise. This, however, is not always to be performed, whatever be the diligence or ability of the writer, for the greater part of mankind "have no character at all," have little that distinguishes them from others equally good or bad, and therefore nothing can be said of them which may not be applied with equal propriety to a thousand more.[3]

Wordsworth counters that "the objects of admiration in human-nature are not scanty, but abundant: and every man has a character of his own, to the eye that has skill to perceive it."[4] But, as it turns out, Wordsworth's defense of epitaph will have little to do with fashioning memorials to worthy "character" in this sense at all. He assents to the obvious point that epitaphs are sometimes properly justified by tribute to "conspicuous or beneficial [acts] of local or general utility," but he does so in passing, and almost grudgingly.[5] Initially, his whole conception of epitaph seems less grounded in social function than in an apparently religious faith, inasmuch as he finds the motivation for epitaph in a transpersonal "consciousness of a principle of immortality in the human soul," without which

> [m]an could never have had awakened in him the desire to live in the remembrance of his fellows: mere love, or the yearning of kind towards kind, could not have produced it.

Wordsworth immediately extends and transcends this claim to assert that the very possibility of social solidarity, and of "sympathies of love towards each other," depend on the belief in some sort of general and persisting human substrate, which he calls "our internal Being":

> [I]t is to me inconceivable, that the sympathies of love towards each other, which grow with our growth, could ever attain any new strength, or even preserve the old, after we had received from the outward senses the impression of death, and were in the habit of having that impression daily renewed and its accompanying feeling brought home to ourselves, and to those we love; if the same were not counteracted by those communications with our internal Being, which are anterior to all these experiences, and with which revelation coincides, and has through that coincidence alone (for otherwise it could not possess it) a power to affect us.... Were we to grow up unfostered by this genial warmth, a frost would chill the spirit, so penetrating and powerful, that there could be no motions of the life of love; and infinitely less could we have any wish to be remembered after we had passed away from a world in which each man had moved about like a shadow. (pp. 51–52)

Wordsworth takes death very seriously. Its sheer irrefutability, its ruthless trivialization of any claims but its own would seem to validate (if it were possible to "identify" with death) a kind of indifference or non-relation to the world, and, most important, toward "each other." The Wordsworthian epitaph attempts not only to counter this despair but also to undermine its very basis: first, appellatively, by starkly making claims upon memory, and claiming the worth of memory; and, second, through a legitimating act of discovering or indexing the immortal—that is, the generally human. In a kind of mirroring or performative tautology, the continuance of epitaph is said to testify to the continuance of our conceptions of human nature, and, by extension, to human nature as such. Yet mere appellation or repetition can hardly be sufficient; the successful epitaph writer must also find a way to appeal poetically to this "internal Being," even if only negatively or through figuration.

The poet's conviction here may well be superstitious, but it seems wrong to call it religious in any strong sense. Although "revelation" is mentioned, neither visions of an afterlife nor divine command significantly energize epitaph for Wordsworth. His "principle of immortality" is a distinctly earthly substrate that both links persons to one another and perseveres beyond all contingent glories (or squalors) of "character" and value:

> [W]e suffer and we weep with the same heart; we love and are anxious for one another in one spirit; our hopes look to the same quarter; and the virtues by which we are all to be furthered and supported, as patience, meekness, good-will, justice, temperance, and temperate desires, are in an equal degree the concern of us all. Let an Epitaph, then, contain at least these acknowledgments to our common nature; nor let the sense of their importance be sacrificed to a balance of opposite qualities or minute distinctions in individual character; which if they do not (as will for the most part be the case), when examined, resolve themselves into a trick of words, will, even when they are true and just, for the most part be grievously out of place; for as it is probable that few only have explored these intricacies of human nature, so can the tracing of them be interesting only to a few. But an epitaph is not a proud writing shut up for the studious: it is exposed to all—to the wise and the most ignorant; it is condescending, perspicuous, and lovingly solicits regard; its story and admonitions are brief, that the thoughtless, the busy, and indolent, may not be deterred, nor the impatient tired: the stooping old man cons the engraven record like a second horn-book;—the child is proud that he can read it;—and the stranger is introduced through its mediation to the company of a friend: it is concerning all, and for all: in the church-yard it is open to the day; the sun looks down upon the stone, and the rains of heaven beat against it. (p. 59)

The epitaph becomes here a virtual agora in which all members of the community can participate, and in ways that, despite all their diversity, somehow also add up to a demonstration of commonality, and indeed an overcoming of social "enmity" (p. 58). In order for this to happen, one might think that an exceedingly complex, almost encyclopedic writing would be required: a kind of book of the world, or perhaps the open, "dialogic" and "genre-less" text sometimes valorized by ideologists of the novel. For Wordsworth, the epitaphic (and perhaps the lyric) path is different, and moves instead toward a kind of reduced surface upon which any number of impulses might play (Wordsworth hopes they will be good ones). This means, on the one hand, that the epitaph should be popular, indeed accessible to the point of banality:

> [I]t is not only no fault but a primary requisite in an Epitaph that it shall contain thoughts and feelings which are in their substance common-place, and even trite. It is grounded upon the universal intellectual property of man;—[...] truths whose very interest and importance have caused them to be unattended to, as things which could take care of themselves. (p. 78)

Wordsworth is aware of the danger of a fabricated or simulated triteness, and insists both that the commonplace "truths" in question be genuine ("instinctively ejaculated, or [...] rise irresistibly from circumstances" [p. 78]) and that they effect some sort of surprise by virtue of their sheer, unexpected, and witless familiarity. At the same time, it would seem that the guarantor of this authentic triteness is not popular reception (however measured) but rather the poem's own proximity, in its corporeal and inscribed plainness, to the vicissitudes of the day, to the sun, the rain, to extra-linguistic being itself. The response to death's socially chilling effect turns out to be a kind of poetic re-appropriation of the inorganic (the realm of the dead), and the re-imagining of its vast indifference as a ground for generalized community. To be a truly popular, universally accessible poetry, the epitaph not only must be "simple" but must sink almost unmarked into the exposed, mute surface upon which it is inscribed: a surface rather like photographic film, one is tempted to say. Might the garden-variety snapshot be the fulfillment of the Wordsworthian epitaph, by managing at once to be common (i.e., trite) and to point to what is common (i.e., that extra-linguistic reality that leaves its (mediated) trace in the photo)?[6]

Yet the crux, as always, lies in the "almost." That such a poetry would run the danger of being passed over as "unremarkable," of being unrecognized as poetry, or indeed (at a certain outer limit) of simply remaining unperceived, is obvious enough. Equally important, Wordsworth makes it clear in a famous passage in the third essay that the epitaph writer has vital cultural work to perform precisely by making language function in this purified, "onto-popular" way. Language, far from constituting an agora by itself, can undermine community as much as reinforce it:

> Words are too awful an instrument of good and evil to be trifled with: they hold above all other external powers a dominion over thoughts. [. . .] Language, if it do not uphold, and feed, and leave in quiet, like the power of gravitation or the air we breathe, is a counter-spirit, unremittingly and noiselessly at work to derange, to subvert, to lay waste, to vitiate, and to dissolve. (pp. 84–85)

The preface to *Lyrical Ballads,* among other texts, leaves us with no doubt as to the historical ground for Wordsworth's reflections on language in the later "Essay on Epitaphs." There the poet is far more explicit about how his own project is ranged against an unprecedented proliferation of discourses, spawned by "the rapid communication of intelligence" and "the increasing accumulation of men in cities"—in short, by modernity itself. By Wordsworth's time, the "multitudes" that Johnsonian epitaph had hoped to animate had become much more diverse and numerous; the likelihood of discovering a common code "exemplary" for one and all, much less.

The problem extended, one should note, even to epitaphic function much more narrowly considered. Thomas Laqueur has shown in his work on the emergence of the modern cemetery in the late eighteenth to the early nineteenth century how "the old community of the dead was breaking down" right at the time that Wordsworth was using the epitaph to reassert community. The cemetery—as opposed to "the lumpy churchyard or the crowded public crypt"—was a middle-class space of "private memory," and "made possible an undreamed of elaboration of personal commemoration and contemplation," and whole new codes of posthumous distinction (and in-distinction).[7] Wordsworth's decision to envision epitaph as pointing beyond codes per se to a corporeality presumably common to all is prompted by factors beyond the strictly poetic but ones that might indeed threaten the very idea of the poetic; his is a historical, here masking as a linguistic, predicament.

On a wider view, Wordsworth's own solution seems to trace out an unlikely space of convergence between the twin antipodes of what we might call (in shorthand) Heidegger-and-Hallmark: that is, the Romantic/post-Romantic "lyric of being" (we might think of writers as diverse as Shelley, Fet, Whitman [at times anyway], Perse, Stevens, and Rilke as representative practitioners) somehow reconciled with its standardized/mass cultural ("trite") opposite:

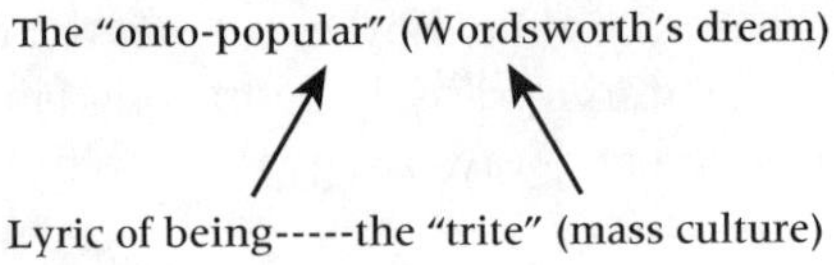

The "onto-popular" (Wordsworth's dream)

Lyric of being-----the "trite" (mass culture)

Yet now is the moment to expand this range of possibilities by reflecting on other counterparts to what we have identified as Wordsworth's two master terms. The "autonomous" (not to say hermetic) quality of the modern "lyric of being" should be set against the possibility of a more anonymous, collective, or "folk" poetry that retains, through its roots in traditional modes of labor (agricultural, craft), some affiliation to the natural world in relatively un-alienated (i.e., non-individualized) form; this horizon can be distantly perceived in a poem like "Michael," for example, and we will see it rather more clearly in the work of some of the early-twentieth-century Russians. For its part, the mass-cultural can be contrasted with the comparably standardized but more class-specific production of official or "elite" verse, very important within old-regime culture right through to the mid-twentieth century and still with us, for example, in the form of occasional monumental inscriptions and in the very category of the "Poet Laureate." We can map out this fuller range of oppositions and label their tentative resolutions in the following way (on the model of the Greimassian "semiotic rectangle"): [8]

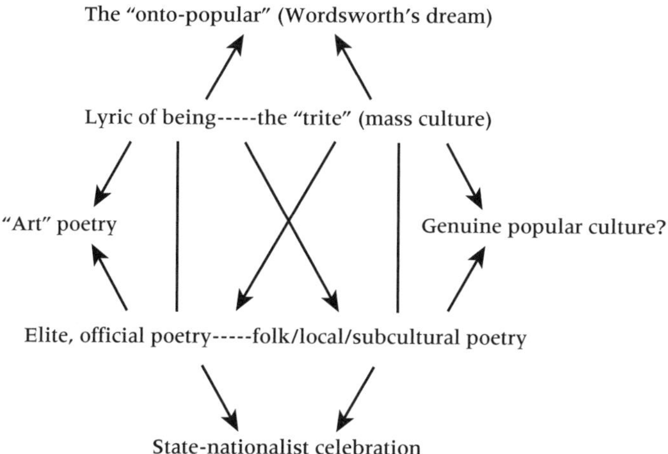

The polarities indicated abstractly here relate to discrete features of the overall post-1789 situation, like subfields within larger social fields of force, all of which overlap in varyingly agonistic ways. The existence of "official" verse is predicated upon the cultural power of both powerful old-regime and newly ascendant (i.e., bourgeois) elites, while its opposite "folk" number points, above all, to the persistence of the peasantry and to the emergence of alternative groupings like, for example, those of artisans, religious dissenters, or ethnic minorities. The "mass-cultural" is, clearly enough, an innovation of industrial, urbanizing capitalist society, an important inaugural movement that Wordsworth was on hand to witness. Meanwhile, the notion of a "lyric of being" has an especially complex intellectual pedigree; on one level, it should be linked (as the case of Shelley will reveal) to those Enlightenment intellectual tendencies—skeptical philosophies, above all, along with the tradition-destroying findings of science (particularly geological and incipient evolutionary science)—that had such corrosive effect upon older (metaphysical, political, ethical) "codes." At the same time, as Wordsworth's example shows, such writing is often motivated by a conservative effort to circumvent the imposition of new codes ("rapid communication of intelligence") by identifying some common base level of being putatively beyond codes as such.

The present chapter is devoted to an exploration of some of the work of a few Romantic-era (John Clare, Percy Bysshe Shelley, William Wordsworth, and Friedrich Hölderlin) and pre-Romantic (Mikhail Lomonosov and James Thomson) poets in light of (but also complicating) this field of creative possibility. Although the poems I discuss are enormously varied, ranging from monumental inscriptions to longer "prospect" poems to short locodescriptive lyrics, they are characterized by some common structuring anxieties: doubts about the nature and availability of audience; a concomitant desire to shape the memories, tastes, and aspirations of that audience; and, finally, a questioning of the rhetorical means used to appeal to audience, and the political implications of those means. As will be seen in later chapters, these are issues that continue, in modified form, to condition lyric production (especially in the inscriptive mode) well beyond the Romantic period and into the twentieth century, though perhaps not beyond it.

Many Dangers Ways

Of the "second-generation" English Romantics—they would include Byron, Shelley, and Keats most prominently—no writer seems more focused on specific locality than the poet and rural laborer John Clare (1793–1864), in his case his native Northamptonshire countryside. His work takes many of the recognizable genres of predecessors like Thomson, Cowper, Gray, Burns, and Wordsworth—I have in mind forms like the "vignette" of rural types (as in "The Woodman" or "The Foddering Boy"), satires (such as "The Cottager" or "The Parish"), the elegy of bygone country life ("Remembrances," "The Flitting"), and locodescriptions of great variety (as in "Emmonsails Heath in Winter" or "The Gypsy Camp")—and imparts to them enormous density of detail, creating the impression (or illusion) of an unusually intense engagement with specific place. An especially fine example is the superbly orchestrated, complexly rhymed "Pettichaps Nest," composed between 1824 and 1832, one of a number of poems on birds' nests that blend locodescription with the "natural-historical" description then in vogue in both prose and poetry, and which Clare practiced seriously:

> Well in my many walks I rarely found
> A place less likely for a bird to form
> Its nest close by the rut gulled waggon road
> And on the almost bare foot-trodden ground
> With scarce a clump of grass to keep it warm
> And not a thistle spreads its spears abroad
> Or prickly bush to shield it from harms way
> And yet so snugly made that none may spy
> It out save accident—and you and I
> Had surely passed it in our walk to day
> Had chance not led us by it—nay e'en now
> Had not the old bird heard us trampling bye
> And fluttered out—we had not seen it lie
> Brown as the road way side—small bits of hay
> Pluckt from the old propt-haystacks pleachy brow
> And withered leaves make up its outward walls
> That from the snub-oak dotterel yearly falls
> And in the old hedge bottom rot away
> Built like an oven with a little hole
> Hard to discover—that snug entrance wins
> Scarcely admitting e'en two fingers in
> And lined with feathers warm as silken stole
> And soft as seats of down for painless ease
> And full of eggs scarce bigger e'en then peas
> Heres one most delicate with spots as small
> As dust—and of a faint and pinky red
> —We'll let them be and safety guard them well
> For fears rude paths around are thickly spread
> And they are left to many dangers ways
> When green grass hoppers jump might break the shells
> And restless sheep around them hourly stray
> And no grass springs but hungry horses bite
> That trample past them twenty times a day
> Yet like a miracle in safetys lap
> They still abide unhurt and out of sight
> —Stop heres the bird that woodman at the gap
> Hath frit it from the hedge—tis olive green
> Well I declare it is the pettichaps
> Not bigger then the wren and seldom seen
> Ive often found their nests in chances way
> When I in pathless woods did idly roam

But never did I dream untill to day
A spot like this would be her chosen home[9]

The poem's surprising recollection of the most primal of all inscriptive settings—the classical roadside marker, with an inscription or meaning here readable only by a literate and attentive naturalist—is probably unconscious (though thoroughly mediated through English poetic sources) but not less striking for that. The association with inscription would seem particularly inadvertent from the bird's perspective, for neither it nor its nest has any interest in issuing an "appellation" to passersby: camouflage, not conspicuousness, is the object. But reading the poem, we feel (perhaps rather like the pettichaps) as though suddenly caught up in an ongoing and hugely lively conversation, as opposed to overhearing some solemn private encounter with an aura-filled memorial. Here Clare forges a rhetorical alliance between (among other discursive levels) the rich orality of much of his best verse and the casual literacy of that dilettante or pre-"professional" natural history that couched meticulous observations in comprehensible style, sometimes (as in Gilbert White's great *Natural History of Selborne* [1789], in the spirit of which Clare began work on a *Natural History of Helpstone* in the 1820s)[10] conveying the "data" in epistolary form.[11] The colloquial conviviality of the tone, its rural urbanity, reminds us (as does Alan Vardy's recent work on the poet's career) that "poor Clare," though in many ways poor indeed, conversed intensely with people of various classes, and sought dialogically to undo his class isolation in life and in verse.[12]

At the same time, the theme of "danger," of the continual proximity of the bird's life to death, surely does carry epitaphic implications, even while the poet's descriptive voice is trying as hard as possible not to be a cold, "anatomizing" one. Yet these two impulses within the poem—the joyous invitation to immersion in living detail, and the far more introverted suggestions of fatality and loss—are better seen as part of a single dialectic that will force us to consider "The Pettichaps Nest" in relation to Clare's historical situation. That situation involves, above all, Clare's own social and creative isolation in the impossible role of "peasant-poet" (i.e., isolation from both middle/upper-class cultural power and his unlettered country neighbors),[13] and his concomitant anxiety, frequently expressed, about the fate of a rural lifeworld passing out of history. "The Pettichaps Nest," I will argue, finds remarkable ways poetically to "resolve" a predicament that proved, for Clare's mind, quite literally intolerable.

We have already spoken, for instance, about how the poem taps into the sensibility of late-eighteenth- and early-nineteenth-century natural history—felt through the wealth of attentive yet colloquial detail about the eggs, the nest, its construction, its setting—in order to project an acute, observant, but potentially enlargeable audience for itself.[14] Surely the inclusion of uncommon words like "pleachy" (bleached) and "dotterel" (pollard tree) implies confidence about the eventual acceptability of this "local" naturalist's observations within a larger community of interest. And yet this is only part of the story, for in Clare's hands naturalist observation undergoes a kind of materialization that moves it well beyond the realm of the simply concrete and anecdotal. The sighting of the nest cannot be extricated from that careful mimicry of a spontaneous flow of observation-in-motion: walking, halting, disturbing, stopping again, and crouching down to touch—motions all sensed to be caught up in the physical flux they seek to apprehend. Syntactically, too, Clare manages to condition if not obstruct our passage through his loping lines, most obviously through his use of the dash (his only punctuation mark here) to mark hiatus and hesitation ("save accident—"; "And fluttered out—"; "Hard to discover—"; "—Stop here's the bird"), and a piling up of modifiers in advance of what they modify, giving them a kind of independence ("the almost bare foot-trodden ground"). These slight blockages reinforce from below, as it were, the central thematic motif of contingency, whose constituent notes—"accident," "had chance not led us," "had not . . . we had not seen," and so on—both recall the primal inscriptive "stoppage effect" and quietly etch instabilities into the poem's iconic "picture of rural life."

Rarely, in other words, is poetic observation more actively corporealized than in Clare, at least among his English Romantic contemporaries. Anyone reading Clare at his best (as here) is struck first by the apparent ability of his language less to "refer" than to make the world's substance seem to appear even through the conventionality of signs.[15] This illusion of phenomenality derives not only from our encountering those thick pockets, striking for this period, of tangled assonance and consonance in the plain style—"rut gulled waggon road," "a thistle spreads its spears abroad," "old propt-haystacks pleachy brow"—but also from the specificity with which the "nest" is made to seem embedded in a field of physical forces with their own impetus (Clare's *Shepherd's Calendar* is probably his culminating achievement in this mode). The presence of the nest is signaled by the movement of the "old bird," and its very substance folds together with the fall of leaves, their decomposition "in the old hedge bottom," the brown-ness of the barren roadway itself; its existence is threatened, but also revealed, by the casual action of insect, animal, woodman, and poet alike.

Yet this particular "field of forces" should remind us to introduce a temporal/historical dimension into our discussion of Clare's poem, if only because the social-phenomenal world of "The Pettichaps Nest"—a world of woodmen, haystacks, and horse-drawn vehicles—is not one within which any present-day reader is likely to have lived. (For whom among us does the name "pettichaps" have any resonance, for instance?) More to the point, how can we understand Clare's "corporeality," together with his related attachment to locale, as a distinct textual response to the poet's own historical horizon (and setting aside questions of strictly "poetic" posterity)? In a 1985 essay on Baudelaire, Fredric Jameson offers the provocative suggestion (not to be verified here) that "before Baudelaire and Flaubert there are no physical sensations in literature."[16] Jameson is thinking above all about those uncannily strong renderings of bodily sense (sight of course, but also touch, hearing, and smell) in the Baudelairean boudoir-world, about which we will have more to say in chapter 2; but his real point concerns an emergence of sensation within poetry as a kind of historical differential, as an effect of the falling away or invalidation of earlier structures, both within language and without. "The older [pre-Baudelairean] rhetoric," he argues,

> was somehow fundamentally nonperceptual . . . even where we are confronted with what look like masses of sense data [as in Balzac], those apparently perceptual notations, on closer examination, prove to be so many *signs*. In the older rhetorical apparatus, in other words, "physical sensation" does not meet the opacity of the body, but is secretly transparent, and always means something else. (p. 253)

I would not hesitate to apply what Jameson describes here—for he is really speaking about a structural/historical effect, rather than about a raw "emergence" at a unique moment—to Clare's intensely somatic and quietly sensational verse (although I will also eventually suggest that these qualities, in turn, "mean something else"). For the necessary historical contrast (and with no invidious judgments intended), consider again the opening inscriptive appellation to Wordsworth's "Michael":

> If from the public way you turn your steps
> Up the tumultuous brook of Green-head Ghyll,
> You will suppose that with an upright path
> Your feet must struggle; in such bold ascent
> The pastoral mountains front you, face to face.
> But courage! for around that boisterous brook
> The mountains have all opened out themselves,
> And made a hidden valley of their own.
> No habitation can be seen; but they
> Who journey thither find themselves alone

With a few sheep, with rocks and stones, and kites
That overhead are sailing in the sky.
It is in truth an utter solitude.... (ll. 1–12)

Wordsworth's lines carry us with simplicity and speed to the place he wants us to be, the place where the inscription is set and will be narratively unpacked. The traditional gesture of "Halt, Traveler!" is considerably naturalized, of course, by the unassertive and even hypothetical mood of the appellative voice ("if from the public way...") and the subtle linking of the scene to a viewing consciousness ("they / Who journey thither find themselves alone..."); compare, for instance, the sharp "Nay, Traveller! rest" that inaugurates "Lines Left upon a Seat in a Yew-tree" (ca. 1797) and the beginnings of many of his other inscriptions. Yet, relative to Clare's lines, Wordsworth's seem post facto rather than the registration of immediate sensation, or of Jameson's "opacity of the body." They stage an introduction to something already known to be greater, to the scene of memory that will also, Wordsworth hopes, persist as his own posterity among "youthful Poets." The description remains (again, relatively) picturesque in diction—"public way," "tumultuous brook," "pastoral mountains"—and there is no sense of possible interruption, or of a lyric observer "left to many dangers way." One should add that the density of local, phenomenal detail in "The Pettichaps Nest" is far from unique to this poem within Clare's oeuvre (here is the opening of the contemporary "Yellowhammers Nest")—

Just by the wooden brig a bird flew up
Frit by the cowboy as he scrambled down
To reach the misty dewberry—let us stoop
And seek its nest—the brook we need not dread
Tis scarcely deep enough a bee to drown
So it sings harmless oer its pebbly bed (p. 141)

—even as the older, Thomsonian rhetoric frequently reappears in unsublimated form (here in a phrase like "oer its pebbly bed").

Any attempt to account for the intense corporeality of Clare's inscription must surely begin with the anxiety his poetry registers, ubiquitously, about the fate of the rural-natural world in the face of historical change, and specifically those social and topographical erasures and re-inscriptions (the notorious enclosures and imparkments)[17] that established new "local" holdings and left Clare and his like in alienation:

Inclosure came and trampled on the grave
Of labours rights and left the poor a slave

. . . .
The sheep and cows were free to range as then
Where change might prompt nor felt the bonds of men
("The Mores," p. 91)

Inclosure like a Buonaparte let not a thing remain
It leveled every bush and tree and leveled every hill
And hung the moles for traitors—though the brook is
running still
It runs a naked brook cold and chill
("Remembrances," p. 150)

Most often, as in "The Pettichaps Nest," Clare's dense observations have a present-tense, documentary quality, as though they were immediate registrations of experience or *plein air* sketches. That we often find the same kinds of descriptions placed in the past tense and given an intense elegiac charge suggests that the overwhelming corporeality of Clare's poetry is best read as shadowed by the disappearance of his physical world, as compensation for a widening absence wrought by historical change. Again, from "Remembrances":

When I used to lie and sing by old eastwells boiling spring
When I used to tie the willow boughs together for a "swing"
And fish with crooked pins and thread and never catch a thing
With heart just like a feather—now as heavy as a stone
When beneath old lea close oak I the bottom branches broke
To make our harvest cart like so many working folk
And then to cut a straw at the book to have a soak
O I never dreamed of parting or that trouble had a sting
Or that pleasures like a flock of birds would ever take to wing
Leaving nothing but a little naked spring (p. 148)

Although the possibility of his voice being read as a "representative" one is not foreclosed—we do get an oblique reference to some commonality of experience ("like so many working folk")—Clare suffers the losses he describes alone. Plainly enough, those markers of dialogue so noticeable in "The Pettichaps Nest" (the recurrent "we," "you and I," the injunction in line 37 to "stop") are likewise motivated by a fear of the loss of all audience. Even this fear carries its own ambivalence, however, for "solitude" (of the type enjoyed by many of Clare's birds, including, in a way, the pettichaps itself) is something the poet also seems to crave.

The contradictions informing this poetry, born of modernity and the imperfect freedoms it brings, are multiple and insuperable. Clare's experience of the rural world enables him to write of it in this dense and "immediate" way, and to defend its importance; yet that rural world was vanishing, even while the new, bourgeois culture that was supplanting it also generated (in the form of new venues of publishing) the very context in which Clare's poetry, already perceived as "nostalgic" perhaps, could be received and read. In other words, the "authenticity" of his inscription projects for his readership the attractive and consumable image of the "peasant poet," a reification that stereotypes the poet but also enables him to have an audience. The more personal ramifications of this situation are not difficult to see: Clarean corporeality at once expresses the poet's anguished attachment to (disappearing) place, and his wish to fashion a persona (again, that of the "peasant poet") that enables an escape from circumscribed place and mute illiteracy into the "autonomous" field of culture.

It might seem that the role of the pettichaps's nest as inscriptive image or paradigm in Clare's poem is to imaginatively resolve these contradictions, to project their solution to the relation between poet and audience within the inscription itself.[18] The nest's location on the "rut gulled waggon road" is enough to surprise the poem's speaker, inasmuch as most nests (including those in Clare's poetry) are found well off the beaten track. Even more surprising, perhaps, is the luxurious interior of the nest ("lined with features warm as silken stole / And soft as seats of down for painless ease"), a haven of romance in the very midst of the destructively mundane. Like Clare's poetry, the nest is "formed" in an unlikely place, in the midst of both natural and human "dangers," but retains nonetheless both its snug integrity and a proximity to the flux of the world.

But as noted already, that proximity is plainly and strongly mediated by an almost impenetrable camouflage, such that it becomes unclear how much further we can extend our analogy; the nest is so "snugly made" that it seems almost indifferent to the kind of audience that Clare ambivalently desires. In the end, the most important projection in "The Pettichaps Nest" is of that audience itself, in the form of the poem's speaker and his hypothetical companion. The poem makes its appeal to a certain kind of observer-reader, someone attentive to and respectful of the negligible, and able not only to wonder at "small things" but also to articulate their value, to make them valid objects of discourse. Most important, perhaps, this reader is mobile, in the sense of being both corporeally responsive to the leadings of "chance" and able to move or mediate between a direct experiencing of nature (characteristic of the peasant) and the discursivities of natural history and poetry, without the one suppressing the other. This "we," this community of response, is a utopian idea, inasmuch as it seeks both to circumvent the complete subsumption of the rural world by external, instrumental categories, and to make rural experience articulate. It is utopian also because it was quite strictly unrealizable within Clare's own lifeworld.

Not a City

Readers familiar with developments in visual studies will already have noticed that the kind of corporealized, mobile gaze structuring Clare's poetry is much like one that has recently been identified as paradigmatic for modernity as such. Jonathan Crary has shown how the camera obscura—a basic optical assemblage known from antiquity, in which an inverted image of "reality" is projected automatically through a small hole inside a darkened interior onto the wall or side opposite—functioned from the late 1500s to the late 1700s as a discursive matrix for perceiving subjectivity in general, a subjectivity characterized by a perfect and instantaneous union of sensory and rational knowledge, a "split between perceiver and world,"[19] and, above all, the independence of perception from the physical body of the perceiver. Beginning in the late eighteenth century, and under the impact of both the Kantian epistemological revolution and emergent physiological science, Crary argues, this matrix is at once de-centered and corporealized:

> In the aftermath of Kant's work there is an irreversible clouding over of the transparency of the subject-as-observer. Vision, rather than a privileged form of knowing, becomes itself an object of knowledge, of observation. From the beginning of the nineteenth century a science of vision will tend to mean increasingly an interrogation of the physiological makeup of the human subject, rather than the mechanics of light and optical transmission. It is a moment when the visible escapes the timeless order of the camera obscura and becomes lodged in another apparatus, within the unstable physiology and temporality of the human body. (p. 70)

Clare can thus be seen as making an intervention within this situation, as fashioning a proposal for a certain kind of disposition toward the world—involving both seeing and reading, and an acknowledgment (in the bird's concealment) of the world's opacity—a proposal whose conditions of possibility are a new sense of "subjective vision" as dependent upon "the composition and functioning of our sensory apparatus."[20] Needless to say, Clare's intervention is a modest one compared to the formidable and quantitative disciplinary optics that (as Crary shows) were emerging around the time Clare was writing, with the aim of harnessing this new dynamic visuality to projects of rationalization and modernization. Clare's mise-en-scène of observation has a preservative motivation as well, of course, inasmuch as it projects a local and rural, and therefore endangered, sort of spectatorship.

For their part, Clare scholars will be reminded here of John Barrell's groundbreaking study of Clarean visuality as it relates to earlier matrices of poetic observation. Barrell situates Clare's mode of description as part of a shift away, within both poetry and painting, from the setting of the *prospect* (from the Latin *pro-spicere:* to look out into the distance) to a much less schematic and more "individualized" mode of seeing. A setting up of perspective often prefaces the traditional lyric-topographical description, as the traveler gains the high vantage point or "prospect" necessary for untrammeled observation and enjoyment. Ideally, this perspective provides both a breadth of vision and a comfortable distance from the actual scene, a vista at once encyclopedic and relaxed, as here (in an example discussed by Barrell, and probably adored by Clare) from the "Spring" section of James Thomson's *The Seasons:*

> Meantime you gain the height, from whose fair brow
> The bursting prospect spreads immense around;
> And, snatched o'er hill and dale, and wood and lawn,
> And verdant field, and darkening heath between,
> And villages embosomed soft in trees,
> And spiry towns by surging columns marked
> Of household smoke, your eye excursive roams—
> Wide-stretching from the Hall in whose kind haunt
> The hospitable Genius lingers still,
> To where the broken landscape, by degrees
> Ascending, roughens into rigid hills
> O'er which the Cambrian mountains, like far clouds
> That skirt the blue horizon, dusky rise.[21]

I should like to emphasize just two aspects of this passage. Like other prospect poems, these lines (although a segment of a much larger whole) constitute an inscription. The poet's response is staged as something provoked by an encounter with the "height," by the attainment of a remarkable view that then elicits lyric commemoration. Such writing recalls the oldest travelers' practices of leaving legible traces on visited places, much as it suggests the guestbook inscription and presages the tourist snapshot; more important for Thomson, certainly, is the whole emergent practice of verse memorialization of journeys, particularly stemming from the "Grand Tour" tradition.[22] Second, a specific matrix of seeing is projected in these lines, one radically different from what we saw in Clare's inscription. While the scene unfolding before the speaker is energized and alive—the prospect "bursts" and "spreads," the columns of smoke "surge"—what dominates is the sense of placedness-within-diversity, a "broken landscape, by degrees /Ascending": the fairly clear stepwise perspectival progression from Hall to hills to mountains, even while punctuated by town and village, heath and dale. Barrell isolates the central import of the passage:

> [T]his insistence on a high viewpoint . . . creates a space between the landscape and the observer, similar in its effect to the space between a picture and whoever is looking at it. So, in this passage, Thomson is able to see the landscape, not as something in which he is involved, and which is all round him, but as something detached from him, *over there* . . .
>
> Thomson . . . feels he must control nature in order not to be controlled by it, and it is in this respect that the, so to speak, moral significance of his insistence on describing landscape from high viewpoint is best understood.[23]

Barrell directly links the structure of the prospect poem to the processes of enclosure: as the prospect-poet represented locality "by applying a more or less arbitrary visual structure to a view," so, too, the enclosers imposed "the landscape of parliamentary enclosure on that of an open-field parish."[24] Thus Clare's corporealizing of lyric observation amounted to a dual act of resistance, an assertion of both poetic and local difference, even as (as we have seen) his very "grounding" of verse description helped to generate and legitimize the marketable category of "peasant-poet."[25]

One could argue, of course, that an abandonment of the high vista—no longer thought of as a literal prospect but rather as the possibility of a comprehensive *theoretical* assessment of a situation within some larger totality—is precisely what leads to this starkly contradictory situation, inasmuch as the reactive turn to literary localism could carry real political efficacy only through a diagnosis of the mechanisms of cultural distribution, and (ultimately) the active fashioning of alternatives to them. At the same time, the dynamic of modernization tends to undermine all "single perspectives" on the social totality, even while it persists as a kind of remote and absolute horizon in relation to which all specific change is merely relative. Those places that Clare (or we ourselves) would deem irreplaceable—that is, as existing within what Henri Lefebvre calls *absolute space*—must at once be considered within a speculative identity shared with their apparent opposite, sheer mobility and exchange. Even contemporary urban space, according to Lefebvre, appears in these "two lights":

> [O]n the one hand it is replete with places which are holy or damned, devoted to the male principle or the female, rich in fantasies or phantasmagorias; on the other hand it is rational, state-dominated and

> bureaucratic, its monumentality degraded and obscured by traffic of every kind, including the traffic of information. It must therefore be grasped in two different ways: as *absolute* (apparent) within the *relative* (real).[26]

And, clearly, imaginings of the general often involve some resettling and amassing of terms, the inscription and arrangement of localities. At the beginning of *The Wealth of Nations,* for example, Adam Smith notes how the scattered distribution of workers, all supposedly laboring toward the ends of a single productive enterprise (and nothing more), has prevented economists from seeing the true nature of the division of labor.[27] A tension exists, therefore, between "place" conceived as self-sufficient and integral, and "place" as a contingent effluvial castoff of theoretical or conceptual frameworks. Theories, for the most part, deny localizations, and what cannot be replaced or reorganized within the general usually ends up in the every-where of assumption or the no-place of exclusion ("irrelevance").

Needless to say (as Lefebvre points out), familiar reserves of the irreplaceable do exist, such as historical sites, monuments, and graveyards. And it gives one a mischievous pleasure to contemplate the obstacles that would be placed in the way of city planning if every street, every building, every parking meter, and every fire hydrant were marked with memorial inscriptions to the local dead, and made the object of ritual visitation and homage. Of course, the memorial is already a paradoxical case, because it is, in fact, itself replacing what it memorializes; the fixedness and prominence of the inscribed object becomes, in a sense, a metaphor for a living integrity that could not be sustained.[28] The ruse becomes obvious when places borrow and conglomerate allegedly "still glowing" details and forms from the past (as in the suspiciously self-conscious and secondhand revelations of most neoclassic architecture) in order to splice together their aura.

From this one might already predict that the periodic discrediting of rational-theoretical frameworks, perhaps extending in radical instances to the invalidation of frameworks per se, might lead to a search for immanent meanings or for particularity beyond significance: in landscapes, in nature, in the "mutely" objective.[29] Place as "simple location" (in A. N. Whitehead's sense) naturally resists replacement by stubbornly asserting, if not accounting for, its own specialness independent of, or even in opposition to, larger schemata. Of course, this specialness can itself seem schematic, observed from a more impinged-upon perspective, from where another self is seen playing Self-Evident. On the other hand, a truly radical particularity would "assert" precisely nothing; like (or almost like) Clare's pettichaps's nest, it would lack all appellative force. But what if the very conditions for "prospective" seeing come into question, as they do within modernity; what if, as happens in Percy Bysshe Shelley's prospective inscription "Mont Blanc" (1816; subtitled "Lines Written in the Vale of Chamouni"), the scene revealed by the prospect is not one that can be described, nor the prospect itself inscribed as a position others might potentially occupy?

All commentators, whatever their other disagreements, maintain that the prospective matrix of Shelley's poem serves to frame a meditation on the relationship between the mind and the external world. Most of them have likewise discovered that the poem seems to say conflicting and various things about that relation. Do mind and nature cohere in exquisite unity,[30] or do they have nothing to do with each other? Is some kind of "interdependence" of the ideal and the material asserted, or does the poet silence nature in order to clear a space for his own freedom?[31]

We would first do well to recall the scene: Shelley, gazing upon Western Europe's highest mountain from a bridge across the Arve River in the Valley of Chamonix, begins by establishing an apparently clear analogy of two relational structures to each other: between the Arve and the valley through which it runs, on the one hand, and, on the other, between the mind and the sensory world ("the clear universe of things around")[32] that provides mind with its raw material or content. As Earl Wasserman has shown, Shelley distinguishes here between "[his] own, [his] human mind" and Mind as such; the Ravine of Arve comes to figure the latter, much as the peak of Mont Blanc figures the inaccessible, quality-less "Power" that is the source of all "things" and impressions of things.[33] The first two lines tell us that "the everlasting universe of things / Flows through the mind," and judging from this it would seem that the relation between Mind and Power is a non-contingent one, as natural as water flowing down a rill. This relationship is one of mutual dependence, for the river requires the ravine for it to be a river, and vice versa. The clamorous life and grandeur of the Ravine—the "mighty swinging" of the "giant brood of pines" (ll. 23, 20), the "earthly rainbows stretched across the sweep / Of the ethereal waterfall" (ll. 25–26)—finds articulate existence only in "the complex interdependence of the mind's darkness and the brilliance of 'things.' "[34]

As in other prospect poems, it is the grandeur of the vista itself, and the knowledge it promises, that is to draw the reader into the inscription. Yet what "Mont Blanc" projects, that remarkable coherence of Knowledge and Being, is shaken near the end of the poem's second section, when the poet inserts his own mind and his own impressions into the analogy.

If the *paysage moralisé* tradition is mobilized here, it is only in order to reflect on that tradition's (conceptual) conditions of possibility:

> Dizzy Ravine! And when I gaze on thee
> I seem as in a trance sublime and strange
> To muse on my own separate phantasy,
> My own, my human mind, which passively
> Now renders and receives fast influencings,
> Holding an unremitting interchange
> With the clear universe of things around [. . . .] (ll. 34–40)

Film theory aficionados might dimly recognize here a scenario rather like cinematic "primary identification" as described by Christian Metz, wherein the prospective unfolding of the film inscribes the viewer into the position of Ideal Spectator;[35] what Shelley seems to perceive in the ravine is nothing less than a corporeal image of Perception itself. Yet as Wasserman and others have noted, it is important that the poet figures this new analogy, or rather the mental conditions under which it is made, as a "trance." The idea of trance suggests self-enclosure, a gazing that is ultimately not related to any outside but is circumscribed by the mind itself. Behind the figure of "trance" lies the realization, I think, that the apparently seamless structure of Mind/World relations just posited has a radically contingent ground. For, after all, the sight of the Ravine, and of the mountain itself, is only another sense impression, merely one more part of that universe of things, and increasingly (as the poem unfolds) a spectacle inimical to projections of any kind. The special meaning imparted to it—its status as an analogue for mind-and-world—has derived not from things but entirely from the workings of the poet's individual mind.[36] As Frances Ferguson has argued, this is not something that the mind can resist doing; but it is also not a practice that leads in and of itself to knowledge of mind and world.[37]

By the time Shelley was writing, political and scientific upheavals had plainly relativized any structure that might be said to inhere within natural or social reality, leading to an ever greater production of theories about what that reality actually was. Perhaps most pertinent for "Mont Blanc," the work of James Hutton and other early geologists had undermined the idea, famously formulated by Thomas Burnet, of a providential order underlying the history of the earth. Suddenly an abyss opened up between cognition and nature, an abyss that also cleared a space for creative engagement with, and reinscription of, nature.[38] Nature, that is, disappears "from experience and [. . .] return[s] as an idea,"[39] or rather as a proliferation of *ideas*. More acutely than most Romantic-era poems,

"Mont Blanc" registers the effects of this separation of natural being from any specific structure of being. It does so by depicting a mind thrown back upon itself, thrust into a radical awareness of dualism, or of the difference between two monisms: that of Mind and that of Nature. If the poem's speaker begins by projecting an order upon what he observes, he ends up by knowing only that he does not know what he is looking at.

The next and concluding lines of the poem's second verse paragraph effect the crucial transition:

> One legion of wild thoughts, whose wandering wings
> Now float above thy darkness, and now rest
> Where that or thou art no unbidden guest,
> In the still cave of the witch Poesy,
> Seeking among the shadows that pass by
> Ghosts of all things that are, some shade of thee,
> Some phantom, some faint image; till the breast
> From which they fled recalls them, thou art there! (ll. 41–48)

The sensory substance of the "wild thoughts" ultimately issues forth from the inaccessible "Power"—from uncoded material flux itself, here affixed with a proper name—but attains the status of "thought" only by virtue of its containment within Mind. But Mind is now figured as decidedly dark, abyssal (the thoughts "float above [its] darkness"); only in the half-light of a poetic/platonic cave might "things" and "mind" be reconciled, even if simply as simulacra, as "shades," "ghosts," or "phantoms." Ultimately, Mind as such is revealed only with the complete retraction or recession of sensory things back to the inaccessible "Power," to "the breast / From which they fled." No image, that is, proves adequate to represent Mind ("thou") or its relationship to Power. Shelley's "nonrepresentational music" (Geoffrey Hartman) finds its origins in the poet's deep skepticism about the mind's propensity to project, to leap to conclusions on the basis of analogy.[40]

Jean-Joseph Goux has analyzed the iconoclasm perceptible in most descriptions of utopia (beginning with the one offered by Thomas More), pointing especially to the utopian desire to abolish systems of "general equivalents" inasmuch as any such systems—especially monetary and conceptual ones—are "instruments of the tyranny of the symbolic."[41] In this light, we might be tempted to relate Shelley's anti-representational negativity to a permanent utopian project as well.[42] Such a reading might generate its own problems, however, for how could humans ever actively engage with the world, whether individually or collectively, without in some way representing that world and the relationship humans have to it? Shelley pursues the radical consequences of his own skepticism in the poem's next section:

> —I look on high;
> Has some unknown omnipotence unfurled
> The veil of life and death? or do I lie
> In dream, and does the mightier world of sleep
> Spread far around and inaccessibly
> Its circles? For the very spirit fails,
> Driven like a homeless cloud from steep to steep
> That vanishes among the viewless gales!
> Far, far above, piercing the infinite sky,
> Mont Blanc appears,—still, snowy, and serene [. . . .]
> (ll. 52–62)

The poet's upward gaze prompts us to think of god-concealing peaks, like Olympus or Sinai, but the allusion is by now grimly ironic. Now, the sight of the mountaintop prompts not comparison but instead a sense of radical separation and dis-analogy. Either the scene before the poet is absolutely distinct from his mind (as life is from death), or (what amounts to much the same thing) his mind and its impressions have trapped him behind the veils of perception and intellection themselves. This possible solipsism is figured not as power or independence but rather as exile ("homelessness"), subjection, and transience. The poet's earlier use of the Ravine to figure Mind proves to have nothing to do with the scene, now grown indifferent to his probings. Indeed, this very indifference, this resistance to interpretation, is the poet's best proof of the existence of the world:

> —Is this the scene
> Where the old Earthquake-daemon taught her young
> Ruin? Were these their toys? or did a sea
> Of fire envelope once this silent snow?
> None can reply—all seems eternal now.
> The wilderness has a mysterious tongue
> Which teaches awful doubt, or faith so mild,
> So solemn, so serene, that man may be
> But for such faith with nature reconciled,
> Thou hast a voice, great Mountain, to repeal
> Large codes of fraud and woe; not understood
> By all, but which the wise, and great, and good
> Interpret, or make felt, or deeply feel. (ll. 71–83)

Ultimately, the mountain relativizes mythic ("the old Earthquake-daemon") and scientific (the vulcanism of the "sea of fire" enveloping the "silent snow") thought alike; even the scene as it now appears before the poet only "*seems* eternal now." The codes of human thought find no Wordsworthian haven in this mute setting.[43] It is by virtue of this extreme de-naturalization of thought that "large codes of fraud and woe," formerly thought to be rooted in natural order, are apparently repealed, de-legitimized.

One might expect this point of transitional resolution in the poem to have an almost comic flavor, as the symbolic network falls away and the material world rises up in near-Bakhtinian fashion. Yet the revolutionary repeal brings with it at least two new, related problems. On the one hand, the possibility of other, non-fraudulent and un-woeful sorts of understanding—of "codes of truth and joy," one might say—is also clearly disabled by the poet's insight. One might reply that codes themselves are the target here, rather than any specific coded content; but then one has to ask about the means by which such a non-coded insight might be "sent forth among mankind."[44] In other words, the question must be raised of the poet's own authority to speak for the mountain, a problem to which (to my knowledge) only John Rieder has paid sufficient attention.[45] Clearly, Shelley appeals to some notion of special authority—the strength of "the wise, and great, and good" (l. 83)—in order to give articulation to the otherwise silent "voice" of the mountain. But the radical poet's anti-authoritarian scruple, and his suspicion of codes, leads him to make his authority a plural one. The mountain's voice is initially "interpreted" by the wise, "made felt" by the great, and "deeply felt" by the good; and yet the real relationship between these levels, and the hierarchy obtaining among them, remains unclear. How can codes, authority, and solipsism be avoided all at once?[46] Where Clare's abandonment of the prospect enables both a new lyric corporeality and its reification within the category of "peasant poetry," Shelley's adoption of the prospect imparts to him an exclusive but skeptical knowledge that leads away from communication and projection alike.

I believe that Shelley offers something like a "way out" of this predicament, but it comes only after a final, traumatic driving home of the corporeal point in the poem's fourth section:

> Power dwells apart in its tranquility,
> Remote, serene, and inaccessible:
> And *this,* the naked countenance of earth,
> On which I gaze, even these primeval mountains
> Teach the adverting mind. The glaciers creep
> Like snakes that watch their prey, from their far fountains,
> Slow rolling on; there, many a precipice,
> Frost and the Sun in scorn of mortal power

Have piled: dome, pyramid, and pinnacle,
A city of death, distinct with many a tower
And wall impregnable of beaming ice.
Yet not a city, but a flood of ruin
Is there, that from the boundaries of the sky
Rolls its perpetual stream; vast pines are strewing
Its destined path, or in the mangled soil
Branchless and shattered stand; the rocks, drawn down
From yon remotest waste, have overthrown
The limits of the dead and living world,
Never to be reclaimed. The dwelling-place
Of insects, beasts, and birds, becomes its spoil;
Their food and their retreat for ever gone,
So much of life and joy is lost. The race
Of man flies far in dread; his work and dwelling
Vanish, like smoke before the tempest's stream,
And their place is not known. (ll. 96–120)

The passage moves relentlessly onward or downward to ever more denuded levels of matter and material force. Power is finally no more than the poet's chosen name for the corporeal but one that at least gives something like depth or perspective to a scene that otherwise overthrows all limits. Beginning again with mythmaking gestures (the glacier-snake, the inhuman city, the personifications of Frost and Sun), the poet again moves to retract any potential for narrative or even figuration, to culminate in a style so plain as to be almost unbearable. Only the Psalmic and Joban allusion of the last, crag-like line—"and their place is not known"—provides any final orientation, inasmuch as it refers not only to annihilation but to the long and lengthening human response to annihilation: to history itself, in other words. The next lines, however, promise something very different:

Below, vast caves
Shine in the rushing torrents' restless gleam,
Which from those secret chasms in tumult welling
Meet in the vale, and one majestic River,
The breath and blood of distant lands, for ever
Rolls its loud waters to the ocean-waves,
Breathes its swift vapours to the circling air. (ll. 120–26)

What enables the astounding shift? The "vast caves" here have affinities not only to "the still cave of the witch Poesy" but also to Demogorgon's cave in *Prometheus Unbound,*

Whence the oracular vapour is hurled up
Which lonely men drink wandering in their youth,

And call truth, virtue, love, genius or joy,
That maddening wine of life, whose dregs they drain
To deep intoxication[.] (II. iii. 3–10)

—and to many other Shelleyan grottoes, like those in "Hymn to Intellectual Beauty," *Hellas*, and *Epipsychidion*.[47]

I would argue that, if any element of what I called "legitimation" is to be found in skeptical "Mont Blanc," it is here, in the cave that mysteriously converts indifferent material into "breath and blood." Through this cave topos—one prevalent in but not unique to Shelley—the poet tries to overcome the antinomies of authority and radical isolation explored in "Mont Blanc." Tilottama Rajan has noted that,

> [Shelley's] characteristic image for inner vision is not the light which radiates outwards [. . .] but the magician groping in his cave, an image that Plato has loaded with skeptical implications[.][48]

It is precisely the darkness of the cave, however, together with its possible proximity to inhuman (whether demonic, volcanic, or revolutionary) power, that makes it suitable as a place (imagined) for an uncoerced, fertile re-union of matter and purpose. The cave is both a site of concentration and of obscurity and risk; the "vast caves" beneath Mont Blanc act as a kind of relay point for amoral Power, converting it into something life-sustaining. This is a true "cave of Poesy" or *making*, from which, crucially, the poet himself with his subjective limitations is absent.[49] Only by the finding or devising of a space protected from chaos but free of codes and conscious strivings—free from repetition, that is—can a "flood of ruin" be turned into "the breath and blood of distant lands," through an ecstatic reworking. Any ominous atavism latent in the conjunction of "blood and breath" with "land" is undone here by making the lands "distant," with source and soil connected but not possessive of each other. The cave's power to rework corporeal flux into an element needed by human communities legitimizes the inscription while apparently avoiding any projection of overall order upon the scene; at the same time, the nature of what happens in the cave remains as exclusive and unknowable as the Power itself.

Excursus 1: Mountains and Caves

In practical terms only the poem itself, a concentrated surface of dead letters, limited in extension but (from the inside) variously navigable, can function as the ultimate referent of the topos. Indeed, the highly complex and irregular rhyme scheme of "Mont Blanc," brilliantly investigated by William Keach, simulates the tension between meaningful order and sheer mindless materiality as an extended prosodic dialectic.[50] As Garrett Stewart has shown, the uneven skein of rhymes compels the reader to scan the poem for "the text's resistance to void,"[51] as, for example, in the poem's last address to the mountain:

> The secret strength of things
> Which governs thought, and to the infinite dome
> Of heaven is as a law, inhabits thee!
> And what were thou, and earth, and stars, and sea,
> If to the human mind's imaginings
> Silence and solitude were vacancy? (ll. 139–44)

The blankness reaffirmed by the rhyme of "sea"/"vacancy" is countered, argues Stewart, by the replenishing linkage of "things"/"imagining"; yet this connection occurs, as with the conversion of fierce glacier into nourishing water in the cave, in a (deliberately) hidden fashion, as though the possibility of the connection were merely inherent in the material letters and sounds themselves.[52]

I would like to pause briefly on this idea of "cave" as imagined space of creative freedom, for it is a fertile topos that comes to be expressed in many forms in later writing: as laboratory, as womb, as "abyss of language" (or just "Language"), even as grave. The potential for demonic and disordering, rather than beneficent, "exhalations" from the cave is always there, of course, but it is essential to the cave topos that the very difference between good and evil, healthy and monstrous, be subject to dissolution, for such binaries constitute the most fundamental and damaging "code" of all. A topos like "cave" is simply a productive surface for exploring various antinomies—such as the question of whether modernity is a space of inchoate, benumbed semi-life or a space of vision and revelation[53]—and not some invariant cultural constant. At various points throughout this book I try to show that "cave moments" are important in modern poetry, because they figure at once a point of possible separation from the world of social effectivity, a vantage for reflection on that world, and a place (like the prospect) where the differences between being and conscious dispositions toward being are erased.

Consider, for instance, this well-known passage from the beginning of Proust's vast novel, one of the great prose place-inscriptions:

> [. . .] when I awoke in the middle of the night, not knowing where I was, I could not even be sure at first who I was; I had only the most rudimentary sense of existence, such as may lurk and flicker in the depths of

> an animal's consciousness; I was more destitute than the cave-dweller; but then the memory—not yet of the place where I was, but of various other places where I had lived and might now very possibly be—would come like a rope let down from heaven to draw me out of the abyss of not-being, from which I could never have escaped by myself: in a flash I would traverse centuries of civilization, and out of a bewildered glimpse of oil-lamps, then of shirts with turned-down collars, would gradually piece together the original components of my ego.[54]

How does this "piecing together of ego" happen? In the absence of sunlight (for we are deep in the middle of the night), the sense of present place issues forth from the entire history, realized and unrealized, of human domestication. While the structure of memory here is a horizontal laying out of past and present moments, memory's content is filled out by that sequence of caves that give some material setting and perimeter to the out-of-place waking subject. It turns out that subjectivity, or the "original components of my ego," is nothing more than the span between the collective recollection of "centuries of civilization" and the first, undifferentiated simplicity.

That memory is a "rope" ("secours") suggests that the slumber cave is a space of bondage, and even more devoid of enlightenment than in the Platonic archetype. Yet the ability of memory to perform this redemptive task, and to synthesize the various places, seems a vertical endowment, "from on high," outside memory itself; the orientation and self-constitution of the subject is made possible because of something beyond the subject rather than within it. Although a place of "destitution" and "not-being," the cave is also the place where this near-miraculous visitation of memory occurs. The cave is thus a place not *of* knowledge but *where* radical knowledge is given or manifested—here, self-knowledge ("who I was"). At the same time, the speaker's reduction to a somnolent and "animal" condition in the cave can be read as a kind of hibernation or respite from the racket of those "centuries of civilization." The "secours," in other words, is doubtless a socially disciplinary memory, which, by virtue of its very urgency, still holds open the passage back into darkness and the womb.[55] The cave works both as a break from all meaning *and* as a theater where the deus ex machina of memory might perform its reconstitutive, signifying labor.

This double structure suggests that the essential theorist of the cave topos remains Porphyry the Neoplatonist, who reads Homer's famous two-portaled cave (in book 8 of the *Odyssey*) as a kind of cosmic recycling chamber where the dialectic of desire, material generation, and liberation takes place.[56] For this processing to go on, however, the cave must also be set at some distance from the everyday world, or at least be guarded from much of the world's noise and activity. For those who venture into the cave, this seclusion in turn often implies a return to a primal simplicity, always complicated (in poetry) by the writing subject's own sophistications and intractabilities.

Paradoxically, however, this very distance suggests that the cave topos may indeed resemble the mountaintop of the prospect poem—its putative topographical opposite—more than might be initially apparent. In *Cave Exits,* his astonishing treatise on the cave topos, Hans Blumenberg stresses the relationship between seclusion and the development of an imagination that can regard itself as productive:

> The primordial cave is a place for the concentration of attention. Both the jungle and the savanna are places of diffuse attention, of subdued wakefulness even in sleep. In the cave there is only one direction for self-preservational attention, namely the opening, which is easy to observe or even to close, and from which everything alien must come hence. [. . .] Only in the study is Faust truly "a Faust"; only there can he be seduced [into pursuing both] what is in the world, and what the world *is.* In *Faust II,* Homunculus announces, as a condition of his own possibility, the law of humanity: "*Whatever is artificial requires enclosed space.*"[57]

The cave for Blumenberg, in other words, is quite precisely the possibility of *observing,* rather than simply undergoing, a separation from being. Speculating on research into the function of cave paintings for the groups who made them, Blumenberg goes so far as to describe the cave as the place where the very idea of possibility vis-à-vis reality, and, by extension, of plans of action, arises. As though inverting Shelley's mountain, Blumenberg's primal cave becomes precisely the vantage point or prospect enabling that distance from objects constitutive of a rational subject.[58] One might thus be tempted to relate the cave topos (in Blumenberg's account) to the Nervalian "ivory tower" so important for post-1848 writers (and perhaps its much later mutation into forms like the literary-critical-pedagogical "profession").[59]

Within Romanticism in particular, the cave topos serves as a field for exploring both the possibility of new, radical, poetic knowledge and the deeply ambivalent attractions of withdrawal and silence. For the poet, descent into the space of the cave involves a certain risk, an abandonment of clarity and orientation, an aleatoric step carrying both threat and promise on all sides. The seclusion of the cave may help to "concentrate attention" or to dissipate it into an absolute relaxation; the poet might emerge from the cave with some communicable booty, or with no more than archaic residues, or his own obscure and foolish projections. Even more than "Mont Blanc," Victor Frankenstein's "workshop of filthy creation," conceived in the shadow of the great mountain, can stand as the apotheosis of the cave paradox: at once the staging ground for the ultimate utopian project—conquering death—and a regression far past the womb into the grave and down to the inorganic.[60]

Excursus 2: On Language and Localization

> Not in Utopia,—subterranean fields,—
> Or some secreted island, Heaven knows where!
> But in the very world, which is the world
> Of all of us,—the place where, in the end,
> We find our happiness, or not at all!
>
> —Wordsworth, *Prelude* 11 (140–44)

My brief treatment of "Michael" in this chapter makes it clear that, like most commentators, I see Michael's predicament, and his project, as analogous to the poet's own. The poem's mode of inscription, in which "Mont Blanc" also participates in a complex way, testifies to the risk involved in the modern—the risk of irrelevance or repetition, within a world now deprived of traditional certainties and thrown into flux. But how might the specific work of writing poetry be thought of in these terms? To answer this question, it will be of value at this juncture to pursue more closely the specifically conceptual implications of this situation for lyric writing. The great burst of aesthetic writing in German during the late eighteenth and early nineteenth centuries is a good starting point. Those foundational modern aestheticians/philosophers (who were sometimes poets as well) were reacting to the same (general) condition of uncertainty, and had to find ways to think of art within a new, more open field of possibility.

The importance of emergent *literacy* is frequently linked to conceptions of modernity, though less often to poetry. Within the modern lifeworld discussed here, the traditional class- and religion-based functions of poetry were felt to be changing, if not yet dissolving utterly—while new forms of language functionality associated with science, commerce, and the state were developing and steadily gaining legitimacy. I would argue that many of the aesthetically gauged reflections of the period are efforts to theorize the kind of literacy that might sustain and be sustained by poetry. In the periods and nations I discuss, literacy is often both a concrete project of reform and reinforcement, and a formal notion of value, a "currency," the meaning of which is a struggle to comprehend: the accepted ways of speaking, reading, and writing language. (Every major work of criticism argues for a distinct vision of literacy.) But literacy is, above all, a standardized knowledge of signs (rather than of, for example, the intricacies of manual craftwork) allowing large groups of people to work together in a coordinated way without continual direct and disciplinary reminders. It is this aspect of literacy which undoubtedly led the anthropologists Scribner and Cole to claim, hyperbolically, that "the primary function of written communication is to facilitate slavery";[61] but literacy is also a famous substitute for mobility, and provides skills that facilitate exploration beyond the prescribed instruction manuals.[62]

The kind of imposed literacy to which Scribner and Cole allude coexists with another, more positive "Enlightenment" notion that regards literacy ideally as a kind of meta-Esperanto. I am thinking (to take one early example) of Leibniz's famous letter to Peter the Great (1716), where he envisions the creation of a Russian Academy that would link the knowledge of Europe and of Asia.[63] In this hypothetical space, all local "ideas" could freely mingle and interact, producing either unpredictable modifications or, as part of the market mechanism of "progress," the gradual improvement of ideas through evolutionary struggle. Behind such truly utopian imaginings lay both the hope that scientific nomenclatures might emerge as a new lingua franca and a belief in the indifference of thought to particular language.[64] Of course, this last assumption generates its own rather familiar antinomies. Faith in the absolute translatability of some logical core is surely inherent in the most monolithic versions of capital-R Reason; yet the same faith can also be seen as informing a great project of converting philosophy into the vernacular—that is, of translating (as advocated by Leibniz and pursued by Christian Wolff) the Latin and Greek "axioma" of thought into quotidian "Lehr-Sätze."[65]

But because it cannot always be easily absorbed into the frameworks of instrumental reason, the activity called poetry (and perhaps all literature) has a difficult time establishing its own form of literacy within the sphere of the modern. Definitions of literacy require some grounding in function, and those for literature tend to break down into two categories. The "positive" variant (which relates roughly to what I have termed "projection") stresses literature's effects of civilizing and edifying, and sustaining or building up some status quo; its conceptual tools range from various versions of "taste" and "sensibility" all the way to *engagement.* Of course (and on the other hand), many since Kant have seen a kind of "(purposeful) purposelessness" as the basic characteristic of art in general. This notion has been elaborated as "resistance to assertion," the "play of language," "what is left outside the margins," and so on, up to and perforce beyond the counter-limit of negativity: pure non-function, agrammaticality, or "illiteracy." That terms like "resistance" or "play" are often used to describe the de-signifying effects of the radical singularity attributed to modern artwork already betrays a desire to propose some *purpose* for the purposeless: its covert re-signification in terms of the critique of Enlightenment. The relationship between the two camps is an extremely fraught and complex one; attempts to bridge the gap, as encapsulated in such phrases as "deconstructive ethics," often seem forced, even oxymoronic. Theodor Adorno, as he does so often, isolates the paradox with precision:

> [I]mmersion in what has taken individual form elevates the lyric poem to the status of something universal by making manifest something not distorted, not grasped, not yet subsumed. It thereby anticipates, spiritually, a situation in which no false universality, that is, nothing profoundly particular, continues to fetter what is other than itself, the human. The lyric work hopes to attain universality through unrestrained individuation. The danger peculiar to the lyric, however, lies in the fact that its principle of individuation never guarantees that something binding and authentic will be produced. It has no say over whether the poem remains within the contingency of mere separate existence.[66]

One of my presuppositions here is that the danger Adorno describes is not one the modern poet has any chance of avoiding, partly because it is also what gives the poetry its "occasion," its opportunity to act. And act it has: for, in fact, poetry within modernity has often proved eminently exploitable, on the one hand, by commercial interests (think of jingles, slogans, song lyrics themselves) and by self-commemorating state power, but, on the other, by subaltern groups and social movements who have used poetry (most often song) as occasions for critique and appellations for unity and struggle. These are the other horizons to keep in mind when considering the difficult question of "lyric language."

* * *

In the German Idealist tradition and its immediate precursors, thought on the topic of poetry is intensely focused on the lyric's affiliation with particularity, with individuality, and with the individual subject. (Such views stand in sharp contrast to earlier emphases on rule, on mimesis [Batteux], and on emotional effect [Klopstock].) And so Friedrich Bouterwek wrote in 1806 that "the essence of lyric poetry is the representation of the poetic nature of the poet himself, of his [own] free view of the world, and of his feeling";[67] Schiller earlier (1791) had pronounced in his review of Bürger that "all that the poet can give us is his *individuality*";[68] Schelling insisted that "particularity" was "the dominant" in lyric;[69] and some of Novalis's "Fragments" convey the same idea with lapidary precision:

> Every poem maintains its own relationships with all its various readers and with all its possible conditions—it has its own environs, its own world, its own God.
>
> The more personal, local, temporal and characteristic [*eigentümlich*] the poem, the nearer it is to the epicenter of poetry.[70]

The first culmination of this tradition is surely Hegel, who in the *Aesthetics* complicates it in a number of ways. He stresses lyric's basis in "subjectivity" and "inner vision"[71] but equally insists that poems possess some "universal validity" (p. 1111). Only by making desire into a comprehensible object can the poet achieve this:

> The blind dominion of passion lies in an unconscious and dull unity between itself and the entirety of a heart that cannot rise out of itself into ideas and self-expression. Poetry does deliver the heart from this slavery to passion by making it see itself, but it does not stop at merely extricating this felt passion from its immediate unity with the heart but makes of it an object purified from all accidental moods, an object in which the inner life, liberated and with its self-consciousness satisfied, reverts freely at the same time into itself and is at home with itself. (p. 1112)

Two questions immediately arise, however: how to ensure that the "object" produced is, in fact, a poem (rather than, for example, a drama, a philosophy, or a utopia); and how to purify the poem "from all accidental moods," to make it coherent. To the first question Hegel responds with a restriction. For a composition to be properly "lyric," it must indeed, as desire "liberated" into object form, display the "inner life" "reverting freely . . . into itself." In other words, the element of projection, and the sense of the possible consequences of this lyric objectification upon the subjectivity that produces (or reads) it, are strictly suppressed:

> [T]his first objectification must not be so far continued as to display the subject's heart and passion in practical activity and action, i.e., in the subject's return into himself in his actual deed [as in drama]. For the primary realization of the inner life is itself still inwardness, so that this emergence from self means only liberation from that immediate, dumb, void of ideas, concentration of the heart which now opens out to self-expression . . . (p. 1112)

This draws a rather tight anti-narrative circle around the lyric and makes us wonder where any "universal validity" (*allgemeine Gültigkeit*) might emerge from such a pure enclosure. Indeed, Hegel has to insist that the inner experiences expressed in lyric be "genuine feelings and meditations" (p. 1111)—although the criteria for identifying this genuineness are never clearly outlined—and that some element of the social, or what he significantly terms the "national," must infuse even the most subjective lyric:

> [I]n lyric both form and content are provided precisely not by the whole external world or by individual action but by the poet himself in his own personal character. But this is not to be understood at all as if, in order to be able to express himself in lyrics, the individual must free himself from any and every connection with national interests and outlooks, and stand on his own feet in abstraction from these. On the contrary if he were thus abstractly independent, nothing would be left for the contents of his poem except a wholly accidental and particular passion, or a capricious appetite or passing pleasure, and unlimited scope would be given to bad and perverse notions and a bizarre originality of feeling. (p. 1123)

To ascertain what might insure such "connection with national interests," Hegel turns briefly to folk poetry, which would seem to offer a clear example of expressed feeling that at once enjoys general comprehensibility:

> [T]he most concentrated deep feeling of the heart can be expressed in folk-song, [but] what is made recognizable in such poetry is not a single individual poet with his own peculiar manner of portraying himself artistically, but a national feeling which the individual wholly and entirely bears in himself because his own inner ideas and feelings are not divorced from his people or its existence and interests. (p. 1124)

This kind of "embryonic" unity with the "people" is, of course, the condition of the *primitive* for Hegel, and such poetry finally holds little appeal for a people that has already passed beyond that state of non-differentiation:

> Therefore, folk-songs are usually trivial in the extreme, and there is no firm criterion of their excellence because they are too far removed from what is *universally* human. (p. 1126)

But, once again, no sense of what that "universal" humanity might mean, or how it might be recognized, is offered. This is left for the poet to discover, and (presumably) for the reader to discern after the fact, although following the stage of folk creativity, the world of prose emerges as a mode of discourse unbound from local attachments. Lyric poetry (which *succeeds* prosaic consciousness, in Hegel's account) tears itself away from that generality, to fashion objects both utterly new and utterly true:

> Folk-song precedes the proper development and presence of a prosaic type of consciousness; whereas genuinely lyric poetry, as art, tears itself free from this already existent world of prose, and out of an imagination

> now become subjectively independent creates a new poetic world of subjective meditation and feeling whereby alone it generates in a living way the true contents of the inner life of man and the true way of expressing them. (p. 1127)

Lacking any universally valid account of the "generally human"—an account that would be fatally subject to reification in any case—the poet is left, in Hegel's treatment, to build his or her "new poetic world" on the basis of an absence. The consequence is clear: as the notion of "generally human" becomes increasingly difficult to fill with any legitimate content, the firm distinction between "new poetic world" and "true . . . inner life of man" becomes impossible to sustain. With this the poet is forced—or freed—to posit the intersection of "truth" and "poetic world" in his or her own oft-times, or even inevitably, "bad and perverse" way. This, needless to say, is not Hegel's own view—he has left us complex descriptions of his sense of the "generally human," including *Phenomenology of Spirit,* to which we will return in the last chapter—but all such descriptions have many, many competitors for our attention.

We would be wrong, however, to focus exclusively on the question of lyric universality in Hegel's aesthetics without making one last mention of the poet's *desire*—"passions" and "feelings," in Hegel's terms. That the lyric imagination generates those true contents "in a living way" depends, indeed, upon a total investment of "pleasure" and "love." For Hegel, every moment of the lyrical poem is absolutely saturated with meaning and relevance, and should draw readerly attention accordingly. Larger ends or "points" are delayed indefinitely, suppressed, or (though Hegel does not go quite this far) discarded altogether.[72] Thus the poem puts into question the very idea of cumulative, sentence-generating syntax, and slows the motion of meaning:

> In a poetic treatment and formulation, every part, every feature must be interesting and living on its own account, and therefore poetry takes pleasure in lingering over what is individual, describes it with love, and treats it as a whole in itself. [. . .] The advance of poetry is therefore slower than the judgments and syllogisms of the Understanding, to which what is important, whether in its theorizing or in its practical aims and intentions, is above all the end result, while it is less concerned with the route by which it reaches it. (p. 981)

The poem withholds a hard totality of meaning from the whole in favor of the "liveliness" of every singular element. It would seem as though Hegel is implying a certain ideal correspondence here between the density of particulars in the artifact and the dilation of readerly response—although too sluggish a pace on either side would no doubt jeopardize "liveliness" (*Lebendigkeit*). Poetry and understanding (*Verstand*) are different modes of thought, with the latter a transparent path from premise to conclusion, the former a rich and infinite tarrying. It is unclear, however—and here we might recall Clare's inscription—how a reader would move from one of the lively particulars to another. How, indeed, does a poem "advance" at all?

It is at this point, in other words, that the motif of the corporeal shows up in Hegel's theory. The problem is related to that of (in)comprehensibility: if the poet's world convinces of its truth, liveliness must be present throughout the work, and with such intensity that the poem's every atom will threaten to become a world on its own, without necessary connection to any "outside." Of course, the extreme point of such fascination would be total occlusion, the bare emergence of the phonic-scriptive elements in the poem, down to the merest blank and letter. Somewhat less absolute, the poem (in fragments or in toto) might coalesce into a fetish, a focal point for readerly and writerly libido, and a moving point of intersection between imagination and what it disavows. Indeed, it might turn out that the poem's radical attention to particularity might alter readerly consciousness itself, bringing to light the possibility (in Rancière's terms) of new "partitions of the perceptible."[73] Thus, in this tension between *truth* and *particularity*, something of the tension between corporeality and mimetic projection can already be traced out in Hegel,[74] and we will explore the consequences of this thought more practically throughout the subsequent chapters.

Meanwhile, my readers will no doubt have noticed that the question of lyric language as such has been approached but not touched upon so far.[75] It is the relative virtue of Friedrich Schleiermacher's later *Vorlesungen über die Aesthetik* (*Lectures on Aesthetics* [1818]) that the author, by sharpening the contradiction between *Verstand* (understanding) and "Poesie" and by de-emphasizing the experiential, pulls the question of language into the foreground. Schleiermacher openly admits that his view of poetry stands at odds with his own theory of language. What he calls "language" is a "logical content" ("ein logischer Gehalt"),[76] meaning the truth-content of any designation in its relation to the law-giving paradigms for either general or particular ideas (both kinds are *gesetzmäßig*, "measurable by laws").[77] But poetry is concerned with the representation of the "totally singular" ("ein schlechthin einzelnes" [p. 408]); how can this be achieved, when words depend for sense and truth upon reference to broader schemata?

> [W]e must entirely remove poetry [from the realm of science (*wissenschaftliche Tätigkeit*)], because anyone can see that its function is in no

> way the reformation toward scientific truth of consciousness's original conceptualizations. Should we now abandon this analogy (because it does not lead to [the realm of] art), nonetheless poetry still has something to do with language—but not insofar as it is the outer representation of any particular mental function related to real Being. In this way we may separate poetic from scientific activity, but our positing remains purely negative. So we must ask whether language is in any way different from what we call (in the largest sense) its logical content; for whatever within language relates to this content is entirely a matter of scientific [knowledge]. Indeed, there is here an entirely analogous [i.e., to poetic creation] supplementing of conceptualization, a supplementing conditioned by the reality of the object—conditioned, that is, by experience, by the mind's free productivity, which posits for itself a form for Being. But this is not artistic productivity, but another kind. What then remains within language, in which poetry might find its own essence? (pp. 396–97)
>
> Language is not made to articulate the determinate quality of the particular thing, but the poet compels it to do so; and therein lies his mastery. (p. 403)

But poetry is surely more than a forceful and punctual exertion, a "compulsion"? Schleiermacher finds a kind of singularity for language in its sound properties—

> melodiousness is something [pertaining to] particulars, and [by concentrating on it] language can fix upon particular determinations. (p. 404)

—but readily admits that these elements alone cannot account for what is usually meant by poetry.[78]

The problem arises in theorizing what Schleiermacher, like Hegel but with a very different slant, calls "expression" or "the representation of the particular determination [certitude]" ("Darstellung der einzelnen Bestimmtheit" [p. 407]). He sees language as a way of reconciling, out of communicative necessity, always specific deployments or expressive acts with linguistic structure per se, a compromise allowing experience to become thought. In speaking of the "totally" specific, one is either introducing a striking innovation into language or moving outside it; Schleiermacher picks the second alternative, although again in a manner different from Hegel's. Whereas Hegel sees the poetic "expression" (*Ausdruck*) as pure representation of extra-linguistic (i.e., phenomenal and intellectual) schemata (for him, the "national"), for Schleiermacher the representation tends, under the pressure (*Druck*) of particularization, toward the concrete lineaments of the referent itself, thought of here as visually apprehended: a *Bild* (picture). Schleiermacher notes that the localizing impulse pushing poems toward the "pictorial" ultimately produces a (real or proximate) nonlinguistic image. Here we are inevitably reminded not only of Lessing's *Laocöon* but of the iconic or pictorial tendency of much Romantic and post-Romantic poetry: the representation of scenes and scenery, singular if often tending toward emblematic status. Pushed to an extreme of singularity, of course, the lyric "picture" would detach itself from any signification whatsoever, to remain an unmeaning corporeal residue:

> Speculative activity stresses only the logical content, poetic activity the expressive elements of language (or its representation of individual determinations). If we want to express this in terms of a still more precise terminology, we will have to fix on something outside of language, in order to regard the *teloi* [of the poetic work] as approximations. Following the trajectory of the poetic leads to the picture; and if we want to distinguish poetry in its essence from philosophy, we have to concentrate on poetry's objective aspect that, as sensuous representation, lies outside of language proper and is irrational relative to language. (pp. 407–408)

Schleiermacher surprises us, however, by then finding in the "image" an odd kinship with its putative antitype, the *mathematical formula.* This latter is a kind of statement where linguistic expression moves outside its own compromise-structure toward the absolute identity with a generality, presumably by means of a univocal nomenclature, or sheer rhetoric:

> On the other hand, as sensuous expression of a particular idea, this [aspect of poetry] bears a similarity to [what might be called the expression of] the pure identity of the particular and the totality: that is, the mathematical formula or construction. We can think [of this construction] as a formula [expressed] within the forms of discrete magnitudes (as in analysis), or as construction of figures within concrete magnitudes. Again, relative to this, language is irrational. (pp. 407–408)

Insofar as poetry *can,* in fact, include projections of various kinds, we might be permitted to think that lyric might indeed tend, at some impossibly distant pole, actually to merge the "mathematical-formulaic" and the "pictorial" modes. This would yield the famous "blueprinting" of the classic utopias, which often contain maps of their domains and charts outlining their elaborate rituals. Something of this tendency can be felt in early-twentieth-century Russian poetry (Khlebnikov, Kliuev), and we need to return to it.

Taken un-dialectically, however, such a view would tend to confirm all the lurid fears of "poetic totalitarianism" that sometimes cluster around the question of "monologic" lyric poetry. And, indeed, Schleiermacher's efforts to solve the problem of poetry's intelligibility might seem to lead him into asserting some kind of preestablished harmony of meaning and matter. He asserts, for example, that poetry is indeed "the singular in its form" (p. 409) but a singular produced out of (nonhuman) matter by human creative activity, and therefore cannot but be informed by "spirit":

> In that this particularity is the expression of an entire life, it is also the expression of the entire human spirit as reflected in a single individual at a single moment, which bears the totality within itself. [. . .] As we have just affirmed, our conceptual activity is the way it is because the totality of the forms of Being, as they appear to us in a particular being, dwell within the human as spirit; [our conceptual activity] is nothing but the temporal production of this spirit (within consciousness) in its encounter with what is given to us from outside [of consciousness]. Just as we posit this form of Being as a totality, the particular, as it is constituted through creative activity, bears the totality within itself. The one [i.e., philosophy] is the totality of spirit conceptualized for itself within the particular; the other [i.e., poetry] is the totality of the relationship of spirit to the corporeal, likewise conceptualized in a particular. (p. 409)

Yet what is really crucial here is "the *relationship* of spirit to the corporeal." The Romantic "order of mind is fundamentally opposed to the order of nature, as inside to outside";[79] its conjectures cannot find perfect alignment with the resistance it encounters in activity. For the corporeal—and this is the real dialectical lesson—resists spirit in its own right. The consequence of this never subsumed exposure to (corporeal) singularities is continuous novelty—

> Thus speculation is language's convergence with the mathematical formula, and poetry its convergence with the picture. The perfect development of the one is philosophy, which provides the type for everything that is scientific; the perfect development of the other is poetry in its continually renewed productions. [. . .] Poetry wants ever to be new, and can achieve this only through ever-varied production. (p. 408)

—except perhaps when, as we have seen, poetry leaps more drastically toward physical or bodily singularity itself.

But perhaps Schleiermacher's most crucial point is his recognition of the odd affinity of both the absolutely general and the absolutely local for some kind of sanctuary outside language, that is, within the conventions and distinctions sustaining abstract systems (like rhetoric) or in material particularity as such.[80] This insight should make us wary of making any strict attributions of locality or generality to a poem—for how can one definitively tell the difference between datum and formula, place and topos? Hans Blumenberg (to take one last and much more recent thinker in the same tradition) expands on the question of these differences in his important essay "Language-Situation and Immanent Poetics,"[81] which presents a more conflictual and historically nuanced notion of the relation between singulars and totalities. For Blumenberg, the poetic expression tends not toward the pictorial expression of the particular but rather consists in particular departures from general linguistic norms. This position recalls that of the Russian Formalists, but Blumenberg explicitly associates this "alienating" procedure with the language situation brought about by the de-ambiguating effects of modern science and technology. These epistemic forces have introduced a new and exclusive idea of valid knowledge and asserted its independence from particular language (Blumenberg calls it "the indifference of information in relation to the word" [p. 148]).

One might, of course, relate this reduction of word to "sheer means" (*bloßes Mittel* [p. 146]) to, among other historical factors, the demystification of sacred language achieved by Protestantism and carried directly into philosophy by Leibniz, Wolff, and their followers. But Blumenberg does not view poetic polysemy as the recovery—in, say, Heidegger's manner—of some more fundamental or "sacred" layer of language hidden and wriggling somewhere in the petrified forest of the *Alltagssprache* ("everyday language"). Instead, polysemy is the breakdown of rigid and artificial generalities that have become identified with language itself:

> The aesthetic effect of the linguistic tendency toward polysemy is, above all, surprise at what has hitherto been familiar; the recovery of self-worth by the sheer means [of language]; the departure of the self-evident out of the sphere of an otherwise unnoticed "lifeworld." Thus it is not something "won back" after having been lost historically through some process of decay (but which might have existed at some time in all its originary presence as some mythic and elementary experience), and which now can be restored. Rather, the poetic function [*Poetisierung*] is entirely bound up with novelty, with first-time-ness. The process of making poetry, carried out in the realm of language, is in this way comparable to the process of theoretical objectification, which is executed in the most elementary sense when the self-evident becomes problematic; when, as here [in the case of poetry], something removes itself from the horizon of the "lifeworld." (p. 146)

Like Schleiermacher, Blumenberg sees in poetry and philosophy a common exilic character; but, like Hegel, he stresses the negativity of this stance, characterized as a resistance to the world's "self-evidence" rather than as a positive drive toward purer forms of representation.

Of course, multiplying meanings against meanings is not in itself constitutive of poetry: and now familiar problems crop up, of which Blumenberg is fully conscious. He also makes recourse to the notion of poetry as "approximation"—not to the impossible *Bild* as in Schleiermacher, but to possible nonsense.[82] A fall into non-meaning is avoided, theoretically, by a structuring that imparts internal coherence of a kind familiar from traditional poetics. At this point, the twin limits of "pure materiality" and a "constellation" carrying its own coherent "self-evidence" emerge explicitly in Blumenberg's discussion:

> The mere acceptance of the reduction of referentiality to the pure materiality of language would provide no criterion whereby entirely self-enclosed meaning and meaninglessness might be distinguished. The oppositional quality of poetic language, which can be inferred from the [general] language-situation, is still not sufficient to produce poetry, for this elementary quality must be brought secondarily into a presentable form. But polysemy is, on the contrary, an atomistic, a destructive notion; it is a [necessary] condition for poetry, but not a factor constitutive of it. [. . .] The structuring through which [the improbability of the poetic] emerges links it to a *probability* which its elements on their own would not have led us to expect: with luck, to [the probability of] evidence. But what is removed from the self-evidence of the lifeworld (and brought into a surprisingly novel form within its own constellation) integrates a context that is continually justified by new and compelling self-evidence. (pp. 149, 153, 154)

Following Valéry (and echoing both Schleiermacher and our discussion of "Mont Blanc"), Blumenberg mentions rhyme and aural harmonizing (*Einklang* [unison]; *Wohlklang* [melodiousness]) as two of the ways poems give the arbitrary a seemingly evidentiary quality. (Of course, he is also playing here with the roots of the German word for probability, *Wahrscheinlichkeit:* the Probable is what "appears true.") But sense is still hard to account for, and we are left again with an unclear relation between a presumed poem and its captivating atoms.

At essay's end, Blumenberg revealingly transforms this relation from a spatial "convergence" (*Annäherung*) to a temporal "anticipation" (*Erwartung*) with unmistakable eschatological—or utopian—overtones. It is a most uncertain waiting, this attendance upon *meaning,* for it is a waiting for something that never was, that has no formal prototype; any manifestation of vision or theophany in the traditional sense is disqualified by Blumenberg's own theories, here and elsewhere.[83] But the key point in Blumenberg is his teasing out of a dynamic latent in both Hegel and Schleiermacher: the theoretical disappearance or withdrawal of whatever in the poem is local or singular. Either it dissolves, that is, into abstract (rhetorical) schemata, or it passes out of representation into concrete material specificity itself. Yet the dissolution in each case might be said to be deliberate. To avoid a mutually destructive antagonism between the particular or eccentric, and (on the other hand) codes of intelligibility, the idea of significant and singular integrity is removed to a limit point of unknown remoteness. This is what Blumenberg, speaking in another context of "self-preservation," calls "der Reduktion der gefährdeten Substanz auf einen intangiblen Kernbestand" ("the reduction of the endangered substance to [endurance within] an intangible core").[84] This movement is often expressed as an inherent "drift" toward knowledge or revelation: "expectation" (*Erwartung*) if located in the observer or reader, "tendency" or "approximation" (*Annäherung*) if we focus on the poem's own inner dynamic.

Look on My Works

Whatever else the topos of the cave might signify, it clearly indexes something like that "point of unknown remoteness" from which an undistorted communication might somehow emerge. This topos stands, in other words, at one extreme of a continuum of possible scenarios of greater or lesser withdrawn-ness, greater or lesser sociability. Its antipode must surely be the topos of the *monument* and the monumental inscription, one of the most public and confidently social—indeed, political—of all modes of poetic writing, one that assumes its own appellative force, and borrows its legitimations from plainly existing sources of power. Such inscriptions are ubiquitous, of course, but how are they to be interpreted within a revolutionary (and counterrevolutionary) modernity?

We will return to this question at the end of this book, through a consideration of Osip Mandelstam's late work; but for the moment, and from out of a million possible examples, peeled off an equal number of busts and pedestals, here is a pre-1789 example, one of Mikhail Lomonosov's fine inscriptions (a sonnet in this case) for a statue of Peter the Great (written between 1743 and 1747):[85]

Se obraz izvaian premudrogo geroia,
Chto, radi poddannykh lishiv sebia pokoia,
Poslednii prinial chin i tsarstvuia sluzhil,
Svoi zakony sam primerom utverdil,
Rozhdenny k skipetru, proster v rabotu ruki,
Monarshu vlast' skryval, chtob nam otkryt' nauki.
Kogda on stroil grad, snosil trudy v voinakh,
V zemliakh dalekikh byl i stranstvoval v moriakh,

Khudozhnikov sbiral i obuchal soldatov,
Domashnikh pobezhdal i vneshnykh sopostatov;
I slovom, se est' Petr, otechestva Otets;
Zemnoe bozhestvo Rossiia pochitaet,
I stol'ko oltarei pred zrakom sim pylaet,
Kol' mnogo est' emu obiazannykh serdets.

This sculpted image of a hero most wise,
Who, for the sake of his subjects, gave up his own peace,
Who took the lowest rank and, while reigning, served,
Who established his laws by his own example;
Born to the sceptre, he stretched his arms towards labor,
Concealing the power of the monarch, to bring learning to us;
When he built the city, directed his efforts into war,
Visited far-away lands and wandered on the sea,
Gathered artists, taught the soldiers,
He conquered both his own people and the enemies abroad;
In a word, this is Peter, the Father of the fatherland;
Russia reveres this earthly divinity,
And as many as there are altars flaming before this image,
So many are the hearts indebted to him.

As with the gravestone inscription, these words are written that they might be attached to something, might become part of a larger complex: the "sculpted image" along with its demonstrative "this." Apparently, Lomonosov wrote the inscription prior to the pouring of the monumental statue itself; there were plans to have two images of Peter made, one mounted and one on foot, and it seems that Lomonosov wrote his lines to fit either possibility.[86] This sort of flexibility is possible partially because the monumental epitaph is very close to conventional panegyric, just as the sculpture itself is often an imitation of its honoree, but with the size exaggerated, scars removed, and posture corrected.

Of course, monumental size and stability serve as the physical analogue for the distinctiveness of the person represented. For surely justified exaggeration is what conventional monuments announce to their audiences most loudly: "what I represent is *not* you, and is larger, greater, more worthy of attention, than you are."[87] We recall James Thomson's tribute in *The Seasons* to the modernizing tsar's supposed ex nihilo creation of a country:

What cannot active government perform,
New-moulding man? Wide-stretching from these shores,
A people savage from remotest time,
A huge neglected empire, one vast mind
By heaven inspired from Gothic darkness called.
Immortal Peter! First of monarchs![88]

No *domestic* god (*lares*) is sculpted in Lomonosov's poem, no privately significant portrait of a successful daughter or fallen uncle; the monument steps outside any localized idolatries to assert itself as the center of a more spacious social domicile. The monument, as Michael North writes in the best study of the monumental impulse in modern poetry, "is the structure made to house both art and society, where each preserves the other in the repetition of worship."[89] Lomonosov's inscription draws out this theme of the monument's relevance—for why should it be standing in everyone's way?—by stressing the extent to which it convinces: beyond his own, indebted people to his very enemies.

In short, we observe in the monumental inscription a fusion of vertical grandeur—the stature of the statue itself—with a lateral extension of relevance in all directions. I borrow this "axial" notion from Harsha Ram's recent work on the Russian "imperial sublime," in which Ram describes a kind of "horizontalizing" of sublime (vertical) energy as central to imperial poetics:

> Poetry encounters history at the intersection of two axes, the point at which the terror of lyric afflatus is resolved in a compensatory and transformative identification with imperial power.[90]

A power that might otherwise prove unsignifiable, and indistinguishable from raw "divine" violence, undergoes a potent ideological conversion through the inscriptive monument-machine, as the statue stretches its arms toward labor and channels corporeal force into national construction. The monument as mechanism is a kind of pivot that can read as turning, unpredictably, toward either the corporeal or projective, depending on whether we emphasize *"the power of the monarch"* or his *"building of the city,"* the creation of a new Petersburg sensorium.

This is not to say that the civic monument might not have its own fragilities. In comparison with caves, for example, monuments are exposed (and this property is deftly aligned by Lomonosov with Peter himself, who supposedly [like Jesus] cast away the robes of monarchical protection) even as they stage their never ending scene of instruction. For this reason they are, like all teachers, the natural targets of erosion and graffiti, and must insist on continual care. Less than most structures does the monument have an apparent use, except from the point of view of pigeons; rather like currency in this respect, it is sustained only by what Slavoj Žižek would call an "enacted" or "performed" ideology, and has little value as scrap metal or stone.

Monuments, in other words, have an unusually close and constitutive relation to their maintenance by the public. Other edifices, such as houses and buildings of various types, are kept in good repair so that they may be inhabited, worked in, entered and exited with a minimum of fuss, and so on; they are kept up so that we may make use of them. Monuments, on the other hand, are there to be preserved: to remind us of memory, one might say. They act as focusing points for the preservative, that is, the memorial, energies of society, and the form these "points" take has much to do with social definitions and justifications. For this reason, of course, the monument's greatest debt is to the inscription that it calls into being. Memorials without some form of inscriptive attachment are sculptures, without any ability to guide memory down particular channels and toward particular names; "inscriptions on State buildings, tombs, and gateways," wrote Mandelstam, "ensure the State against the ravages of time."[91]

* * *

The utopian aspect of the political monument inscription—its longing to order the world around itself—is obvious, and today appears rather unattractive to many of us, who want our inscriptions to rely on less "tendentious" forms of legitimation. The monument's corporeality can reemerge, as suggested above, when its two structural axes of vertical concentration/horizontal dissemination begin to fall apart or fail to coincide. This happens with the appearance in poetry of those backgrounds and those histories—of instantiation and reception—on which monuments depend but invariably obscure. Here we find the basic instrument for any anti-monumentalizing cultural strategy, and the most concentrated example of, and meditation on, this strategy remains, in my view, that high school classic, Shelley's magnificent sonnet, "Ozymandias" (1817–18):

> I met a traveller from an antique land,
> Who said—"Two vast and trunkless legs of stone
> Stand in the desart.... Near them, on the sand,
> Half sunk a shattered visage lies, whose frown,
> And wrinkled lip, and sneer of cold command,
> Tell that its sculptor well those passions read
> Which yet survive, stamped on these lifeless things,
> The hand that mocked them, and the heart that fed;
> And on the pedestal, these words appear:
> My name is Ozymandias, King of Kings,
> Look on my Works, ye Mighty, and despair!
> Nothing beside remains. Round the decay
> Of that colossal Wreck, boundless and bare
> The lone and level sands stretch far away."[92]

The sonnet's first line reminds us both of the memorial and of the obstructing functions of the monument (Latin *monumentum*, from *monere*, to remind). "I met a traveller from an antique land": in monument poems an encounter occurs where one party, often the poet's "I," is largely silent, at least initially,[93] and where the speaker, or often an inscription, speaks for or out of the past. But there is a layering of encounters or blockages here. They begin with a reader's encounter with the poem, which we will not discuss for the moment. (In general, as we have said, monuments (and other inscriptions) obstruct the horizontal path of human strivings and words, if only by sticking up out of the ground. Indeed, it has been suggested that the piling up of attenuated lines characteristic of lyric stanzas is partly an attempt to verticalize or monumentalize language.)[94]

Although dramatized as an oral report, the traveler's description itself, in its directness and columnar compactness, resembles a verse inscription. On the sonnet's "pedestal" is, of course, another pedestal, on which "words appear." The traveler is both reader and bearer of messages: the message read is an artifact's self-identifying or introductory gesture ("My name is . . . "); the one borne or uttered includes this first message and much else—although not, significantly, the traveler's own name. Thus it could be said that the palimpsest of voices here deflects some of the monument's centrality; the king's inscription is interrupted before it even begins.

Perhaps the most striking interruption is that of the sculptor, for his hand intervenes in the very expressive substance of the monument. Like the traveler and ourselves, the sculptor is a reader and, we are told, a good one. Apparently the traveler infers from both the bulk of the visible fragments and the proud, disdainful tone of the inscription that the artist's portrayal of regal scorn shows not just skill but understanding as well. But this palpable medium, the artist, deflects the direction in which we "remember" Ozymandias. Placing the hypothesis about the sculptor's relation to the king's "passions" prior to the inscription immediately gives the statue the particularized, subjective quality of a portrait, the product of local encounters between artist and subject, hand and stone—we can almost hear the emergence of an ironic, Browning-like dramatic monologue.

Yet, ideally, the monumental artifact provides a transparent medium between viewer and retrieved memory, excluding other pathways. Indeed, what is recalled should, as far as possible, materially manifest itself in the artifact as the monarch's motive force, "stamped on these lifeless things," that shapes image and attention: an indwelling and governing spirit, as it were, imposing itself on the rock. Here, paradoxically, the very strength of the expressive rendering breaks up this impression of identity, drawing attention to the artist's, rather than the king's, mastery. The shaping hand becomes a possible punster; did the artist mock (that is, imitate), or mock? The traveler reads an alternative will out of the once single-minded, now "shattered" visage.

This hidden fragmentation within what is remembered (what are "my Works"?) is presented as a kind of virus of irony that presages the monument's final failure: its neglect and collapse. Thus the poem, on one level, is clearly about the de-monumentalizing of an artifact; the king's representation is not the unmediated exertion and expression of a singular will. In this respect, it can be argued that the poem remains, despite its irony, a projective work of art in that it implies a "configuration of the perceptible" (Rancière) far more heterogeneous than the one that Ozymandias's kingly power would propose. The sonnet, with its layering of inscriptions, replaces Ozymandias's voice—authoritative, limiting—with the "material ideality of language" and its unpredictable effects.[95] Nonetheless, in the end, "*Nothing beside remains.*" On the one hand, the king's pride has become the victim of time; on the other, only this decrepit trace remains to attest to how "much of life and joy is lost." It would be wrong to conclude from this, however, that "the lone and level sands" are thereby converted into a negative monument to the silenced and powerless. Instead, the horizontalizing of state power crucial to the classic monumental inscription drifts away into the senseless corporeality of sand. As for many (though not all) other moderns, the monument topos is not recoverable for Shelley; it can only be subjected to a critical, *material* humiliation.

Dark Chamber

But is this a humiliation of *creativity* as such, in the end? Ozymandias, like Michael in this respect, seeks to generate "works," creations that were never there before; the post-Napoleonic Shelley, supremely conscious of the barbaric subtext of cultural documents and hostile to idolatry, allows creativity to emerge only ironically, as the traces of the work that Ozymandias would efface. We see here that highly productive anxiety surrounding the New, and with that which might prevent the emergence of the New, that characterizes all the poets and theorists we have looked at, and marks their work as quintessentially modern in spirit. On one side, the creation of some "new poetic world" is not only possible for them but is necessary, given the absence of binding standards.[96] On the other, there is a manifest concern, within a social and cultural sphere not already saturated by signification, for the relationship of poetic to other worlds, indicated most obviously in the preoccupation with lyric intelligibility and with audience. Looking carefully into this duality, we see that it offers a way into one temporality specific to the modern lyric: a tension between the new construction or development, and whatever that new construction leaves behind, destroys, or expels in the process of constituting itself.

Thus *memory* emerges as one of the central fields for poetic exploration during the whole period. The clearest instances are perhaps found in those locodescriptive inscriptive lyrics described by M. H. Abrams according to the model of "Tintern Abbey":

> "Tintern Abbey" [...] inaugurated the wonderfully functional device Wordsworth later called the "two consciousnesses": a scene is revisited, and the remembered landscape ("the picture of the mind") is superimposed on the picture before the eye; the two landscapes fail to match, and so set a problem ("a sad perplexity") which compels the meditation.[97]

And so we find Wordsworth returning to his earlier happy haunts near the abbey, unable to recover those "coarser pleasures" of his boyhood but ready to articulate (in the poem itself) the shape that "abundant recompense" in adult life might take. This mediation is needed because novelty risks abandoning all anchoring in (social) discourse. At the same time, another, non-discursive kind of "communality" can also be discerned in Wordsworth's poem. The connecting distance between the poet's present "chastened and subdued" condition and his earlier "animal" state is not just time but also quite precisely the *corporeal*—"the mountain, and the deep and gloomy wood"—which exists but ultimately falls outside representation. "I cannot paint/What then I was."

The tensions between memory and novelty, on the one hand, and the corporeal and the projective, on the other, are perhaps the central features of the great Romantic inscriptions, and in concluding this chapter I explore their dynamic through readings of two remarkably comparable Romantic-era poems—Wordsworth's "Mark the concentred hazels" (composed between 1807 and 1814) and Hölderlin's "Der Winkel von Hardt" ("The Shelter at Hardt" [1803–1805]):

> Hinunter sinket der Wald,
> Und Knospen ähnlich, hängen
> Einwärts die Blätter, denen
> Blüht unten auf ein Grund,
> Nicht gar unmündig.
> Da nämlich ist Ulrich
> Gegangen; oft sinnt, über den Fußtritt,

Ein groß Schicksal
Bereit, an übrigem Orte.[98]

The forest sinks off
And like buds, the leaves
Hang inward, to which
The valley floor below
Flowers up, far from mute,
For Ulrich passed through
These parts; a great destiny
Often broods over his footprint,
Ready, among the remains.[99]

The place referred to here is a "Winkel" in both prevalent senses of that German word. The site of the legendary "Ulrichstein" near the town of Hardt, it consists of two large, long slabs of rock that lean against each other at the top to form a narrow angle or corner (Winkel). This configuration of stone has the protecting, cavelike, half-enclosed character of a nook or shelter (Winkel), and was used as such in 1159 by its most renowned tenant, Prince Ulrich of Württemburg, who successfully concealed himself there from pursuing enemies; local legend holds that an indented rock next to the slabs bears the imprint of Ulrich's "Fußtritt" ("footprint").[100]

These two meanings of "Winkel" pertain, respectively, to physical form and to pragmatic function and, by virtue of this ambiguous if undemonstrative structure, prompt reflection on the relation of a place's structure or shape to its real or potential significance, point, or relevance. Common sense would suggest that the relation is a purely contingent one, dependent entirely, on the one hand, upon circumstance and human interests, and, on the other, on the pliancy or recalcitrance of the pertinent piece of natural world. And, oddly enough, the poem never mentions, and only indirectly depicts, the stones making up the empirical "Winkel": they are, perhaps, too dumbly and flatly *there* to quibble about how they will be descriptively used.

In any case, it does seem that the poem that follows is an imagining of a relation between the place and possible modes of occupation, and that the shelter proper is somehow not fully adequate to this idea. We find instead an analogizing account of expressive peripheries implied by or implicated in the primary structure; that is, the enclosure as described in the poem seems shaped by the activity of surrounding vegetation, by what one might almost call the *sense* of vegetation. A principle of movement, if not of directed action, precariously shapes and sustains this "pleasant grove." "Sinks off" introduces the forest, ominously, as a vestigial and waning appearance, yet the turn to the inward-hanging leaves, nearly possessed of their own inherent blossoming energy ("like buds"), retards this downward motion without reversing it. Even more daring, however, is the image of the very ground's directed exertion into flower. It is hard to find the right verb to describe the relation of this ground to the leaves; to say that it meets the leaves would outrun the poem, that it tends toward them seems too reticent. What is clear is that the use of directional markers ("hinunter sinket" ["sinks off"], "hängen / Einwärts" ["hang inward"], "denen" ["to which"], "unten auf" ["below... up"]) together with the language of "blooming" gives the scene a certain tension and even *in*tention that a bare account of the shelter's stone frame would not have. (One is reminded of Mandelstam's call at the end of his "Conversation about Dante" for the conversion of all substantives into the dative case.)[101]

The effect is strong enough to warrant describing the scene as "nicht unmündig," a phrase that suggests a whole cluster of meanings: "not mute," "not without power," "not not-of-age." And yet these trends and danglings are precarious, because as vegetable motion they carry the possibilities of erosion or overgrowth; they can bring the structure down as easily as sustain it, in a duality crucial to the poem's inner dialectic. Indeed, the tendency of the scene toward internal closure is immense. The forest and the ground are like the lids of a seeing eye about to clamp shut, or (to link up with "mündig") a speaker's lips falling together—so that the space of the "Winkel" is kept open only by the inscription of the footprint, and (perhaps) the poet's superscription. The intensely focused dynamic that turns the shelter into an ecstatic *region* (in Heidegger's sense)[102] also portends something like an overwhelming of the site by material energies.[103] At the poetic heart of all the tension is the simple "Da," which seems to suggest both of its primary senses simultaneously, "there" and "for, because."[104] The footprint, in other words, is the indefinitely drawn-out *material sustaining of a cause*—both a senseless mark and a relic saturated with meaning for both the past and (especially) the future.

At this point, however, we need to acknowledge (with Wolfgang Binder and other critics) that a formative historical moment is being recalled, a powerful entry into the scene that established its center of gravity. What kind of power is needed to inscribe a footprint into stone? A supernatural power, we might reply, or, what would have been less imaginable for Hölderlin than for us, an industrial one. The violence surrounding Ulrich's original flight to the shelter, as well as the strength involved in rendering his trace—and the place—indelible, haunts it as past and as future. It is strength exceeding the narrowly "human," and would apparently persist even in the absence of human attentions—even though local legend is presumably what brings the poet to the site. Similarly, the very senselessness of Ulrich's trace recalls the non-literacy of the heroic culture that produced it; the footprint retains a warrior sternness, insofar as we feel it to be an inheritance from that culture. Viewed in these terms, the poem seems torn in two equally undesirable directions: toward a memory of repellent historical violence or (on the other hand) a thinly disguised "völkisch" drumming up of heroic bombast ("a great destiny"), the desire of inscription to recovery some of its authentic, divine, legitimating power.

This indeed is part of the poem's risk, although we would do better, in alluding to the question of politics, to recall Hölderlin's deep sympathy with the democratic aspirations of the French Revolution, and his surprising definition (in "Das Werden im Vergehen") of that most troubling word "Fatherland":

> Nature and humans, insofar as they interact in a particular way [*in einer besonderen Wechselwirkung stehen*].

Pierre Bertaux glosses as follows:

> A particular connection among things, a (little) world. Today we would say, "the environment, insofar as it coheres, of the particular—and insofar as it is experienced as coherent by the individual living within it, without irreconcilable inner contradictions and conflicts."[105]

These terms help us to see more clearly the question raised by "The Shelter at Hardt": what enables that (political) "environment" to "cohere," or rather what has to *happen* for it to cohere, what might "coherence" cost? The footprint sign is peculiar in that it must wait for fulfillment or fate ("Schicksal," destiny) rather than interpretation. It might be said that the fate awaited here is simply the legendary story of Ulrich—now become *his* fate and conventionally implied by the footprint—or the dissemination of it. Yet here Hölderlin almost washes the story off the footprint; he works backward, and tries to depict the "fateful" trace as though it had never been framed by a specific narrative: as though to imagine an inherent speaking potential (or "Mündigkeit") in the scene rather than the actual tale. Doubtless there is an ironic recollection here of Kant's famous sentence: "Aufklärung ist die Befreiung des Menschen von seiner selbstverschuldeten *Unmündigkeit*" ("Enlightenment is the liberation of the human from an *immaturity* for which he is himself responsible"). The superstition-laden place is speechless without being mute, pre-modern without being premature. Hölderlin still needs the name, of course ("Da *nämlich* ist Ulrich gegangen"), but comes close to converting the place into a pure omen.

An omen purified, that is, of everything except the energy of anticipation itself, which might feed any number of "vegetable growths." The rigor of the refusal of any content preset for the place, and the equally absolute insistence on its singular potential and coherence, marks the inscription as profoundly modern in the terms we have laid out. And yet in that very refusal—by never merely taking up the setting as a background for imaginative fantasy, or interpretation—the poet implies that nothing less than some actual intervention would suffice as "destiny." The projective machinery stops short of offering any kind of internal legitimation. As so often in Hölderlin, there is a sense that the poet is anticipating a kind of visionary subjection (we think of "Heidelberg," or the hymns in general). But eschatology could go two ways, it seems: either toward some renewal, heroic or otherwise, of the "remains," or (more likely, perhaps) toward absolute closure of the situating consciousness itself ("The forest sinks off") that, in its rigor, exposes the old "fate" of a sheer materiality.

The Wordsworth inscription, sharing so much with Hölderlin's, could scarcely provide a more illuminating contrast:

> Mark the concentred hazels that enclose
> Yon old grey Stone, protected from the ray
> Of noontide suns:—and even the beams that play
> And glance, while wantonly the rough wind blows,
> Are seldom free to touch the moss that grows
> Upon that roof, amid embowering gloom,
> The very image framing of a Tomb,
> In which some ancient Chieftain finds repose
> Among the lonely mountains.—Live, ye trees!
> And thou, grey Stone, the pensive likeness keep
> Of a dark chamber where the Mighty sleep:
> For more than Fancy to the influence bends
> When solitary Nature condescends
> To mimic Time's forlorn humanities.[106]

The key motif linking the two poems is "protection." The "Winkel" served as a quite literal protection from enemies, just as shelter in general protects against nature (without destroying access to it). What protects in Wordsworth's sonnet? The trees obviously recall a feudal (and no doubt national-bardic) entourage, epitaphic guardians who, like the words on Jonson's funerary tablet for Elizabeth Chute, "keepe the Rowle." But the main "marking" or circumscription of the place is a noticing (or a "re-marking," as Marshall Brown terms it in his superb extended reading of the poem)[107] rather than a fencing off; the concentricity of the stone's surroundings are at least partially generated by sight rather than activated from within. A typically Wordsworthian series of co-centers are set up, beginning, perhaps, with the attentive enclosure of the sonnet itself by reading: the hypothetical spectators (poet and beckoned reader) wrapping their attention around the hazels, which hang like sentinels over the stone; that sleepily brooding stone, which "houses" the mighty (and fictional) dead but which also, like an old gray head, sits pondering the very circle of the earth. But as the centering imagination is brought into the constitution of the place, so are less sober, extraneous elements—the "beams that play / And glance," the "rough wind"—which the structure only partially excludes.

The poem is as much an inscription on the experience of a certain seeing as on the scene itself. Protection is circular: the protective or "embowering" attitude both protects and is protected by the "scene," for Wordsworth, in the wake of his own political and personal disappointments, is enjoining his own imagination to "live" as much as the trees. The implied *remark* shifts its place of inscription subtly, moving from the carving on the trees suggested by "mark" (which also recalls "Nutting," as Brown notes) to the implication of a *frame* surrounding an *image* of the trees. The poem is thus an unusual ekphrasis, an explanatory comment appended to a picture that does not yet exist. But there is no chopping up of the trees for use as picture frames here; they are urged to "live" as trees, ultimately resistant to Fancy but "bendable" to it, at least on occasion. Nature "con-descends" as the hazels "con-center"; that is, as part of what is imagined as a meeting of various and expanding centers: trees, eyes, Fancy, and "more than Fancy."[108]

One apparently rather modest "utopian" impulse in the poem can thus easily be located: it is asserted that, if only properly *perceived,* untouched, existent nature will dilate the imagination. Thus the poem is indeed, as Brown maintains, a Bloomian "scene of instruction," and its teaching is a *cognitive* lesson:

> Humanity lies neither in matter, which is fixed, nor in movement, which cannot be fixed, but in the understanding that generates the accord of matter and movement, energy and form, variety and unity.[109]

But I think we can push our description of the dynamics of imaginative desire here a step further. What Wordsworth is actually striving for is a situation where the understanding's correct calibration with nature paradoxically opens at once a vastly broadened space ("*more* than Fancy") for imagination. *Poetry will, under such conditions, write itself*—or, rather, emerge as a normal consequence of conscious, forlornly human interaction with the world. Such, too, is the properly utopian consequence of writing poetry in a language really used by men (as advocated in the preface to *Lyrical Ballads*), and it is important not to blunt the force of the poet's aspiration by a positivistic stress on his poetry's obvious divergence from "real" colloquiality. All that need happen is that the scene be marked in order that it might yield up its vision; in a world of such "accord of matter and movement," poetry would be everywhere, with no damage done to the vernacular or to poetry. (Although, of course, "poetry" would no longer mean what it does now, would no longer need to be fenced off as property—Wordsworth points to a rather different "end of art" than that envisioned, perhaps, by Hegel.)

Much later in this volume (chapter 3) we examine the far more explicit development of the same implicit idea in some twentieth-century Russian poets. Meanwhile I would like to add a final complication to this reading by focusing again on the poem's pictorial thematic. "Image," "frame," "mimic" all sanction, I think, our reading the phrase "dark chamber" as a somewhat surprising pun—inasmuch as "dark chamber" is a direct translation of the Latin *camera obscura.* Wordsworth would have known about the camera from his readings of William Gilpin and elsewhere; in "Mark the concentred hazels," the "framed" quality of the scene and—more important—the control exerted upon light conspire to suggest that primeval image-generating apparatus. Yet Jonathan Crary's historical outline of early-nineteenth-century visuality, and of the superceded place of the camera obscura within that new discursive order, helps us to see just how past-directed (and metapoetic) Wordsworth's inscription really is. Here Wordsworth is modeling an inscriptive poetry that would align vision with world in such a way that authentic vision—the "Mighty" sleeping in their chamber—would appear, through the spontaneous cooperation of nature with this simplest of utopian representational machines. Poetry (on the model of the camera, and of the "concentred hazels") could indeed fashion a space in which a unity of human meaning and natural being could become literally perceptible, outside all the noise of modernity and its novel physical and cognitive stresses.

That the mimicry is of "Time's forlorn humanities" suggests typically Wordsworthian doubt about the possibility of such vision, of course. And although the inevitable inversion of images in the camera goes unmentioned, that fact recalls both the distance between imagination and nature and the corporeality that Wordsworth's resignifying efforts involuntarily recall throughout.[110] There is still artistic work to be done, in other words—unless, of course, the inscriptive apparatus is allowed to *substitute* for creation, rather than enabling it. This last thought suggests another kind of "noise"—the visual noise of reproduced photographic images—than Wordsworth could have known but that could still emerge out of the longing to preserve this quietest of settings, "among the lonely Mountains."[111] A less sympathetic reader than I might even find some foretaste of the "trite" (in the sense of mass-produced art) in Wordsworth's own locodescription here, nearly objectified as it is into a static emblem.

In contrast to Wordsworth's elaboration of ekphrastic inscription—involving a reflection on both its procedures and its motives—Hölderlin's poem seems a near reduction to the more primal form of the roadside inscription as such, with its densely archaic horizon. In "Der Winkel von Hardt," we sense that the description leads either to further waiting, or to action, but not to more description or re-description. In Wordsworth, what is awaited are more occasions for "pensive likenesses" to take shape. It is hard to know on what such occasions depend, although they surely involve the retention of some sense of a "dark chamber" unfilled by the "ray / Of noontide suns," which the poet hopes to provide through his own inscriptions. That an invalidated and archaic culture can be sustained (only partially, to be sure) by the marks and within the frames provided by the modern, literate imagination is Wordsworth's fancy in this sonnet, whereas Hölderlin, more preoccupied with traces of real power, points to a less accommodating and usable past. On the other hand, Wordsworth's meticulous marking-centering-sustaining runs the risk of mere repetition of a specific set of forms, in spite of a desire to open "mimicry" up to something "more than Fancy." Hölderlin, like Shelley but still more negatively, tempts muteness or despair.[112] We will see a similar array of possibilities throughout later modern poetry, depending on whether the writing aims at (cognitive) effects that writing might attain, or whether it will be satisfied by nothing less than an *event,* with the New as such.

— 2 —

Empty and Full

Poetry, Self, and Society in Lamartine, Baudelaire, and Poncy

> Ivresse religieuse des grandes villes.—
> Panthéisme. Moi, c'est tous; Tous, c'est moi.
> Tourbillon.
>
> Religious drunkenness of great cities.—
> Pantheism. I—am everyone; everyone—is me.
> Turbine.
>
> —Baudelaire, "Fusées"

Benjamin

Though it can do many things, the locodescriptive poem most typically involves the return of a speaker, usually presented in the first person, to a former haunt or habitation. Change is noted, place is compared to remembered place, self to remembered self, and the poem becomes the scene of an imaginative trial, as the speaker tries to extract continuities and consolation from a landscape filled with omens of mortality.

Our reading of Shelley suggests that "continuity" should be conceptualized along at least two axes: that of identity (particularly self-identity) over time, and that of the connection of self and setting. The self cannot witness itself, or its own change, except punctually, and by comparison with externalities. Yet some kind of connection between the person and the setting must be conceivable in order for an analogy to be made. So that sense of self, its history and sense of constancy, can be read or made only through having a *relevant* context. It must be possible for the self to understand something about itself and its history by looking outside; for this knowledge to be other than pure projection, the disposition of the world toward the self must be, in some sense, real.

By "continuity," I mean more here than the bald, statistical fact of being-located, as though within a grid; more, too, than the shared affinities of habitat and biological organism. I mean, instead, a sense of relevance within and to the place. From out of woods and wastes a gesture, like a handshake—or a menacing claw!—is offered by the world to its inhabitants, and perseverance of self over time is recognized, countersigned by the self's surroundings. My feet extend to the ground, and the ground rises to meet my feet.

Of course, claims of this kind are incredible. How can the reciprocal importance of humans to setting be asserted without recourse to (pseudo-religious or racialized) myths of autochthony? One more or less sophisticated solution is the projection of continuity into a sphere outside the visible and mutable phenomenal world, a warm force of abstraction collecting persons and things into one colossal, immanent, and living memory. Thus Wordsworth, returning to the beloved area "a Few Miles above Tintern Abbey," tries to point outside the altered scene to a "remoter charm," to connection itself:

> a sense sublime
> Of something far more deeply interfused,
> Whose dwelling is the light of setting suns,
> And the round ocean and the living air,
> And the blue sky, and in the mind of man:
> A motion and a spirit, that impels
> All thinking things, all objects of all thought,
> And rolls through all things. (ll. 95–102)

But the last movement of Wordsworth's meditation suggests a different, less ambitious, more narrowly human and social kind of "interfusion." Without annulling his vision of an "interest / Unborrowed from the eye," he sees his sister; her enjoyment of the scene recalls his own, thereby verifying, through a validating repetition, his experience.

> [. . .] and in thy voice I catch
> The language of my former heart, and read
> My former pleasures in the shooting lights
> Of thy wild eyes. Oh! yet a little while
> May I behold in thee what I was once,
> My dear, dear Sister! and this prayer I make,
> Knowing that Nature never did betray
> The heart that loved her [. . . .] (ll. 116–23)

As he does so often, Wordsworth voices his hope in the mode of petition and "perchance," not of confident assertion. Yet Dorothy's "wild eyes" give more palpable, if also more mediated, evidence of a natural bond than does that "something far more deeply interfused"; continuity with nature is demonstrated by the continuity of a human response to nature. "Tradition" is one possible name for this kind of continuity, in the sense of a knotted string of responses that allude to, struggle with, and reinforce one another: "like ivy around a wall," as Walter Benjamin said of the relation of moral proverbs to the events they commemorate.[1] It is a changing record, one that obscures nature but also, perhaps, grows in accord with nature's own changes. "[O]n the banks of this delightful stream / We stood together [. . .]": the poet brings others into the uncertain region between experience and setting—other writers will try to cram in whole nations—in the hope of confirming it as a world, a "force field" of connection.[2]

The contextualizing critic, who would weigh texts and contexts against each other in search of understanding, faces some analogous problems. How can the "situation" of the poem—thought of in terms of historical (including literary-historical), social, religious, or personal settings—be comprehended as a real relation? Analogizing again from Wordsworth's poem, we discern a pair of possible answers, obscurely related to each other. Perhaps the poem manifests "trends" or deeper tendencies in the surroundings, to which the features of the text are related as symptoms are to syndromes; the "trend" in its turn is first pointed to, if not entirely clarified, in the poem, to which it owes initial articulation. (Of course, it should be granted that Wordsworth's "feeling of presence" is primarily intuitive, a spiritual experience; it is mingled nonetheless with reflection on experience, with a sobered, comparative mode of thought wherein what is immediately apprehended is not unity, but a longing for unity.) Trends are manifestly demonstrated in relevant "structures" or "forms" within the poem, which are concrete intimations *of* rather than analogues *to* more general, less tangible principles.[3] Or the critic can reflect historically on interpretations of the work, comparing their various styles of contextualizing in search of a consistent line of response or, as in the case of many histories of criticism, simply allowing commentary to cluster around and adumbrate its object, like a thick frame of marginalia. Or perhaps the better analogue for "the mind within *us*" is the more immediately interactive, conversational side of critical labor: teaching. Of course, it cannot be assumed that these two forms of continuity—the intense products of solitary theorizing, and looser, larger, polyglot growths of comment—will be finally compatible.

In both cases the critic acts as the poem's unseen guide, who leads it back to its own atmosphere, where, it is hoped, text and context will meet in mutual, articulate recognition. The poem should then sing its own understanding, without the help of ventriloquists.[4] In "Tintern Abbey" the unseen guide of the poet is, of course, memory; and we might say that the critic's role is a memorial one as well, as he or she "re-calls" the text to its source.[5] Yet the analogy of memory to guide is not perfect, for memory is more than a nostalgic and unidirectional backward pull. It is itself a continual return, or an imagining of the past—full of affective and cognitive content—which precedes, or at least "half creates," the zone of historical understanding it seeks to establish.[6] (A preoccupation with this problem is part of what leads to a "personal" criticism and, further, to the regressive search for origins: what pulls the critic back to a specific question, to a particular discursive setting?) And the need for scholarship, for a studied reconstruction of context based on recorded knowledge, reminds us that memory, simultaneously the canvas and the frame for any image of the past, must itself be assembled, mustered together from repositories lying at various, and perhaps indeterminate, distances from the critical object. For it is never fully inside the understanding it grounds.

> You cannot come to unity and remain material[7]

Perhaps the difficulty of speaking of "validity in interpretation" stems from this necessary imaginary element in all critical rememberings.

* * *

> The shock experience which the passer-by has in the crowd corresponds to what the worker "experiences" at his machine.[8]

In Walter Benjamin's dense, idiosyncratic essays on Baudelaire's poetry, lyric poems are considered as products of and responses to processes of commodification, urbanization, and industrialization that touch on all aspects of economic, social, and psychological existence. But the bond, the "impulsion" that continues through all these levels of life, is not easy to isolate with precision. It emerges only gradually and obscurely out of Benjamin's well-known, provocative theses about a palpable impoverishment of experience and a narrowing of imaginative horizons in the modern, urban environment built up by capitalism—specifically, "the Paris of the Second Empire in Baudelaire." Within this setting, knowledge is flattened into information, persons into "physiological types," experience into forgetful repetition, things into commodities, time into empty succession. For each item on this list (and it could be extended or rephrased) the translation of the first term into the second involves the withdrawal of any uniquely and recognizably significant accumulation of time, of any "breath of prehistory" (*CB*, "Some Motifs," p. 145), from objects, persons, thoughts, or moments.

The task of the critic is thus to bring time back into the object, or bring the object back to time—without, however, forcibly or dishonestly resettling it into a recovered wholeness, a plenitude that could only be "mythic" in the very worst sense. This would be especially true in the case of Benjamin's Baudelaire, who, though thoroughly part of and shaped by the city, "battled the crowd—with the impotent rage of someone fighting the rain or the wind" (*CB*, "Some Motifs," p. 154). So the goal is to recover not time lost but the losing of time: to see how context can help explain a poetry to which it does not, in a sense, relate. Benjamin's famous and controversial "montage" method of presentation—that is, the juxtaposition of document with historical/economic and literary analysis—is really, as in Dziga Vertov or Chris Marker, an exploration of how knowledge might be created under such conditions. What is sought is some complex ideogram that might represent historical process and contradiction rather than static analogy or unruffled continuity.

This teasing out of discontinuity as a principle coexists with the second, more properly inscriptive alternative we identified—the communing of responses around a common object that they help to establish, or what might be called "setting-as-testimony." Poe, Hugo, Proust, Valéry, Hoffmann, Engels, Simmel, Freud are just a few of the voices in this colloquy on the city; Benjamin sought significant coherences among the most disparate thinkers—literary, historical, philosophical, sociological, political, psychoanalytical, revolutionary.[9] A comprehensiveness that might be dismissed, from an anti-intellectual perspective, as "mere" erudition or as the product of a somewhat irrational collector's instinct, is better explained in terms of a project of reconstituting the city, its intricate, broken contours, through multiple analyses and accounts of lived experience. The essays are a venue for a community of response that the highly developed urban division of labor itself made impossible. Comparative studies of the specialized disciplines might provide the image, if not the impetus, for a new (or perhaps, depending on how nostalgic one sees Benjamin, a *lost*) synthesis of the theoretical knowledge of society with workaday practice.

> Interacting with one another, [soul, eye and hand] determine a practice. We are no longer familiar with this practice. The role of the hand in production has become more modest, and the place it filled in storytelling lies waste. [. . .] In fact, one can go on and ask oneself whether the relationship of the storyteller to his material, human life, is not in itself a craftsman's relationship, whether it is not his very task to fashion the material of experience, his own and that of others, in a solid, useful, and unique way.[10]

Thus testimony, or the atmosphere in which it could exist, had to be fashioned by the critic, in the absence of any legitimate traditional account of the emergence of the modern city. Considered in this way, criticism becomes a political act, in the sense of gesturing toward, or perhaps performing, a community.[11]

* * *

I suggested in chapter 1 that a basic conceptual feature of Romanticism, one stemming from shifts in society, technology, and philosophical thought, is the consciousness of a new separation of (natural, social) being from any specific lawful structure that might inhere within being. This does not mean that being loses all shape and predictability for human beings, but rather that being becomes separable from structure old and new, for a time at least. Structure is relocated (though never totally) into consciousness; imagination, or consciousness considered under the aspect of agency, becomes the only force capable (or thought to be capable) of a reattachment of being and structure—while proving equally capable of driving them apart even further.

The succeeding epoch would seem to make this separation even more acute and insurmountable. Patricia Parkhurst Ferguson has shown how "the debacle of 1848 and the radical disruption of urban renewal in the Second Empire" converted the *flâneur* or "genial ambulatory philosopher of the July Monarchy into a key figure of loss within a larger 'discourse of displacement.' "[12] Benjamin is the great historian of this loss, and Charles Baudelaire (1821–1867) its best-known artist-witness. Yet what often seems to emerge in "the Paris of the Second Empire in Baudelaire" is something like a new nature, a re-fusion of structure and being within the cities of high capitalism. This is a fusion, moreover, that is perceived as inevitable, indeed as occurring apart from any visible, creative intervention, whether individual or collective, in the shaping of social reality. In truth, of course, the new, orderly, "Haussmannized" Paris that emerged during the post-1848 period was not only very much a *project*, as David Harvey and others have shown in detail; it was a project that divided elite and dominated groups internally, even while the very prospect of alternative sorts of intervention (a prospect more and more often given the name of "socialism" by this point) became both more palpable and more terrifying.[13]

The new situation does not entail, for all the infusions of order, any deceleration of the pace of modernization; indeed, circulation and near-infinite replaceability become axiomatic for the new order. The result, judging from much of the most powerful poetry of the period, is an ongoing crisis or separation within consciousness, following upon the earlier, greater scission within nature. Vast amounts of accumulated, now increasingly invalidated knowledge and practice—what might be called memory, and which Benjamin relates to "experience"[14]—are broken off from present, moment-by-moment conscious existence and become residual or meaningless. This last disintegration is, I think, precisely what Benjamin means by *shock:* the modernization of the mind, involving simultaneous evacuation and reinscription. A major response to this situation was, of course, the conscious reappropriation of motifs and imagery of the past, in order to create fantasy buffers against the effects of change.[15]

The idea of the city as a new "nature"—the scare quotes are meant to point up the notion as ideological—is an important and dialectical notion in Benjamin.[16] Many philosophers of the metropolis, like Georg Simmel, stress the abstraction and "intellectuality" of city life, which leads to the suppression of other, more natural human impulses.[17] But the accidental quality of the urban community, the lack of any self-defining project consciously negotiated among its members, suggests the "natural" in a broader sense: indifferent to human plans and ideas, a brute presence of humans living within a system as transcendent and immutable as physical law itself. This tableau is part of the larger canvas Benjamin draws of urban nature,[18] although its inner structure and relation to bourgeois thought was best outlined by Georg Lukács, under whose influence Benjamin probably wrote:

> [T]he contradiction [. . .] between subjectivity and objectivity in modern rationalist formal systems, the entanglements and equivocations hidden in their concepts of subject and object, the conflict between their nature as systems created by "us" and their fatalistic necessity distant from and alien to man is nothing but the logical and systematic formulation of the modern state of society. For, on the one hand, men are constantly smashing, replacing and leaving behind them the "natural," irrational and actually existing bonds, while, on the other hand, they erect around themselves in the reality they have created and "made," a kind of second nature which evolves with exactly the same inexorable necessity as was the case earlier on with irrational forces of nature (more exactly: the social relations which appear in this form).[19]

This paradoxical image of the modern—made by/not made by humans, lawful yet anarchic—takes on crucial, deeply structural importance in poetry of the mid-nineteenth-century city, and tracing out some of its variants is the central purpose of this chapter.

The work of Baudelaire, particularly in its Benjaminian redaction, has long been a centerpiece for discussions of changes in poetic subjectivity in the mid-nineteenth century. In this chapter I recur to this work as well, although only as one of a set (not exhaustive, to be sure) of possible responses—represented by Baudelaire, Alphonse de Lamartine (1790–1869), and Charles Poncy—to the evacuation of historically grounded experience brought about by modernization. Where Baudelaire splits the social off from the aesthetic realm (while also relentlessly exposing the performance of that fissure), the populist-aristocratic Lamartine, fully confounded by the new situation, oscillates between envisioning the urban social space as a kind of moral and sensory catastrophe (as in his long narrative poem, *Jocelyn*) and imagining an alternative pastoral (and perhaps authoritarian) utopia. For his part, the worker-poet Poncy points to a new, participatory imaginative relation between the new city space and the people who actually build and live in it. Thus, in contrast to more monographic approaches—where Baudelaire is all too often taken as the singular exemplar of mid-nineteenth-century poetic modernity, joined perhaps by Rimbaud—I will read inscriptive poems by these very different authors in order to sketch out a variegated force field of possibility. It would seem that the "Second Empire" city would throw into question the possibility of inscription either shaping or sustaining community. This is indeed the case, and in this chapter I hope to show that the (projective, appellative, legitimating) aspirations of inscriptive writing persist either as institutionalized nostalgia (Lamartine), or in the complex form of a reappropriation of both urban existence and inscriptive technique, in order to make the isolated poem a pure object of attraction (Baudelaire) or reconceived as part of a specific community's self-constitution (Poncy).

* * *

It is not true, of course, as some have suggested, that the city first appears in poetry in the nineteenth century (and with Baudelaire). For earlier writers, the city was either inimical or (more rarely) useful to poetry. Juvenal, for example, speaks through the voice of his friend, Umbricius (in the well-known third Satire "Against the City of Rome") of the noise of the city ("'Here in town the sick die from insomnia mostly'"),[20] of the turmoil of traffic in the streets. Eventually he announces his intention to move. Victor Hugo, in his poem "A Villequier," expressed his visionary relief at the city's absence:

> Maintenant que Paris, ses pavés et ses marbres,
> Et sa brume et ses toits sont bien loin de mes yeux,
> Maintenant que je suis sous les branches des arbres,
> Et que je puis songer à la beauté des cieux;
> [. . . . .]
> Je viens à vous, Seigneur, père auquel il faut croire[.][21]
>
> Now that Paris with its paving-stones and marbles
> And its fog and its roofs are far away from my eyes;
> Now that I am beneath the branches of the trees

> And can think on the beauty of the skies;
> [. . . . .]
> I come to you, Lord, father in whom one must believe.

Yet the image of the city as plenitude, as "achieved centre,"[22] as the oasis that "receives its form from the desert it opposes,"[23] is also familiar. Boileau famously advised:

> Etudiez la Cour, et connoissez la Ville.
> L'une et l'autre est toûjours en modeles fertile.[24]
>
> Study the court, and know the city.
> Both the one and the other are always rich in forms.

Thus the traditional city of poetry is centrally a place of variety and multitudinous "forms." But either that variety is a stimulus to imagination, or an *over*-stimulus, a proliferation that allows poetic consciousness no prospect and no cave in which to settle. In Benjamin's Baudelairean city the poles of this duality move closer to each other: the novel energies of modernization break down old orders, while installing new "rational systems of nomination"[25] to replace an older, situated knowledge. Poetry in this situation is squeezed into an infinitely small space between instrumentality and residuality; the poet is no longer a visionary, or even a "minstrel," but simply "a representative of a genre" (*CB*, "Some Motifs," p. 109), if a highly suspect one within the dominant system. And it is precisely here, as it turns out, that Benjamin's great motif of *aura* finds its relevance.

Benjamin's second Baudelaire essay incorporates a significant citation from Valéry:

> We recognize a work of art by the fact that no idea it inspires in us, no mode of behavior that it suggests we adopt could exhaust it or dispose of it. We may inhale the smell of a flower whose fragrance is agreeable to us for as long as we like; it is impossible for us to rid ourselves of the fragrance by which our senses have been aroused, and no recollection, no thought, no mode of behavior can obliterate its effect or release us from the hold it has on us. He who has set himself the task of creating a work of art aims at the same effect.

Benjamin comments:

> According to this view, the painting we look at reflects back at us that of which our eyes will never have their fill. What it contains that fulfills the original desire would be the very same stuff on which the desire continuously feeds. What distinguishes photography from painting is therefore clear, and why there can be no encompassing principle of "creation"

applicable to both: to the eyes that will never have their fill of a painting, photography is rather like food for the hungry or drink for the thirsty. (CB, "Some Motifs," pp. 146–47).

The comparison here is, of course, between painting, not poetry, and photography; and it is difficult to identify precisely that new mode of representation that stands in the relation to poetry that, according to Benjamin, photography does to painting. (Perhaps the similarly columnar pillars of text in newspapers?) But more important than specific analogues is the structure of the difference between "mechanical" photography and "auratic" painting, a difference that, in Benjamin's account, mingles object and response inextricably. The painting elicits admiration by its very existence; it creates, out of itself, a need that it never entirely fulfills. In contrast, the photograph satisfies desires—for information, for disclosure, for veracity, for "exhibition"[26]—deriving from extrinsic scarcities. It exists in order to be totally consumed and forgotten, leaving behind only products that are reabsorbed into the system: conversations, legal decisions, or statistical data on its exploitation.

Whether or not one agrees with Benjamin's specific distinction between painting and photography (and clearly it involves a reductive view of photography's techniques and possibilities), the more general point of his historical axiology is important and unmistakable. A sense of "uniqueness" once proper to entities has been utterly destroyed by the commodification accompanying the growth of capitalist economies.[27] So it might be said that the perception of *distance* that Benjamin elsewhere identified as essential to aura[28] really involves the perceived resistance of the object to sense organs grown acquisitive or consumerist, and particularly to sight.

In this case his idea would represent an innovation in the history of *aesthetic distance,* "from its appearance as the 'rule' of *éloignement* in classical poetics [and traceable to Aristotle][29] right down to its 'politicization' in the dramatic theory of Bertolt Brecht."[30] The importance of such an innovation for thinking about configurations of space in poetry (like the prospect or anti-prospect poem, and the inscription generally) should be apparent. The usual notion of distance is a kind of strategic sobriety, the refusal of the artist or the reader/viewer/listener to be absorbed by moments of pathos or captivating detail: this, in order to preserve the integrity and independence of a rational subject capable of ranging inclusively over its objects.[31] One is almost tempted to call "Benjaminian distance" the inversion of this and other intervals of safety laid out for the sake of judgment and vantage point. For the aura is actually a kind of protection of the object *against* the mind, a "shell" (to use one of Benjamin's own metaphors)[32] on which strategies masticate. At the same time, of course, the aura imparts a certain reflexive protection upon the mind as well, as the positive consequence of the prohibition upon any colonizing omniscience.

Such an idea is alien to the mainstream of secular, post-Cartesian thought. Indeed, Benjamin's aura seems to insert an ineluctable taboo element into the more or less formal divide separating observer and object. The separation of subject-object is in a sense maintained, but the agency of the separation is displaced into objects, including poems. Unlike most written language, the auratic is quickened from the inside; it relates poetry to the sheer recalcitrance or independence of things, resistant and potentially threatening in their secret animation. Of course, "animation" may be too strong a word: in noting the demise of aura, is Benjamin really mourning "die entgötterte Natur" (the "dedivinized Nature"), elegizing a landscape where

> Jener Lorbeer wand sich einst um Hilfe,
> Tantals Tochter schweigt in diesem Stein,
> Syrinx' Klage tönt' aus jenem Schilfe,
> Philomelas Schmerz aus diesem Hain[?][33]
>
> That laurel once writhed for help;
> Tantalus's daughter lies silent in this stone;
> The plaint of Syrinx sounds from this reed,
> And Philomena's pain from this grove [?]

Certainly, statements about the ability of aura-invested objects "to look at us in return" (*CB*, "Some Motifs," p. 148) are initially puzzling; we seem driven toward superstitious imaginings. Perhaps the most relevant available sense of the—animation? sanctity? aura? (of course, it *should* be difficult to find the right word)—of things is the Hebraic one, where God's law shapes concrete human dealings with the world, and where relations to objects—precisely *relations,* rather than points on a hieratic map—are not a matter of indifference. The lineaments of the world precede any human trailblazing: "the rabbis included the Torah among the beings which existed before creation."[34] Human sovereignty over nature is conditioned by a sense of nature's peculiar autonomy, which everyday practice, made cautious through law, continually recalls:

> Open my eyes and I shall fix my gaze
> on the wonders of your Law.
> Wayfarer though I am on the earth,
> do not hide your commandments from me.
> (Psalm 119:18–19)

Limited in my understanding both of Judaism and of Benjamin's relationship to it, I can only gesture vaguely in this direction. What is important is that "the return of the look" is primarily constitutive of distance by virtue of resistance, rather than a warm responsiveness. Like God's law, a reply of eyes compels, if not submission, at least hesitation before the pounce; distance is less a fixed span than a moment of backing away, and (potentially) the axis across which a non-coercive relation of subject and object might emerge.[35]

This notion of aura as withdrawal returns in altered form in Benjamin's discussion of the Baudelairean poet as "hero," and the hero's relation to the famous "correspondances." By taking up "the refuse of the city" and attaching it to some "dat[um] of remembrance" (*CB*, "Some motifs," p. 141), the poet resists (futilely, of course) the annihilation of experience both through his ironic ennobling of "refuse," and, more important, through his recovery of the "antique" itself, a recovery that points only to loss. Baudelaire's poetry is devoid of the "neoclassical" fusions of mid-nineteenth-century architecture (and later music) that pretended to assert real continuities.[36] The past lives on in *Les Fleurs du Mal* only in permanent recession, in the way the "correspondances" register not some allegorical absorption of the old into the new but the waning of the old and its replacement by allegories of "antiquity." Thus aura undergoes a fundamental structural change in the mid-nineteenth century. From being the "unique phenomenon of a distance," or sense of awe or "primordial shudder"[37] in the face of the object's authority and integrity, the distance proper to aura becomes a recession of the object into the infinity of "bien d'autres encor" ("Le Cygne"), a radical negativity that prompts flight or pursuit rather than reflection.[38]

This structure of withdrawal or retreat has its effects on the level of subjectivity as well, and nowhere more clearly than in the well-known "poetics of the dandy" in Baudelaire. I follow Benjamin, Sartre, Peter Nicholls, and others in identifying a thoroughgoing rejection of the useful—of social effectivity in general—as dandyism's central tenet. Sartre characterized the dandy cult as a deliberate recoil from social usefulness even more pure, because more parasitic, than the refusals of the artist.[39] The social background to this refusal is well known: the banner of "utility" had been seized in Baudelaire's day by a rising bourgeois class, and the time of the barricades had conclusively demonstrated that stratum's imaginative limitations and authoritarian proclivities.[40]

At the same time, I would argue that the profusion of artificial detail in Baudelaire's verse—furniture, perfumes, cordials, boudoir bric-a-brac of all sorts, and the city itself—betrays a deep fascination with the productive powers of the modern, with creation untrammeled by natural restriction.

Des meubles luisants,
Polis par les ans,
Décoreraient notre chambre;
Les plus rares fleurs
Mélant leurs odeurs
Aux vagues senteurs de l'ambre,
Les riches plafonds,
Les miroirs profond,
La splendeur orientale,
Tout y parlerait
A l'âme en secret
Sa douce langue natale.[41]

[Shining furniture, polished by the years, would decorate our room; the rarest flowers, mingling their scents with the vague perfume of ambergris; the rich ceilings, the deep mirrors, the oriental splendor, everything would speak to the soul in secret its sweet native tongue.][42]

The "douce langue natale" becomes the property not of landscape, as in Romanticism, but of *stuff.* Sartre, again, has expressed it best:

> In [Baudelaire's] eyes cosmetics, finery and clothes were a sign of the true greatness of man—his creative power. [. . .] A city is a perpetual creation: its buildings, smells, sounds and traffic belong to the human kingdom. Everything in it is poetry in the strict sense of the term. It is in this sense that the electrically operated advertisements, neon lights and cars which about the year 1920 roused the wonder of young people were profoundly Baudelairean. The great city is a reflection of the gulf which is human freedom.[43]

Thus one finds in Baudelaire a co-presence of the visionary with refuse, "forts parfums" wafting amid the "poudre" (dust) in which the wretched, displaced swan flaps its wings. Between these poles, effectivity or use—including the audience-forming projects of inscriptive poetry—would seem to drop out entirely.

Most interesting is the way that the new consciousness, bifurcated between an endlessly present stream of data and a receding past, participates in the (a)social logic of dandyism. Again, memory (in Benjamin's experiential sense of *Erlebnis*) becomes the realm of the residual, as here in the iconic inscription "Spleen":

> J'ai plus de souvenirs que si j'avais mille ans.
>
> I have more memories than if I were a thousand years old.[44]

Already in this first line, memory is felt as a burden; that the poet is *not* "a thousand years old" suggests that his memory is prematurely over-laden, that it has become a dumping ground for fugitive recollections. Later, the poet explicitly compares his memory to what is passed and passing:

> Je suis un vieux boudoir plein de roses fanées,
> Où gît tout un fouillis de modes surannées,
> Où les pastels plaintifs et les pâles Boucher,
> Seuls, respirent l'odeur d'un flacon débouché.

> I am an old boudoir full of withered roses, where lie disorderly heaps of out-of-date fashions, where the plaintive pastels and faded Bouchers alone breathe in the odor of an unstoppered scent bottle. ("Spleen," p. 75)

The conclusion to be derived from these lines—lines at once grim and ridiculous—is unmistakable. A portion of consciousness, that link between "collective and individual" pasts underlying earlier modes of experience, has been converted into a *thing* related to memory only as the outmoded is to the past. Experience is "preserved," in other words, only by being carefully corporealized into discrete items, at once residual and (as representations) superbly laid out in perfectly modulated couplets. At the same time, the scent emanating from the "unstoppered" bottle seems to carry some promise of real experience, if only because the surroundings are "withered" ("fané") and of use to no one. The next lines indicate that the progressive reification of consciousness at once paradoxically clears the way for some intimation of immortality:

> Rien n'égale en longueur les boiteuses journées,
> Quand sous les lourds flocons des neigeuses années
> L'ennui, fruit de la morne incuriosité,
> Prend les proportions de l'immortalité.
> —Désormais tu n'es plus, ô matière vivante!

> Nothing equals the length of the limping days, when, under the heavy flakes of the snowy years, tedium, born of dull incuriosity, takes on the proportions of immortality. Now you are no longer, o living matter[!] ("Spleen," p. 75)

Ennui is consciousness as inorganic thing, or (more precisely) memory that has lost all relation to present practice, and become utterly inert.[45] Yet, for Baudelaire, this non-effectivity merely purifies the material, clearing the way for an unexpected revelation, and an odd recollection of monumental inscription:

> —Désormais tu n'es plus, ô matière vivante!
> Qu'un granit entouré d'une vague épouvante,
> Assoupi dans le fond d'un Sahara brumeux;
> Un vieux sphinx ignoré du monde insoucieux,

Oublié sur la carte, et dont l'humeur farouche
Ne chante qu'aux rayons du soleil qui se couche.

> Now you are no longer, o living matter, anything but a block of granite surrounded by a formless fear, lying torpid in the furthest reaches of a misty Sahara; an old sphinx unregarded by the careless world, forgotten on the map, and whose unsociable whim it is to sing only to the rays of the setting sun. ("Spleen," p. 75)

Ennui, it might be said, is a purgative mechanism that clears language and consciousness of any "sociable" strivings or interest in history. The old sphinx in the desert twilight is no historical recollection but a total image, one whose indifference to audience ("l'humeur farouche") is matched by its irresistible beauty. It is also a projection of radical freedom, but one whose only realization is at the level of the poem itself as independent and "immortal" inscription.

In his accounts of the waning of experience, Baudelaire both embraces the de-structuration of consciousness attendant upon modernity and rejects it through his fashioning of aesthetic substitutes for aura, even while that very act of substitution is thematized over and over again. This "solution" presages the preoccupations of later modernism, on both the Left and the Right; as a whole, the antinomy of asociality and aesthetic ambition confirms Sartre's thesis about Baudelaire's "bad faith," his incoherent but very modern insistence on receiving social recognition for his alienated "autonomy" as it precipitated out into his poems. The poet, writes Sartre, "wanted to be a *freedom-thing*."[46] But Baudelaire's utter rejection of the Useful also puts into question the very possibility of inscription as transformative, and of aesthetic practice within modernity as bearing any positive relationship to "the careless world."

Building on the work of Benjamin and others, Jacques Rancière has argued that modern poetry ("Romantic poetics," in his terms) converts ordinary things into "point[s] of heterogeneity in the commerce of everyday life,"[47] repositories of historical/social knowledge and foci for interpretive activity:

> In the show-rooms of Romanticism, the power of [Schiller's] Juno Ludovisi is transferred to any article of ordinary life which can become a poetic object, a fabric of hieroglyphs, ciphering a history. [. . .] [Romantic] poetics makes everything available to play the part of the heterogeneous, unavailable sensible. By making what is ordinary extraordinary, it makes what is extraordinary ordinary too. [. . .] "Prosaic" objects become signs of history, which have to be deciphered. So the poet becomes not only a naturalist or an archaeologist, excavating the fossils and unpacking their poetic potential. He also becomes a kind of symptomatologist, delving into the dark underside or the unconscious of a society to decipher the messages engraved in the very flesh of ordinary things.[48]

Most important about Baudelaire's work, I will argue, is the way that its "knowledge effects"—the social symptoms it enables us to discern—are absolutely cut off from the new sensoria, the configurations of affect and perception, that the poetry attempts to produce. The hieroglyphic sphinx of "Spleen" is typical inasmuch as its message is not one of correspondence between ancient and modern but rather of the *failure* to establish such a correspondence. There is no vital mystery to be read, only a "farouche," auratic beauty at once magnetic and impossible to decode. It is this failure that we are given, over and over, as a purely negative sign for the social symptom dominating the poetry, namely, the evacuation of experience grounded in any kind of common history. At the same time, we will see that the poetry, through its very technical control, evokes reconfigurations of experience so radical that they lose all discursive outlet and become (as in "A une passante," analyzed below) flashes of private, incommunicable, transitory psychic being. Thus Baudelaire seems to straddle the abyss separating two kinds of modern poetry, and two ways of reading modern poetry: a broken writing that in its fragmentation offers nothing but symptom, nothing but heterogeneity, versus an autonomous poetry entirely discrete and resistant to cognition.

Baudelaire's complex response to modernity proves singularly important in later years, but it is, as I have indicated, only one of many options that emerge in poetry in mid-nineteenth century France;[49] no account of these options can be exhaustive, but some rough map of the wider dialectical field of possibility needs to be sketched out. Thus, alongside Baudelaire's ambivalent refusal of the new functional order, we also find the de-structuring of older social life interpreted not in terms of any emergent replacements but as a kind of return to the primordial, and terrifying (if also ecstatic) loss of all social and cognitive moorings. This response, which oscillates with the desire for renewed order, is explored here through the example of the poet-politician Alphonse de Lamartine. Finally, we find in the work of the largely unknown worker-poets—Charles Poncy is my example here—something like a poetry of effectivity, one that seeks to imagine an inscriptive reappropriation of the "new nature" of the city through agencies different from solitary poetic consciousnesses.

Lamartine

It is difficult to imagine two figures more antipodal than Baudelaire and Lamartine. Saint-Beuve wrote that Lamartine, aristocratic poet–turned–de facto leader from February to July 1848, "did not foresee [. . .] that he would be the Orpheus who later, for a time, would direct and govern, with his golden lyre, this invasion of barbarians."[50] Lamartine's role in the upheavals of 1848, so famously "de-politicizing" in their effect upon Baudelaire, is notoriously ambiguous. His political career is marked, on the one hand, by support of religious authority, public rejection of the red banner in favor of the tricolor, absurd, providential mysticism ("democratic lyricism"), and lack of political savvy; but, on the other, by a longstanding (though inconsistent) resistance to state terror and paternal maintenance of social welfare programs.[51] With Baudelaire he shared an enthusiasm for the ultra-conservative thinker Joseph de Maistre, "founder... of an imperishable school of high philosophy and Christian politics";[52] at the same time, he wrote of his own era as "one of the great periods... of social renovation."[53]

For Benjamin, Lamartine's "politico-poetic program" was nothing less than the "model for fascist programs of today." He cites the poet's "Des Destinées de la poésie" as proof of this:

> The ignorance and timidity of governments... has the effect, within all the parties, of disgusting one by one those men endowed with breadth of vision and generosity of heart. Each, in his turn, disenchanted with the mendacious symbols that no longer represent them, these men are going to congregate around ideas alone.... It is to help bring forth conviction, to add one voice more to this political group, that I temporarily renounce my solitude.[54]

Presumably, Benjamin has in mind the obvious rhetoric of elitism, the appeal to a self-appointed vanguard "bringing forth conviction" and preserving "ideas" against "mendacious symbols," and the implied call for a Republican government by and for the strong and wise (rather than the masses). On a philosophical level, Lamartine was always at particular pains to maintain the "aristocratic" separation of mind from matter; in the wake of 1848 (and probably earlier as well), Lamartine was convinced that "materialist" philosophy—whether of liberal or socialist coloration—was the central source of "atheism" and disorder among working people.[55] At the same time, he apparently maintained that a materially "rooted" agrarian existence was the best guarantor of the piety and patriotism required for social stability.

The poetic consequences of these doctrines will become apparent in a moment when we examine sections from his *Jocelyn* (1835); but beyond these patently limited views, more interesting are the poet's democratic "effusions," his (as I take it) genuine if confused or mystified interest in "the 'totally moral conditions' created by the revolution" and "the 'social discoveries' of 1848."[56] What might "social renovation" have meant to the man who wrote that poets, rather than "scaling some stormy peak," should, instead,

> [. . .] plonger ses sens dans le grand sens du monde;
> Qu'avec l'esprit des temps notre esprit s'y confonde!
> En palper chaque artère et chaque battement,
> Avec l'humanité s'unir par chaque pore [. . . .][57]
>
> [. . .] immerse [their] sense in the great sense of the world,
> That our spirit might merge with the spirit of the age!
> And by examining by finger each artery, each blow,
> To unite with humanity in every pore [. . . .]

To be sure, at the end of the same poem (the quasi-Saint-Simonian "Utopie") Lamartine argues that poet and social world are separable, or rather that the poet can and should choose his modes of dealing with the crowd:

> Il faut se séparer, pour penser, de la foule,
> Et s'y confondre pour agir![58]
>
> To think, one must separate oneself from the crowd,
> And merge with it in order to have effect!

In the central section of the poem, Lamartine draws a detailed picture of a society for the sake of which a poet might agitate. It combines anti-urbanism and universalized Christianity (dominated by "le verbe pur du Calvaire") with a lifting of the burdens of labor and "equality under God":

> Ils ne vivent pas dans les villes,
> Ces étables des nations;
> Sur les collines et les plaines,
> L'été, comme des ruches pleines,
> Les essaims en groupe pareil,
> Sans que l'un à l'autre l'envie,
> Chacun a son arpent de vie
> Et sa large place au soleil.
>
> Les éléments de la nature,
> Par l'esprit enfin surmontés,
> Lui prodiguant la nourriture
> Sous l'effort qui les a domptés,
> Les nobles sueurs de sa joue
> Ne vont plus détremper la boue
> Que sa main doit ensemencer,
> La sainte loi du labeur change,
> Son esprit a vaincu la fange,
> Et son travail est de penser.

[. . . . .]
Votre tête est découronnée,
Rois, césars, tyrans, dieux mortels
À qui la terre prosternée
Dressait des trônes pour autels
Quand l'égalité fut bannie
L'homme inventa la tyrannie
Pour qu'un seul exprimât ses droits,
Mais au jour de Dieu qui se lève
Le sceptre tombe sur le glaive,
Nul n'est esclave, et tous sont rois! . . . (pp. 1153–54)

They live not in cities,
Those stables of the nations;
In summer, like hives full of bees,
Like swarms grouped together,
On the hills and plains,
Each one has his acre of life
And a broad place under the sun
Without the one envying the other.

The elements of nature
Are finally surmounted by the [human] spirit,
And produce food for spirit
Having been subdued by its effort;
The noble sweat of its brow
Will no longer mix with the dirt
That its hand must seed;
The sacred law of toil changes,
For the spirit has conquered the mud,
And now its work is thought.
[. . . . .]
Kings, caesars, tyrants, mortal gods
To whom the prostrate earth
Erected thrones as altars—
Your head has been uncrowned.
When equality was banished
Man invented tyranny
That one man alone might express his rights;
But on the day that God will rise,
The scepter will fall to the sword—
None are slaves, and all are kings!

The attack on kingship here seems worthy of Shelley—but how do we get to this stage of liberation? Later in the poem Lamartine stations himself between those who "deny movement" and those who would "blow all into powder at a single blow" (pp. 1155–57). "La patience est sa vertu," and underlying the poet's march toward "the certain goal" is a providential notion of history that precludes revolutionary anger. Like rulers, the comrades of the poet are to "live in everything": "C'est tout porter en soi comme l'âme suprême" ("To carry all within the self like the supreme soul").

More difficult to see, perhaps, are those classically Saint-Simonian "separations of spheres" covertly furrowing the utopia. Mud and mind are absolutely distinguished, and each person, fitted in place according to natural aptitude, would have his own "acre of life." Concealed here, in other words, is a naturalized *bureaucracy,* the Saint-Simonian ideal of a society not ruled but administered: natural capacity guarantees the fit of person and occupation, with those fitted to administration "naturally" rising to positions of control.[59]

The trope of "tous sont rois" clearly shows the tension in Lamartine's thought between his aristocratic background and his democratic fantasies: for him, freedom is imaginable only as kingship universalized, though within careful strictures. As in the far more extreme case of the Marquis de Sade (as described by Sartre), Lamartine uses the forms of democracy in order to preserve, in utterly distorted form, his "rights" as a nobleman:

> [This is an] attempt [. . .] already permeated with bourgeois subjectivism; objective titles of nobility are replaced by an untrammeled superiority on the part of the Ego.[60]

In real life, this contradiction manifests itself as Lamartine's well-known and sometimes embarrassing "effusiveness" and fondness for the public stage. The aristocratic poet exercises his right to prolixity before the crowd, a practice that leads ultimately, in the changed post-1851 circumstances, to his sad conversion into a prolific literary hack.[61]

* * *

The Lamartinian stress on "the idea" and on separation reminds us of the structure of the classic prospect poem; and, indeed, Lamartine was one of the last great Romantic practitioners of that inscriptive matrix in a relatively pure form, as in the famous "Les Laboureurs" section from the ninth "époque" of *Jocelyn*:[62]

> La tiède attraction des rayons d'un ciel chaud
> Sur les monts ce matin m'avait mené plus haut,
> J'atteignis le sommet d'une rude colline
> Qu'un lac baigne à sa base et qu'un glacier domine,
> Et dont les flancs boisés, aux penchants adoucis,
> Sont tachés de sapins par des prés éclaircis.
> . . . .

J'y pouvais, adossé le coude à leurs racines,
Tout voir, sans être vu, jusqu'au fond des ravines.
Déjà, tout près de moi, j'entendais par moments
Monter des pas, des voix et des mugissements:
C'était le paysan de la haute chaumine
Qui venait labourer son morceau de colline,
Avec son soc plaintif traîné par ses boeufs blancs,
Et son mullet portant sa femme et ses enfants. . . .(pp. 362–63)
. . . .
Et pour consacrer l'héritage
Du champ labouré par leurs mains,
Les bornes firent le partage
De la terre entre les humains,
Et l'homme, à tous les droits propice,
Trouva dans son Coeur la justice
Et grave son code en tout lieu,
Et pour consacrer ses lois même,
S'élevant à la loi supreme,
Chercha le juge et trouva Dieu!

Et la famille, enracinée
Sur le coteau qu'elle a planté,
Refleurit d'année en année,
Collective immortalité!
Et sous sa tutelle chérie
Naquit l'amour de la patrie,
Gland de people au soleil germé!
Semence de force et de gloire
Qui n'est que la sainte mémoire
Du champ par ses pères semé! (p. 366)

The mild attraction of the rays from the hot sky
Above the mountains led me higher this morning.
I reached the summit of a rough hill,
With a lake swimming at its base, dominated by a glacier,
And the gentle slopes of whose wooded sides
Are spotted with fir trees ranging across the bright meadows.
. . . .
Here, leaning my elbow against [the roots of trees],
I could see everything without being seen, down to the base of the ravines.
Already, very near, I heard at times the sound
Of climbing steps, of voices and the lowing of cattle.
It was the peasant from the cottage above
Who had come to work his piece of hill
With his wretched plow pulled by his white oxen,
And his mule carrying his wife and children.
. . . .
And to consecrate the legacy
Of fields worked by their hands,

The boundary stones affirm the partitioning
Of earth among human beings.
And the man, who looks favorably upon all rights,
Finds justice in his heart,
And engraves its code in every place;
And to sanctify the laws himself,
Rising toward the law supreme,
He seeks the judge, and discovers God!

And the family, rooted
On the hillock it had planted,
Blossoms year to year,
A collective immortality!
And under its dear tutelage
Is born the love for country:
Acorn of the people, germinated by the sun!
Seed of force and glory
Which is nothing but the holy memory
Of the fields sown by their fathers!

A more perfect demonstration of the logic of the prospect poem—of that untrammeled vision that enables the spectator (here the priest Jocelyn himself) to inscribe an interpretation on the scene that seems to "emanate" from the scene itself—could hardly be imagined. Here the inscription's striving for both separation and community is sensed all too clearly, as the scene of the poem comes to incorporate first one peasant plot, then many (harmoniously separated by boundary stones), and finally the nation as such, all bound by a single "law."[63] The passage forces one to recall Benjamin's insistence on Lamartine's "proto-fascism," as well as the now much-studied kinship between landscape representation and national ideology. Less obvious, however, is that "Les Laboureurs" is in fact a compensatory vision, situated immediately following an astonishing, little-known section from the eighth "époque" of *Jocelyn* that at once vividly exposes the substratum of anxiety about modern community that both "Utopie" and "Les Laboureurs" struggle to conceal, and displays the terminus for the older prospect matrix in its confrontation with the new content of the city.

In this section the title character, a priest with a complicated past who lives in the mountains, has brought his sister back to her husband and family in Paris. They convince him to remain in the city for a few days, both to mollify the sad effect on his sister of his necessary departure, and to savor the tempestuous scenery and wild sublimity of the city. The section begins from a prospect:

Pour qu'avant de rentrer dans mon obscur réduit
Mon oreille du monde ait entendu le bruit,

Comme au pied de la dune on monte sur la crête,
Pour écouter la vague et pour voir la tempête.[64]

So that before returning to my obscure corner
My ear might hear the sound of the world,
As one climbs on foot to the top of the dune
To hear the waves and hear the storm.

The most interesting examples of urban prospect verse reveal something about the need for the separation of observer from observed, as in Hugo's "Le jour s'enfuit des cieux" (1828):

Oh! qui m'emportera sur quelque tour sublime
D'où la cité sous moi s'ouvre comme un abîme!
Que j'entende, écoutant la ville où nous rampons,
Mourir sa vaste voix, qui semble un cri de veuve,
Et qui, le jour, gémit plus haut que le grand fleuve,
Le grand fleuve irrité, luttant contre vingt ponts!
[. . . . .]
Que la vieille cité, devant moi, sur sa couche
S'étende, qu'un soupir s'échappe de sa bouche;
Comme si de fatigue on l'entendait gémir!
Que, veillant seul, debout sur son front que je foule,
Avec mille bruits sourds d'océan et de foule,
Je regarde à mes pieds la géante dormir! (pp. 31–32)

Oh! who would carry me to some sublime tower
From where the city would open like an abyss below me!
So that, listening to that city where we crawl,
  I would hear
That great voice dying, the voice that resembles
  the cry of a widow,
And which, during the day, moans more loudly than
  the great river,
The great and agitated river, struggling against
  20 bridges!
[. . . . .]
So that the old city would extend before me
  on its couch,
That a gasp would escape from its mouth;
As though one heard it moaning from exhaustion!
So that, standing alone before that face I pursue,
With a thousand dull sounds of ocean and of the crowd,
I would see the giantess sleeping at my feet!

These lines express, of course, a *wish* for a prospect, for a place from which to see and hear the place, or rather the abyss where, as Hugo says, "we crawl" ("nous rampons"). The motivation for the imagined climb seems devotional: to be a witness to a widow's mourning, or to her own death (or near-death) by exhaustion. The city is a vast voice tending toward a single inarticulate moan, a sort of dying chaos of which no impression can be gained from the inside (which is, of course, where the poet remains). What is left is a cluster of possible figures for the hypothetical "foule": the exhausted sleeper (a worker), the giant (single-bodied, mythic), or the ocean, the very image for that which is "without form and void," but also for a destructive potential.

As we shall see, Jocelyn's experience of the city is much less scenic even than this; but immediately after his account of the city he gives us, in contrastive recollection, a picture of his own Alpine home, which mingles standard aspects of the landscape panorama with the *locus amoenus:*

> Oh! nuits de ma montagne, heure où tout fait silence
> Sous le ciel et dans moi; lune qui se balance
> Sur les cimes d'argent du pâle peuplier,
> Que l'haleine du lac à peine fait plier;
> Blanches lueurs du ciel sur l'herbe répandues,
> Comme du lin lavé les toiles étendues;
> Des brises où de l'eau furtif bruissement,
> Des chiens par intervalle un lointain aboiement,
> Le chant du rossignol par notes sur des cimes,
> Silence dans mon âme ou quelques bruits intimes
> Qu'un calme universel vient bientôt assoupir,
> Et qu'un retour vers Dieu change en pieux soupir.
> Ôjours d'un saint labeur! douces nuits de Valneige!
> (p. 722)
>
> Oh nights upon my mountain, oh hour where all
> falls silent
> Under the sky and within me; the moon, swaying
> Above the silver peaks of the pale poplar
> Which the breathing of the lake barely causes to bend;
> White flickerings of sky extend across the grass,
> Like stretched-out sheets of washed linen.
> Furtive rustling of breezes or of water;
> At intervals, the far-off barking of dogs;
> The notes of the nightingale's song among the branches;
> Silence in my soul, or a few intimate sounds
> Which a universal calm will soon subdue
> And which a return to God converts to pious sighs.
> O days of holy drudgery! sweet nights of Valneige!

"Silence," "calme," "balance": more a soundscape (silence-scape?) than a landscape, this is a mutedly harmonious vision of cooperation. As "les laboureurs" emit sounds "par moments," so here the nightingales sing "par notes," the dogs bark "par intervalles"; noise itself seems dainty and "intime," and only a slight hint of indolent sensuality in any way disrupts the scene's chaste placidity. For this is "*his* mountain," an image of ideal proprietorship. The notion of *property*—in both the obvious and metaphysical senses—is the oft-noted cornerstone of Lamartine's democratic vision, wherein Enlightenment equality and rationality is translated into the generalization of the privileges of ownership.[65]

More centrally, however, the passage is the memory of an exhausted mind, meant to contrast maximally with the preceding lines, where the balance of static perceiver and remote and compliant object is gradually, completely undone by Paris.

> Oh! que le bruit humain a troublé mes esprits!
> Quel ouragan de l'âme il souffle dans Paris!
> Comme on entend de loin sa grande voix qui gronde,
> Pleine des mille voix du peuple qui l'inonde,
> Semblable a l'Océan qui fait enfler ses flots,
> Monter et retomber en lugubres sanglots!
> Oh! que ces grandes voix des grandes capitales
> Ont des cris douloureux et de clameurs fatales,
> D'angoisses, de terreurs et de convulsions!
> On croit y distinguer l'accent des passions
> Qui, soufflant de l'enfer sur ce million d'âmes,
> Entrechoquent entre eux ces hommes et ces femmes,
> Font monter leur clameur dans le ciel comme un flux,
> Ne forment qu'un seul cri de mille cris confus,
> Ou qu'on entend le bruit des tempes de la terre
> Que la fièvre à grands coups fait battre dans l'artère.
> (p. 721)

> Oh! how the human noise troubled my spirit!
> What a hurricane of the soul is breathed in Paris!
> As though one hears that great, groaning voice from
> far away,
> Filled by the thousand voices of the people flooding it,
> Like the ocean that augments its streams,
> Makes them rise and fall again in lugubrious gasps!
> Oh! how much sorrowful crying and fatal clamor,
> How much of anguish, of terror and convulsion
> Have the great voices of the great capitals!
> One seems to discern the accent of passions
> Which, breathing of hell above this million souls
> And hurling these men and women among themselves
> Makes their clamor rise into the air like a flux,
> Forming one single cry from a thousand confused cries;
> One seems to hear the sound of the earth's temples,
> The sound of their arteries pummeled by huge blows
> of fever.

Sounds, mobile and congested, are difficult to designate here. There is something unsettling about a "*human* noise": what might emerge choir-like from the "thousand voices" as a single "grande voix" instead roars and sighs incomprehensibly; the sounds of the city are sensed as physical shocks, "à grands coups," rather than articulated speech. Images of ocean and flood in Romantic poetry are often (as in Byron and Pushkin) metaphors for liberty or heroic destiny, but here they function almost *de*-anthropomorphically, linking the "bruit" to a raw din of nature and nearly depriving "ces grandes voix" of human owners. "Almost" and "nearly," because the poet also uses the more creaturely figure of the anguished or terrified "cry," which might be described as a sound mid-way between speech and the sounds of inanimate nature, or as speech on its way to becoming mindless rustling.

Yet this tumult, though "fevered" and frenetic, has a hellish intensity suggestive of strength rather than weakness and infirmity. Pity, aloofness, and condescension become postures more difficult for the protagonist to sustain:

> Quel poids pèse sur l'âme en entrant dans ces murs?
> En voyant circuler dans ces canaux impurs
> Ces torrents animés et cette vague humaine
> Qu'un courant invisible en sens contraire entraine,
> Qui sur son propre lit flotte éternellement,
> Et dont sans voir le but on voit le mouvement!
> Quel orageux néant, quelle mer de tristesse,
> Chaque fois que j'y rentre, en me glaçant, m'oppresse!
> (p. 721)

> What weight presses on the soul when entering
>   into these walls?
> Watching these animated torrents and this human wave
> Circulate through these impure canals,
> It is as though some invisible current pushed in
>   an opposite direction,
> Floating eternally above its own proper bed,
> And of which one sees the motion without seeing
>   its goal!
> What stormy nothingness, what a sea of sadness
> Oppresses, intimidates me each time I enter it!

Despite the omen-like intimation of a "current" running above and counter to the eddies of the crowd, this is a landscape from which no providential pattern emerges—although perhaps a call for authoritarian, ordering intervention is distantly implied.[66] Crowds surge like a natural torrent, directed but unmeant; indeed, the question "what weight?" concerns the mystery of this "human wave" as much as its magnitude. Why should massed humanity, allegedly adding up to an "orageux néant" ("stormy nothingness"), have such an "oppressive" psychic effect; is the "animation" of the torrent a motive force, or merely motion?

These questions are not, perhaps, finally answerable, but part of a response may be suggested by Lamartine's account of the fortunes of the soul ("âme"), a word frequently used here. The images of natural tumult suggest that souls are reduced by their accumulation, that the whole is somehow de-souled. Not merely individual subjectivity but the idea of soul itself seems threatened, but in a perversely, feverishly seductive way. Jocelyn perceives something in the city that "weighs" on his soul, even as he abandons the high perspective of the prospect poem and enters the soul of the scene.

> Il semble que ce peuple où je vais ondoyer
> Dans ces gouffres sans fond du flot va me noyer,
> Que le regard de Dieu me perd dans cette foule,
> Que je porte à moi seul le poids de cette houle,
> Que son immense ennui, son agitation
> M'entraînent faible et seul dans son attraction,
> Que de ses passions la fièvre sympathique,
> En coudoyant ce peuple, à moi se communique,
> Que son âme travaille et souffre dans mon sein,
> Que j'ai soif de sa soif, que j'ai faim de sa faim,
> Que ma robe en passant se salit à ses crimes [. . . .]
> (p. 721)

> It seems as though this mass, on which I shall float,
> Will plunge me into the bottomless abysses
> of the stream;
> That God's eye loses me in this crowd;
> That I carry by myself the weight of this tide;
> That its immense ennui, its agitation
> Pulls me, weak and alone, into its attraction;
> That the sympathetic fever of the passions of the mass
> Is transmitted to me as I touch it;
> That its soul labors and suffers within my breast;
> That I partake of its thirst, partake of its hunger,
> That my robe, as I pass, is soiled with
> its crimes [. . .]

There is a fascinating mixture of images of unwilling absorption into the crowd ("its agitation/Pulls me, weak and alone," "the sympathetic fever") and of the priest's absorption of the crowd into himself, a bearing-of-the-sins-of-the-world ("partake of its thirst, partake of its hunger," etc.), a self-consuming texture that recalls the Pauline kenotic paradigm of Philippians 2.[67] In other words, the experience of "communication" seems describable as both radical sympathy and as a traumatic bombardment: a triumph and a defeat, like a martyrdom.

The possibility of true martyrdom would depend on some higher equilibrium or plausible redemptive hope from which resolution or edification could emerge. But Jocelyn senses that God's own eye cannot cope with this new landscape. This loss severs the line to any renewed elevation, as do the priest's own demerits—his avowed weakness, palpable disgust for the crowd, and oddly excited fascination for what appalls him. The appeal of immersion in the crowd would seem in some sense aesthetic, but Jocelyn cannot detachedly savor a sublime thrill or come away from the crowd—as one can, say, from the sea—with new metaphors for the soul's own immensity. The merging with another order and his opposition to it become more and more absolute; his own nature seems altered by a new kind and intensity of contact.

> Et que, tourbillonnant dans ses mouvants abîmes,
> Je ne suis pas pour lui plus qu'une goutte d'eau
> Qui ne fait ni hausser, ni baisser son niveau,
> Un jet de son écume, un morceau de sa vase,
> Une algue de ses bords qu'il souille et qu'il écrase,
> Et que si je venais à tomber sous ses pas
> Cette foule à mes cris ne s'arrêterait pas,
> Mais comme une machine à son but élancée
> Passerait sur mon corps sans même une pensée! . . .
> (p. 721)
>
> And that, whirling within those moving abysses,
> I am no more [to the crowd] than a drop of water,
> Able neither to raise nor lower its level.
> A spray of its foam, one piece of its vase,
> An alga on its side that it soils and crushes;
> And if I were to fall beneath its feet,
> This crowd would not be stopped by my cries;
> But like a machine, shooting forward toward its goal,
> Would pass over my body without a single thought!

Jocelyn changes, and very rapidly, with the growing vigor of the crowd's motions and the silencing of its "voice." The absence of discernable order within these movements deprives him of agency, and perhaps of responsibility; having been observer and martyr, he ends as mere victim. Nor, it would seem, is the "foule" (crowd) culpable. We are presented here with the paradox of souls without soul, or, more precisely, a purely corporeal human mass—can it be called "community"?—perceived as inorganic force. The runaway or renegade machine expresses this paradox perfectly, for it is the very figure of human technology pursuing non-human and mindless ends ("sans même une pensée!" [without a single thought!]), detached beyond indifference, like material nature.

Yet the opposition of crude "machine" to shocked "pensée" also recalls the ancient distinction between intellectual and manual labor, or, more specifically, between the "artes *liberales*"—that is, occupations "worthy of a free [person]," the trivium and quadrivium (grammar, rhetoric, dialectic; arithmetic, geometry, music, astronomy)—and the "artes *mechanicae*" which, together with sheer bull work, are the characteristic activities of the "foule."[68] Here, in Lamartine, this and other distinctions seem to be breaking down.

> Une poignante angoisse
> De chaque aspect pour moi sort et vient m'assaillir,
> J'entends des sons de voix qui me font tressaillir.
> J'entends des noms qui font rougir jusqu'à mon âme.
> Je frémis de lever les yeux sur une femme.
> Je tremble qu'à son front, rencontré par hasard,
> Mon coeur ne meure en moi, foudroyé d'un regard;
> Puis je rentre, l'esprit courbé de lassitude,
> Mais poursuivi des cris de cette multitude,
> Trouvant l'isolement mais jamais le repos,
> Le coeur amer et vide, et plein de mille échos;
> Le bruit assourdissant de l'humaine tempête
> Monte, gronde sans cesse et m'enivre la tête;
> Et seul, sans qu'il me tombe une goutte de foi,
> J'entends à peine, hélas! mon coeur qui prie en moi.
> (p. 722)

> From every appearance
> A sharp anguish emerges for me, threatens to assail me;
> I hear the sounds of voices that make me tremble,
> I hear words that make me blush unto my very soul.
> I shudder to raise my eyes toward a woman.
> I tremble to think that on seeing her face,
> encountered by chance,
> My heart would die inside me, blasted by a glance;
> Thus I return, my spirit bent by fatigue,
> But pursued by the cries of that multitude,
> Finding isolation but never repose,
> The heart bitter and empty, and full of
> a thousand echoes;
> The deafening sound of the human storm
> Grows, ceaselessly groans and intoxicates my head;
> And alone, without a drop of faith falling to me,
> Alas! I barely hear my heart, supplicating me.

Simmel suggests that the psychic and social life of the city is threatened, on the one hand, by the blind indifference of humans to one another wrought by a total discontinuity of their individual strivings and, on the other, by the over-imposition of novel stimuli and "unwished-for suggestions," to the point of cowing or stupefying the city dweller.[69] The usual preventive is a more or less stable antipathy, which might be called a midpoint between indifference and exposure—a willingness to shun others as obstacles while muttering against them for being that way—but Jocelyn has not achieved this functional median. Anything but indifferent, he is crushed anew by every atom of the crowd. Sounds, words, and faces invade him even in their absence, and, presaging Baudelaire, he is suddenly susceptible to what Benjamin would call "sexual shock." Women, accidentally encountered, become Medusas of the street. His excitation ("me [faire] tressaillir" ["makes me tremble"], "Je tremble," "m'enivre la tête" ["intoxicates my head"]) is again difficult to characterize, for it seems to involve pity, fear, and a distressingly sexual hyperstimulation. Most puzzling is the coexistence of devastation and plenitude in Jocelyn's self-description—"Le coeur amer et *vide*, et *plein de mille échos*" ("the heart bitter and *empty, and full of a thousand echoes*"; my emphasis). The experience of the city renders him empty but full, defeated yet intoxicated: how are we to understand this "stormy nothingness"?

Later in the section Jocelyn finds a resolution in traditional terms of piety:

> Ainsi, Seigneur, tu fais d'un peuple sur la terre
> L'outil mystérieux de quelque grand mystère [. . . .]
> (p. 724)
>
> Thus, Lord, you make of a people on the earth
> The mysterious tool of some great mystery [. . . .]

But the culminating lines of his city chronicle suggest a different possibility:

> Et seul, sans qu'il me tombe une goutte de foi,
> J'entends à peine, hélas! mon coeur qui prie en moi.
>
> And alone, without a drop of faith falling to me,
> Alas! I barely hear my heart, supplicating me.

Jocelyn never "merges" with "l'humaine tempête." Yet his fears point to two aspects of what such a merging might mean. First, the city is not a community, a self-consciously collective creation, but a return to a preconscious state of nature. Carried to its extreme, this kind of regression would lead to a total de-centering of consciousness, of which

Jocelyn has keen intimations. But (second) the solitary "heart" is swept away and replaced by a different kind of experience, born of a different imposition of the human environment on its constituent members within modernity.

The culminating lines describing Jocelyn's ordeal and return to his room are effectively borrowed from Saint-Preux's seventeenth letter to Julie in *La Nouvelle Héloïse*. There, in one of the Ur-scenes of the modern, the writer describes his "shock" in the face of that torrent of words and impressions that is Paris, and uses the same language of plenitude and vacuum as Jocelyn does to describe his soul:

> Confused, humiliated, struck with consternation over feeling human nature in me being degraded, and seeing myself fallen so low from that innate greatness to which our impassioned hearts had reciprocally raised us, I return in the evenings pierced by a secret sorrow, overwhelmed by a mortal disgust, my heart empty and puffed up like a balloon full of air.[70]

But earlier in the same letter, Saint-Preux acknowledges the appeal of this loss of self within urban flux, figuring it (as Lamartine will later do) in terms of "giddiness," intoxication:

> However, I am beginning to feel the intoxication into which this busy and tumultuous life plunges those who lead it, and I am becoming giddy like a man before whose eyes a multitude of objects is made to pass rapidly. None of those which impress me engage my heart, but all together disturb and suspend its affections to the point that sometimes I forget what I am and whose I am.[71]

Faced with the possibility of experiential annihilation in the city—which is, again, the vanishing of the past within practical consciousness—Jocelyn, like Saint-Preux but far more drastically, can find no mediation between full abandonment of experiential moorings and a return to providential authority. It is unclear, in short, whether we are to interpret Jocelyn's experience as a true breakdown or whether (in the wake of the revolution) it is better read in de Maistrean terms, as a punishment but also a purgative bath out of which the poet-priest (and his nation) might "regenerate."[72] What is clear is that the raised standpoint of the prospect—which determines the speculating poet's position in a work like "Utopie," for example, and for which Lamartine so ardently yearns—is impossible within the city; as we have seen, the devastation represented in *Jocelyn* can only be contained through a nostalgic appeal to a timeless rural order, where the bond between human project and corporeal reality is so tightly bound as to require no legitimizing argument.

BAUDELAIRE

> No gaps, hence no surprises.
>
> —Baudelaire, "The Painter of Modern Life"

Baudelaire did not regard Lamartine very highly. But I would like to think that his prose poem, "Les Foules," contains an ironic allusion to Jocelyn and his hermitage. After having spoken of the "jouissances fièvreuses" enflamed by wandering in the crowd, Baudelaire surmises that:

> Founders of colonies, pastors of nations, missionary priests exiled at the far ends of the earth, no doubt know something of such mysterious transcendences, and in the heart of the vast family created by their genius, must sometimes laugh at those who pity their unquiet fortunes, and their chaste lives.[73]

In this last sentence Baudelaire directly relates the poet's metempsychotic ability to "commune" with the crowd to the *projects*—the "génie"—of colonists and the missionaries who accompanied them. These projects are the plans inscribed on the "vacant" landscapes and populations of the dominions; and the passage suggests that the logic of colonial expansion always involves some originary nihilism, the insistence that there was nothing there before the settlers made the desert bloom. The flâneur-poet takes up that logic, and explicitly enjoys the crowd "at the expense of the human race." The poet is the genius of all loci; for him "tout," except that which isn't worthwhile, "est vacant" ("everything is a vacancy"):

> Multitude and solitude are equal and interchangeable terms for the active and productive poet. [. . . .] The poet enjoys the unique privilege of being both himself and other people, at will. Like those lost souls which wander in search of a body to inhabit, he can enter the personality of anyone else, whenever he likes. (p. 59)

There is a powerful identification here of poetic consciousness with the nihilism of modernity—and particularly, again, the nihilism of colonialism—inasmuch as that nihilism involves a denial of the historical substance of whatever it encounters. The simile of "lost souls," of course, introduces another valence: is the poet's "errance" ("wandering") a power of centered self-dissemination comparable to colonial exploration, or is it the homeless meanderings of a soul damned to eternal vagrancy? The wandering soul is traditionally the unburied soul with no epitaph or the soul undomesticated by funeral rites. Its situation here is describable in terms of both systematic domination and radical powerlessness. Indeed, despite the ascription of "vacancy" to the poet's surroundings, wandering through the city is actually a continual confrontation with entities:

> He can make every profession his own, and make his all those joys and miseries that circumstance may bring his way. (p. 59)

Thus vacancy here is double: the real, empty space of the universal exchange/replacement of "professions" (or, rather, "real-abstract," to use Alfred Sohn-Rethel's more appropriate term)[74] is the poet himself.

Colonialist nihilism is a necessary cognitive step toward the fulfillment of a vast array of aims: the acquisition of goods, markets, of "living space" in general. What does the poet gain by his alignment with its logic? Again, we see that nothing remotely useful is sought. Rather, "the solitary and thoughtful stroller draws a *unique intoxication* from this universal communion."[75] The qualities of this intoxication are difficult to discern, for it is "unique" intoxication, part of an "*ineffable* orgy." Starting from a productive if ruthless nihilism, the poet moves past the whole realm of conventional utility into immediate and absolute expenditure. Absolute, because his intoxication eludes any element of "feedback" into a larger economy: neither moral effect nor possible gains in urban knowledge (even of a "physiognomical" type) play any role here.

At the same time, the absence of the "middle realm" of social effectivity is made palpable through the very strength with which it is elided. What, after all, could the poet's "appropriation" of professions really amount to, devoid as it is of any specific knowledge of those professions and their "joys and miseries"? In another iteration of the theme of colonialist nihilism, we find still stronger examples of Baudelaire's elision of social effectivity in the prose version of "Invitation to the Voyage," which fantasizes about "ships glutted on the produce of the East" as they bring their wares to

> A true land of Cockaigne [. . .] where everything is rich, tidy, and glossy, like a clean conscience, like a magnificent array of kitchen utensils, like splendid silverware, like colorful jewelry! The world's treasures pour in there, as into the house of a hard-working man who deserves the whole world's best.[76]

A caesura—the caesura of modernization itself—falls between the production of "treasures" and enjoyment of them. In other words, the relationship of productive energy to expenditure in Baudelaire is an allegorical one: the glutted ships float without mediation into "the house of a hard-working man"; nowhere does production as such intercede, as the reference to the hard-working man only underscores. The modern in Baudelaire emerges quite precisely as this still incomplete historical amnesia, the undoing of coherent links between experience/presentness, productive energy/expenditure, seemingly thwarting all efforts to reforge them. At the same time, this discovery of caesura, together with its interpretation, is precisely the way that criticism seeks to reinsert the poem back into the full historical reality from which (on my reading) it tries to withdraw. In this sense, analysis of the Baudelairean phantasmagoria, which seems on first glance to be "demystification," is also another way of ensuring the temporal fullness of the artifact, a tacit insistence on art's suitability as a passageway to the totality of life. It is therefore wrong to think that an ironic, excavating, de-idealizing criticism is the inversion or opponent of modern (post-Romantic) poetics; it is, rather, one of the culminations of this poetics—this, in contrast to Baudelaire's poetry as such.[77]

* * *

The hiatus- or caesura-structure of "Les Foules" is an important one in Baudelaire, never more obviously so than in the following famous sonnet "A une passante" (from the "Tableaux Parisiens" of 1861):

> La rue assourdissante autour de moi hurlait.
> Longue, mince, en grand deuil, douleur majestueuse,
> Une femme passa, d'une main fastueuse
> Soulevant, balançant le feston et l'ourlet;
>
> Agile et noble, avec sa jambe de statue.
> Moi, je buvais, crispé comme un extravagant,
> Dans son oeil, ciel livide où germe l'ouragan,
> La douceur qui fascine et le plaisir qui tue.
>
> Un éclair... puis la nuit!—Fugitive beauté
> Dont le regard m'a fait soudainement renaître,
> Ne te verrai-je plus que dans l'éternité?
>
> Ailleurs, bien loin d'ici! trop tard! *jamais* peut-être!
> Car j'ignore où tu fuis, tu ne sais où je vais,
> Ô toi que j'eusse aimée, ô toi qui le savais! (p. 69)
>
> The [deafening] street was howling around me
> When a woman passed on her way, so tall and slender,
> All in black mourning, majestical in her grief,
> With her stately hand lifting, swaying the scallop
> and hem,
>
> Light-footed and noble and with a statuesque leg.
> And I, tense as a man out of his wits, drank from

her eye—
A pallid sky in which a tempest brews—that gentleness
Which bewitches men, that pleasure which destroys.

A flash of light—then darkness! O vanishing beauty,
Whose glance brought me suddenly to life again, shall I
Never see you [again] except in eternity?

Elsewhere, far from here, too late, or perhaps never?
For whither you fled I know not, nor do you know
whither I
Am bound—O you whom I could have loved, O you
who knew it![78]

Several features of this sonnet link it to inscription, not least of which is the allusion to the primal appeal to a passerby (a *viator* or *passant*) in the title itself. To summarize my argument aggressively: the poem illustrates (among other things) Baudelaire's complete refusal of any "prospective" attempt to fashion an inscription that might be open to "all," in Wordsworth's terms. The way out of the "deafening street" is to mobilize the resources of poetry to project an inscribed object—the poem itself—that carries its own absolute justification. To show how this works, some analysis is required.

The setting here is both a place and the *noise* of "la rue assourdissante" ("the deafening street"). Whether because of self-canceling cacophony or through the languishing of ears, the howling street seems to resonate with a rapt and solemn quiet. Indeed, its formless "howl" suggests that the street has returned to the primal soup, to the pure non-differentiation before creation.

Et sur ces mouvantes merveilles
Planait (terrible nouveauté!
Tout pour l'oeil, rien pour les oreilles!)
Un silence d'éternité.
("Rêve Parisien," p. 76)

And, most terrible novelty of all,
With everything for the eye and nothing
For the ear, a silence of eternity
Hovered over all those moving wonders. (p. 201)

But the "deafening street" also bears some affinity to *religious* settings. Like a hurricane, the street roars "autour" ("du moi"), leaving an eye or clearing in the center wherein the Event might be staged. In contiguity with the obvious ritual garb and ceremonial pace of the *passante,* street noise comes to resemble the rumbling ground tones of an organ.

In this weird cultic setting, again recalling the basic ritual scenario of roadside inscription and strangely made possible by an extreme intensification of worldly activity,[79] the stage is set for the reappearance of "first things."

As befits a priestess, or ritually clothed sacrifice, the *passante* is impersonal, inexpressive, and virtually faceless; we are given no sense of how the "douleur majestueuse" shows up on her face. Rather, she is a catalogue or montage of parts and adjectives, hems and gestures. Words of the body ("tall, slender"; "light-footed and noble"; "stately hand") are spliced together with suggestions of ceremonial objects and the role of mourning ("all in black mourning, majestical in her grief"; "swaying the scallop and hem"; "statue"). Like a complex ideogram, she seems capable of "passing" into very different realms. If we ask what energizes this mix of decorum and sensuousness, we notice the similarity between the germinating "hurricane" in her eye and the tumult on the street. This suggests a paradoxical affinity between the auratic rite and its secular context—the city in the furious throes of commerce—and between her spirit and the surrounding city. Here again, the sacred or "antique" object's contours cannot contain its burning desire to be consumed, for immediate integration with the tide of products.

Needless to say, the poet's own posture is not that of a buyer coldly examining saleable items, although the form of his description of the woman vaguely resembles an inventory. The poet's appreciation primarily recalls the "convulsions" of religious enthusiasm, or perhaps a Dostoevskian epileptic fit. ("Un éclair... puis la nuit!") Yet, as Hartman has noted, his devotion is oddly smeared, chewed up by a consumer's visual rapacity.[80] As with the *passante,* the poet works to annihilate the gap between sacred and profane rapture. The moment of their communion is reduced to a flash, apparently the only form—an illegible form—in which it can be preserved. At the heart of the scene's everyday-ness is something that inextricably confuses consumption of (visual) commodity with radical, unspeakable sensorial novelty.

It will prove illuminating, at this point, to go back to the theme of aesthetic education—seemingly left so far behind—and compare the scene of Baudelaire's sonnet with what Jacques Rancière calls "the 'original scene' of aesthetics," Schiller's introduction of the notion of "play-drive" through a description of an aesthetic encounter with the Greek statue of the Juno Ludovisi.[81] Rancière elaborates as follows:

> The statue is "self-contained," and "dwells in itself," as befits the traits of the divinity: her "idleness," her distance from any care or duty, from any purpose or volition. [...] [T]he spectator who experiences the free play

> of the aesthetic in front of the "free appearance" enjoys an autonomy of a very special kind. It is not the autonomy of free Reason, subduing the anarchy of sensation. It is the suspension of that kind of autonomy. It is an autonomy strictly related to a withdrawal of power. The "free appearance" stands in front of us, unapproachable, unavailable to our knowledge, our aims and desires. The subject is promised the possession of a new world by this figure that he cannot possess in any way. The goddess and the spectator, the free play and the free appearance, are caught up together in a specific sensorium, canceling the oppositions of activity and passivity, will and resistance. The "autonomy of art" and the "promise of politics" are not counterpoised.[82]

Brought by chance into the poet's purview, the *passante* is indeed a "free appearance," unrelated to her admirer in any necessary way. In turn, however, the "flash" experience recounted by the poet can hardly be called a new sensorium: it seems too temporary, too discontinuous, too detached from time and space to carry any promise of "a new world," much less any repeal of "large codes of fraud and woe." To this extent, the autonomy of which the poem speaks is radically self-enclosed and hard to relate to any legible cognition. Yet, at the same time, the poem openly acknowledges that the encounter is owing to the crowd—that the crowd brings poet and *passante* together. There is a rift here between what we might call the sensory and the epistemological aspects of the aesthetic experience: within the scene of consumption, bared and in full view, is an irreducible, unsignifying core.[83]

We might see in this double heterogeneity a weird fulfillment of Schleiermacher's postulate of the dual tendencies of poetry toward the pictorial (toward pure presence) or the mathematical (toward pure differential). And certainly we should extend the relevance of this duality to Baudelaire's poem itself, which also purports to offer a unique experience within the wider production and exchange of cultural products. I would like to hazard a hypothesis and argue that Baudelaire's inscription, in the way it offers dazzling perceptual novelty through technical control, presages the dualism inherent in the work of the sublime pointillist Seurat, as described by Jonathan Crary:

> Seurat's work . . . [holds] at least the promise or dream of a fully unalienated, instinctual aesthetic gratification, yet [this] could only be imagined through the impoverished systematizing of drive or of affect into a quantifiable and manageable economy of excitation, within an "organized" and controllable body. . . . even to attempt the creation of [Seurat's] luminous effect [meant] bringing into the work the forms of rationalization that eradicated aura in the first place.[84]

As Seurat fashioned the stunning surfaces of *La Grande Jatte* through a hyper-mechanical deployment of color technique, so, too, the assembly of the *passante* out of an array of affecting elements—leg, hem, mourning veil—generates the luminous "éclair." From a metapoetic standpoint, in other words, the *passante* figures the inscription itself as technical apparatus, though one less elaborate to be sure than Seurat's calculus of color; for its part, the poet's "extravagant" response is the inscription's aesthetic discharge, utterly unique if still impossible without the city. The Baudelairean modern poem enters life, as most everything else does, through the market; yet because the experience it offers is non-exchangeable, the poem as aesthetic event finds its only posterity in the subjunctive mode of melancholy, as a permanent "I could have loved." Thus the poem is also quite precisely a "freedom-thing," inasmuch as it claims to insert a radical autonomy within a wider system of equivalences, without aspiring productively to alter that system in any generally aesthetically educational way.[85]

In other words, the very non-meeting of *passant* and *passante* preserves the precious experience from the social even while the social is fully present as that from which the "flash" is wrested. There is, however, a further implication to be drawn from the *temporal* duality (of modernity/antiquity) inherent in the allegorical structure of the *passante*. On the one hand, as suggested, she is figured as a ceremonial object and, as such, registers the "fugitive beauté" of vanishing sacral forms. On the other, her "vanishing beauty" is that of the urban crowd, the beauty of *fashion*, of that which sets itself apart (momentarily) from the shapeless and "deafening street." In a famous section from "The Painter of Modern Life" that echoes many of the sonnet's motifs, Baudelaire relates both fashion and "the eternal" to modernity and the project of a modern art:

> The aim for [the modern artist] is to extract from fashion the poetry that resides in its historical envelope, to distil the eternal from the transitory. [. . .] Modernity is the transient, the fleeting, the contingent; it is one half of art, the other being the eternal and the immovable. There was a form of modernity for every painter of the past; the majority of the fine portraits that remain to us from former times are clothed in the dress of their own day. They are perfectly harmonious works because the dress, the hairstyle, and even the gesture, the expression and the smile (each age has its carriage, its expression and its smile) form a whole, full of vitality. You have no right to despise this transitory fleeting element, the metamorphoses of which are so frequent, nor to dispense with it. If you do, you inevitably fall into the emptiness of an abstract and indefinable beauty, like that of the one and only woman of the time before the Fall. [. . .] The draperies of Rubens or Veronese will not teach you how to paint watered silk *à la antique*, or satin *à la reine*, or any other fabric produced by our mills, supported by a swaying crinoline, or petticoats of starched muslin.[86]

The terms "transitory" and "eternal" are placed in slightly misleading opposition here, for Baudelaire argues that what is transitory is *also* eternal—not particular "fleeting elements" but the transitory as such. Modernity is the very phenomenal situatedness of an object, that which cannot be distilled out of appearances and moved about; it is, in short, what is irreplaceable about the object and cannot survive the resettlements of modernization. Yet, paradoxically, that irreplaceability is itself in continual flux. This means in part that the recessive negativity characterizing residues of past modes of life is part of the *present* as well. The artist seizes upon memories of the present as upon precious fragments of an auratic past—indeed, in a complete rejection of any neoclassical allegoreses, here the modern *is* the antique.

More broadly considered, the eternal flux of fashion requires that the artist be vigilant and active in identifying that "fleeting element" proper to any given present, no doubt a temporally impossible task.[87] The artist is asked to grasp the essential-transitory forms with a *prophetic* speed that outruns change itself:

> If in a shift of fashion, the cut of a dress has been slightly modified, if clusters of ribbons and curls have been dethroned by rosettes, if bonnets have widened and chignons have come down a little on the nape of the neck, if waist-lines have been raised and skirts become fuller, you may be sure that *from a long way off his eagle's eyes will have detected it.*[88]

Thus the modern artist, and perhaps the modern critic as well, is charged with determining (or *pre*determining) what is new, what is living, and what is dead at any given moment. The waning and devaluation of the past and the inability to intervene in the social sphere are both to be compensated for by *an absolute knowledge of the (always-already superseded) present:* only such a presentist, "cultural" knowledge can in any way reattach the now *déclassé* artist to the whole, to the lived "vitality" of a society shedding one body after another.

Of course, this knowledge is no less fleeting than its objects. Nothing but the momentary, explosive, and consuming attention it pays to "la transitoire" distinguishes it from the deracinating logic of modernization as such. The moment of unalienated wholeness virtually coincides with the reduction or absolute dissolution of both object *and* subject into unstructured being ("a flash—then night"). The effect is quite precisely *fetishistic* in Georges Bataille's sense (here, as interpreted by Denis Hollier):

> The fetish [in Bataille] is the irreplaceable, untransposable object. [. . . .] The transposed fetish is the fetish that no longer works as a fetish: it has been discarded and framed to be put on the market; it has been degraded to become a commodity. It is no longer used but collected.[89]

Hollier concludes his discussion of Bataille's apocalyptic notion of fetishistic use-value with an explicit allusion to Baudelaire:

> A materialism of use-value, it defines the material as what does not last. [....] The material is expended integrally, without remains, without leaving anything behind, not a ghost, not an heir, not a double. A flash—then night.[90]

Paradoxically enough, modern sonnet writing strives to build a *monument to a fetish,* to convert the experience of the fetishist into a nagging memory, whose very obscurity ("...puis la nuit!") communicates an essential uncommunicability.[91] It is clear to us, as it undoubtedly was to Bataille, how Baudelairean modernity could eventually generate the absolutely resistant objects of surrealism. In relation to later writing, however, Baudelaire's work has no location but is rather like a flash separating the poem-as-commodity from the modernist fetish-poem—while joining them as well.

* * *

(Deeply anxious) nostalgia and (a highly complex and fraught) aestheticism: were these the only possible responses to the new difficulty facing inscriptive verse, a difficulty rooted in an increasing inability to imagine audience (and community)? Along with Jacques Rancière and others, the historian William H. Sewell Jr., has recovered for us the largely forgotten "worker-poet" movement in France in the 1830s and 1840s and, in so doing, adds a vital nuance to our reading of mid-century poetic modernity, and the relationship of modern inscription to self-conscious group formation.[92]

The worker-poets, usually dismissed as authors of "inferior imitations of Lamartine,"[93] strove through the very fact of their poetic work toward an overcoming of old divisions of intellectual and manual labor:

> That manual laborers were capable of poetry [...] signified that the long-presumed opposition between vile labor and lofty creativity was false, that labor and poetry were not opposite but basically the same.[94]

In this poetry, the moment of (socially effective) *production* is reinserted with a vengeance. Doubtless, some of the workers' poems even prefigure the more ponderous hortatory features of later "proletarian" poetry, including the early Soviet variety with its cult of metal and machine:

> Armons nos bras des sonores marteaux,
> Et, pour la gloire et le bonheur du monde,
> Donnons la vie aux rebelles métaux.

> [Arm ourselves with sonorous hammers,
> And, for the glory and the happiness of the world,
> Give life to rebellious metals.][95]

These lines were written by the Toulon stonemason Charles Poncy, one of several worker-poets patronized by Baudelaire's spiritual nemesis, George Sand. Poncy published his collection *La Chanson de chaque métier* in 1850 to represent "the spirit and situation of the workers during [1848]" for a posterity that might otherwise know only of the revolution's failure.[96] His work celebrates the unity and the diversity of the various trades, the "moral heroism"[97] of the workers' struggle against poverty, and the centrality of labor as the foundation of human social life. For all his insistence on the "life-giving" powers of work, however, his lines give equal time to the traditional, religious foundations of the laborer's self-conception. The result is a potentially uneasy cooperation of Christian with modern, self-assertive canons of value:

> Que ta voix de fer, mon marteau, résonne
> Pour glorifier le Travail et Dieu,
> Le Travail et Dieu.
>
> Let your voice of iron resound, my hammer,
> To glorify Labor and God,
> Labor and God.
>
> Oui, que pour le bonheur de tous
> Le travail s'organise,
> Et que du Seigneur, parmi nous
> Le regne s'éternise.
>
> Yes, for the happiness of all
> Let labor be organized,
> And let the Lord's reign
> Be eternal among us.[98]

Can "the Lord" and "organized labor" be praised as equals in a single breath? The dualism concisely expresses many of the anxieties surrounding the *identity of the people*—the working masses—from Wordsworth's through Baudelaire's time and beyond. How really different was the new, "deafening" urban culture from what had gone before; how much of earlier modes of life and thought would persist, how much would change, be abandoned or simply repeated? What would the "Lord's reign" look like in a world dominated at present by "Roberts & Co. . . . the lightning-rod . . . the Crédit Mobilier"?[99]

We will return to Poncy at the end, but it behooves us first to consider one more Baudelaire lyric, the great and puzzling "Les Sept Vieillards"

("The Seven Old Men," from *Tableaux Parisiens*), perhaps Baudelaire's most revealing poetic response to this unreadable social situation:

> Fourmillante cité, cité plein de rêves,
> Où le spectre en plein jour raccroche le passant!
> Les mystères partout coulent comme des sèves
> Dans les canaux étroits du colosse puissant.
>
> Un matin, cependant que dans la triste rue
> Les maisons, dont la brume allongeait la hauteur,
> Simulaient les deux quais d'une rivière accrue,
> Et que, décor semblable à l'âme de l'acteur,
>
> Un brouillard sale et jaune inondait tout l'espace,
> Je suivais, roidissant mes nerfs comme un héros
> Et discutant avec mon âme déjà lasse,
> Le faubourg secoué par les lourds tombereaux.
>
> Tout à coup, un vieillard dont les guenilles jaunes
> Imitaient la couleur de ce ciel pluvieux,
> Et dont l'aspect aurait fait pleuvoir les aumônes,
> Sans la méchanceté qui luisait dans ses yeux,
>
> M'apparut.
> (p. 64)
>
> O swarming city, city full of dreams,
> Where ghosts accost the passers-by in broad daylight!
> Mysteries flow everywhere like sap
> In the narrow veins of this mighty giant.
>
> One morning, when in the dingy street
> The houses seemed to be stretched upwards
> By a mist and looked like the two quays
>   of some swollen river,
> And when—a background not unlike an actor's soul—
> A dirty yellow fog flooded the whole of space,
> I was making my way, heroically steeling my nerves
> And arguing with my already weary soul,
> Through the suburbs which were shaken
>   by ponderous tumbrils.
>
> Then suddenly an old man whose yellow rags
> Were the same color as the rainy sky, and
>
>   whose appearance
> Was enough to invite showers of alms were it not
> For the wicked glint in his eyes,
>
> Hove in sight. (Baudelaire, *Complete Verse,* pp. 177–78)

In the first lines we get yet another ambiguous representation of primordiality: the city as a soup both void and hyper-saturated. The opening invocation emphasizes a fullness in the city ("fourmillante" ["swarming"], "plein" ["full"], "en plein jour," "partout coulent" ["flow everywhere"], "colosse puissant" ["mighty giant"]), yet it is a fullness of dreams, of ghosts and mysteries: a plenitude of fantasy, not of people. As the curtain rises on the narrated "scene" with its hero, a river of fog inundates the street; the décor resembles "the soul of an actor" because, presumably, it is a blank nothing, and absorbs, like that of the poet, all professions, joys and miseries.

The bent-up old man appears entirely punctually, "tout à coup," not clearly related to the place described—in contrast to, say, what we see in classic pastoral descriptions like Lamartine's "Les Laboureurs," where land and laborer meet in perfect coherence. Whether beggar, worker, or simply inhabitant, Baudelaire's old man is certainly another *passant.* His appearance is followed by two other, more perplexing "mysteries": his own sevenfold reduplication, and (in another echo of *La Nouvelle Héloïse*) the poet's intense, bifurcated reaction to it:

> Exaspéré comme un ivrogne qui voit double,
> Je rentrai, je fermai ma porte, épouvanté,
> Malade et morfondu, l'esprit fiévreux et trouble,
> Blessé par le mystère et par l'absurdité!
>
> Vainement ma raison voulait prendre la barre;
> La tempête en jouant déroutait ses efforts,
> Et mon âme dansait, dansait, vieille gabarre,
> Sans mâts, sur une mer monstrueuse et sans bords!
> (p. 65)
>
> Irritated beyond endurance like some drunkard
> seeing double,
> I went home and locked my door, terrified and nauseated
> And depressed, my mind feverish and disturbed,
> Hurt by this enigma, this absurdity.
>
> My reason tried to take over, but in vain:
> Its efforts were all thwarted by the storm,
> And my soul danced and danced like some old
> mastless barge
> Heaved on a monstrous shoreless sea. (p. 179)

In this poem, the city crowd is refigured not as a "mass" but as a series of terrifying repetitions, described as alternatively natural or artificial in origin. On the one hand, that "this sinister old man . . . replicates himself" ("ce sinistre vieillard . . . se multipli[e]") suggests non-natural reproduction, the eternal sameness of the assembly line. At the same time, the old man is "son and father to himself" ("fils et père de lui-même"), and thus bizarrely reintegrated into a "familial" model of generation, however motherless. As he does so often, however, Baudelaire uses tropes of the mythic and antique to cut through simple natural/artificial dichotomies, to obscure the object's origins and identity by wrapping it in a mantle of mythic time. For the old man is also a "dégoutant Phénix" ("a disgusting Phoenix"), a creature that proliferates by virtue of the agency of some inhuman (and *non*-human) mechanism. "The seven monsters had an eternal air about them," implying that their essence lies somehow beyond the reach of practical and theoretical knowledge alike.

No doubt Baudelaire needed to see the working masses in this way in order to posit his own radical difference from them, but the complexities of response here preclude our explaining the poem simply in terms of the author's attempts at solipsism. For one thing, the self-generation of the old man ("fils et père de lui-même") surely resonates with the poet's own ambitions of simultaneous mastery and autonomy. The old men are wretched, "broken" ("cassés") indeed—but they are also strangely fertile, filled with energy, and seized with an annihilating fury directed at the past and at nature. For this reason, Benjamin's notebook comparison of the old men with "chorus girls" strikes me as too moralizing, too exclusively focused on the pathos of the scene.[100] The first "vieillard," progenitor of the rest, walks

> Comme s'il écrasait des morts sous ses savates,
> Hostile à l'univers plutôt qu'indifférent. (p. 65)
>
> As if he were crushing the dead beneath his shoes,
> Hostile to the universe rather than indifferent. (p. 179)

In a very Lamartinian locution, Baudelaire describes the "cortège infernal" as "walking at the same pace toward an unknown goal" ("Marchaient du même pas vers un but inconnu"). But here the Enlightenment myth of progress is at once affirmed and shattered. Not only is the goal unknown but the nature of the "cortège" is also indeterminate. The relentless, irrational, forward march of modernizing rationality leaves behind broken-down old men but also produces new kinds of people, whose dwelling is a new nature.

Clearly, however, this new nature is truly a mystery, a phenomenon that confounds all previous standards of judgment. The poet is faithful to his incomprehension when he writes:

> Vainement ma raison voulait prendre la barre;
> La tempête en jouant déroutait ses efforts,
> Et mon âme dansait, dansait, vieille gabarre,

Sans mâts, sur une mer monstrueuse et sans bords!
(p. 65)

My reason tried to take over, but in vain:
Its efforts were all thwarted by the storm,
And my soul danced and danced like some old
  mastless barge
Heaved on a monstrous shoreless sea. (p. 179)

Reason, especially the reason that discerns or posits social function and effectivity, is pushed aside by a soul in the negative ecstasies (*ek-stasis*) of modernization. The poet's schizophrenia corresponds to what Peter Wollen years ago identified as the fissure between the "functional" and the "visionary" that opened up within Soviet avant-garde practice starting in the late 1920s—although the eventual consequence there was a reverse valorization of the *functional*.[101]

The goal of utopian thinkers of the late nineteenth and early twentieth centuries, of course, will be precisely to fuse the functional and the visionary together in some way. We might even regard Charles Poncy's poetry as gesturing in that direction—as the attempt, by imagining labor as linked to both experience and future aspirations, to create inscriptions that actually *work* to summon a community. Here his "young stonecutter" wanders through a utopian landscape, where mute material has indeed been infused with social meaning in which the maker-observer participates:

Le coeur plein d'avenir
Partout, sur son passage,
Salue un souvenir.
Il lève la paupière,
Et lit, d'un oil joyeux,
Ces poèms de pierre,
Ou'ont écrits ses aieux.

His heart filled with the future
At each step of the way,
He greets a [memory].
He raises his eyelids,
And reads with joyous eye,
Those poems of stone,
That his elders have written.[102]

The project of Wordsworth's Michael, it might be said, finds its true fulfillment here; work itself, far from being mere production, links the worker to the work(er)s of the past and the works that are not yet here.

The bitter counterargument would be that writers like Poncy are kidding themselves, that they are idealizing one of the classes most thoroughly harrowed by modernization and most thoroughly deprived of experience—their own. From our vantage point, it is indeed difficult to read Poncy's lines and not think not only of Lamartine's blood-and-soil proclivities but also of later histories fabricated by states (with the help of archives) on behalf of their now "proletarian" citizens, and inscribed as heroic bas-reliefs on public walls (or movie screens). But we ourselves continue to live squarely within the Baudelairean gap between vision and function, of course, and to that extent remain blindly modern: the persistent critical dichotomy of authentic versus "useful" (or "tendentious") poetry is one small proof of that. Our "critique" of figures like Poncy remains uncritical unless it is felt to contain a judgment upon our own limitations as well.

For writers after Baudelaire, the new mass quality of social life retained the nature of a risk, of a flowing enigma that might be variously conceptualized, even if only (to adopt Flaubert's expression) as the shit pounding against the walls of the ivory tower. What kind of place would the "new people" (to use a cliché phrase of Russian radicals) create and live within? What was of immediate importance for the successors of Baudelaire, Lamartine and Poncy was the question of what might reconstitute or (if necessary) substitute for experience within newly emergent, modernizing, heterogeneous (national, proletarian, colonized) groups. Thus the notion of culture, rather than nature or even subjectivity per se, becomes the central preoccupation of late nineteenth and twentieth-century modernism: the question of what literacy should be, of how poetry might participate in it, and who if anyone should (or could) control it, "prendre la barre."

— 3 —

Kernels of the Acropolis

Poetry and Modernization in Blok, Kliuev, and Khlebnikov

> All our lyric verse from Walther von der Vogelweide to Goethe and from Goethe to the poems of our dying world-cities is monologue, while the Classical lyric is a choral lyric, a singing before witnesses.
>
> —Spengler, *The Decline of the West*

> Hee-Haw! Click-Clack! And Cock-a-doodle-doo!
> —Wull Gabriel in Esperanto cry
> Or a' the warld's undeemis jargons try?
>
> —Hugh MacDiarmid, "Gairmscoile"*

Palaces Out of the Ground

Alexander Blok's lyric poetry is filled with spectral presences, with that of Baudelaire among the more obvious ones. An inventory of props common to the two poets might include:

— enigmatic black-clad women whose eyes unfold onto sublime and terrible visions;
— intense, random encounters in the city street;
— representations of the "I" as a shaken, solitary observer of urban turmoil;
— an atmosphere of "mysterious vulgarity";[1]
— a primarily ocular sexuality, rapt and revolted.

*The title "Gairmscoile" means "poet's school" in Gaelic; the word "undeemis" in the poem means "countless."

Adrian Wanner's fascinating recent study of *Baudelaire in Russia* contains its own list of "correspondances,"[2] together with the acknowledgment that these lists explain little about how the specific philosophical and figural textures of Baudelaire and Blok might merge or diverge.

Glancing at Blok's early biography, one is tempted to describe his relation to Baudelaire as virtually familial: both his mother and grandmother were early translators and enthusiasts of the French poet. Wanner points out several other, equally remarkable biographical commonalities.[3] Yet, in spite of these "family ties," Blok only rarely refers to Baudelaire in his prose works, nowhere discusses Baudelaire's poetry at length, and produces, at eighteen, a single overtly Baudelaire-inspired poem, a parody of "L'Albatros," naughtily inserted into a letter to his grandmother.[4] And, of course, any consideration of Blok's reception of Baudelaire as it relates to Blok's representation of city life has to remain aware of other factors—historical-political (the chaotic Petersburg of the revolution and the years leading up to it), cultural-philosophical (Vladimir Solovyov, Viacheslav Ivanov, Johann Honegger, Nietzsche), and literary (above all, Dostoevsky)—that imposed themselves upon him and to which he responded.

Avril Pyman, for example, has already pointed to Blok's veiled description of Petersburg's invasion "by the semi-peasant masses from industrial islands,"[5] in the quasi-mythic allegory "Podnimalis' iz t'my pogrebov" (1904) ("They emerged from the darkness of cellars"):

> Podnimalis' iz t'my pogrebov.
> Ukhodili ikh golovy v plechi.
> Tikho vyrosli shumy shagov,
> Slovesa neznakomykh narechii.
>
> Skoro pribyli tolpy drugikh,
> Volochili kirki i lopaty.
> Raspolzlis' po kamniam mostovykh,
> Iz zemli vozdvigali palaty.
>
> Vstala ulitsa, serym polna,
> Zatkalas' pautinnoiu priazhei,
> Shelestia, pribyvala volna,
> Zatrudnaia protok ekipazhei.
>
> Skoro den' gluboko otstupil,
> V nebe dal'nem rasstavivshii zori.
> A nezrimyi potok shelestil,
> Prolivaias' v nash gorod, kak v more.
> My ne stali iskat' i gadat':
> Pust' zameniat nas novye liudi!

V tekh zhe mukakh rozhdala ikh mat',
Tak zhe nezhno kormila u grudi...

V pelene otkhodiashchego dnia
Nam byla eta uchast' poniatna...
Nam poslednii zakat iz ognia
Sochetal i sotkal svoi piatna.

Ne stereg isstuplennyi drakon,
Ne pylala nad nami geenna.
Zatopili nas volny vremen,
I byla nasha uchast'—mgnovenna. (p. 328)

They emerged from the darkness of cellars,
And their heads were set low on their necks;
The sound of their footsteps grew louder,
And the [words] of their strange dialects.

Then legions of newcomers followed,
With pickaxes and shovels in hand.
They went swarming all over the roadways
And raised palaces out of the ground.

Then a street rose up, [filled with] gray,
With spidery threads interwoven.
The tide flowed along with a murmur,
And the coaches could hardly keep moving.

Day retreated far into the distance,
A red glimmer was all we could see,
But the unseen flood flowed into
Our city as into a sea.

We abandoned our quests and surmises:
Let our places be taken by [new people]:
They were born in like sorrow, and suckled
With like joy at the breasts of their mothers [...]

In the [shroud] of the daytime's departing
Our own destiny's meaning was clear:
The last sunset combined and wove
All its colors for us out of fire.

We were guarded by no raging dragon.
We endured no Gehenna of torment.
Time's waves [...] quickly engulfed us;
We were fated to last but a moment.[6]

The poem's inscriptive horizon is visible only at the end, when its desperately ironic self-epitaphs come into full view. Yet this epitaphic tablet comes close to denying itself any possible audience, insofar as it memorializes not a person but some older version of the "public" as such. The pessimism, self-parodying though it surely is, had its own distinct historical motivation in the social, political, and economic turmoil afflicting St. Petersburg and Russia during Blok's entire lifetime (1880–1921).[7] The spread of factories throughout St. Petersburg in the late nineteenth century, and the attendant growth of the labor market, led to a huge inflow of peasants (especially after the lifting of restrictions on rural-urban migration in 1906) fleeing even worse conditions in the countryside. "By December of 1910," writes James Bater, "69 per cent of the city's 1.906 million inhabitants were peasants."[8] This, along with chaotic zoning practices, led to the volatile mingling of rich and poor, of residence and factory:

> In the early 1900s upper class residential areas were no more than discontinuous pockets within the urban environment. They consisted of areas of living space on the second, third and sometimes the fourth floors of the built environment. They tended to be more ubiquitous than spatially segregated—and so, therefore, were their more affluent occupants. Cellars had long since been occupied by the poor, though they were steadily becoming more crowded. The middle classes and the affluent, figuratively speaking, pushed the poor upward and outwards. Zoning had succumbed to industrialization and factories were to be smelled, if not seen everywhere. Tucked away in inner courtyards, or occupying whole buildings, they had in a real sense changed the face of the city. Limited spatial mobility precluded a rapid and extensive decentralization of factories and workshops, along with their work-forces.[9]

The "new people," and the obscuring of the old shapes of the city, are major themes in Blok's Petersburg lyrics. The second part of his essay "Hard Times" ("Bezvremen'e" [1906], a perversely celebratory description of urban poverty and vagrancy) begins with the sentence: "But in the square the [female] spider celebrates."[10] As in Baudelaire and Lamartine, the crowd is sub-humanized, here in the direction of the "swarming," industrious arachnid; "the voice of the storm drew them from their spider-shelters," wrote Blok of tramps wandering through Petersburg's blizzards (p. 31). Yet what emerges from the basements of "Podnimalis' iz t'my pogrebov" is not simply a leveling flood, even if the trope of inundation has provided the capital city's privileged form for catastrophe since (at least) the time of Pushkin. The "wave," the unseen stream, is also responsible for weaving a whole new city, one that occludes but will also replace the life of the old city, a life condensed in the pronoun "we." Indeed, the appearance of new palaces suggests the possible emergence of a whole new array of civic or monumental inscriptions, to be written in "strange dialects."

The "we" introduces a dichotomy of collectives crucial to Blok's poetry of the city. The poet presumes to speak for an established group that we might name in various ways—the old world, the intelligentsia, individualism, civilization—a collective identity that is about to be replaced by something larger, more vital, less readable. Here we should take care to remember that the new sense of crisis extended to the question of reading itself: as the urban proletariat that Slavophiles like Aleksei Khomyakov had so dreaded started to take shape,[11] newly literate peasants began to read secular, commercial writing, radical ideas began to spread, and (in general) older sources of cultural authority, religious and otherwise, began to lose their grip on the population. Entering into this breach was a variety of projects to condition the culture of the emergent "new" population (including government-sponsored cultural centers and libraries, and Leo Tolstoy's Posrednik [Intermediary] publishing house [founded in 1884]).[12] Blok's poem would seem to be the opposite of an intervention, although as epitaph it could be read as having a mournful appellative function for the superceded "we," itself apparently a recently formed entity ("We were fated to last but a moment").

In contrast to Baudelaire's persona, the "I" (here exclusively a first-person plural) in Blok begins to play a self-consciously representative role in a pessimistic pageant of historical and cultural change. Rather than the fate of subjectivity in the face of urban shock, the destiny of culture, sometimes projected against a lurid horizon of class conflict, emerges with increasing overtness both as Blok's theme and the theme of much of the greatest Russian poetry that follows in his wake.[13] (Indeed, it may be said that Blok's "I" comes to stand in for subjectivity itself as a "doomed" though not, of course, irrelevant category.)[14] The victor in this process (one Blok chooses to mystify as quasi-natural) is only obscurely and tentatively a human force, despite its artisanal labors; the new constructions have a disruptive effect (on traffic, at least) barely distinguishable from natural disaster.

Recalling the motif of the holy "wanderer" (*strannik*) familiar from Tolstoy, Dostoevsky, and Leskov, among others, Blok, in "Hard Times," describes the city's poor vagrants as part of the "thousandfold eye of Russia." Their paths smudge the "straight lines of the city" and reconnect Petersburg with the supposedly wild, swamp-like and mystical obscurity of the essential Russia (pp. 32–34). Yet the ambivalence of trope here—is the "gray street" an annihilating flood ("time's waves") or a fertile infestation, producing its own webs and "hive-life" (Tolstoy)?—cautions us not to regard Blok as a mere prophet of *Untergang*, despite his irrational, reactionary impulses. The deliberately offensive condescension of his description of the gray, inarticulate builders as having "their heads set low on their necks" implies that they are troglodytes, struggling in quasi-evolutionary fashion toward emergence and eventual dominance. Dominance indeed, for this is a paradoxically constructive flood, a disaster that leaves behind not ruins but spidery palaces.

This chapter will be preoccupied with the way the emergent "communities"—the word has to be set in scare quotes—that seized Blok's imagination entered into early-twentieth-century Russian poetry as stimuli to reflections on other possible literacies. Were the language and subjectivities generated by modernity utterly novel; were they translations of older modes; or were they a new *non*-literacy (à la Lamartine)? The inscriptive mode, even if present only in residual, deeply sublimated or ironically distorted form, will turn out to be an imaginative matrix through which poets continue to reflect on these questions of audience, and to project their own answers. Common to the three writers I examine in this chapter (the Symbolist Blok, the "peasant-poet" Nikolai Kliuev, and the Futurist Velimir Khlebnikov) is a concern about the degree to which the very medium of poetic appellations and projections—for them, the Russian language itself—could both accommodate the proliferation of new discourses and preserve the old, and I will argue that both Kliuev (in his ekphrastic inscription, "Where heaven is enameled" [1916–17]) and Khlebnikov (in the great meta-inscription "Incantation by Laughter" [1909]) see their own poetic work as precisely helping to fashion a linguistic agora of this capacious sort. Their solutions, however, never manage to unite the "new" and "old" particulars into a single, seamless legitimating structure; in this they remain within the same contradictions that drove their pessimistic predecessor Blok into (among other stances) an ambivalent populism, lucidly documented by Yuri Lotman,[15] as a way of responding to this situation of radical instability and openness. The famous appearance of Christ after all the barbarity of "Dvenadtsat' " ("The Twelve")—an appearance truly ironic in its larger resonances—should stand as the apotheosis of Blok's anxiety rather than as a facile affirmation of continuity.

Blok's best poetry, as here in the ironic prospect poem "Neznakomka" ("The Stranger" [1906]), registers that anxiety in unforgettable terms:

Po vecheram nad restoranami
Goriachii vozdukh dik i glukh,
I pravit okrikami p'ianymi
Vesennii i tletvornyi dukh.

Vdali, nad pyl'iu pereulochnoi,
Nad skukoi zagorodnykh dach,
Chut' zolotitsia krendel' bulochnoi,
I razdaetsia detskii plach.

I kazhdyi vecher, za shlagbaumami,
Zalamyvaia kotelki,
Sredi kanav guliaiut s damami
Ispytannye ostriaki.

Nad ozerom skripiat ukliuchiny,
I razdaetsia zhenskii vizg,
A v nebe, ko vsemu priuchennyi,
Bessmyslenno krivitsia disk.

I kazhdyi vecher drug edinstvennyi
V moem stakane otrazhen
I vlagoi terpkoi i tainstvennoi,
Kak ia, smiren i oglushen.

A riadom u sosednykh stolikov
Lakei sonnye torchat,
I p'ianitsy s glazami krolikov
"In vino veritas!" krichat.

I kazhdyi vecher, v chas naznachennyi
(Il' eto tol'ko snitsia mne?),
Devichii stan, shelkami skhvachennyi,
V tumannom dvizhetsia okne.

I medlenno proidia mezh p'ianymi,
Vsegda bez sputnikov, odna,
Dysha dukhami i tumanami,
Ona saditsia u okna.

I veiut drevnimi pover'iami
Ee uprugie shelka,
I shliapa s traurnymi per'iami,
I v kol'tsakh uzkaia ruka.

I strannoi blizost'iu zakovannyi,
Smotriu za temnuiu vual',
I vizhu bereg ocharovannyi
I ocharovannuiu dal'.

Glukhie tainy mne porucheny,
Mne ch'e-to solntse vrucheno,
I vse dushi moei izluchiny
Pronzilo terpkoe vino.

I per'ia strausa sklonennye
V moem kachaiutsia mozgu,

I ochi sinie bezdonnye
Tsvetut na dal'nem beregu.

V moei dushe lezhit sokrovishche,
I kliuch poruchen tol'ko mne!
Ty pravo, p'ianoe chudovishche!
Ia znaiu: istina v vine. (pp. 391–94)

In the evenings, above the restaurants,
The air is hot and thick and wild,
And with drunken cries
A putrid springtime spirit rules.

Far away, above the dust of side streets,
Above the tedium of country cottages,
The bakery-pretzel shines slightly golden,[16]
And the crying of a child is heard.

And every evening, past the barriers,
Tipping their bowler hats,
Well-tried wits go strolling with ladies
Along the canals.

Oarlocks creak above the lake,
And a woman's shriek is heard;
In the sky, accustomed to everything,
The [moon's] disc bends senselessly.

And every evening, I see my only friend
Reflected in my glass,
And, like me, he's numbed and subdued
By the tart, astringent liquid.

Nearby, at the neighboring tables,
Sleepy waiters hang around,
And drunkards with the eyes of rabbits
Cry "in vino veritas!"

And every evening, at the appointed hour
(Or do I only dream it?)
A girlish form, wrapped in silks,
Moves in the misty window.

And slowly moving through the drunkards,
Always alone, without escorts,
Exhaling perfumes and vapors,
She sits next to the window.

And ancient superstitions flutter
From her supple silks,
From her hat with its feathers of mourning,
From her slender hand, with its rings.

And seized by a strange nearness
I look beyond the dark veil,
And see an enchanted shore,
And a distant, enchanted prospect.

Obscure mysteries are vouchsafed me,
I've been entrusted with someone's sun,
And bitter wine has flowed
Through all the windings of my soul.

And ostrich feathers, bending,
Sway inside my brain,
And blue and bottomless eyes
Blossom on the far shore.

In my soul there lies a treasure,
And the key is given to me alone!
You're right, you drunken monster!
Now I know: there's truth in wine.

"Neznakomka" is built upon the almost grotesque inversion of the structure of a prospect poem: beginning with an "overhead" view of the scene, it works its way downward to the benumbed speaker, to whom a new "distant, enchanted prospect" will be uniquely revealed. Plainly enough, the mimetic vantage point on the physical (and social) scene has been decisively broken away from any topographically visionary perspective. Yet this appropriation of an old form for landscape poetry is only one of the poem's many ironies, though not the least significant. On one level, this is a poem about a *translatio*, and, in that sense, it constitutes a minor modernization in its own right: an ancient cliché ("in vino veritas," from Pliny's *Natural History*) finds its way into Russian ("istina v vine"). The instructor in Latin truths is, surprisingly, the "drunken monster," the celebrant of the "putrid springtime spirit" hovering over all the "senselessness." It should be noted that the setting here is a liminal one, something like a holiday *prigorod* (suburb), lodged between city and country, and perhaps between "people and intelligentsia" as well: a place where leisure and suffering, civilization and decay, seem to fold into each other.[17] (The spirit is "putrid" *and* "springtime"; the pretzel-sign twists commerce, infant hunger, and (by an implied allusion to the golden "cupola" on churches) religion into a single crusty knot.) It seems as though things can pass easily into other things here—infant cries into women's shrieks, Latin into Russian, wine into "inspiration."

The main point of passage is the *passante*-like "stranger" herself, through whom "enchantment," "superstition," and "distance" (but also "strange closeness") are recovered; she is quite literally a "medium," and empty, in the sense of being transparent, rather than a surface on which plans are projected. Clothed in a manner that codes her socially as a prostitute, her provision of spiritual insight seems dependent upon her physical props (rings, veil, and so on) and techniques. The moment of deepest connection is a kind of strange brain surgery or trepanation ("ostrich feathers . . . inside my brain"), when fashion or "le transitoire" directly stirs the cerebral cortex into non-ocular vision (of course, the two meanings of "dukh" [soul and "vapor" or perfume] are part of this, too). Blok's work is part of a moment when "mystery" is on the verge of being re-described in entirely corporeal/somatic terms, in a manner we have already seen suggested in our Proust example (on the "cave" of memory) in chapter 1. Meanwhile the corporeal, in its own right, is clearly being flattened into commodity—pretzels, feathers, bowler hats.

Yet this generalization is in need of nuance. We might say that the banal, almost empty nature of the vision—"enchanted shore," "obscure mysteries," "someone's sun," "bottomless eyes"—reflects its inarticulate corporeal basis. But we also notice its repetitiveness ("every evening, at the appointed hour"), which the beginnings of the stanzas reflect not only on the level of sense (in the repetitions of "and every evening") but also in obsessively iterated stress units ("I kázhdyi," "I kázhdyi," "A riádom," "I kázhdyi," "I médlenno," "I véiut," "I strànnoi," "I pér'ia"). If the revelation itself is devoid of communicable content, the occasions of revelation are multiplied ad infinitum. Visionary experience, in contrast to the radical singularity of the Baudelairean *éclair*, is now a regularized rapture, almost a kind of work (at which one must arrive "at the appointed hour") rather than a conversion or intervention that orients future action in a novel direction. Epiphany becomes a habit much like drinking, but one difficult to distinguish from numb inertia.

The proffered revelation, however, is as "private" as it is incommunicable. Why is the speaker not able to participate in the drunken springtime revelry, and why are the "obscure mysteries" and their associated rituals—the poem's central legitimations—so exclusively his property? It may be simply that he is a representative of a Spenglerian "dying culture," mourned by Blok's *passante;* he retreats from the surrounding *narod*—a "monstrous" social form speaking not Russian but a Bacchic Latin—into fetishes of distant enchantment. But we might want to complicate this schematic (and rather sentimental) reading by making brief reference to one of the obvious precursor poems of "Neznakomka," Mikhail Lermontov's "How often, surrounded by the motley crowd" ("Kak chasto, pestroiu tolpoiu okruzhen" [1840];

here translated in full), a poem produced in an utterly different (pre-emancipation, pre-industrialization) era:

Kak chasto, pestroiu tolpoiu okruzhen,
Kogda peredo mnoi, kak budto by skvoz' son,
Pri shume muzyki i pliaski,
Pri dikom shepote zatverzhennykh rechei,
Mel'kaiut obrazy bezdushnye liudei,
Prilich'em stianutye maski;

Kogda kasaiutsia kholodnykh ruk moikh
S nebrezhnoi smelost'iu krasavits gorodskikh
Davno bestrepetnye ruki,—
Naruzhno pogruzhas' v ikh blesk i suetu,
Laskaiu ia v dushe starinnuiu mechtu,
Pogibshikh let sviatye zvuki.

I esli kak-nibud' na mig udastsia mne
Zabyt'sia,—pamiat'iu k nedavnei starine
Lechu ia vol'noi, vol'noi ptitsei;
I vizhu ia sebia rebenkom; i krugom
Rodnye vse mesta: vysokii barskii dom
I sad s razrushennoi teplitsei;

Zelenoi set'iu trav podernut spiashchii prud,
A za prudom selo dymitsia—i vstaiut
Vdali tumany nad poliami.
V alleiu temnuiu vkhozhu ia; skvoz' kusty
Gliadit vechernii luch, i zheltye listy
Shumiat pod robkimi shagami.

I strannaia toska tesnit uzh grud' moiu:
I dumaiu ob nei, ia plachu i liubliu,
Liubliu mechty moei sozdan'e
S glazami, polnymi lazurnogo ognia,
S ulybkoi rozovoi, kak molodogo dnia
Za roshchei pervoe siian'e.

Tak tsarstva divnogo vsesil'nyi gospodin—
Ia dolgie chasy prosizhival odin,
I pamiat' ikh zhiva ponyne
Pod burei tiagostnykh somnenii i strastei,
Kak svezhii ostrovok bezvredno sred' morei
Tsvetet na vlazhnoi ikh pustyne.

Kogda zh, opomnivshis', obman ia uznaiu,
I shum tolpy liudskoi spugnet mechtu moiu,
Na prazdnik nezvanuiu gost'iu,
O, kak mne khochetsia smutit' veselost' ikh
I derzko brosit' im v glaza zheleznyi stikh,
Oblityi gorech'iu i zlost'iu! . . .[18]

How often, surrounded by the motley crowd,
When before my eyes, as though through a dream,
  Accompanied by the noise of music and dancing,
And the savage whispering of speeches learned by rote,
I glimpse images of soulless people,
  Their masks tightly fixed by propriety;

When the long since dauntless hands of urban beauties
With careless audacity touch
  My cold hands,—
And apparently absorbed in their brilliance and
  vanity,—
In my soul I fondle an old dream,
  The holy sounds of bygone days.

And if somehow I manage for a moment
To sink into a reverie,—[suspended] by memory I fly
  Like a free, free bird to days of old, still fresh.
I see myself as a child; and around me
All my native places: the high manor-house
  And the garden with the ruined hothouse.

The slumbering pond is covered with a green net
  of grasses,
And beyond the pond floats the smoke of the village—
  In the distance rise mists above the fields.
I walk into a dark avenue; through the bushes
Peers a ray of evening, and yellow leaves
  Rustle under [my] timid steps.

And a strange longing already seizes my breast:
I think of her, I weep and I love,
  I love the creation of my dream
With her eyes, filled with azure fire,
With her pink smile, like the first gleaming
  Of the day beyond the grove.

Thus the omnipotent master of a marvelous kingdom—
I sit long hours alone,
  And their memory is alive to this day . . .
And amid the onerous storms of doubt and desire,
Like a cool island on the sea,
  Flowering unharmed in the watery desert.

And when, having come to my senses, I recognize
  the deception,
And the noise of the human crowd scares away my dream—
  An uninvited guest at the party—
O, how I want to disrupt their gaiety
And impertinently cast an iron verse before their eyes,
  Covered with bitterness and spite!

In both poems the speakers are, to all appearances, part of the crowd. Lermontov (to substitute the poet's names for their protagonists, out of convenience) is "apparently absorbed," and Blok is drunk like everyone else. But Lermontov has a memory of his own, excited by weariness and boredom, whereas Blok's imagination seems more dependent upon external "stirrings." "How often . . ." is indeed a poem about distinctions, and the central one is that between the artificial (high society, aristocracy) and the genuine. The latter is generally found (in Lermontov) in some version of either the "people" or the Transcaucasian "native"; but here genuineness for Lermontov is not lodged Rousseauistically in nature or the people or the "village" as such but rather in the poet's own creation ("the creation of my dream"). His creation pretends to be of an entirely different order of value than the social order he participates in; the sole mediation between the two is provided by invective (the "iron verse" forged at the end) or the hope of invective: an outburst that betrays a desire to seize some public space for "dreaming." Yet Lermontov still seems resentfully powerless relative to his social surroundings, whose main power is to "wake" him to his primary asset: his individuality itself.

Sixty years later, in Blok, the polarities of genuine/false, power/non-power are more intricately knotted. Visionary individuality has been comprehensively ironized, and the antithesis of the vital and the non-vital has replaced that of the artificial and the genuine. As we have seen, Blok often urges a decision, an identification of these two poles (vital = genuine) but not here. Vitality, or Hegelian "Lebendigkeit," is not ultimately readable or localizable. Nothing, perhaps, separates the drunkard from the drunkards, which are also his "reflection"; it is not clear whether what the drunkard sees—that is, the forms the new social vitality will take—are "old superstitions" or just "thick and wild" enjoyment or "obscure mysteries": beliefs and practices hitherto unknown. Surface and depth, hat and spirit, perfume and belief: Blok's poetry moves into a social setting where these and other distinctions will have to be abandoned, complicated, or hardened.

Lenin, the Father Superior

> Even the dream of a "better humanity" in which our children would "have a better life" is only a sentimental fantasy [. . .] when it is not, at bottom, the dream of a better nature in which they would live. (Herein lies the inextinguishable claim of the Fourierist utopia, a claim which Marx had recognized [and which Russia had begun to act on].)
>
> —Benjamin, *The Arcades Project*

Blok's preoccupation with the historical continuity of "culture" through a revolutionary flux within communities was, of course, common to many late-nineteenth- and early-twentieth-century Russian writers; figures as disparate as Vasilii Rozanov, Viacheslav Ivanov, Nikolai Zabolotsky, Vladimir Mayakovsky, and Osip Mandelstam could be studied through the prism of this problematic. As we have seen, Blok came to expect some kind of renewal of "cultural energy"—if not of the very forms of the older culture—from the uneducated masses, or *narod,* who, for Blok along with his fellow "Scythians" (primarily Pilniak, Ivanov-Razumnik, and Bely), meant, above all, the peasantry. It was in the peasantry that the essence of Russian culture, obscured by centuries of bureaucracy and Westernization, could be recovered—or so the story went for some in this time of intense cultural-nationalist pathos.[19]

The story that emerged eventually as dominant was, of course, very different indeed:

> "I don't want a commune without a stove-bench."[20] But a commune with a stove-bench is not a reconstruction of all the foundations of life in accordance with reason, with compass and yardstick in hand, but just the same old peasant paradise.[21]

Here Leon Trotsky (in his great and greatly biased 1924 overview of contemporary Russian writing, *Literature and Revolution*) cites the first line of a 1918 poem by the "peasant-poet" Nikolai Kliuev (born 1884). Kliuev was hounded and ostracized by Soviet authorities from the mid-1920s on, and ultimately shot in October 1937 as an alleged "active sectarian ideologue" in the "Union for the Salvation of Russia," a group that never existed.[22] Here are the poem's first two stanzas:

Ne khochu Kommuny bez lezhanki,
Bez khrustal'noi pesenki uglei!
V stikhotvornoi tiagostnoi viazanke
Dumnyi khvorost, burelomnik dnei.

Ne svalit' i v Krasnuiu Gazetu
Slov shchepu, opilki zapiatykh,
Nenavisten mudromu poetu
Podvorotnyi, tiavkaiushchii stikh.[23]

I don't want a commune without a stove-bench,
Without the crystal song of the coals!
In the onerous bundle of poetry
Is thoughtful brushwood, the fallen trees of days.

Don't pile up the Red Gazette
With the kindling of words, the sawdust of commas,

A begging, yelping poem
Is hateful to a wise poet.

Trotsky's reading of Kliuev, though hostile, is not imperceptive. He attacks both the poet's love of detail, decoration, and color, and his celebration of a peculiarly lush, utopian, strangely "decadent" peasant culture; to blame are the presumed acquisitiveness and complacency of "kulak" patriarchy, and (consequently) a wary, conservative inertness on the plane of culture:

> There is too much decoration in Kliuev's poems to allow any movement—heavy brocades, semi-precious stones, and the like; here one has to move with care, to avoid any breakage or loss.[24]

Kliuev is certainly both ornamental and, in many poems, a panegyrist of ornament, particularly of the wooden carvings adorning peasant huts. And it is hard to miss a certain "parochialism," both personal and poetic, in Kliuev's outlook. He was, in fact, from the remote village of Koshtug in the northern Olonets region; he dressed like a peasant (largely for show, it seems) and, according to Anna Akhmatova, exaggerated the unreduced "O" of the northern dialects when speaking. (A trait rendered by Akhmatova in her memoirs by inserting large *O*'s where they appear in citatiOns Of the nOrthern pOet's wOrds.)[25] His poetry borrows freely from "localisms" of various types: regionalisms, terms associated with peasant life, with Russian paganism, and the language of marginalized (and often geographically segregated) Christian religious sects.

Trotsky noticed that Kliuev did not appropriate just *any* sort of ornament, and accused him of "[typically] peasant" narrowness, especially in comparison with the urban proletariat and its supposedly cosmopolitan revolutionary energies.[26] Indeed, in the same poem, Kliuev casts doubt on the value of a socialist city-culture, here troped as "gifts" brought by "the guests from Berlin":

Ikh dary—magnit i grad kolbasnyi,
V buterbrodnoi banke Parsifal' [. . . .][27]

Their gifts are the magnet and a sausage-city,
And Parsifal in a sandwich container [. . . .]

Nonetheless, the poet's "sectarianism" is of an individual sort. Kliuev is perhaps best known for his sympathy for and interest in radical Christian religious dissenting groups, including the notorious *skoptsy* (self-castrators), in tribute to whom he wrote some of his most astonishing verses. Yet he was hardly a functionary of any sect, and seems to have been primarily interested in using Old Believer and sectarian motifs as part of a rhetorical "sacralizing" of rural life, of nature, and particularly (and hubristically) of his own speech, rather than the other way around.[28]

Against the presumed "localist" grain, and perhaps more surprising, his poetry often openly asserts a kind of mystic internationalism linking the Russian peasant world to an array of "exotic," often (though not always) non-European, and even non-Christian settings. Just some of the places he mentions are Sudan, "Nubia," Egypt, Mecca, Siam, Chile, in the "wigwam painted with bison" ("V raspisnom bizon'em vigvame"),[29] areas in Central Asia, and particularly India.[30] The poem discussed by Trotsky ends with the following stanza:

> To moia zavetnaia lezhanka,
> Karavannyi araviiskii shliakh,—
> Nesprosta nubiika i slavianka
> Vorozhat v olonetskikh stikhakh.[31]
>
> Thus my cherished stove-bench
> Is as an Arabian caravan-highway—
> It's not for nothing that a Nubian woman and Slavic woman
> Practice sorcery in verses from Olonets.

Kliuev's religious interests and "ruralism" must also be considered in light of his political activities.[32] He had been jailed in 1906 as an antitsarist activist and later took active part in illegal meetings held in Petrozavodsk.[33] In 1917 he wrote enthusiastically of revolution, managing to suspend his usual antipathy toward the city in verses directed toward his urban "Tovarishch" ("Comrade"). There he makes it clear that he identifies the difference between city and country with the poles of sacred and secular: "Hurrah and Hosanna . . . the iron factory and the hut of the steppes . . . two brothers of wind."[34] His "Lenin" cycle of 1918 was apparently the first major poetic tribute to the new Soviet leader, although the language of Kliuev's panegyric, as Trotsky pointed out, suggested a sensibility not entirely in step with Leninist orthodoxy:

> Est' v Lenine kerzhenskii dukh,
> Igumenskii okrik v dekretakh,
> Kak budto istoki razrukh
> On ishchet v "Pomorskikh otvetakh."
>
> Muzhitskaia nyne zemlia,
> I tserkov'—ne naimit kazennyi,
> Narodnyi ispod shevelia,
> Nesetsia glagol krasnozvonnyi.[35]

There is in Lenin a Kerzhenskii spirit,
A Father Superior's cry in his decrees,
As though he sought out the sources of ruin
In the "Pomorskie otvety."[36]

Today the land is the muzhik's,
And the church is not a state hireling.
A beautifully ringing word is spreading,
Stirring the underside of the people.

The comparisons here may seem either naive or, as Trotsky implied, secretly derisive, but Kliuev would have taken these toponyms and allusions very seriously indeed. By figuring Lenin as an Old Believer *pop* (priest)—or, rather, as a dissenting, polemicizing monk—the poet associates him with the long and troubled history of dissent in Russia instead of drawing an abstract and absolute line of dialectical *preodelenie* (overcoming) separating Bolshevism from earlier, "feudal" forms of opposition. The revolution is interpreted not as a pure outcome of the mechanics of class struggle but rather as the co-creation of a diverse activism, including religious activism.[37] And viewing events from the other direction, we see that Kliuev likewise regarded the "local" concerns that preoccupied him—concern for religious freedom for the dissidents, for more land and power for the peasants—as having some affinity to urban-based social movements, without being subsumable by them.[38] Needless to say, Kliuev's position on the revolution later changed drastically indeed.[39]

* * *

In the introduction to this book I argued for the inclusion of a fourth parameter, modernization, as overlapping with Perry Anderson's master triangle of those political, cultural, and technological forces that determined the protean shape of modernity. By this I mean a consideration not of specific change itself but to the absoluteness and ubiquity of that change: could a space be imagined where existing forms of life and new forces of change might meet on something like equal terms? A focus on modernization as poetic problem may enable a re-conception of the apparently wholly nostalgic preoccupations of Kliuev and his fellow "peasant poets." We might imagine that their concern with things rural might have been part of a halting, uncertain gesture toward the conception of a new and unprecedented mass culture. Now that the full incorporation of the peasantry into that mass was inevitable, how could it occur without destructive and total canceling out of older ways, or the explosion of reactionary antagonisms?[40] That the mass culture that finally emerged was born largely at the cost of those older ways does not really distinguish the Soviet story from other tales of modernization, although its human cost was appallingly, if not uniquely, high (roughly 15 million dead between 1917 and 1933, according to an authoritative recent estimate), and was not borne by the peasantry alone.[41] But it is true that one partial and negative definition of modernization might simply read: "the end of the peasantry." It would be absurd to present the Stalinist outcome as inevitable; Kliuev, after all, could not have imagined it in 1917. Yet, as historical horizon, it represents a certain extreme resolution of the contradictions of modernity, to which must be juxtaposed other, unrealized solutions posited during the early revolutionary years. For what kind of say might members of a "pre-modern" group have regarding the form their own obsolescence would take?[42]

Katerina Clark has shown how authoritative Soviet policy on "language in literature" moved from the radical utilitarianism and opposition to ornament found in Trotsky's early-1920s "Promethean" pronouncements on language[43] to Gorky's influential advocacy of a kind of epic purity in his 1931 article "Concerning Work with Language."[44] Though sharing a common purgative impulse, the hypothetical result of these normative suggestions would not be identical: Trotsky's ideal Russian was precise, economical, scientific, and, above all, standardized, while Gorky's proposals led to the adoption of a (no less standardized) "incongruously bookish language" for literature.[45] Such standardization, of course, had long been a feature of modernization, and in the most varied contexts; we need only think of the hostility to figuration and "obscurity" common to much Enlightenment speculation on language,[46] and pre-Fordist attempts to replace verbal interaction in the workplace with "instruction cards."[47]

But "flattening" had been an object of poets' concern for some time as well. The work of Robert Burns marks perhaps the modern beginning of a vital line of poetic anti-standardization, including John Clare, the Provençal revivalist Fredéric Mistral, Hugh MacDiarmid, and many others. Most of these names could be associated, inevitably, with various localisms/nationalisms and the ambiguous relation of those ideologies to both liberatory and authoritarian politics. Looking further, we might also adduce the more dialectical resistances of Wordsworth and Whitman, who both trust in and seek to purify the vernacular.

Among the participants in the great Russian modernist flush of literary/linguistic experimentation—names such as Mayakovsky, Bely, and Guro also come immediately to mind—Kliuev and the *budetlianin* (Futurist) Velimir Khlebnikov stand near the furthest remove from language-functionalist dicta, if only because of the relentlessly, stubbornly anachronistic or "sectarian" quality of their language. Their work is therefore notoriously hard to read—this is, inevitably, the first impression it creates—and especially so for non-native speakers. Although a knowledge of Slavic roots can help with guessing, no one should approach these writers without keeping close at hand the great dictionary of Vladimir Ivanovich Dal′ (from which the poets themselves drew, and to which I shall again refer). In his discussion of Calvinist ethnography, Michel de Certeau writes critically of the traditional reduction of all cultural differences to *"a language to be translated"*:[48] the lines of Kliuev and Khlebnikov are filled with small-scale resistances to translation—into their "own" language![49]

I would like to consider the "archaizing" linguistic practice of Kliuev and Khlebnikov—who were exact contemporaries, the first born in 1884, the second in 1885—in light of the problematic of the modern, and of the form that a mass literacy might take. Briefly, I argue that the two poets, both inveterate word hoarders and devotees of Slavic mythology, sought contrasting if comparably radical solutions to the problem of the linguistic flattening that came along with utilitarian culture building. "Russian" for these poets is not reducible to any one lexicon but rather involves entire varieties of practical literacy, living, dead, and not-yet-born; it is the medium in which, in a time of both rapid change and large-scale archiving the life or death of cultural forms remains discernable.

But Khlebnikov welcomes, indeed celebrates, modernizing trends, including the radio, "world languages," and unifying technologies of all sorts (although not, interestingly enough, the book as such). At the same time, and apparently paradoxically, he calls for the abolition of "language" itself, for "an end to language conceived as a duty," for the shattering of "the shell of language everywhere and forever." "Languages for present-day humans," he wrote, "are a claw on a bird's wing: an unnecessary remnant of prehistory. . . ."[50] Khlebnikov's hopes for a resolution of the paradox seem to lie in the possible discovery, rather than the creation, of an international (or at least pan-Slavic) "trans-sense" language, one grounded not in local derivations and vocabulary but in a recovery of the free productive capacities of linguistic expression from within standardization itself. The science of chemistry is possibly the master model for Khlebnikov's procedures: idiosyncratically, he seeks out the basic phonemic and morphemic *elements* of words, which he then will release into new compounds. But his surmises—Trotsky thought them "considerably imbued with the archaic"[51]—blur the usual distinctions between the outdated and the updated. On the one hand "antiquarian," in the sense of a philological return to Slavic (and other) "roots," the combinations finally produced are no calque-like derivations from preexisting abstractions—say, from Greek or German—but are entirely new formations which, in a sense, precede their meanings or leave their meanings up for negotiation.

Kliuev, on the other hand, *situates* himself and his work (the overused verb is appropriate in his case) within a hugely complex, self-devised framework of mythic, religious, and dialectal references embedded in the traditions and aspirations of the Russian peasantry from whose ranks he emerged. Attracted by defunct language, parochialism, sects, and the archaic in general, he often seems to be striving toward the creation of a "dissenter's" model of literacy, a center of culture only partially but very palpably distinct from the official one (whether that be Western, tsarist, Soviet, or of the "intelligentsia").

Taking just the few lines already quoted, "lezhanka" ("stove-bench," obviously a term associated with the peasant domicile), "dumnyi" (in the sense of "pensive, thoughtful"), and "burelomnik" (either "fallen trees" or "cruel wind") are all examples of diction outside (or, rather, lagging behind) the contemporary norm. On one level, the poetry can be read as a vast fabric of citations, pointing not to a single textual source but to historical categories: to the provincial and the passé as such. He rehabilitates nonstandard or dated forms of *parole* rather than setting familiar morphemes into entirely new kinds of action, à la Khlebnikov. Of course, when out-of-date provincialisms are not replaced by adequate "vernacular" paraphrases, charges of mere "ornamentalism" are invited. What Kliuevan diction emphasizes are historic types of language practice associated with now "abnormal" communities of users. Yet his incorporation of these "idiosyncrasies" within verses formally recognizable as secular rather than "folk"—he was discovered as a poet by Blok and began his career with some fluent imitations of that poet—seems to advocate that the norms of literacy open themselves to other norms, or to the coexistence of other norms, rather than, as in Khlebnikov, exploding the vernacular from within.

Pinewords, Bearthoughts

There can be no doubt that the dialectal density and abstruseness we find in Kliuev's later works, above all *Pogorel'shchina* (*The Burned Ruins*), were the product of a long labor of word hoarding and study; by no means was Kliuev's poetic vocabulary his only or his "everyday" one, as his letters show. Clearly, he sensed a kind of tension separating the various literacies among which he wandered, a tension thematized in the following poem (written in 1916–17):

Gde rai finiftianyi i Sirin
Poet na vetke raspisnoi,

Gde Pushkin govorom prosviren
Pitaet dukh vysokii svoi,

Gde Mei iarovchatyi, Nikitin,
Velesov pervenets Kol'tsov,
Tuda bredu ia, likom skryten,
Pod noshei varvarskikh stikhov.

Kogda slozhu svoiu viazanku
Sosnovykh slov, medvezh'ikh dum?
"K kostru gotov'tes' spozaranku,"—
Gremel moi praded Avvakum.

Sgoret' v metel'nom Pustozerske
Ili v chernilakh utonut'?
Slovopoklonnik bogomerzkii,
Ne znaiu ia, gde orlii put'.

Poet mne Sirin izdalecha:
"Liubi, i zvezdy nad toboi
Zapolykhaiut krasnym vechem
Gde serdtse—kolokol zhivoi."

Nabat serdechnyi chuet Pushkin—
Predvechnykh sladostei poet . . .
Kak iablonovye makushki,
Blagoukhaet zvukotsvet.

On v beloi bukve, v aloi strochke,
V fazan'i-pestroi zapiatoi.
Moia dusha, kak mokh na kochke,
Prigreta pushkinskoi vesnoi.

I pod luchom kudriavo-smuglym
Dremucha glub' torfianikov.
V mozgu zhe, roscherkom okruglym,
Stanitsy tianutsia stikhov. (*Pesnoslov,* p. 93)

Where heaven is enameled, and Sirin
Sings on a painted branch,[52]
Where Pushkin nourishes his exalted spirit
With the talk of a woman making communion bread—

Where bright Mei is, and Nikitin,
And Kol'tsov (the firstborn of Veles)—[53]
There I wander, with concealed visage,
Under the burden of barbaric verses.

When will I make up my bundle
Of pinewords, of bearthoughts?
"Get ready for the furnace in the early morn,"
Thundered my great-grandfather Avvakum.[54]

Shall I burn in stormy Pustozersk[55]
Or drown in inks?
A word worshiper, impious, I don't know
Where to find the eagle's path.

Sirin sings to me from afar:
"Love, and above you, stars
Will blaze like a red tocsin
Where the heart is a living bell."

Pushkin—poet of everlasting sweetnesses—
Senses the alarm bell of the heart . . .
The soundcolor is as fragrant
As the tips of apple-trees.

It is in the white letter, the crimson line,
And in the comma, motley as a pheasant.
My soul, like moss on a hummock,
Is warmed by a Pushkin-spring.

And dense is the depth of peat bogs
Under that curly-haired, dark-complexioned beam.[56]
In the brain, with a rounded flourish of pen,
Poems extend in flocks.

The first phrase ("Where heaven is enameled") signals the poem as both projective—indeed, almost utopian—and ekphrastic in a unique way: what Kliuev gives us here is a hypothetical "enameled" picture or relief upon which his particular version of cultural synthesis might be painted. The poem is a mise-en-scène of Kliuev's particular "heaven," almost an ekphrastic manifesto, and its appellation consists precisely in its offer of this pointedly framed vision.[57] Needless to say, Kliuev's "great-grandfather Avvakum" would not be pleased with his descendant's indiscriminate mixing of Christian piety with Russian paganism and (even more shocking) an aesthetic paganism of poetic divinities whose company the author clearly seeks. Nor can we reduce, by some process of allegoresis, the disparate imagery to a religious message; on one level this is, unavoidably, a poem about poetic ambition.

The first two stanzas imagine a kind of sublimity linked both to terms of traditional rural and religious (and visual) cultural production—enameled sky, painted branch—and to the secular "canon" of literary values, represented, above all, by Pushkin, who here both gives and receives inspiration. The central question for Kliuev—the co-habitability of these putatively distinct cultural norms, the degree to which they could communicate—is idealistically figured here by a "nourishing" conversation between modern Russia's arch-poet and a peasant woman, presumably a figure for Pushkin's nursemaid and herself a maker within a (vanishing) rural lifeworld.[58] The heaven projected here is indeed this imagined space of communication, which Kliuev's inscription hopes to instantiate.

The poetic heaven Kliuev sought is occupied by some predecessors: Mei, Nikitin, Kol'tsov—all either peasant writers or writers who took peasant life as a significant part of their subject matter. The poet's barbaric "burden," contritely borne, is really his key into that realm of the elect. But the idea of "burden" has an additional importance here in that it alludes to the historical specific gravity of what Kliuev is proposing to bring to poetry in his "bundle" (again, "viazanka"): his words are "pine," his thoughts, "bear." I have chosen to translate his adjective-noun pairings here ("sosnovye slova," "medvezh'ie dumy") as single words—*pinewords* and *bearthoughts*—in order to highlight Kliuev's insistence on the intimate relationship of his language and sensibility to the material conditions of his own early life and locale. The deliberate, corporeal opacity of these figures—for what could "bearthoughts" be, much less "pinewords"?—seems to stem from their very typically Kliuevan revision of standard anthropomorphism: what we have is not a speaking pine, an inspirited tree of some sort, but rather the words, the terms of pine itself, uttered in pine's own (to us) unimaginable tongue.

What would it mean for bears not to speak but to have *their own language*? Nowadays, of course, in the age of Care Bears and an all-colonizing animation-through-technology, this question has a naive and comical ring to it. And, doubtless, Kliuev's own celebration of enamel, Sirin, and painted branches intimates a later, full-scale kitschification of folk material—the whole souvenir world of lacquered boxes, balalaikas, kerchiefs, and *matrioshki* (nested ornamental dolls). We might recall, in this connection, Wordsworth's interest in what I termed the "onto-popular," with the additional observation that, by Kliuev's time and with the commodification of "folk" trappings of all sorts, any effort to recover a primal simplicity for poetry came to run the danger of seeming "trite" in a more damaging sense than before. This overtone is real, but it should not, I would argue, blunt our sense of Kliuev's utopian yearning here. For one thing, the goal of cultural synthesis is transected by a "decadent" refusal to sublimate, by an insistence on a place, if not a meaning, for each "white letter and crimson line."[59]

The "bundle" is a kind of message, and we can easily see how the implied antithesis here between "barbarism" and "civilization," or even between "bear" and "thought," could generate the peasant-poet as a "Scythian" mediator between nature and culture. They have become Babels to each other, but the peasant may be able to "bundle" (or "slagat' "—also a word for the writing of poetry) their scripts together. The final metaphor of poems as "flocks" could be seen as the image of a rural poetic produce, entering into trade on an equal basis with the city. But the poem is doubtful about the possibility of synthesis, at least initially. If Mei, Nikitin, and Kol'tsov provide Kliuev with images of success, his true ancestor remains the dissident Avvakum, for whom death was preferable to any form of accommodation: a martyr, not a mediator. The fearful alternatives—either misunderstanding and exile to "stormy Pustozersk" from the communicative and evaluative norms of literate culture *or* complete conformity with them ("drowning in inks")—recall our earlier reflections on truth and particularity in lyric. Yet the mention of Avvakum and his fate charges these options with urgency more than usually political. The implication is that a world, and not an entirely personal or invented world, is at stake in Kliuev's words; Kliuev would make his poetry into a test of both his own ability and the receptivity of his audience.

The specific message of Sirin (in the fifth verse) is far less important than the appearance of myth itself—the gap between Pustozersk and Petersburg is to be filled by myth, or rather a couple of myths. The first is, of course, Sirin, who represents the oldest and most resilient stories, whose name (though little more than that) links sacred and secular times. The production of this kind of continuity is arguably the prime function of the modern notion of myth, which allows history and comparative generalization to develop only after the basic elements of some presumed Ur-narratives have been excavated by structural analysis.[60]

The second myth is that of Pushkin himself, who incorporates several mythic strands at once. He is the legendary poet, the inspirer who himself (particularly in *Ruslan and Liudmila*) made use of Russian myth; he is, perhaps, a Christ figure pasturing new "flocks" of poetry; he is the exotic part-African ("curly-haired, dark-complexioned") who distantly (though corporeally; i.e., racially) connects the peasant-poet with the much sought after "oriental" sources of creative fructification; he is Kliuev's version of Blok's "Stranger," a muse and stirrer of poets' brains ("And ostrich feathers, bending, / Sway inside my brain"). As myth, he is constituted as much by what precedes him—his origins—as by his own achievement. Indeed, the important thing about these myths—about *myth* in general—is that they are felt to underlie and predate both "barbaric" and literate poetic modes. They, rather than language per se, are Kliuev's shared medium through which communication across gaps in time or "development" (which is a notion allowing a kind of mapping of time onto localities) is supposedly possible. On the other hand, language for Kliuev serves largely to sustain distinctions erased in part through the sharing of (national, cultural, religious) myths, and in part through the mediation of the poet. By poem's end, sunlight and bog maintain a parity of depth, nothing is lost—the writing, as it flourishes, keeps the ornamental hues of white and red, the "burdensome" texture of a pheasant.

Perhaps we may be allowed to translate this final process of fertilization or "soundflowering" into more prosaic terms, knowing as we do of the poet's intensive (if informal and idiosyncratic) study of folklore and dialect.[61] Kliuev's path to and from the past—and certainly our path to his poetry—would seem to depend not upon some form of mystic fusion but rather upon philology, and specifically upon some form of lexicon. This may be a dictionary or collection of proverbs, whether a private cache of words or Dal"s colossal (if also amateur) map of Russian in Russia.[62] It is specifically the historical or dialectal rather than the normative dictionary that enables Kliuev's bundle of old words to enter literacy for the first time; without such a philology, Kliuev's language would be merely "illiterate," deprived of all authority for its citations.[63]

And here we might speculate on the historical lexicon's surprising liberatory potential as well. The authority of the normative or "instruction manual" dictionary is partially grounded in its coherence with actual linguistic practice, which it can both shape and stabilize but which can also (hypothetically) correct *it* in the event of a mistake. In the case of archaisms or stubbornly local variants, no easy verification is possible; indeed, one can imagine a fraudulent "lexicon of archaisms" entirely composed of phony words, plausibly etymologized and documented. In other words, this second model for the dictionary—obviously the one more immediately applicable to Kliuev—frees up the word-hoarding poet to modulate meanings, to recover useless linguistic junk, and even (at a certain outer limit) to engage in out-and-out fabrication.[64]

Thus the advantage of the lexicon (and especially the historical dictionary) as a cultural authority might lie in the relative neutrality and capaciousness of its disposition of terms—relative, that is, to manuals produced by epistemological (e.g., liturgical, scientific, political) authorities.[65] Again, even in relation to orthography, a work like Dal"s would suggest a proliferation—and a "proliferatability"—of variants rather than a restriction of them. Perhaps this potential for a creative dialectic between history and invention was part of what stimulated Osip Mandelstam to place the dictionary at the center of his vision of a future "culture":

> [. . .] [W]e all have the desire to live in history; and in each one of us there is an invincible need to find the solid kernel of a Kremlin, an Acropolis; it doesn't matter whether that nucleus is called "state" or "society." [. . .] We have no Acropolis. Even today our culture is still wandering and not finding its walls. Nevertheless, each word in Dal's dictionary is a kernel of the Acropolis, a small Kremlin, a winged fortress of nominalism, rigged out in

> the Hellenic spirit for the relentless battle against the formless element, against nonexistence, which threatens our history from every side.[66]

Without philology, Kliuev's language would be merely "illiterate," deprived of all authority for its citations. Indeed, the complex inscription known as "dictionary" enables Kliuev's bundle of old words to enter literacy for the first time.

Absolutely Mundane Language

> At no point in time, no matter how utopian, will anyone win the masses over to a higher art; they can be won over only to one nearer to them.
>
> —Benjamin, *The Arcades Project*

As already mentioned, the arch-neologizer Khlebnikov was a kind of philological nationalist, intensely interested in Slavic mythology and language, and committed (as he indicated in a letter to Vyacheslav Ivanov) to the creation of an "'all-Slavic language'" and the cleansing of "the Russian language of foreign borrowings."[67] This meant a highly idiosyncratic delving into sounds and morphemes—what he called the "simple names of the language"[68]—and exploration of their permutations (as in the famous "Incantation" [1909] built from words derived from "smekh" ["laugh"], a poem often cited but rarely read):

O, rassmeites', smekhachi!
O, zasmeites', smekhachi!
Chto smeiutsia smekhami, chto smeianstvuiut smeial'no,
O, zasmeites' usmeial'no!
O, rassmeshishch nadsmeial'nykh—smekh usmeinykh smekhachei!
O, issmeisia rassmeial'no smekh nadsmeinykh smeiachei!
Smeivo, smeivo,
Usmei, osmei, smeshiki, smeshiki,
Smeiunchiki, smeiunchiki.
O, rassmeites', smekhachi!
O, zasmeites', smekhachi![69]

O, laugh it out, you laughsters!
O, laugh it up, you laughsters!
So they laugh with laughters, so they laugherize delaughly.
O, laugh it up belaughably!
O, the laughingstock of the laughed-upon—the laugh of
belaughed laughsters!

O, laugh it out roundlaughingly, the laugh of laughed-at laughians!
  Laugherino, laugherino,
  Laughify, laughicate, laugholets, laugholets,
    Laughikins, laughikins,
  O, laugh it out, you laughsters!
  O, laugh it up, you laughsters![70]

"What bounty and what sweet spell there are in our Slavic idiom!" was the reaction of critic Kornei Chukovsky to Khlebnikov's experiment.[71]

Part of Khlebnikov's intent was to demonstrate the resourcefulness of his discovered Slavic—apparently a purely latent language, a language that never existed as *parole.* Thus the inscribed location of this poem is a pure hypothetical, that "bonfire of humanity" from out of which (according to a later poem) the world language would rise like "the stupidest tear-stained child."[72] On the surface, his plan recalls the efforts of Leibniz and Christian Wolff to establish a German suitable for thought, or indeed the earlier efforts of Church Slavonic and Russian wordsmiths.[73] This aspect of Khlebnikov's art was dedicated to both the purification and expansion of the hypothetical "Slavic" (perhaps not exclusively Russian) vernacular; ideally, his verbal creations would be comprehensible to anyone familiar with the basic "units"—Vladimir Markov describes their effect as "transparent obscurity."[74]

Nonetheless, the difficulty of Khlebnikov's verse, alongside his frequent denunciations (mentioned above) of "language as such," should make us pause before simply assuming, as is usually done, that the poet was simply out to both purify and "universalize" the Russian language. In one recent essay, for example, Andrew Wachtel argues that, because Khlebnikov sometimes offers "translations" into Russian of his "trans-sense" works, the latter represent "a sort of deep structural code that mediates between different versions of the same thought" rather than "a random nonsense language." Because the poet finds "equivalence" between "trans-sense" and Russian, Wachtel concludes, his linguistic investigations ultimately seek "to recognize in modern Russian the outline of a universal language (one that had existed in the past and would do so again in the future)."[75] However, and as Wachtel acknowledges, no final or fully legible code for translating into/out of "trans-sense" language is actually offered by Khlebnikov. This absence, among other features of the poet's work, allows us to develop a somewhat differently inflected interpretation of "trans-sense," one that is at once more sympathetic to Khlebnikov and considerably more radical in its implications. The context for the emergence of "trans-sense," I would argue, was at once Russian imperialism (cultural and otherwise) and the entrance of vast numbers of people into literacy within Russia itself; his work is best read as a uniquely probing reflection on what this heterogeneous context might mean.

Much of the obvious "incantatory" effect of the "laughter" poem comes from the modulated repetition of the root, rather than from the fantastic words: "rassmeiat'sia" ("laugh it out") and "zasmeiat'sia" ("laugh it up") are not even neologisms, of course. Yet in contact with the other, less immediately comprehensible terms (like "usmei," "osmei," for instance), they come to seem less like vocabulary items and more like expressive possibilities, hardly less contingent than the unfamiliar words surrounding them. The effect is quite precisely the double one of estrangement (*ostranenie*), inasmuch as we perceive at once the de-signified material stuff of language ("sme-") *and* are granted new knowledge: here, knowledge of the relativity of significations themselves. In a strange temporal twist, *everything* becomes neologism—or perhaps (who knows?) archaism, newly recovered by the poet. A word like "smeianstvovat' " ("laugherize"), for example, seems to substantivize the "laugher" into something resembling a profession (on the analogy of "uchitel'stvovat'," "akterstvovat'," and so on). Meanwhile, the implied allusion to the fabled "Tsarevna-*nesmeiana*" ("the princess who doesn't laugh") of the fairy tale simultaneously thrusts the reference of this "new" word back into the past—here a projected, an unrealized past. If we read in this way, we are suddenly reminded of the affinities of the "Invocation" to the most archaic inscriptions: its appellations ("O, laugh it out, laugh it up!") mimic in the strongest way the primal imperative call to a passerby; yet here is an inscription whose "original" setting seems to straddle all points along the time line. It might have been equally carved in birch bark, or scored under the wing of a spaceship. In Khlebnikov's most daring experiments, the "temporalities of art" are multiplied in a way "that renders [art's] boundaries permeable."[76]

This multiplication is generated through Khlebnikov's extraordinary privileging of the corporeality of text over any authoritative, normalizing pedagogical voice: "*mute graphic marks,*" he writes in his essay "To the Artists of the World," "will reconcile the cacophony of languages."[77] A poem like "Incantation," susceptible to virtually infinite readings, essentially attempts to enforce "the democracy of the book" (Rancière)[78] by internally relativizing all its diction. Khlebnikovian "trans-sense," on this reading, is neither the crypto-Russian *Urform* of all languages nor, in Wachtel's words, "a random nonsense language." Rather, it acts as a kind of linguistic agora, a space wherein meanings are up for discussion, even those proposed by the poet himself. It has to be stressed, qualifying readings like that of Wachtel, that the central difference between the word-creating projects of Khlebnikov and those of someone like Leibniz is the absence in the former of any unambiguous translation from a prior authoritative model. Indeed, it seems to me that Khlebnikov's fabrications are precisely an effort to bypass entirely the need for dictionaries, calques, or any other kind of standardization. Only the most indispensable and uncontroversial linguistic education—in the basic roots, the "atoms" of the Russian language—would be needed to begin to grapple with his constructions. Armed with knowledge of these very basic parts and their combinatory principles, even words completely unheard of would be both "understandable" and producible. Khlebnikov wants a language that carries its own validity, comprehensibility, and rightness *while being* infinitely productive of new expressions: a language entirely mundane and entirely projective, as Mandelstam realized:

> [. . .] Khlebnikov can be compared [. . .] to a situation in which our language, like a righteous man, could have and should have developed, unburdened and undesecrated by historical necessity and adversity. Khlebnikov's language is so completely the language of the laity, so completely secular, that it seems as if neither the monks, nor Byzantium, nor the literature of the intelligentsia had ever existed. His speech is the absolutely secular and mundane Russian language, resounding for the first time in the history of Russian letters. If we accept this view, there is no need to regard Khlebnikov as a sorcerer or a shaman. He projected different paths of development for the language, transitional and intermediate paths, but the historically unprecedented path of Russia's oral destiny was realized only in Khlebnikov's work. It took hold there in his trans-sense language, which meant no more than those transitional forms which succeeded in not being covered by the semantic crust created by the properly and correctly developing language.[79]

By analogy, we can say that the structure of the Futurist poet's project resembles what might be called the central cultural problematic of a radical democracy. How might access to the resources of "cultural capital"—to *vocabulary* in the largest sense—be equalized and rationalized without hollowing out those resources into a boring and simplified sameness (given the scarcity of available time for study)? More drastically than Wordsworth's "language of common men," Khlebnikov's experiments point to the radical meaning of "vernacular": not a vocabulary which is limited to (and limits) some hypothetical "standard" of everyday communication but rather a supply of endlessly fertile (because *dead*) linguistic atoms, common to all speakers, which enables an elimination or severe reduction of "vocabulary" as such.[80] We ignore this core implication of his work at the price of impoverishing our readings of it.

Of course, the question of the possibility of interaction between different linguistic "sets," whether across time or place, finds no answer here, thereby pulling the poem back into contradiction. Plainly enough, the aspiration to extinguish the differences between bygone and contemporary language worlds within the space of inscription—deriving from Khlebnikov's famous non-Euclidean, "Lobachevskian" attitude toward temporality, wherein putatively distinct historical layers do eventually meet, including past and present[81]—both gives inscription too much credit and tries to overcome the passage of time through a spatialization presaging a postmodern flattening of historical difference.[82] More important, perhaps, the very possibility of legitimating such an inscription falls profoundly into question. Either the projections discussed above occur freely—legitimated, that is, by none but other readers/producers of the text—or else Khlebnikov's new inscriptive projections are given their social guarantee (and guarantee of comprehensibility) by some outside agent, whether a group of expert specialists or (if this were possible) by the "language" itself, inconceivable except as a locally or nationally based entity. Thus it might indeed be said that the freedoms enabled by Khlebnikov's new technology of writing could find their meaningful ground only in that national and exclusive language that enables the inscriptions to be "read."

We should slightly qualify our anxiety even here, for obviously Khlebnikov's project would radically destabilize any easy "analogy between an ethnicity, a nation-state, and a national language" by depriving that language of any proper boundaries and giving it a productive energy that could not but have radical effects on every level of social life and communication.[83] It is more useful, I believe, to think of this contradiction in terms of the antinomies of the audience projected by modern poetry: is "trans-sense" language designed to be finally read by a clique of experts—here, either a macro-clique comprised of Russian (or "Slavic") speakers, or a micro-clique of academic Khlebnikov specialists ("khlebnikovovedy")—or is it destined to be an unclosed field of linguistic exploration for its readers? That neither the latter aspiration nor Kliuev's groping toward a kind of cohabitation of alternative vocabularies was taken as a model for (in Trotsky's phrase) a "reconstruction of all the foundations of life" is, of course, a matter of history. And how could it have been otherwise? With this closure, the fields of possibility opened up by early modern instability have come to seem archaic to us from our own *less* open, that is, fully modernized, perspective.

— 4 —

Unkind Weight

Mandelstam, History, and Catastrophe

Say on, sayers! sing on, singers!
Delve! mould! pile the words of the earth!
Work on, age after age, nothing is to be lost,
It may have to wait long, but it will certainly come in use,
When the materials are all prepared and ready,
    the architects shall appear.

—Whitman, "A Song of the Rolling Earth"

Poetic culture arises from the attempt to avert catastrophe, to make it dependent on the central sun of the system as a whole, be it love, of which Dante spoke, or music, at which Blok ultimately arrived.

—Mandelstam, "Badger Hole"*

Center and Periphery

Writing about the end of the novel, in an essay so titled, in 1922, Osip Mandelstam identifies the reasons for what he regards as the novel's decline in an apparent disappearance of novelistic subject matter: not simply of narrative material but of the social basis of character. The classic realist novel, according to Mandelstam, requires a dynamic between actor and setting, or the sense that personal life retains some individuality in and through its submersion in the social:

> The measure of the novel is the personal biography, or a system of biographies. Taking his first steps, the new novelist already sensed that a separate,

*Mandelstam's article, "Badger Hole," was written in August 1922, on the first anniversary of Blok's death.

> particular fate does not exist, and [therefore] tried to extract the social plant he required roots and all, retaining all its attributes and concomitants. In this way, the novel always offers us a system of phenomena, guided by a biographical linkage, measured by a biographical standard. The novel holds together compositionally to the extent that the centrifugal thrust of the planetary system lives within it; to the extent that in a given society such systems exist at all; to that extent the centripetal force, the force pulling the periphery to the center, has not finally conquered the centrifugal.[1]

In abstract terms, the centrifugal force is describable both as the resistance of particulars to insertion within a system, and as a persisting diversity of forces weakening the dominance of the center (whether a state or economic order). But it is intriguing and paradoxical that, for Mandelstam, the original model of "separate, particular fate" is the life of Napoleon, a figure who was also the activator of one of the most centripetal, imperial projects in modern European history:

> The flowering of the novel in the 19th century should be regarded as directly dependent on the epic story of Napoleon, which raised the share-price of the personality-in-history to an extraordinary extent, and which (through Balzac and Stendhal) manured the soil [in preparation] for the entirety of the French and European novel. The typical biography of Bonaparte, invader and "lucky fellow," ended up spreading out in Balzac across scores of so-called "romans de réussite" ("novels of success"), where the fundamental motivating theme is not love but career: that is, the attempt to force one's way out of poverty, from the middling social strata all the way to the top. (p. 202)

This *model for the individual*—the description already contains a paradox—is the same man chosen by Hegel to represent the "cunning of Reason," as Susan Buck-Morss has recently reminded us:

> Writing *The Phenomenology of [Spirit]* in his Jena study in 1806, Hegel interpreted the advancing army of Napoleon (whose cannons he could hear roaring in the distance) as the unwitting realization of Reason.[2]

In his choice of Napoleon, Mandelstam is ultimately suggesting a quite Hegelian point: that Napoleon's story demonstrates less the ability of individuals to triumph within an antagonistic system than the way such triumphs reinforce system itself, even through radical changes in content.

The heyday of the particular personality-in-history has passed, says Mandelstam, as impersonal forces—geopolitical and economic, above all—render the individual personality less and less socially effective. Napoleon is representative of a transitional period that has now found its resolution, according to Mandelstam.[3] He notes that "the greatest event of the end of the 19th century—the Paris Commune—has still not found a sufficiently convincing representation in novel form," presumably because the Commune was a truly collective event, lacking a single, personal center (p. 203). Indeed, perhaps the Commune's central creative act (apart from helping to inspire the poetry of Rimbaud) was a clearing rather than a building: the destruction by the "autonomizing crowd" of the Vendôme monument—famously crowned by a statue of Napoleon, built to honor the Grand Army—on May 16, 1871. Only after that pole of authority was removed, writes Christopher Winks, "in the rubble strewn about the newly cleared space of the Place Vendôme," did the crowd itself commence "[the cultivation of] a *topos*, in an atmosphere that can rightfully and without exaggeration be termed poetic."[4]

In Mandelstam's account, however, it would seem that the possibilities for a collective cultivation of space have been drastically reduced after the Commune's demise, and only partly because of the notorious crackdown that culminated (as one writer informs us) with "more people [dying] in the final week of May 1871 than in any of the battles of the Franco-Prussian War, or than in any of the previous 'massacres' (for example, the Terror) in French history."[5] As the dialectic of general/particular slips away from any kind of individual or collective agency, writes Mandelstam, a crisis in artistic representation ensues:

> In our day, Europeans have been hurled out of their biographies, like balls from the pockets of billiard tables. [. . .] A person without a biography cannot be the thematic core of a novel, and the novel for its part is inconceivable without an interest in individual human fate, in the individual human story and everything that goes along with it. Beyond this, an interest in psychological justification, by means of which the novel in its decadent phase managed to preserve itself so skillfully, senses its own imminent downfall; it has been undermined at its core and discredited by the helplessness of psychological motives in the face of forces of reality, already fully present, whose reprisals against psychological justification are becoming more and more cruel by the hour. The very notion of *action* for a [given] personality is being replaced by another notion, with socially richer content: the notion of *adaptation* [*prisposoblenie*]. (p. 204)

Mandelstam's choice of words here suggests that the change he is describing is at once mechanical (with personalities subjected to "billiard-ball causality"), inevitable, and pitiless (with psychological motivations as the object of "reprisals"). The "notion of adaptation" (as opposed to action) implies nothing less than social life become fully natural, a realm of immutable process in regard to whose larger contours humans lack all control. Of course, Mandelstam was writing these words in the immediate wake of the catastrophes of the Great War, the Russian civil war, and the attendant waves of epidemic and famine. With millions of refugees wandering through the country, it might indeed have been thought that the traditional notion of biography had lost some of its legitimacy as a generic category.[6] In light of this new social configuration and within the sphere of (what had been called) the literary, there would seem to be little room for projective thinking as we have been discussing it; the writer as "individual" has been as biographically compromised as everyone else. Indeed, "it is obvious," writes Mandelstam, "that, through force of circumstances, the contemporary prose writer is becoming a chronicler, and the novel is returned to its sources: [. . .] to the chronicle, to hagiography" (p. 205). The specific form of adaptation open to prose writers is apparently a stance of accommodation, and a return to what would most likely be either sheer inventories of calamity or monumental histories of the present order.

Mandelstam's express topic here is the novel; but we have seen (in our examination of German Romantic and pre-Romantic thought on poetry, and of mid-nineteenth-century French poetry) that the question of the "active individual subject" is an absolutely central preoccupation of modern lyric as well. In this last chapter I use Mandelstam's comments on the novel as a starting point for discussing the poet's own theoretical and lyric production in light of the modernity upon which he reflected and within which he lived. The greatest poet-theorist in modern Russian literature, Mandelstam both participated in the flush of cultural speculation characterizing Russia's high utopian moment (ca. 1905–28) and (like Nikolai Kliuev and many others) ended up a victim of a coercive modernization (usually called "Stalinism") that helped put an end to the centrifugal unevenness and utopian imaginings of the core modern period.[7]

But throughout his life and in response to devaluations of experience (in Benjamin's sense), Mandelstam ceaselessly tested various cultural models—"planetary systems," in his terms—as matrices through which the changing relationship of writing and audience might be considered. In this chapter I outline Mandelstam's struggle, in his theory and his poetry, to define a creative practice that would accept the need radically to make anew while refusing the destructive attitude toward the past and existing norms so characteristic of modernization globally. As we will see, the inscriptive mode in all its dimensions—its community-shaping appellations, imaginative projections, grounding legitimations, and corporeal substrata—offers one of the crucial horizons for Mandelstam's thought on the possibility of audience and poetic effectivity within modernity. The familiar topoi of his thought—among others, the tension between organization and organism; poetry as architecture or as time capsule—can be read as a powerful meditation, within the tradition of European post-Romantic inscriptive poetics, on the antinomies of modern culture building. To be sure, his speculations leave his readers with no easy answers, for in his late work Mandelstam envisions nothing less than the terminus for specifically modern poetic consciousness and practice. His account of this end point requires us to examine at some length his "Verses about the Unknown Soldier" (written in 1937, during the Stalinist Terror), perhaps his final major poetic statement and an inscription ranking with the greatest European Romantic and post-Romantic examples. As it turns out, it will also compel us to return to Napoleon, to Romanticism, and to Hegel.

Forever on the Road

> In fact, one can go on and ask oneself whether the relationship of the storyteller to his material, human life, is not in itself a craftsman's relationship, whether it is not his very task to fashion the raw material of experience, his own and that of others, in a solid, useful, and unique way.
>
> —Benjamin, "The Storyteller"

That we need constantly to recollect the origins of the modern in Romantic and pre-Romantic notions of aesthetic education is not surprising, of course. Indeed, it could be argued that the real questions pressing upon writers like Blok, Kliuev, Khlebnikov, and Mandelstam were the same ones that preoccupied Schiller and his successors a century or more earlier. What kind of literacy can and should develop in tandem with the radically new technologies of labor generated by social and scientific change? What balance should be sought out, what primacies established among the various knowledges required (and valued) by professional/occupational specialties, including the scientific; by government and its agencies of legitimation; by more traditional spheres of culture (religion, the arts, sport) which had enjoyed (or suffered) a certain amount of autonomy from political authority; and by some notion of speculation or critical thought, which struggles to provide a synthetic vision of knowledge while never entirely pulling free of the local concerns and vocabulary (aesthetic, religious, scientific, economic, etc.) of one or more of the dominant discursive formations?

The crucial point in all this, I believe, is the conjunctural one made by Perry Anderson. Russia and the Soviet Union (along with other nations) were at a stage of technological development and historical and administrative self-consciousness at which these questions could be asked. The knowledge of other models, and the sense that remodeling was possible, stimulated minds to imagine the most varied corrections (informed by varying degrees of nostalgia) of what Schiller had called "disorganization" ("Zerrüttung"):

> This disorganization, which was first started within man by civilization and learning, was made complete and universal by the new spirit of government. It was scarcely to be expected that the simple organization of the early [Roman] republics should have survived the simplicity of early manners and conditions; but instead of rising to a higher form of organic existence it degenerated into a crude and clumsy mechanism. [. . .] State and Church, laws and customs, were now torn asunder; enjoyment was divorced from labour, the means from the end, the effort from the reward. Everlastingly chained to a single little fragment of the Whole, man himself develops into nothing but a fragment; everlastingly in his ear the monotonous sound of the wheel that he turns, he never develops the harmony of his being, and instead of putting the stamp of humanity upon his own nature, he becomes nothing more than the imprint of his occupation or of his specialized knowledge.[8]

Poets, although understandably concerned with the future role of their own specialty, did not confine their speculations to poetry alone. Indeed, Mandelstam was singularly prolific on the subject of social organization—indeed, one might say that education in the broadest sense is the dominant underlying theme of many of his essays.

For instance, Mandelstam, like many of his contemporaries, was fascinated by the collective movement therapy of Dalcroze and his followers, which involved the coordinated performance of rhythmic exercises.[9] Might it not be the case that the Dalcrozian experiments attracted such attention because they provided an unusually clear *Darstellung* of what a successful mass literacy might mean: a coordination of inner, individual impulse and acting body together with the direction of the group?

> If rhythmic education is to become nationally accepted, a miracle must occur that transforms the abstract system into the people's flesh. Where yesterday there was only a blueprint, tomorrow the dancers' costumes will flash colorfully and song will resound. School precedes life. School sculpts life in its own image and likeness. The rhythm of the academic year will be determined by accents that fall on the holidays of the school Olympic games; rhythm will be the instigator and organizer of those games. On such holidays we shall see a new, rhythmically educated generation freely proclaiming its will, its joys and sorrows. Harmonious, universal, rhythmical acts, animated by a common idea, are of infinite significance for the creation of future history.[10]

All too "harmonious," we murmur now: and doubtless Mandelstam later lost much of his optimism regarding the possibility of a liberated collective (the essay was written in 1920). Within the Dalcrozian utopia, all need for inscribed texts is abolished, insofar as audience and project have been fused within matter (the "flesh") itself. Yet it is not entirely surprising that a poet would entertain a theory that elevated *rhythm* to a place where it could actually give people conscious possession of their collective will, their "own image and likeness."

What, indeed, will be the role of poetry, with its rhythms and lines and allusions and tropes and visionary pretensions, in a "future history"? The commonsense answer might be, "Much the same role it has always played—a very small one." But again, as with social planning in general, the interest of the question lies in the possibility of asking it; historical opportunities do present themselves where it seems that poetry (and other arts) might be made much more important or vanish altogether in a storm of instrumentalization. Mandelstam, who died because of his poetry, was concerned not only with poetry's survival but also with poetry itself as a mode of survival, as a kind of space where existing forms of life and new forces of change could meet on something like equal terms.

A theorist thoroughly informed by Western European aesthetic, philosophical, and historical thought, Mandelstam offers us an unusually self-aware reflection on what modernization might mean for poetry. On the one hand, Mandelstam, like many of his contemporaries, argued that aesthetic activity could transform not only art but the whole of lived experience as well. In the work of some of his Futurist peers (like Khlebnikov, for instance) this aspiration took the form of the most uninhibited utopian speculations. The Acmeist Mandelstam's own projective impulse was directed toward theorizing what he called (with only apparent modesty) a new "domesticity." He sometimes presented this valorized dailiness in the guise of "Hellenism," as in the great essay "On the Nature of the Word":

> Hellenism is the conscious surrounding of man with domestic utensils instead of impersonal objects; the transformation of impersonal objects into domestic utensils, and the humanizing and warming of the surrounding world with the most delicate teleological warmth. (p. 127)

Despite all appearances to the contrary, nostalgia plays no major role in Mandelstamian Hellenism. What is of interest to him, as in the case of the Romantics and pre-Romantics, is the "Greek idea" of a "[self-sufficient] collective life that does not rend itself into separate spheres of activities."[11] To achieve this life requires creative action ("surrounding," "humanizing," "transformation") rather than mere restoration of older norms. In this crucial respect, Mandelstam is at one with his avant-garde contemporaries working across the arts. Poetry has consequences beyond poetry, and the wider social metamorphoses of language have consequences for poetry in turn. In opposition to all neoclassicism, Mandelstam's home building takes place within the Rancièrean "aesthetic regime," wherein

> the allegedly "pure" practice of writing is linked to the need to create forms that participate in a general reframing of the human abode. [. . . .] Both industrial production and artistic creation are committed to doing something else than what they do—to create not only objects but a sensorium, a new partition of the sensible.[12]

As we will see, Mandelstam's version of this reframing stressed the latent potentialities and integrity of everyday language rather than either linguistic archaism or experimentation in the Khlebnikovian manner.

The Acmeist polemic also involved a rejection of the brittle metaphysics of much of the poetry produced by the Russian Symbolists, with (in Mandelstam's view) its largely sterile gestures toward a "transcendent" world. In contrast, Mandelstam advocates a humanizing of life and art, and of life and art through each other:

> The key to [Acmeism's active love of literature] was precisely a change in taste, the indomitable will to create a man-centered poetry and poetics, with man as master of his own home, not man flattened into a wafer by the horrors of pseudo-Symbolism; genuine Symbolism surrounded by symbols, that is, by domestic utensils having their own verbal representations, just as men have their own vital organs. ("On the Nature of the Word," p. 131)

However, the insistence on "active love of literature" seems to move us toward a very different set of concerns. For, by "literature," Mandelstam quite precisely means a certain tradition: "because a new taste arose in Russia at the beginning of the century," he writes in the sentence immediately preceding the citation above, "such massifs as Rabelais, Shakespeare, and Racine were moved from the bases and came to pay us a visit" (p. 131). Indeed, Mandelstam's concern for past writers—Dante, Villon, Pushkin, and Annenskii are just a few of the eminences in his pantheon—is such that he is frequently thought of as a traditionalist above all else, a poet who set himself the task simply of preserving the "great works" in a time of danger. I will argue, however, that Mandelstam's creative/renovative and restorative/past-oriented impulses are to be regarded as very much of a piece. On the one hand, the concern for what we might call "humanized construction" answers to the familiar call for the New, for a creative occupation of the spaces opened up within modernity. On the other, and perhaps more important for Mandelstam, attention to past works both enriches the field of possibilities and relativizes the present itself, preventing its unilateral hypertrophy and chastening its tendency toward nihilistic projection. For Mandelstam (to apply Ranciére's words),

> [b]eing a matter of art turns out to be a kind of metamorphic status. The works of the past may fall asleep and cease to be artworks, they may be awakened and take on a new life in various ways. They make thereby for a continuum of metamorphic forms. According to the same logic, common objects cross the border and enter the realm of artistic combination. They can do so all the more easily in that the artistic and the historical are now linked together, such that each object can be withdrawn from its condition of common use and viewed as a poetic body wearing the traces of its history.[13]

Assisted by the notion of the "metamorphic work," Mandelstam envisions an internally self-correcting modernity, one that suppresses any monumentalization of past, present, or future.

On the level of the poetic work itself, the lyric's focus on humble particulars expands, rather than constricts, awareness, or so Mandelstam argues in his greatest theoretical tract, the "Conversation about Dante" (1933):

> [W]hen we enunciate the word "sun," we do not toss out an already prepared meaning—this would be tantamount to semantic abortion—rather we are experiencing a peculiar cycle. Any given word is a bundle, and meaning sticks out of it in various directions, not aspiring toward any single official point. In pronouncing the word "sun," we are as it were undertaking an enormous journey to which we are so accustomed that we travel in our sleep. What distinguishes poetry from automatic speech is that it rouses us and shakes us into wakefulness in the middle of a word. Then it turns out that the word is much longer than we thought, and we remember that to speak means to be forever on the road. (p. 407)

Thus the new poetic sensorium is to be produced through heightened attention to the words that exist, an attention that "wakens" and opens up enormous spaces for movement "in various directions." The inscriptive stoppage effect is not, for Mandelstam, sheer disengagement from meaning but rather the prerequisite for consciousness or "wakefulness" itself. As for Kliuev and Khlebnikov in their very different ways, language for Mandelstam is at once "alive" in practice and sedimented with earlier practice. For Mandelstam's ideal poet Dante, "time is the content of history understood as a simply synchronic act" ("Conversation about

Dante," p. 420); poetry is not merely a "time-machine" but a way of recovering and perhaps redeeming past, unfinished creative projects.[14]

But the poem is a passageway not only to different temporalities but to other, extra-artistic forms of life as well. Mandelstam reproaches Symbolism for its preoccupation with mere "ideas," contrasting it with an Acmeism "not concerned with world views, but [...] with [...] *a host of new taste sensations,* much more valuable than ideas" ("On the Nature of the Word," p. 131; my emphasis). This aspiration toward the creation of taste links Mandelstam to a long utopian strain in Romantic poetics, and indeed to the originary reflections of Kant on artistic experience as a point of passage between perception and ethical cognition:

> [W]e often describe beautiful objects of nature or art by names that seem to put a moral appreciation at their basis. We call buildings or trees majestic and magnificent, landscapes laughing and gay; even colors are called innocent, modest, tender, because they excite sensations which have something analogous to the consciousness of the state of mind brought about by moral judgments. *Taste makes possible the transition, without any violent leap, from the charm of sense to habitual moral interest,* as it represents the imagination in its freedom as capable of purposive determination for the understanding, and so teaches us to find even in objects of sense a free satisfaction apart from any charm of sense.[15]

In other words, taste would be a sphere wherein the relationship of forms ("charms of sense") to values ("moral interests") might be reflected upon, negotiated, played with. In one form or another, the possibility of fabricating this sphere of "taste," a utopian inscriptive mechanism if there ever was one, is probably the key preoccupation of modernist cultural theory; the Dalcrozian lockstep of "flesh" with "abstract system" is only the reductio ad absurdum of this project, just as the Khlebnikovian destruction of language would be its sublation. Mandelstam seeks a different solution, wherein the objects available to taste would be multiplied rather than reduced, in an effort to fend off the impoverishment of the sensorium.

The Reality of the Material

The problem of continuity-within-modernity is hardly peculiar to Russia, of course. In the U.S. context one associates it particularly with the preoccupations of the Whitmanian tradition: of Hart Crane, for instance, whose poetics sometimes seem remarkably Mandelstamian:

> For poetry is an architectural art, based not on Evolution or the idea of progress, but on the articulation of the contemporary human consciousness

> *sub specie aeternitatis*, and inclusive of all readjustments incident to science and other shifting factors related to that consciousness. [. . . .] [C]ontrary to general prejudice, the wonderment experienced in watching nose dives is of less immediate creative promise to poetry than the familiar gesture of a motorist shifting gears. I mean to say that mere romantic speculation on the power and beauty of machinery keeps it at a continual remove; it cannot act creatively in our lives until, like the unconscious nervous responses of our bodies, its connotations emanate from within—forming as spontaneous a terminology of poetic reference as the bucolic world of pasture, plow and barn.[16]

For Crane, what demonstrates the successful absorption into poetry of elements of radically new lifeworlds is fusion within something like a *body*. One side of the fusion involves "inner emanation," a notion recalling the alliance of poetic language with the corporeal: the physicality of rhetoric and rhythmized language; the sculptural potential of the shaped line, culminating in pictorial poetry; the dangerous ecstasies of the Bacchic chorus; and, at the utopian limit point, the poem as charm or creative word, the poem that moves matter. The other side is habituation, or rather the rhythmic incorporation of new into old experience, into an already existing vocabulary rooted, in turn, in various histories and practices.

As it turns out, the crucial distinction between Crane and Mandelstam is that the Russian poet situates the "body" or "storehouse" of poetic reference in the word itself rather than in a trans-historical human consciousness. For Crane, an instrumental use of language would be just another transitory vocabulary, whose lasting elements—useful for poetry, in the long run—would settle out over time, like a sediment. For Mandelstam, on the other hand, purely utilitarian language is anti-language. Words in his poetics carry with them human history, human community; to neglect their multivalent connection to historical life—or what the poet calls their "resistance"—is to drain language, the very stuff of human relations, of its substance:

> What madman would agree to build if he did not believe in the reality of his material, the resistance of which he knew he must overcome? A cobblestone in the hands of an architect is transformed into substance, but a man is not born to build if he does not hear metaphysical proof in the sound of a chisel splitting rock. [. . . .] Tyutchev's stone, which "having rolled down the mountain, lay in the valley, torn loose itself, or loosened by a sentient hand," is the word. ("Morning of Acmeism" [1913], p. 41)
>
> The life of the Russian language in Russian historical reality outweighs all other facts in the abundance of its properties, in the abundance of its

> being. Such abundance appears to all the other phenomena of Russian life as but an inaccessible outer limit. [. . . .] [T]he Russian language is historical by its very nature, since in its totality it is a turbulent sea of events, a continuous incarnation and activation of rational and breathing flesh. No language resists more strongly than Russian the tendency toward naming and utilitarian application. Russian nominalism, that is, the idea of the reality of the word as such, breathes life into the spirit of our language. ("On the Nature of the Word" [1922], pp. 75–76)

Mandelstam speaks of "language," not "Spirit," as his arch-medium of history, but the near-Hegelian quality of his thought here should not be missed. He recruits Hegel implicitly at the beginning of "On the Nature of the Word" in his attack on the "bad infinity" of empiricist/evolutionist/progressivist science, a science incapable of discovering any kind of "synthesis or inner structure" linking the world's phenomena (p. 73).[17] Later, Mandelstam recalls Hegel's discussion of "Observing Reason" in the latter's *Phenomenology of Spirit* when he writes approvingly of a psychology moving away from a study of subjectivity through mere "objectification of [mental] representations" to a "humanized science," which examines things mental not only as "objective given[s] of consciousness" but as "human organs, exactly like the liver, the heart" (p. 81). Like Hegelian "Spirit," too, Mandelstamian language cannot be objectified and yet is retentive, is continually "in motion" and yet saturated by the entire history of language use.[18] Finally, Mandelstam insists that we are given language not as an immediate object of thought but as a product of reflection or philology—meaning both literal "wordlove" and the more familiar and laborious academic practice without which the kind of language-memory he speaks of is impossible.[19]

In his essay, "On the Nature of the Word," Mandelstam does not consider language in isolation from its historically conditioned uses but rather sees it as the very fabric constituting those "conditions of use." The utilitarian applications against which he defends "the language of the people" (p. 75) include equally "the tendency toward [using] telegraphic or stenographic codes for the sake of economy" (p. 76) and the sacrifice of language to the "mystic intuitions" and "anthroposophy" of Russian Symbolism.[20] In describing Russian as "a continuous incarnation and activation of rational and breathing flesh" (p. 80), Mandelstam is using Christian notions of "the incarnate Word" in an exclusively secularizing way;[21] he is at pains to define something like a persistent vernacular, which would not be an object but rather an environment for thought and communication, conditioning and conditioned by humans.

Moving closer to Mandelstam's own moment, we might again draw a comparison between the word-based "event" and the Benjaminian story, that verbal creation in which "life," "counsel," and "situations" reside, in whose "gentle flame" the storyteller "could let the wick of his life be consumed completely [. . .]."[22] Language becomes part of the substance of the "human material" itself—particularly in its historical and communitarian aspects—and poetry a protected space for reflecting upon it. By insisting on the saturation of language by both past and present practice, Mandelstam links his theory of the word to the very highest political stakes, a connection that can be foregrounded by contrasting his ideas with the (conscious or unconscious) source of all such tropes of "building" and "craftsmanship," Schiller's Fourth Letter:[23]

> When the artisan lays hands upon the formless mass in order to shape it to his ends, he has no scruple in doing it violence; for the natural material he is working merits no respect for itself, and his concern is not with the whole for the sake of the parts, but with the parts for the sake of the whole. When the artist lays hands upon the same mass, he has just as little scruple in doing it violence; but he avoids showing it. For the material he is handling he has not a whit more respect than has the artisan; but the eyes [that] would seek to protect the freedom of the material he will endeavor to deceive by a show of yielding to this latter. With the pedagogic or the political artist things are very different indeed. For him Man is at once the material on which he works and goal towards which he strives. In this case the end turns back upon itself and becomes identical with the medium; and it is only inasmuch as the whole serves the parts that the parts are in any way bound to submit to the whole. The statesman-artist must approach his material with a quite different kind of respect from that which the maker of Beauty feigns towards his. The consideration he must accord to its uniqueness and individuality is not merely subjective, and aimed at creating an illusion for the senses, but objective and directed to its innermost being.[24]

Plainly, the difference between the two poet-theorists hinges on contrasting conceptions of "art" and "respect." Schiller never speaks of other, more cautious dispositions of the maker toward the material that might merit the name of "respect": the artisan, too, needs to concern himself with the intrinsic properties of the substance—grain of wood, weight of clay—before inscribing it or shaping it into something useful.

Mandelstam's crucial innovation is his placement of the "word"—the "material" of poetry—into the same sphere of respect as Schillerian "Man," who is the stone of the "statesman-artist." He makes it quite clear that the specific activity of the writer—of any user of language—is no more separable from the social whole, no less participatory in that whole, than so-called political art. The conclusion to be reached from this is, I think, quite inescapable: Mandelstam's vision of a vernacular resistant to instrumentalization amounts to a politicization of language, in the sense of linking the fate of language to the fate of the polis as such. As we shall see, the thingly independence theorized by Benjamin as aura becomes for Mandelstam a property of all historical residues of human activity; silent, corporeal material can never "die" but only fall dormant, even while its significance when active cannot be exhausted.

Equal Honor

> Mineral rock is an impressionistic diary of weather accumulated by millions of natural disasters; however, it is not only of the past, it is of the future: it contains periodicity. It is an Aladdin's lamp penetrating the geological twilight of future ages.
>
> —Mandelstam, "Conversation about Dante"

Mandelstam's consciousness of the value-laden nature of language was not unrelated to his having strong values of his own. As his attitude toward "material" and his appreciation of Kliuev imply,[25] Mandelstam was concerned with taking diverse resistances to modernizing change into account, with recognizing (as he says in "The Horseshoe Finder" (1923), arguably his greatest poem) that,

> Raznoobraznye mednye, zolotye i bronzovye lepeshki
> S odinakovoi pochest'iu lezhat v zemle [. . . .]
> (pp. 148–49)
>
> Various tablets of copper, gold and bronze
> lie in the earth with equal honor.

He was clearly enchanted by what he regarded as the independent, even conservative and separatist character of Armenian and (here) Georgian culture:

> Georgians keep wine in long, narrow jugs buried beneath the earth. Therein lies the prototype of Georgian culture—the earth has preserved the narrow but noble forms of its esthetic tradition, and has sealed the vessels full of fermentation and fragrance. [. . . .] Russian culture has never imposed its values on Georgia. Russification of the region never exceeded administrative formalities. Although Russian administrators, led by Vorontsov-Dashkov, mutilated the region's economic life and suppressed its communal organizations, they never managed to encroach upon its life-style, treating it with reluctant respect. ("A Word or Two about Georgian Art" [1922], p. 101)

I would argue that what is crucial for Mandelstam here is the form—the vessel—that allows for both the development and the (eventual) mobility of tradition; the form's hollowness ensures variety. But what distinguishes "form" from "value" in this case: could the third sentence be changed to "Russian culture has never imposed its *forms* on Georgia"? We might say that value is always assessed relative to some standard—more or less flexible, abstracted from experience and training—which represents a hardening of feeling into communicable judgment. Form in this sense is the measure of value, and one can see why the preservation of form is so often a matter of debate and battle: as Kant saw, it enables judgment in the broadest sense.[26] The ends of this argument do seem eventually to meet; the hypothetical standard finally overlaps entirely with value, as in the case of liturgical norms, at which point the two can be teased apart only by historical investigation, and even then with difficulty.

But this clinging to forms, making them irreplaceable, generates familiar problems of rigidity, on the one hand, and of a gradual draining away of relevance, on the other. How is it possible, within modernity, to protect language or any other "independent" sphere without constricting and reifying it, as both Kliuev and Khlebnikov might be read as doing? This difficulty is felt with an unusual intensity, perhaps, in the Russian and Soviet contexts, where Western modernization has been perceived as both a leveling and an enlightening force. David Quint, for example, has shown (in a brilliant discussion of Eisenstein's "Russian medieval epic," *Alexander Nevsky*) how the Marxist critique of the self-universalizing and "cosmopolitan nature of bourgeois society" could paradoxically lead, under the conditions of Stalinism, to renewed localism and a once revolutionary art turned "nationally one-sided and narrow-minded."[27]

Needless to say, this type of parochialism is the last thing anyone would associate with Mandelstam's art and thought. He could never have imagined himself, as Kliuev seemingly did, as "consecrated by the people" ("posviashchennyi ot naroda"), even if Kliuev sees "the people" as stretching well beyond Russia to Mecca, Algiers, China, and Chicago.[28] Of Central European Jewish descent, born in Warsaw, raised in St. Petersburg, educated in Western Europe, Mandelstam was quite self-consciously a poet without a single, local dialect. One of his foremost interpreters, Gregory Freidin, calls him a "cultural orphan":

> Only a cultural orphan growing up in [Russia's] revolutionary years could possess such an insatiable need for a continuous construction of a gigantic vision of culture meant to compensate for the impossibility of belonging to a single place.[29]

Yet the poet's defense of language as the medium and circumference of culture may be difficult to distinguish from more garden-variety separatism in practice. In his comments on "the word," for example, Mandelstam seems to regard Russian as a peculiarly resilient and thickly retentive soil. The cultural-political subtext of his remarks is not too difficult to discern: Russia's relative "backwardness," especially in terms of economic and technological development, finds philological and cultural compensation in a language "abundant" in historical continuity.

But as we will see, Mandelstam's description of language as *historical* entity is motivated not by antiquarianism but by a concern about the potential impoverishment of the present and future. He implies that the collapse of value into form is what allows values to have a kind of semi-autonomous history. This history is precarious, of course, for the difference between form as latent value, as encryption of meaning, and form as mere material inscription, is not a difference that can be predicted. But we have seen in Kliuev how, within a culture of symbolic equivalency, an entire philosophical and historical narrative, distinct from the dominant one, can be woven around irreplaceable objects. The Mandelstamian hope seems to be that language would provide a basis for cultural critique, inasmuch as it preserves the historic forms surpassed by modernity, and thus productively relativizes modernity itself.[30] In a passage that (I suspect) informed Mandelstam's well-known preoccupation with the medium of stone, Schiller described this trans-historical political function of art:

> The Roman of the first century had long been bowing the knee before his emperors when statues still portrayed him erect; temples continued to be sacred to the eye long after the gods had become objects of derision; and the infamous crimes of a *Nero* or a *Commodus* were put to shame by the noble style of the building whose frame lent them cover. Humanity has lost its dignity; but Art has rescued it and preserved it in significant stone [*die Kunst hat sie gerettet und aufbewahrt in bedeutenden Steinen*]. Truth lives on in the illusion of Art, and it is from this copy, or after-image, that the original image will once again be restored.[31]

The artwork's "noble style"—its projections, now virtually indistinguishable from its corporeal perseverance—preserves the work's integrity independently of both its creators/patrons and specific recipients. Schiller's plan for aesthetic education is, among other things, an effort to create a social form—or *taste:* a form for forms—where such a conception of art might be sustained. Artistic form becomes the historically traceable implication of an alternative measuring of value.

Radical Classicism

> Imagine a granite monument erected in honor of granite, as if to reveal its very idea.
>
> —Mandelstam, "Conversation about Dante"

In terms of practical poetics, the question of language-memory in Mandelstam studies has quite properly focused on the intensive use of citations in his writing. The work of scholars such as Kirill Taranovsky and Omry Ronen has established the quest for intertext as an axiomatic methodological starting point. Indeed, in Ronen's treatment, quotation—recast as "memory" or "literary recollection"—is the very subject of Mandelstam's poetry (and of Acmeist poetry in general).[32] Ronen cites a passage from Mandelstam's essay, "Storm and Stress" (1923), to justify this interpretation:

> A revolutionary reappraisal of the past preceded the creative revolution. Affirmation and justification of the real values of the past is just as revolutionary an act as the creation of new values. Unfortunately, however, memory and action quickly parted company and ceased to go hand in hand. (p. 110; last sentence not quoted in Ronen)

This raises the difficult question, unanswerable here in any satisfactory way, of how citation of past literary works, or their modified incorporation into present writing, could constitute "affirmation and justification of the real values of the past." Perhaps poems are tiny archives, the records of a private (or localized) set of readings and choices, passed on in a form different from that of the public archive, possibly a cryptic form. But what is that "different form," and how is it related to value?

One of Mandelstam's best-known metaphors for poetry is, of course, the famous image of the "plough" in "The Word and Culture" (1921):

> Poetry is the plough that turns up time in such a way that the abyssal strata of time, its black earth, appear on the surface. There are epochs, however, when mankind, not satisfied with the present, yearning like the ploughman for the abyssal strata of time, thirsts for the virgin soil of time. Revolution in art inevitably leads to Classicism, not because David reaped the harvest of Robespierre, but because that is what the earth desires. (p. 70)

This passage—also cited by Ronen—binds the idea of excavation to that of preparation. Soil is tilled not merely to expose "abyssal strata" but in order to ready the land for sowing, and improve conditions for growth.

Mandelstam blurs agency here by ascribing the desire for tillage to both the earth—that is, the vast repository of time—and to the poet-ploughman, who seeks fresh, renewing depths by trying to inscribe himself into the material traces of the past. Clearly enough, we can see here again how Mandelstam is at pains to avoid the implication of any "exploitative" relationship to time. But what is the "black earth" or "virgin soil"—the second phrase recalls a well-known cliché of socialist realism—of time, and what is to be sown upon it? To the first question Mandelstam responds: a source beneath our sources.

> One often hears: that is good but it belongs to yesterday. But I say: yesterday has not yet been born. It has not yet really existed. I want Ovid, Pushkin, and Catullus to live once more, and I am not satisfied with the historical Ovid, Pushkin, and Catullus. [....] The silver trumpet of Catullus—*Ad claras Asiae volemus urbes* [Let us wish for the famous cities of Asia Minor]—alarms and excites us more forcefully than any Futurist riddle. Such poetry does not exist in Russian. Yet it *must* exist in Russian. I chose a Latin line because it is clearly perceived by the Russian reader as a category of obligation: the imperative rings more vividly in it. Such an imperative characterizes all poetry that is Classical. Classical poetry is perceived as that which must be, not as that which has already been. ("The Word and Culture," p. 71)

It would be a mistake to describe Mandelstam's desire to be classical as simply the strain of an anxious and ambitious consciousness under the "burden of the past," or as a tendency toward "absolute forgetting." He is imagining a context in which all the humanistic labors of the past, all the collecting and arranging, could be moved from archives into present spheres of creation. As in Benjamin, this is a vision of the present, with all its resources of collection, organization, and distribution, as an area for the broad recovery of lost cultural aspirations rather than the blind execution of mechanical directives. Here the obligation is to *translate:* not specific lines of poetry but the entire creative project—in some way reconstructed—which the older poets failed to realize.

The continuation of the Latin poem cited here (Catullus's "Carmen 46") suggests that Mandelstam is also alluding to the "Progress of Poetry" myth—from whose standard versions the Russian lands were, of course, excluded—with its mixed historical movements of appropriation and visitation, of communing between kinds of alienness:

> Let's fly to the famous cities of Asia!
> Now our minds are ready to wander,
> our very feet are restless and strong.
> Farewell to your sweet companionship, friends.

We left on our distant journey together;
various roads are taking us back.[33]

The "now" of Catullus's poem is the rejuvenescent spring. The motivation for Mandelstam's ploughing is likewise the promotion of a kind of new growth; it is as though poetry's digging is really the precondition for certain kinds of (for Mandelstam, positive) development, from behind which poetry itself will follow. "The Word and Culture" begins with this optimism:

> Grass on the streets of Petersburg—the first sprouts of a virgin forest that will cover the site of modern cities. This bright, tender verdure, astonishing in its freshness, belongs to a new, inspired nature. Petersburg is truly the most advanced city in the world. Speed, the pace of the present, cannot be measured by subways or skyscrapers, but only the cheerful grass thrusting itself forth from under city stones.
>
> Our blood, our music, our State—all will be continued in the tender life of a new nature, a nature-Psyche. In this kingdom of the spirit without man every tree will be a dryad and every phenomenon will tell of its own metamorphosis. (p. 69)

"Advance" becomes the turn not to an old state but to a "*virgin* forest," a "*new* [. . .] nature." The "kingdom of the spirit" will advance "without man," in the directions provided by an anti-individualistic social organization ("subways or skyscrapers"), but retain, with poetry's help, both animation and historical memory of specific "metamorphosis." It is implied that the stakes for "literary recollection" are very high indeed; how can we imagine it as the soil for this "cheerful grass"?

* * *

Mandelstam's other well-known metaphors for poetry—those of the "message in a bottle" (later made famous by Paul Celan) or "Egyptian funerary vessel" and "architectural construction"—all play in fundamental ways on the matrix of inscription. They help to elaborate the tensions between continuity and creation generated by the "plough." On the surface, it seems that the "bottle/vessel" notion is in open contradiction to the idea of poetry-as-excavation; the poem is buried or cast to the mercy of the waves rather than brought into social light:

> Every man has his friends. Why shouldn't the poet turn to his friends, to those who are naturally close to him? At a critical moment, a seafarer tossed a sealed bottle into the ocean waves, containing his name and a message detailing his fate. Wandering along the dunes many years later, I happen upon it in the sand. I read the message, note the date, the last will and testament of one who has passed on. I have the right to do so. [. . . .]

> Reading [a] poem of Baratynsky, I experience the same feeling I would if such a bottle had come into my possession. The ocean in all its vastness has come to its aid, has helped it fulfill its destiny. And that feeling of providence overwhelms the finder. ("On the Addressee" [1913], pp. 44–45)
>
> Once more I shall liken a poem to an Egyptian funerary ship. In that ship everything is provided for life, nothing is forgotten. ("On the Nature of the Word," p. 83)

But just as the "black earth" is upturned only that it might be covered again by growth, so the poem, entombed or buried in water, is submerged in order to be found, "fulfilled" by a reader. Of course, this double movement of concealment and exposure, or the dialectic of latency, connects Mandelstam with the long modern concern with poetic posterity, perhaps best expressed in Shelley's "Defense of Poetry."[34] Within Mandelstam's poetics, neither life nor death is an absolute attribute of any *thing*.[35] Of more immediate interest, however, is the distinction between the two metaphors of "burial" which Mandelstam offers us, both of which are actually variants on the classic place-inscription.

The second seems the less provocative, if only because the fate of the funerary vessel depends on something arguably even more precarious than good luck, namely, religious certainty. Without the gods, this vessel remains a museum's relic. Yet this predicament points clearly to the tension between faith and intervention implied by Mandelstam's allegory of writing and reading. The funerary chamber housing the vessel is, of course, a kind of cave, and the vessel is designed to ensure that, whatever happens inside that space, what emerges from it will be something human. The vessel can thus be seen as a kind of minimal insertion of technique, intended to conduct the forces of the Unknown down a specific river.

Both metaphors emphasize solitude, of course, and surrounding the small hope for "friendship" and "life" is a vast sea of muteness. It is odd and sad to think of the "message in a bottle" as a poet's appellation to "friends"—the situation of the seafarer certainly suggests the absence of proximate friendship. Among the several different genres of writing with which this "testament" has affinities, the most obvious is the letter; here, indeed, is an urgent *"correspondance"* trying to preserve experience in some "crisis-proof form" (Benjamin).[36] For the message is explicitly the product of crisis and need; it is not difficult to see its similarity to petition or prayer. Yet it is also a strangely mobile and imperiled kind of epitaphic inscription—but much more hidden, much closer to silence—a memorial *Tafel* tossed to the waves for protection. The bottle-bearer of the message is wholly unconscious, and at great risk; it is hardly distinguishable from other flotsam or sea trash; yet its containment of the testament secures at least the chance of some kind of arrival. Faith is reduced to fortune, but not, perhaps, secularized out of existence.

The poem seems to be little more than a gesturing toward a possible arrival or response, and it is important to notice that Mandelstam's larger development of the metaphor emphasizes reception rather than production. One meaning of the seafarer's gesture is, of course, the abandonment of an impossible situation, an abandonment that is then re-imagined as providing an escape route or passage for a precious value. This escape route, or reception, is again a fragile and fortuitous matter, and can occur only on the inhospitable, unlikely, bastard soil of the beach, neither land nor sea; the imagined recipient for poetry is a shoreline bottle-picker, a quite literally marginalized figure. The compensation for this destitution arrives at the nearly inconceivable moment of "correspondence": finding and reading a poem become nothing less than providential events. Through this trope of providence, Mandelstam acknowledges that the transition between poetic work and "life"—the path of comprehension that needs to be opened through the vacuum of a not-yet-existent sensorium—is difficult to realize. For it is surely the poem, not the manifesto, which has the real work to do.[37]

Rational Abyss

As so often in Mandelstam's theoretical work, however, one finds for one topos—here the "providential bottle"—a kind of antithetical double. This is, of course, the much discussed trope of architecture—chronologically the earliest of Mandelstam's metaphors for poetry—which offers a vision of poetic communication unfolded not against a horizon of isolation but imagined as a complete context for creation, response, and development.[38] Commentary on Mandelstam often seems to explain his notions of "construction" as merely another metaphor for poetic craftsmanship, but certainly the architectural work (except in its ruined form, perhaps) has social-organizational aspirations beyond its own contours, as Suzanne Langer's useful (if idealized) summary reminds us:

> Architecture creates the semblance of that World which is the counterpart of a Self. It is a total environment made visible. Where the Self is collective, as in a tribe, its World is communal; for personal Selfhood, it is the home. [. . . .] [T]he human environment, which is the counterpart of any human life, holds the imprint of a functional pattern; it is the complementary organic form. Therefore any building that can create the illusion

> of an ethnic world, a "place" articulated by the imprint of human life, must seem organic, like a living form. "Organization" is the watchword of architecture.[39]

Of course, buildings provide shelter above all, and thus do not merely demarcate but enforce distinctions between humans and the surrounding organic life. Yet built places must yield to the "imprint of human life," says Langer, so that their rigid walls may "create the illusion of an ethnic world." In trying to resolve the contradiction between unnatural form and "life," Langer makes use of the etymology of "organization" (which relates, of course, to "organ," "organic," etc., its customary meaning notwithstanding), just as Mandelstam had announced the Acmeist "love for the organism and for organization" in "Morning of Acmeism" (p. 42).

In what does this strange love actually consist? That which is organic is born, not made; growing, metabolizing organisms have no built-in future, except death, and are therefore always trying to seize a new beginning, whether through procreation or some other kind of dissemination. Organisms appear as un-self-conscious accidents, although it is always presumed that these flukes find their explanations within some much larger economy of nature, which is neither born nor made but is simply "there." Organization, on the other hand, is a subjection of particulars to some kind of arrangement—this, in order that they might be used in some specific way, or produce a certain effect. Organizations, as the experience of modernization continues to show, are about enabling deeds or events to happen—that is, they are about the future—and are basically indifferent to survival in the organismic sense; they represent, but do not have, will.[40] (Poems can surely be seen as types of organizations—"designed" to give pleasure, at least—but this does not really distinguish poems from pies, or port.)

Langer explicitly states that the successfully constructed "place" must be organized to create the effect of the organic, the famous "living form": organizations can imitate organisms, if the organizer is a Sullivan or a Frank Lloyd Wright. The critical principles by which this living form might be recognized are never really clarified by Langer, but it is, in any event, "an illusion," presumably "begotten by the visible expression of a feeling," but really a matter of technique.[41]

Mandelstam's thinking on the relation between organization and organism is more difficult. His discussion of Gothic "divine physiology" involves the three components of edifice, individual, and society, all linked by the "body" metaphor:

> What in the thirteenth century appeared to be the logical development of the concept of the organism—the Gothic cathedral—now has the

> esthetic effect of something monstrous: Notre Dame is the triumph of physiology, its Dionysian orgy. [. . . .] The Middle Ages, defining the specific gravity of man in its own way, sensed and acknowledged it for each individual regardless of his merits. The title of maître was given readily and without hesitation. The humblest artisan, the lowest ranking cleric possessed the secret knowledge of his own true worth, of the devout dignity so characteristic of that epoch. [. . . .] From this stems the aristocratic intimacy uniting all people, which is so alien in spirit to the "equality and fraternity" of the French Revolution. ("Morning of Acmeism," p. 42)

Between the "concept of the organism" and "the humblest artisan" intercede both the cathedral and an "intimacy uniting all people"; the cathedral, it is implied, is a society's representation of itself, complete with saints and angels, peasants and monsters. The reactionary tenor of this longing for "aristocratic intimacy" notwithstanding, it is clear that the category of the *social* provides the real mediation—which threatens to vanish into the "body" metaphor—between the abstract "organization" implied by the cathedral (including the "definition" provided by the Middle Ages, the "title of maître" it readily imparts) and the "specific gravity" of individual organisms. It is not implausible to see the "Dionysian orgy" of Notre Dame as a code word for something like Ivanov's *sobornost'* (spiritual fellowship), in which the collective becomes the object of each individual creative libido.[42]

On one level, this "society-organism" is a politically inflected expansion of the familiar Romantic anti-self-consciousness principle—but if the collective exists, then why is the cathedral necessary at all? The specific professions Mandelstam mentions—maître, artisan, cleric—are either builders or functionaries of the temple, both humble men and "masters." The distinction between the primary meaning of the church building (as a social order's self-referential icon, an artifact made by artisans) and the secondary meaning (i.e., as Society itself) is deliberately blurred but never abolished. Thus the temple in Mandelstam represents at once the social order and the devices, the labors that make and sustain the social order, including art and technology.

As already mentioned, Mandelstam's later poetry expresses much less optimism about the possibility of any kind of building on solid and public ground. This is not to say that the early architectural poetry (located for the most part in *Stone*) is placidly monumental. It contains, rather, a difficult and wide-ranging meditation on creation, order, and value, perhaps nowhere more suggestively than in the much discussed "Notre Dame," an expanded architectural inscription in the classic mode:[43]

> Gde rimskii sudiia sudil chuzhoi narod—
> Stoit bazilika, i radostnyi i pervyi,

Kak nekogda Adam, rasplastyvaia nervy,
Igraet myshtsami krestovyi legkii svod.

No vydaet sebia snaruzhi tainyi plan,
Zdes' pozabotilas' podpruzhnykh arok sila,
Chtob massa gruznaia steny ne sokrushila,
I svoda derzkogo bezdeistvuet taran.

Stikhiinyi labirint, nepostizhimyi les,
Dushi goticheskoi rassudochnaia propast',
Egipetskaia moshch' i khristianstva robost',
S trostinkoi riadom—dub, i vsiudu tsar'—otves.

No chem vnimatel'nei, tverdynia Notre Dame,
Ia izuchal tvoi chudovishchnye rebra,
Tem chashche dumal ia: iz tiazhesti nedobroi
I ia kogda-nibud' prekrasnoe sozdam. (pp. 83–84)

Where a Roman judge once judged a foreign people,
A basilica stands and,—first and joyful—
Like Adam once did, spreading his nerves,
A light groined vault frolics with its muscles.

But from the outside a secret plan gives itself away:
Here the strength of arches like saddle-bands
Ensured that the weighty mass didn't crush the walls,
That the battering ram of the haughty vault
remains idle.

Elemental labyrinth, inscrutable forest,
Rational abyss of the Gothic soul,
Egyptian power and Christian shyness,
The oak stands next to the reed; and everywhere,
the tsar is a plumb line.[44]

But the more attentively I studied
Your monstrous ribs, O stronghold of Notre Dame,
The more often I thought: someday I too
Will make something beautiful from unkind weight.

The poem invites comparative speculation on the two terms it hovers between: "creation" and "judgment." The judgment with which the poem opens is both a creative and destructive act: it creates the Gaulish "foreign people"—creates them, at any rate, as "foreign"; it establishes the Roman legal authority, crushing whatever codes had been in place among the natives; it creates the city as the seat of legitimate judgment.[45] The newly created Adam does not seem immediately comparable to this kind of legal creation, for he is apparently enjoying a pre-lapsarian frolic, *prior* to the judgment that created the "Old Adam." Then comes the "basilica" itself, whose well-nigh biological mysteries are apparently just the cunning calibrations of the "plumb line." Finally, we have an "I," presumably the poet, promising or perhaps threatening to join the throng of creators.

It might be useful to provide a rough schema for these disparate levels and relationships, with "creators" on the left side, "creations" on the right:

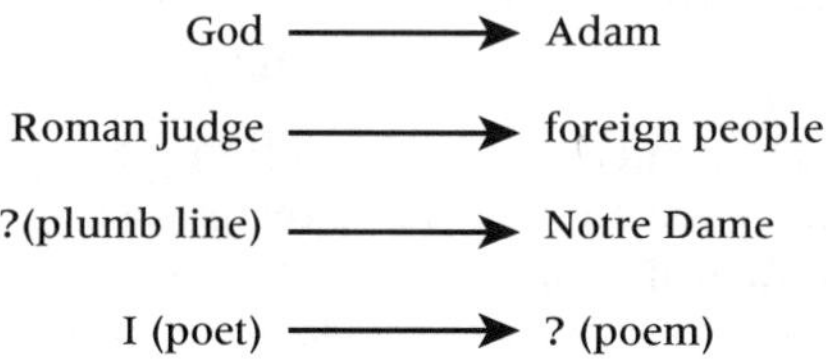

In each case, creation rather traditionally involves forming something out of "unkind weight" or unwilling dross: clay, Gauls, stone, and (perhaps) words. But with the possible exception of God, all the "creators" seem to create with the help of some recognizable technique, such as the law or measurement, and it is this technique rather than the actual maker that connects the material to the "plan." God's plan is a more mysterious imposition, but even here the reference to "muscles" and "nerves," conjuring up a lithe daVincian anatomical drawing, implies some ultimately extractable and understandable physiology. The poem imagines created structures as both endlessly complex and perfectly fathomable; the body-church is a "rational abyss." "The enigma [of the structure]," as I. Gurvich puts it, becomes "a clearly *discernable* property of the polysemic image."[46] "Mystery" ("taina") as such has moved from the inside of the church to the outside, from the hidden sacristy to the exposed ribs.

But that startling image of the "monstrous ribs" suggests death as well as vastness. Together with the novel appearance of the "I" in the last stanza, the suddenly dinosaurian cathedral—a skeleton in the midst of all the bodily energy—suggests that some time has passed since its "Adamic" heyday. The cathedral reveals itself to be not even a crypt but the corpse itself, the sheer weight of the material world. Even the sublime, nearly oxymoronic diction betrays a certain anxiety here, for the poet is surrounded by corporeal magnitudes in excess of what might be moved or decrypted through the work of inscription: "weighty mass," "elemental labyrinth," "inscrutable forest," even "rational abyss." The poet's insistence on placing everything at his own disposal—from Adam through the

Middle Ages to the contemporary world of "plans" and historical consciousness—threatens to overwhelm the creative task set for the poem.

In the end, the poem seems to suggest at least two ways to lighten this overload, neither of them quite mutually exclusive. The oxymoron of a "rational abyss"—a cave figure if there ever was one—suggests some immanent, self-organizing tendency in the material that the "plan" merely activates. On the other hand, the final turn to the lyrical "I" suggests that the planner's authority is primary, although Mandelstam is careful to make the planner's skill inseparable from all the knowledge sedimented within the weighty mass itself. Much depends, indeed, upon the feeling that the plan is somehow "given away" by the cathedral and that the building participates, however blindly, in its own posterity. The line of descent is unclear, but the poem seems to imply some kind of historical, as well as purely formal, continuity among types of creation.

And yet the little diagram above, you will have noticed, contains some blanks. The plumb line is the tool used to build Notre Dame, but who/what *builds* it? The previous line of the schema provides a possible answer, of course, in the shape of that "foreign people" legislated into existence by Rome, now craftsmen and creators themselves. We already know the poet's description of the Gothic cathedral as an icon of medieval social order; here it would seem that the creative agency of this new entity called the *people* is obscured by the omnipresence of technique, the "tsar–plumb line."

And yet we can turn the cathedral inside out again, as it were, and show how the poem's diction points beyond an architectural to a social/political dynamic. For starters, it is odd for a building to incorporate its natural enemy, the "battering ram" ("taran"), as its apex (the "haughty vault"). "Taran," of course, is also a pun on "tiran" ("tyrant"), and the wordplay suggests a fairly specific characterization of authority: as aggressive, charged with concentrated power, and potentially self-destructive. Surrounding this dome is the "weighty *mass*" ("massa gruznaia") itself, whose domesticated bulk, the very stuff of the edifice, carries an even greater potential threat. "Taran/tiran" and "massa"—the allegory of government and people—are in no internal equilibrium; arches outside the building, stability's visible secret, hold the thing together like disciplinary "saddle bands."

But to what does the arches' "strength" ("sila") really refer? Finding a direct "social" analogue for these buttresses is more difficult than for the church's vault and substance—indeed, our descriptions of the latter slide all too easily perhaps between architectural and political metaphors. "Tsar–plumb line" is the axis along which that slide occurs, and the arches seem to be another trope for the same fusion of knowledge with authority. For, in the end, the arches are more than contrived supports, representing, in the most general sense, *techne,* the not-so-secret plan itself. Technique, mastery, and learnable strategy are apparently what hold together both cathedral and political community, rather than any internally established balance. I have already suggested "discipline" as a possible placeholder for this *techne;* its answering term on the level of poetry would be poetic technique itself, the ability to inscribe effective projections.

We might append a corollary and say that technical knowledge, the knowledge of the creator, erases the distinction between the making of organism (Adam) and the founding of organization (nations, buildings), as all phases of creation collapse into know-how. This, alas, implies in turn a separation of function—the roles of all the "parts" of the building—from the larger vision informing the structure as a whole. More acutely than in Shelley's "Mont Blanc," the question of authority imposes itself on this vision of comprehensive unity, as the self-assertive author/creator projects his shadow across the living history he celebrates: the hidden glue of sheer corporeal force.

The third stanza still manages, beautifully, to soften this structure by naturalizing it ("elemental," "forest," "reed and oak"), implying that inscribed order is suffused through, but will never emerge from, that labyrinthine "abyss." Only "someday," says the speaker of the last stanza, will he make "something beautiful" ("prekrasnoe"). We see here a poet, of course, hypothesizing about his own craft and ambitions—but is his withholding of an overt comparison of the cathedral with poetry simply a matter of tact? (Kliuev, we recall, releases poems in flocks at the end of his poetic "manifesto.") I am inclined to read the ending instead as poised somewhere between a savoring of new knowledge and the possibilities it brings, and a kind of shudder or reluctance to burden his new understanding with a project.

Because a project of aesthetic education informs his inscriptions, the pursuit of creative knowledge is also a pursuit of power in Mandelstam, and therefore inseparable from questions of artistic, philosophical, and political authority. This is, of course, a problem for a poetry that seeks (as "On the Addressee" insists) "originality and unexpectedness" from its interactions with readers, and indeed with language itself. Mandelstam's aspiration toward a de-monumentalizing poetry of the unexpected is revealed by the negative or "unclosed" ending of "Notre Dame," but such a moment is certainly typical of Mandelstam's "buildings" themselves, which are ultimately impossible, floating, liberated structures. I am thinking of Hagia-Sofia, "swimming in the world" ("kupaiushchiisia v mire" [p. 83]), or of the last stanza of the poem on Petersburg's Admiralty building, where the imagery recalls the very differently nuanced liberating flight of Baudelaire at the end of "Les Sept Vielliards"):

> Serdito lepiatsia kapriznye Meduzy,
> Kak plugi brosheny, rzhaveiut iakoria—
> I vot razorvany trekh izmerenii uzy
> I otkryvaiutsia vsemirnye moria! (p. 88)
>
> The capricious Medusas cling, angrily;
> the anchors rust like discarded plows—
> and here the bonds of three dimensions snap,
> the entire world's seas are opened wide!

The grand structure proffers an invitation to "universal" exploration, and the motif of the breakout into sea travel recalls both the building's institutional purpose—to house the Admiralty—and the imperialist opening of "windows onto Europe" (Pushkin) and elsewhere. Yet it seems that the poet is subjecting the building to an ironic kind of reading, in order to wrest the "Admiralty" from the Admiralty. Medusas are famous precisely for their petrifying power, but here what they are forced to adorn contradicts all rigidity, and promises a complete revision of Medusan identity. Indeed, this snapping of bonds appears perilously like the building's full self-suppression as building—the opening up onto "universal seas," for example, is made possible by the partial ruin of the structure, the rusting of its anchors. Neither Medusas nor anchors are discarded, however, and the Admiralty is never quite allowed to devolve into chaotic materiality à la Shelley but instead is rendered metamorphic for and by the imagination: either "frigate or Acropolis," as the poem's third line would have it.

The human world constitutes, according to the third stanza, a "fifth element," made by the "free person" ("svobodnyi chelovek"). The simple epithet "person" manages to capture the generic or generally human source of this world while not generalizing that source into a single "humanity" ("chelovechestvo"); the fifth element is the co-creative product of many human creators. Of course, the second stanza had already de-monumentalized the edifice, so as to unveil and pay tribute to the creative labor informing it:

> Lad'ia vozdushnaia i machta-nedotroga,
> Sluzha lineikoiu preemnikam Petra,
> On uchit: krasota—ne prikhot' poluboga,
> A khishchnyi glazomer prostogo stoliara. (p. 88)

> Boat of air and sensitive mast,
> Serving as a measuring-rule for Peter's successors,
> It teaches that beauty is not a demigod's whim,
> But the sharp, rapacious eye of a simple joiner.

The anonymity of the "simple joiner" is one with that of the "free person," and seems to be Mandelstam's way of conceiving a creator whose authority, like that of Benjamin's storytellers and craftsmen, is inseparable from his lived experience and the nature of the material with which he works.[47]

Years later in the "Conversation about Dante" (1933), Mandelstam offered his final theoretical word on the relationship of the poet-creator to his words and his audience, but with the figure of the conductor replacing that of the joiner. He makes it clear during the course of the conversation that he rejects the notion of an "anarchic" or "conductorless" poetry:

> An orchestra without a conductor, as a long-cherished hope, belongs to the same order of vulgar pan-European "ideals" as the international language Esperanto, symbolizing the linguistic teamwork of all mankind. (p. 426)

It would seem at first glance as though Mandelstam were merely repeating the openly reactionary argument offered by Gogol in *Selected Passages from Correspondence with Friends,* where the "conductor" simile is famously used to justify autocracy.[48] The intertext, too plain to be denied, is an alarming one, given the date at which Mandelstam was writing. Although the basis of Mandelstam's own rejection is not fully clear, it seems that what offends him about Esperanto is that it is a mere symbol of linguistic teamwork—a thinned-out simulacrum of a common language lacking the richness to do anything but "symbolize" (like the Symbolists) that toward which it aspires.[49] Poetry, on the other hand, involves a different kind of collective sensorium, which Mandelstam evinces through depiction of a special kind of scene:

> When you read Dante with all your powers and with complete conviction, when you transplant yourself completely to the field of action of the poetic material, when you join in and coordinate your own intonations with the echoes of the orchestral and thematic groups continually arising on the pocked and undulating semantic surface [. . .] then the purely vocal, intonational and rhythmical work is replaced by a more powerful coordinating force—by the conductor's function—and the hegemony of the conductor's baton comes into its own, cutting across

> orchestrated space and projecting from the voice like some more complex mathematical measure out of a three-dimensional state. (p. 425)

The conductor's baton seems to figure that very expansion of dimensions proclaimed at the end of the "Admiralty": the unpredictable consequence of the structure rather than its plan. The rhetoric of coordinated intonation surely recalls the earlier interest in Dalcroze, but here the emergence of the "conductor's hegemony" is plainly dependent upon readerly effort and focus, and is inseparable from that conscious engagement of reader with material. And yet the "more powerful coordinating force" of the baton is something that appears belatedly and in transcendent form; its leadership is like that exerted by mind over material:

> The conductor's baton was badly overdue when it was born: the chemically radioactive orchestra anticipated it. The usefulness of the conductor's baton is far from being its only justification. The chemical nature of orchestral sounds finds its expression in the dance of the conductor who stands with his back to the audience. And this baton is far from being an external, administrative accessory or a distinctive symphonic police which could be done away within an ideal state. It is no less than a dancing chemical formula which integrates reactions perceptible to the ear. [. . .] In a certain sense this invulnerable baton qualitatively contains in itself all the elements in the orchestra. But how does it contain them? It gives off no smell of them, nor can it. It does not smell of chlorine, as the formula of ammonium chloride or ammonia does not smell of ammonium chloride or of ammonia. (p. 426)

In our terms we can say that the conductor's baton is at once the inscribing pen and Mandelstam's trope for the significance that (he hopes) will emerge from the aesthetic experience—precisely experience, and not simply the artwork itself. Even better than "rational abyss," the figure of the baton as "dancing chemical formula" captures this well-nigh oxymoronic idea, with the physicality of the dance and the conceptuality of the formula contaminating each other utterly. As formula, the baton synthesizes all the material ("chemical") elements in the orchestra without reducing them; as visible, legible pattern, it acts as the conduit of expression between material sounds and the perceiving ears and minds of the audience. The "conductor," like Hegelian Spirit, is the product of historical development—here, of the diverse and "chemically radioactive orchestra"—rather than some eternally hegemonic and always persisting *logos*. Yet it is not clear how we should read the conductor's pose, as he stands with his back to the audience. Does this stance represent a self-effacement of the artist-leader before the elements swirling around him on all sides, or is it a mystified figure for necessary, nearly invisible (though also ubiquitous) authority? The image of "dancing chemical formula" expresses a problem and a contradiction rather than a solution. No inscription, however reduced in form or capacious in intent, can avoid the authoritarianism involved in the inscriptive act itself; the latter is never identical to the corporealities and projections with which it is engaged. Mandelstam is unsentimental about this fact, even as he pays grand tribute to diversity in the very style in which his treatise is written, a free crisscrossing between criticism, philology, autobiography, exhortation, and (even) poetry—a mode profoundly at odds with the "centripetal" tendencies of the time in which the "Conversation" was produced.

Conclusion

The Place of the Skull

Etot vozdukh pust' budet svidetelem,
Dal'noboinoe serdtse ego,
I v zemliankakh vseiadnyi i deiatel'nyi
Okean bez okna—veshchestvo. . . .

Let this air, its long-range heart,
Act as a witness.
The ocean in dugouts—omnivorous,
Active, windowless—is a substance.

Do chego eti zvezdy izvetlivyi!
Vse im nuzhno gliadet'—dlia chego?
V osuzhden'e sud'i i svidetelia,
V okean bez okna, veshchestvo.

How denunciatory are these stars?
For what reason must they see [into] everything?—
Into the censure of judge and witness;
Into the windowless ocean, the substance.

Pomnit dozhd', neprivetlivyi seiatel'—
Bezymiannaia manna ego,—
Kak lesistye krestiki metili
Okean ili klin boevoi.

That ungracious sower, the rain, remembers—
Its anonymous manna—
Remembers how the ocean, or the wedge of battle,
Was swept by the forest of little crosses.

Budut liudi kholodnye, khilye
Ubivat', kholodat', golodat'
I v svoei znamenitoi mogile
Neizvestnyi polozhen soldat.

Cold and sickly people
Will kill, starve, grow cold.
And in his famous grave
Is laid the unknown soldier.

Nauchi menia, lastochka khilaia,
Razuchivshaiasia letat',
Kak mne s etoi vozdushnoi mogiloi
Bez rulia i kryla sovladat'.

Teach me, sickly swallow,
Who has forgotten how to fly—
Teach me how, lacking rudder and wing,
I am to control this grave of air.

I za Lermontova Mikhaila
Ia otdam tebe strogii otchet,
Kak sutulogo uchit mogila
I vozdushnaia iama vlechet.

And I will give you a strict account
Of Lermontov, Mikhail—
Of how the grave instructs the stooping one,
And of the attraction of the airy pit.

Sheveliashchimisia vinogradami
Ugrozhaiut nam eti miry
I visiat gorodami ukradennymi,
Zolotymi obmolvkami, iabedami,
Iadovitogo kholoda iagodami—
Rastiazhimykh sozvezdii shatry,
Zolotye sozvezdii zhiry. . . .

These worlds threaten us
Like rustling vines.
Tents of tensile constellations,
Golden fats of constellations
Hang like stolen cities,
Like golden slips of the tongue, like slander,
Like berries of toxic cold. . . .

Skvoz' efir desiatichno-oznachennyi
Svet razmolotykh v luch skorostei
Nachinaet chislo, oprozrachnennyi
Svetloi bol'iu i mol'iu nulei.

Through the ether, a decimalized light,
Made of velocities ground into a beam,
Begins its count, made transparent
By bright pain and the mole of zeros.[1]

I za polem polei pole novoe
Treugol'nym letit zhuravlem,
Vest' letit svetopyl'noi obnovoiu,
I ot bitvy vcherashnei svetlo.

And beyond the field of fields flies
A new field, like a triangular crane.
The news flies like a glittering new toy,
And it is bright from yesterday's battle.

Vest' letit svetopyl'noi obnovoiu:
—Ia ne Leiptsig, ia ne Vaterloo,
Ia ne Bitva Narodov, ia novoe,
Ot menia budet svetu svetlo.

The news flies like a glittering new toy:
"I am not Leipzig, not Waterloo,
Not the Battle of the Nations: I am something new.
Because of me the world will become bright."

Araviiskoe mesivo, kroshevo,
Svet razmolotykh v luch skorostei,
I svoimi kosymi podoshvami
Luch stoit na setchatke moei.

An Arabian jumble, a medley,
A light made of velocities ground into a beam—
And with its slanting soles
The beam stands upon my retina.

Milliony ubitykh zadeshevo
Protoptali tropu v pustote,—
Dobroi nochi! vsego im khoroshego
Ot litsa zemlianykh krepostei!

Millions, killed cheap,
Tramped down the path in nothingness—
Good night! All the best to them
From the face of earthen fortresses!

Nepodkupnoe nebo okopnoe—
Nebo krupnykh optovykh smertei,—
Za toboi, ot tebia, tselokupnoe,
Ia gubami nesus' v temnote—

Incorruptible sky of the trenches—
Sky of vast, wholesale deaths,—
For you and behind you, o integral one,
I drift on my lips in the darkness—

Za voronki, za nasypy, osypi,
Po kotorym on medlil i mglil:
Razvorochennykh—pasmurnyi, ospennyi
I prinizhennyi—genii mogil.

Beyond the craters, beyond the embankments and screes,
Along which he tarried, darkened:
The sullen, variolic, and humbled
Genius of the graves of the smashed.

Khorosho umiraet pekhota,
I poet khorosho khor nochnoi
Nad ulybkoi pripliusnutoi Shveika,
I nad ptich'im kop'em Don-Kikhota,
I nad rytsarskoi ptich'ei pliusnoi.

The infantry dies well,
And the night choir sings well
Over Schweik's flattened smile,
And over Don Quixote's birdlike spear,
And over the knight's birdlike metatarsus.

I druzhit s chelovekom kaleka—
Im oboim naidetsia rabota,
I stuchit po okolitsam veka
Kostylei dereviannykh semeika,—
Ei, tovarishchestvo, shar zemnoi!

The cripple befriends the human—
There'll be work for both,
And on the outskirts of the century
Knocks the little family of wooden crutches,—
Hey, fellowship, the globe!

Dlia togo l' dolzhen cherep razvit'sia
Vo ves' lob—ot viska do viska,—
Chtob v ego dorogie glaznitsy
Ne mogli ne vlivat'sia voiska?

Is it for this, that the skull must develop
Into a full forehead—from temple to temple,—
So that the troops could not but pour
Into his precious eye sockets?

Razvivaetsia cherep ot zhizni
Vo ves' lob—ot viska do viska,—
Chistotoi svoikh shvov on draznit sebia,
Ponimaiushchim kupolom iasnitsia,
Mysl'iu penitsia, sam sebe snitsia,—
Chasha chash i otchizna otchizne,
Zvednym rubchikom shityi chepets,
Chepchik schast'ia—Shekspira otets. . . .

From the beginning, the skull develops
Into a full forehead—from temple to temple.
It mocks itself with the purity of its seams,
Appears like a comprehending cupola,
It foams over with an idea, dreams of itself—
The cup of cups and the fatherland to the fatherland,
A cap sewn with a starry hem,
The little cap of happiness—Shakespeare's father. . . .

Iasnost' iasenevaia, zorkost' iavorovaia
Chut'-chut' krasnaia mchitsia v svoi dom,
Slovno obmorokami zatovarivaia
Oba neba s ikh tusklym ognem.

Clarity of ash-tree, sharp-sight of sycamore,
Slightly red, rushes into its house,
Glutting both skies with their dull fire
As though with fainting spells.

Nam soiuzno lish' to, chto izbytochno,
Vperedi ne proval, a promer,
I borot'sia za vozdukh prozhitochnyi—
Eta slava drugim ne v primer.

We are united only with abundance,
Ahead lies measurement, not downfall,
And fighting for enough air
Is a glory unlike any other.

I soznan'e svoe zatovarivaia
Poluobmorochnym bytiem,
Ia l' bez vybora p'iu eto varevo,
Svoiu golovu em pod ognem?

And, glutting my consciousness
With half-unconscious being,
Will I have no choice but to drink this swill,
To eat my own head beneath the fire?

Dlia togo l' zagotovlena tara
Obaian'ia v prostranstve pustom,
Chtoby belye zvezdy obratno
Chut'-chut' krasnye mchalis' v svoi dom?

Was this tare of fascination
Prepared in empty space,
So that the white stars (slightly red)
Rushed back into their house?

Slyshish', machekha zvezdnogo tabora,
Noch', chto budet sechas i potom?

Listen, stepmother of the starry gypsy camp,
Night: what will be, both now and in the future?

Nalivaiutsia krov'iu aorty,
I zvuchit po riadam shepotkom:
—Ia rozhden v devianosto chetvertom,
Ia rozhden v devianosto vtorom. . . . —
I v kulak zazhimaia istertyi
God rozhden'ia—s gur'boi i gurtom

Ia shepchu obeskrovlennym rtom:
—Ia rozhden v noch' s vtorogo na tret'e
Ianvaria v devianosto odnom
Nenadezhnom godu—i stolet'ia
Okruzhaiut menia ognem.

Aortas are filled with blood,
And it is heard through the ranks, in a whisper:
"I was born in '94,
I was born in '92 . . . —"
And, clenching a worn-out birth tag
In my fist, I murmur with bloodless lips
Along with the crowd, en masse:
"I was born during the night, between the second
And third of January in the irresponsible year
1891—and the centuries
Surround me with fire."

—Mandelstam, "Stikhi o neizvestnom soldate"
("Verses about the unknown soldier"), 1937

* * *

Although [our] native land's [own] singer
  Has sung of him more than once,
A song is still a song, and life, life still!
  He sleeps his final sleep.

—Lermontov, "Mogila boitsa"
("The Warrior's Grave"), 1830

An Idea is a concept perfected to the point of irony.

—Friedrich Schlegel, "Athenäum Fragments"

In this book I have repeatedly argued that the modern is not marked by punctual closures. Unevenness remains the "formal principle" of its history, making any attempt to assign beginnings or endings to the modern period a purely contemplative and academic exercise. If I *were* to choose a poem with which to mark the end of the modern, however, it would have to be Mandelstam's 1937 "Verses about the Unknown Soldier" ("Stikhi o neizvestnom soldate"), written in the midst of the Stalinist Terror, seven years after Mandelstam had resumed writing poetry (following a five-year hiatus) and not long before the poet's own death. Both extreme in its difficulty—a consideration of it allows us to revisit and summarize virtually the entire trajectory of the present book—and (as Irina Semenko has pointed out) oddly direct,[2] Mandelstam's "Verses" are, among other things, a reflection upon a new impossibility of inscriptive verse within a modernity that at once creates and annihilates its publics.

No single reading can hope to exhaust the complexities of this poem, although a host of crucial intertextual discoveries (revealing the presence of Byron's "Vision of Judgment,"[3] Camille Flammarion's "Récits de l'infini" [1872],[4] Lermontov's "Demon,"[5] anti-utopian reworkings of Nikolai Fyodorov's utopian writings,[6] and Khlebnikov's "A War in a Mousetrap,"[7] among other texts) have sharpened our sense of its conceptual undercurrents—notions of apocalypse, of war without heroes and quasi-industrialized mass death, of divine judgment, of wholly new kinds of time and space, of poetry's attempts to set up bridges across gulfs of historical catastrophe. No one has succeeded, however, in linking all the implied argumentation, allusive textures, and the crisis situation of the poem itself into an integral reading; nor do I hope to produce such a reading. My own comments will focus exclusively on the poem's implied reflections on modernity, which involve complex references to modernity's discursive beginnings in the Romantic and pre-Romantic periods, and particularly to Hegel.[8]

As a whole, "Verses" most obviously invokes the setting so unforgettably described in Benjamin's "The Storyteller"—the Great War's antiworld of trenches and destruction, the catastrophe commemorated by the original monument (erected in 1921 in Paris) to the Unknown Soldier:

> For never has experience been contradicted more thoroughly than strategic experience by tactical warfare, economic experience by inflation, bodily experience by mechanical warfare, moral experience by those in power. A generation that had gone to school on a horse-drawn streetcar now stood under the open sky in a countryside in which nothing remained unchanged but the clouds, and beneath these clouds, in a field of force of destructive torrents and explosions, was the tiny, fragile human body.[9]

The first stanza sets up the poem's fundamental problem of trying to imagine death on a scale so great that it has no outside, and no real witnesses. The militarized air over the trenches is called upon apostrophically to attest to the disaster, but the request only underscores the absence of any commemorating or historical consciousness on the scene. In Mandelstam, even the clouds are mobilized into absolute flux:

> Etot vozdukh pust' budet svidetelem,
> Dal'noboinoe serdtse ego,
> I v zemliankakh vseiadnyi i deiatel'nyi
> Okean bez okna—veshchestvo. . . .

> Let this air, its long-range heart,
> Act as a witness.
> The ocean in dugouts—omnivorous,
> Active, windowless—is a substance.

Following Nadezhda Mandelstam, Irina Semenko has pointed out how the "windowless" ocean substance is a reference not only to poison gas but to the "windowless" Leibnizian monad.[10] The allusion suggests that the new "public" created by war has been in some sense re-naturalized into pure "simple substance," for the windowless monads are "the true atoms of nature and, in brief, the elements of things." Regarding them, Leibniz adds,

> There is also no dissolution to fear, and there is no conceivable way in which a simple substance can perish naturally.[11]

The quest for the basic "elements of things" is of course one of the great passions of Enlightenment: to recover natural Being through the workings of analytic intelligence itself. That the warring human mass has become monadic (as well as nomadic) suggests that the familiar modern problem of alienation from nature has found an appalling resolution, as technologized conflict brings humans "back" to some corporeal substrate.

The result, of course, is the complete disappearance of anything like participation of humans in the making of their own histories. Instead, there is a de-coupling of material existences (and annihilations) from the meanings assigned them by state power. This de-coupling is indicated by the absolute conceptual caesura—one far more brutal than any Baudelairean hiatus—in the middle of the following quatrain, from which the action of military geopolitics is elided:

> Budut liudi kholodnye, khilye
> Ubivat', kholodat', golodat'
> I v svoei znamenitoi mogile
> Neizvestnyi polozhen soldat.
>
> Cold and sickly people
> Will kill, starve, grow cold.
> And in his famous grave
> Is laid the unknown soldier.

For the poet, the problem arises of how "Verses," inscriptive in intent, might be written about this soldier. There is, in effect, no public left to be drawn into (or, just as important, reject) the inscriptive appeal; the only verses to be written on such a monument are purely official in character, inasmuch as the signification of death here has been entirely predetermined and instrumentalized.

> Nauchi menia, lastochka khilaia,
> Razuchivshaiasia letat',
> Kak mne s etoi vozdushnoi mogiloi
> Bez rulia i kryla sovladat'.

Teach me, sickly swallow,
Who has forgotten how to fly—
Teach me how, lacking rudder and wing,
I am to control this grave of air.

Traditional symbol of poetry, the swallow is "sickly" like the people laid in the "grave of air." But a new kind of poetry is required here, one that at once takes into account the need to memorialize, the impossibility of any representation of the memorialized, and the imperative to resist the easy commemoration typical of official inscriptions. Possibly Mandelstam was thinking of Arkadii Shteinberg's "The Grave of the Unknown Soldier" ("Mogila Neizvestnogo Soldata"), published in *Molodaia gvardiia* in 1933, as exemplifying the kind of tribute he did *not* want to write:

Kogda boevye znamena vzletiat
I grianet v litavry narodnaia zloba,
Ia—staryi fantom, bezymennyi soldat—
Voskresnu iz mertvykh i vyidu iz groba.

Ia snova pushchus' po reke krovianoi,
V sherengakh druzei i vo vrazheskom stane,
Vezde, gde proidut za poslednei voinoi
Poslednie volny poslednikh vosstanii.[12]

When the banners of war rise up
And the people's anger crashes out on kettledrums,
I—the old phantom, the nameless soldier—
Shall rise from the dead and emerge from my grave.

Again I'll set out along the river of blood,
Amid ranks of friends and in the enemy camp—
Everywhere, where the final waves of the final insurrections
March past toward the final war.

Mandelstam's poem refuses this sort of reanimation of anonymous corpses as actors in a patriotic chronicle history. The result is a new level of irony, a new suspicion of meaning, a representation of catastrophe from within catastrophe itself.

Writing about the dismantling of monuments after the fall of the USSR, Mikhail Iampolskii noted the strange novelty of statue-less monuments, memorials reduced to pure pedestal:

> Of what is the pedestal a monument, if there is no figure on top of it? The answer is, apparently, the stability of time, a stability completely autonomous of any hero or any event, simply stability as such.[13]

Something similar might be said about "monuments to unknown soldiers," which have figures and pedestals but cannot be related to any heroes or even events. The danger is great, in other words, that the poet will be so overwhelmed by his task that the unknown soldier will indeed seem inchoate, elemental, "stability as such": a windowless ocean. Later on, indeed, we find the *genius loci,* legitimating link between specific place and the wider history of commemoration,[14] become but another drop in the sea of crippled refugees that people the poem:

Za voronki, za nasypy, osypi,
Po kotorym on medlil i mglil:
Razvorochennykh—pasmurnyi, ospennyi
I prinizhennyi—genii mogil.

Beyond the craters, beyond the embankments and screes,
Along which he tarried, darkened:
The sullen, variolic, and humbled
Genius of the graves of the smashed.

The genuine u-topia (no place) achieved here is characterized, above all, by a total, blinding "real subsumption" (Gramsci) of material reality to a system of rational calculation. The corporeal world has become entirely malleable, and the difference between sky and earth, weapon and victim, is lost in the crucible of machinery and combat:

Skvoz' efir desiatichno-oznachennyi
Svet razmolotykh v luch skorostei
Nachinaet chislo, oprozrachnennyi
Svetloi bol'iu i mol'iu nulei.

Through the ether, a decimalized light,
Made of velocities ground into a beam,
Begins its count, made transparent
By bright pain and the mole of zeros.

Nepodkupnoe nebo okopnoe—
Nebo krupnykh optovykh smertei,—

Incorruptible sky of the trenches—
Sky of vast, wholesale deaths,—

Yet the poem finds ways to chronicle, and not simply respond to, the loss it records. On the phonic-scriptive level, of course, materiality rises before us in every line and portion of line, like a forest of impenetrable thickness. The poem possesses a phonetic/graphemic texture so complex that one would need a multileveled chart or diagram to plot out all the echoes, overlaps, and overtones (my rough graphic notations here do not begin to do even these lines justice):

Skvoz′ efir desiati*chn*o-ozn*achenn*yi
Svet razmolotykh v lu*ch* **sko**rostei
*Nach*inaet *ch*islo, oproz*rachnenn*yi
Svetloi bol′iu i mol′iu nulei.

Nepod *kup* **noe nebo** o*kop***noe**—
Nebo *krup*nykh optovykh smertei,—

Mandelstam's "shamanic" side, so illuminatingly explored by Gregory Freidin, finds concrete realization here: poetry burdened with the charge of imagining total deracination manages a mode of expression so internally "grounded" and impossible to paraphrase that it comes to feel like ritual-mnemonic formula.

It is on the level of allusion, however—often complexly fragmented and veiled—that "Verses" reintroduces the historical fabric that the poem's representational "scene" threatens to obliterate. These allusions, as previous scholarly work has shown, are often of Romantic-era provenance (Byron, Lermontov, Napoleonic echoes; I will add some of my own), which in and of itself suggests that Mandelstam is returning to a kind of primal scene of modernity in order to develop a grasp of present catastrophe. Sometimes the echoes are direct and palpable, as in the way the whole notional shape of this stanza (about which more later)—

Dlia togo l′ dolzhen cherep razvit′sia
Vo ves′ lob—ot viska do viska,—
Chtob v ego dorogie glaznitsy
Ne mogli ne vlivat′sia voiska?

Is it for this, that the skull must develop
Into a full forehead—from temple to temple,—
So that the troops could not but pour
Into [its] precious eye sockets?

—explicitly recalls Lermontov's appropriately elegiac "The Warrior's Grave" (1830):

Na to l′ on zhil i mech nosil,
   Chtob v chas vechernei mgly
Sletalis′ na kurgan ego
   Pustynnye orly?

Was it for this that he lived and bore a sword,
   So that, at the hour of evening darkness,
Desert eagles would land upon
   His barrow?

Indeed, the entire bygone history of Romantic heroic (and anti-heroic) poetic commemoration informs the poem, as though executing a single grand allusion back to formative moments of post-Napoleonic states, modern national and international literary cultures, and projects of aesthetic education.[15] Many of these subtexts are deeply rooted in the inscriptive mode, as we will see. Among the most striking (hitherto unnoticed by commentators, to my knowledge) are the following two famous stanzas from the third canto of Byron's *Childe Harold's Pilgrimage*, where "self-exiled Harold" meditates on Napoleon's defeat:

> Stop!—for thy tread is on an Empire's dust!
> An Earthquake's spoil is sepulchred below!
> Is the spot marked with no colossal bust?
> Nor column trophied for triumphal show?
> None; but the moral's truth tells simpler so.—
> As the ground was before, thus let it be;—
> How that *red rain* hath made the harvest grow!
> And is this all the world has gained by thee,
> Thou *first and last of Fields*! king-making Victory?
>
> And Harold stands upon this *place of skulls*,
> The grave of France, the *deadly Waterloo*!
> How in an hour the Power which gave annuls
> Its gifts, transferring fame as fleeting too!—
> In "pride of place" here last the Eagle[16] flew,
> Then tore with bloody talon the rent plain,
> Pierced by the shaft of banded nations through;
> Ambition's life and labours all were vain—
> He wears the shattered links of the World's broken chain.
> (canto 3.st. 17 and 18; my emphasis)[17]

Beyond the apparent shared themes of Waterloo and impossible (or negative) monumentalizing, the phrase "first and last of Fields" seems to be taken up in Mandelstam's

> I za polem polei pole novoe
> Treugol'nym letit zhuravlem[.]
>
> And beyond the field of fields flies
> A new field, like a triangular crane[.]

—while "place of skulls" resonates, as we shall see, with the larger cranial pathos of the poem.

Of course, these echoes all work by contrast rather than pure similarity. At least Lermontov's warrior has a story, a record of achievement, for nature and forgetfulness to dishonor; Byron's "skulls," too, are still recalled as part of a larger history of thwarted ambition and international conflict. Byron, indeed, was in the situation of (as Francis Berry has stressed) "addressing an assured audience about an event of public importance."[18] The speaker in Byron's poem is, as G. Wilson Knight argues, "superbly conscious of the whole of Europe"; although he does regard the continent "as one vast theatre of tombstones," it is clear that, "through his touch the dead are temporarily raised, and in the poetry there is no futility."[19] But Mandelstam's battle is waged on "a new field," and the Romantic inscriptions are invoked largely as chiaroscuro, in order to stress that a new order of Being has arrived:

> Vest' letit svetopyl'noi obnovoiu:
> —Ia ne Leiptsig, ia ne Vaterloo,
> Ia ne Bitva Narodov, ia novoe,
> Ot menia budet svetu svetlo.
>
> The news flies like a glittering new toy:
> "I am not Leipzig, not Waterloo,
> Not the Battle of the Nations: I am something new.
> Because of me the world will become bright."

* * *

The Napoleonic theme is, of course, of special consequence within a Russian context, for it was the invasion of 1812 that, perhaps more than any other event, shook the Enlightenment faith of the Russian educated classes and to some extent provoked those novelistic critiques of Enlightenment (Dostoevsky, Tolstoy) that had such a colossal and enduring effect in the West.

Napoleon has also had his advocates, to be sure, although not many in Russia. Hegel, as we have already noted, apparently thought that the battle of Jena, "which occurred while the *Phenomenology* was being finished," enabled him to see "Napoleon, that 'world-soul' on horseback."[20] I recollect Hegel and *Phenomenology* at this point, because it seems that the richest and most extraordinary of Mandelstam's allusions within the poem are taken from that great work, specifically (but not exclusively) from its famous concluding paragraph on the subject of "Absolute Knowledge." Here is that paragraph (in the original and in English):

> Das Ziel, das absolute Wissen, oder der sich als Geist wissende Geist hat zu seinem Wege die Erinnerung der Geister, wie sie an ihnen selbst sind und die Organisation ihres Reichs vollbringen. Ihre Aufbewahrung nach der Seite ihres freien, in der Form der Zufälligkeit erscheinenden Daseins ist die Geschichte, nach der Seite ihrer begriffenen Organisation aber die Wissenschaft des erscheinenden Wissens; beide zusammen, die begriffene Geschichte, bilden die Erinnerung und die Schädelstätte des absoluten

Geistes, die Wirklichkeit, Wahrheit und Gewißheit seines Throns, ohne den er das leblose Einsame wäre; nur—

Aus dem Kelche dieses Geisterreiches
Schäumt ihm seine Unendlichkeit.[21]

[The goal, Absolute Knowing, or Spirit that knows itself as Spirit, has for its path the recollection of the Spirits as they are in themselves and as they accomplish the organization of their realm. Their preservation, regarded from the side of their free existence appearing in the form of contingency, is History; but regarded from the side of their [philosophically] comprehended organization, it is the Science of Knowing in the sphere of appearance: the two together, comprehended History, form alike the [recollection] and the Calvary [*Schädelstätte,* skull-place] of absolute Spirit, the actuality, truth, and certainty of his throne, without which he would be lifeless and alone. Only

From the chalice of this realm of spirits
Foams forth for Him his own infinitude.[22]

Although I suspect that motifs from *Phenomenology* help to illuminate a number of the poem's details, the allusive heart lies in the following two stanzas (st. 17 and 18 in the Nerler edition):

Dlia togo l' dolzhen cherep razvit'sia
Vo ves' lob—ot viska do viska,—
Chtob v ego dorogie glaznitsy
Ne mogli ne vlivat'sia voiska?

Razvivaetsia cherep ot zhizni
Vo ves' lob—ot viska do viska,—
Chistotoi svoikh shvov on draznit sebia,
Ponimaiushchim kupolom iasnitsia,
Mysl'iu penitsia, sam sebe snitsia,—
Chasha chash i otchizna otchizne,
Zvednym rubchikom shityi chepets,
Chepchik schast'ia—Shekspira otets. . . .

Is it for this, that the skull must develop
Into a full forehead—from temple to temple,—
So that the troops could not but pour
Into its precious eye sockets?

From the beginning, the skull develops
Into a full forehead—from temple to temple.
It mocks itself with the purity of its seams,
Appears like a comprehending cupola,
It foams over with an idea, dreams of itself—

The cup of cups and the fatherland to the fatherland,
A cap sewn with a starry hem,
The little cap of happiness—Shakespeare's father. . . .

As far as I can tell, no previous interpreter of the poem has mentioned Hegel in connection with it; nor is Hegel referred to by name in Mandelstam's own prose works. Nonetheless, and well beyond the level of imagery, the similarities are unmistakable, and we will dwell on some of them at length.[23]

The allusions are arrayed, as will be seen, in collage form, closer to Eliot's montage textures than to Joycean punning or Wordsworth's more muted references to the generic horizon of inscription. As usual, however, the Mandelstamian allusion proves to be less a simple reference than a Chinese box or *matrioshka,* layering intertexts within intertexts. For it would appear that most of the points of resemblance on Hegel's end are concentrated in the two lines of poetry ending *Phenomenology,* lines misquoted (or adapted) in their turn from the ending of Schiller's "Die Freundschaft." In that early (1781) poem, Schiller celebrates the "all-powerful drive/That forces hearts together/Into the eternal assembly of Love's celebrants" at the expense of those who find order in the universe by projecting "laws" upon it. Here are the last two stanzas of that proto-Romantic poem:

Arm in Arme, höher stets und höher,
Vom Mongolen bis zum griechschen Seher,
  Der sich an den letzten Seraph reiht,
Wallen wir, einmüthgen Ringeltanzes,
Bis sich dort im Meer des ewgen Glanzes
  Sterbend untertauchen Maß und Zeit.—

Freundlos war der große Weltenmeister,
Fühlte *Mangel*—darum schuf er Geister,
  Selge Spiegel *seiner* Seligkeit!
Fand das höchste Wesen schon kein gleiches,
Aus dem Kelch des ganzen Seelenreiches
  Schäumt *ihm*—die Unendlichkeit.[24]

Arm in arm, higher and ever higher,
From the Mongol to the Greek seer,
  Who follows the last seraph,
We surge, a unanimous ring-dance,
Until Time and Measure sink down to death
  In a sea of eternal glory.

The great Master of the world was friendless,
Felt a *lack*—so he created spirits,
  The blessed mirror of *his* blessedness!

The highest Being had found no equal;
Out of the chalice of the whole realm of spirits,
  Eternity foams up to *him.*

Clearly the crucial references to the "chalice of spirits" (Mandelstam's "cup of cups" ["chasha chash"]) and to the "foaming infinitude" of ultimate, self-conscious unity (Mandelstam: "foams over with an idea" ["mysl'iu penitsia"]) are already found in "Die Freundschaft." Indeed, the whole synthetic trajectory of Hegel's vast work is contained *in nuce* in these last stanzas, as the problem of finding unity within diversity is overcome by a grand, ongoing sublation of all history into something called "the Spirit that knows itself as Spirit." This is precisely why Hegel concluded his work with these lines; and, of course, the entire Hegelian project is partly a critical reaction to Schiller's hopes for the creation of a coherent, participatory public sphere through the agency of art.[25]

Mandelstam, in "Verses," offers his own devastating version of the Schillerian "ring-dance," a vision of a mass unanimity of broken, ruined bodies forced to the outskirts of history:

I druzhit s chelovekom kaleka—
Im oboim naidetsia rabota,
I stuchit po okolitsam veka
Kostylei dereviannykh semeika,—
Ei, tovarishchestvo, shar zemnoi!

The cripple befriends the human—
There'll be work for both,
And on the outskirts of the century
Knocks the little family of wooden crutches,—
Hey, fellowship, the globe!

Mandelstam's poem, however, contains a more explicit (and complexly ironic) allusion to the progress of self-conscious Spirit than the reference to Schiller alone can account for: specifically, the skull "mocking" and "dreaming of" itself ("draznit sebia," "sam sebe snitsia"), and indeed the wider motif of the skull itself. This motif, made famous within the Hegelian corpus by the discussion on phrenology at the end of the section on "Observing Reason," is released at the end of *Phenomenology* through the name "Calvary"—the place where Jesus Christ was crucified—whose German rendering "Schädelstätte" preserves the sense of the probable Aramaic source, *Golgotha* or "skull-place," alluded to in the passage from *Childe Harold* as well.[26] It is within Hegel's place of the skull, a place of simultaneous unification and subsumption, where Mandelstam's reflections on modernity find their appropriate setting.

We should pause, however, to determine how well Mandelstam might have known Hegel's *Phenomenology* in the first place, for such an inquiry will prove instructive in more ways than one. It should be noted, first of all, that Mandelstam can hardly have been unaware of the great Hegel revival occurring in literary-intellectual circles in the USSR from the mid- to late 1930s; the *Aesthetics,* to take only one example, was published in serial form in mid-decade in the important journal *Literaturnyi kritik.*[27] Beyond this immediate context, I think it is likely that the poet read all or part of the German original during (or after) his studies in Heidelberg in 1910. Mandelstam's energies there were directed primarily toward art history and literature, but according to his fellow student, Aaron Steinberg, he did attend lectures by Wilhelm Windelband, author of the once famous and much translated *Lehrbuch der Geschichte der Philosophie.*[28] However, a more important source of things Hegelian (and then teaching in Heidelberg) might have been Emil Lask, whose thinking, according to Steinberg, "will be shown by further research to have had a deep influence on the poet's world view."[29] An important neo-Kantian philosopher, Lask was born of a Jewish family in Wadowice near Krakow in 1875, and—significant for a consideration of "Verses"—died in battle in Galicia in 1915 during the Great War.

Lask conducted a course during the winter semester of 1909–10 on "the history of modern philosophy up to and including Kant," and it seems likely that Mandelstam was in attendance.[30] Although it is clear from the title of the course that Hegel was not the focus of the lecture series, Lask's published works on Kant, Fichte, and other pre-Hegelian philosophers are punctuated by frequent references to Hegel, who was then enjoying a renaissance at Heidelberg and toward whom Lask was respectfully, if critically, disposed. And on the occasion of his inaugural lecture on January 11, 1905 (published soon afterward by the university), Lask chose to speak on "Hegel in his relationship to the worldview of the Enlightenment," focusing on Hegel's reflections on the historicity of values. One passage from the conclusion of the essay is of particular interest:

> Especially in his lectures on the history of philosophy, Hegel dealt with the difficult question of the development of values. How do the Eternal, the Changeless, the timeless world of thought come to have a history? History as an object of empirical-historical representation depicts only a series of superseded and bygone forms that have been pushed aside by other ones. In regard to these forms, says Hegel, it is correct to say that the feet of those who will be carrying you away are already standing before the door. By contrast, history conceived as an object of pure speculation—that history, [in other words], which is philosophy itself—can have nothing to do with

> whatever is passé. Thus, according to Hegel (more or less), the deeds of world-historical individuals and heroes of thought are not laid down in some temple of recollection, like pictures from time past, but are just as present and as alive as at the time they appeared. They comprise effects and works that are neither transcended nor destroyed by what follows. Comprehended history is the recollection and the Golgotha of the absolute Spirit [Die begriffene Geschichte ist die Erinnerung und die Schädelstätte des absoluten Geistes]. In another place, Hegel compares this history with a Pantheon filled with images of gods.[31]

Lask insists that Hegel's concern for history is far removed from the "glorification of the past" typical of certain "Romantic and Restoration [thinkers]" (p. 341). Instead, Hegel is engaged in a thoroughgoing critique of the structure of values as propounded by Enlightenment philosophy:

> [Hegel] directs a continual polemic against the formlessness, abstractness, and emptiness of the standards of value [upheld during] the Enlightenment. [. . .] The rationalist method of the eighteenth century had seen only the frame, the naked scaffolding of the upper floor of value, but had not understood how to value the architectonic magnificence of the whole richly arranged construction. Thus formalist ethics extracts only particular abstract moments from out of the heterogeneity of the living human world[.] [. . . .] Entire regions of value remain, so to speak, undiscovered. (p. 343)

And yet, despite Hegel's hostility to any attempt to make "abstract norms into a rule," his interest in the "customary world" (*sittliche Welt*) and its history is in no way directed toward a petrification of time and process, all "conservatism" notwithstanding.[32] Instead, suggests Lask, by continually posing historical process and existing value against each other, Hegel seeks their mutual enrichment:

> To any mere tarrying in the past or clinging to abstract and frozen forms, [Hegel] always opposed the ongoing *process* of reason's development toward new levels—the drifting of the concrete World-Spirit, and the scent of the spiritual world, which (he says) penetrates even into the most far-flung solitudes. (p. 345)

The tropes of "drifting" (*Wehen*) and "scent" (*Duft*) are meant to suggest the continual movement of thought: not necessarily direction-less movement but certainly lacking in preset destination. Thus Lask's Hegel offers a vision of temporal motion fully burdened by history, of spirit "remaining itself in its alienation,"[33] of history as phenomenological rather than logical.

In other words, Lask gives us a reading of Hegel that (anachronistically) we can only call Mandelstamian. We easily recognize some of the poet's best-known preoccupations there in *Urform:* his rejection of conventional progress (and obsolescence), his non-dogmatic drive toward synthesis and comprehensiveness, his non-antiquarian concern for the past and the uses made of the past. It is therefore legitimate, I would maintain, to regard Hegel in the Laskian account as a kind of notional *Hintergrund* to Mandelstam's poetic theory and reflections on culture, early and late. But even assuming that enough time has passed since Karl Popper to allow us to consider a "Mandelstamian Hegel" seriously,[34] what does all this have to do with the poem? In the final section that follows, I attempt not to apply Hegel to Mandelstam but to think of the poetry of *Phenomenology* through that of the (ultimately anti-Hegelian) "Verses," in order to achieve some sense of where Mandelstam sees the "concrete World-Spirit" actually getting *to,* by 1937.

* * *

Let us return to the seventeenth stanza:

Dlia togo l' dolzhen cherep razvit'sia
Vo ves' lob—ot viska do viska,—
Chtob v ego dorogie glaznitsy
Ne mogli ne vlivat'sia voiska?

Is it for this, that the skull must develop
Into a full forehead—from temple to temple,—
So that the troops could not but pour
Into its precious eye sockets?

The opening formula of "is it for this" recalls the rhetoric of public lament, as well as the theatrical and visual-arts tradition of meditation upon the *memento mori,* with *Hamlet* (5.1) providing the classical example. Yet the trajectory of the meditation here seems rather different from what we find in Shakespeare and elsewhere. Musing on Yorick, Hamlet reads the skull emblem as a token of decay, of the final victory of corporeality, asking,

> Why may not imagination trace the noble dust of Alexander, till 'a find it stopping a bunghole?[35]

We might in turn read the troops pouring into the eyeholes of Mandelstam's skull as a simple figure for mass mortality, the fate of the millions who died (and would die) in modern war. But this reading simplifies the larger meaning of the tropes of skull and eyes as developed within the poem. In the second stanza, the stars in the militarized ether—possibly death-dealing projectiles—are troped into all-seeing eyes:

Do chego eti zvezdy izvetlivyi!
Vse im nuzhno gliadet'—dlia chego?

How denunciatory are these stars!
For what reason must they see [into] everything?

Later, the speaker's own eyes are effectively occluded by the new techno-military "mass," now fully unified, rationalized, and purified into a blinding beam of light:

Araviiskoe mesivo, kroshevo,
Svet razmolotykh v luch skorostei,
I svoimi kosymi podoshvami
Luch stoit na setchatke moei.

An Arabian jumble, a medley,
A light made of velocities ground into a beam,
And with its slanting soles
The beam stands upon my retina.

The "slanting soles" are the shoes of those "millions, cheaply killed" who "tramped down the path in nothingness" ("protoptali tropu v pustote"). They lack all real distinctiveness and represent either a simple quantity (pure light) or a compound so complicated that Observing Reason is utterly overwhelmed by it:

Iasnost' iasenevaia, zorkost' iavorovaia
Chut'-chut' krasnaia mchitsia v svoi dom,
Slovno obmorokami zatovarivaia
Oba neba s ikh tusklym ognem.

Clarity of ash-tree, sharp-sight of sycamore,
Slightly red, rushes into its house,
Glutting both skies with their dull fire
As though with fainting spells.

The two "skies" are the militarized ether overhead and the "incorruptible sky of the trenches." In a recuperation of the stellar and "constellation" imagery, earthly vision (the sight of "ash-tree" and "sycamore") vanishes from the skies back into its astrological "house," worn out and reddened (like the war planet Mars) by the excess of "decimalized" light. The next mention of stars clarifies their connection both to vision and to the skull that houses them:

Dlia togo l' zagotovlena tara
Obaian'ia v prostranstve pustom,
Chtoby belye zvezdy obratno
Chut'-chut' krasnye mchalis' v svoi dom?

Was this tare of fascination
Prepared in empty space,

So that the white stars, slightly red,
Rushed back into their house?

The syntax ("was this . . . ?") recalls both the skull (now a "tare of fascination") and the eye sockets, with the eyes ("white stars, slightly red") removed or rather pursued into recession by the "beam of velocities." The implied question ("was it for this?") thus seems to become: does the skull, the "house" of human vision, exist ultimately to house not seeing eyes but rather a homogeneous radiance—the compounded light of anonymous troops—in excess of any vision?

The crucial eighteenth stanza answers with an anguished, ironic *no*, but this reply becomes audible only gradually:

Razvivaetsia cherep ot zhizni
Vo ves' lob—ot viska do viska,—
Chistotoi svoikh shvov on draznit sebia,
Ponimaiushchim kupolom iasnitsia,
Mysl'iu penitsia, sam sebe snitsia,—
Chasha chash i otchizna otchizne,
Zvednym rubchikom shityi chepets,
Chepchik schast'ia—Shekspira otets. . . .

From the beginning, the skull develops
Into a full forehead—from temple to temple,—
It mocks itself with the purity of its seams,
Appears like a comprehending cupola,
It foams over with an idea, dreams of itself,—
The cup of cups and the fatherland to the fatherland,
A cap sewn with a starry hem,
The little cap of happiness—Shakespeare's father. . . .

In her discussion of Benjamin's treatment of the skull motif in the German allegorical poets, Susan Buck-Morss notes that,

> The emblem of the skull can be read in two ways. It is human spirit petrified; but it is also nature in decay, the transformation of the corpse into a skeleton that will turn into dust.[36]

There is, we might add, a duality within this duality: the skull as "spirit" is human but frozen, whereas the skull as emblem of decay, though ruined, is still an object in motion. This kind of synthetic duality is characteristic of the skull-as-symbol and is partially captured by the traditional Latin designator: *caput mortuum*, the "dead head." Surely Hegel's culminating reference to the "skull-place" of Golgotha—the *locus calvariae* cohabited by death and resurrection (or better, "abolition" and "preservation")[37]—takes particular advantage of the skull's peculiar status as both mute residue and meaning-filled hieroglyphic.

Hegel's critique of phrenology contributes its own version of the contradictory cranium, inasmuch as the skull becomes for him both the dead end of Observing Reason and the means by which Spirit comes to find itself, however inadequately, in being. Phrenology—the correlation of human character traits with bumps on the skull—is an attempt by reason to create an adequate, objective self-portrait, and to understand itself through this depiction. Thus it might be thought of as a reductio ad absurdum, standing in the same relation to phenomenology as Dalcrozian exercises do to Kantian taste. And yet, Hegel argues, such an absurd depiction has a certain value, and not just insofar as self-consciousness "must have a foothold somewhere in the crust of material thinghood."[38] Self-consciousness does have a seat in the brain, but the real truth that emerges from identifying Spirit with the skull is the notion that Spirit—always mobile, infinitely elusive[39]—*is:*

> Observation has here reached the point where it openly declares [. . .] that the certainty of Reason seeks its own self as an objective reality. Of course, the intention here is not to state that Spirit, which is represented by a skull, is a Thing; there is not meant to be any materialism, as it is called, in this idea; rather Spirit must be something more and other than these bones. But to say that Spirit [merely] *is,* means nothing else than that it is a Thing. When *being* as such, or thinghood, is predicated of Spirit, the true expression of this is that Spirit is, therefore, the same kind of being that a *bone is.* It must therefore be regarded as extremely important that the true expression has been found for the bare statement about Spirit—that it *is.* (*PS,* p. 208)

As always in Hegel, the moment of insight both exhausts the value of that aspect of Spirit under discussion (here, Observing Reason) and opens up a new stage. Unable "to find itself immediately," consciousness now aims "to produce itself by its own activity" (p. 209),[40] leading to the "actualization of self-consciousness" and ultimately to true Spirit, wherein what is active and negative ("being-for-itself") is perpetually reconciled with the substance of the living world ("being-in-itself").

I recapitulate all this not to suggest that Mandelstam had Hegel's *arguments* firmly in mind when writing "Verses"—a most doubtful proposition—but rather to give some definition to those Hegelian *motifs* that are indeed introduced allusively and figuratively. What is clear, first of all, is that the skull of the poem becomes much like Spirit itself in Mandelstam's treatment. Beginning as a living thing (the phrase "from the beginning" literally reads "from life" ["ot zhizni"]), the skull mutates into a changing cultural object, winning the Mandelstamian tribute of an oxymoronic architectural metaphor ("comprehending cupola"). Indeed, the stanza can be read as a kind of rough mini-history of the development of Spirit, moving from material immediacy to Observing Reason ("mock[ing] itself with the purity of its seams") to self-consciousness ("dream[ing] of itself") to the capaciousness of absolute Spirit ("cup of cups," "fatherland to the fatherland"). The last two lines reintroduce the element of contradiction, and thus totality as well: the "starry-hemmed cap of happiness" seems to mean at once a crown, a fool's cap, and the skull, suggesting that Skull-Spirit is big enough to contain them all. Meanwhile, the sudden reference to "Shakespeare's father" recalls both the author "Shakespeare" as a stand-in for Spirit's grandest achievements, and the specific, suffering fathers in the plays themselves.

The tragic associations of the latter, however, bring us back to the grim overall pathos of Mandelstam's "Verses." We have already seen how the general situation of the eighteenth stanza recalls the Yorick setting, an allusion made stronger by reference to the "little cap." *Hamlet,* of course, is very much a play about fathers and the ruination of fathers, with dead jester Yorick (who carried young Hamlet on his back) combining skull, father, and fool in a single cluster. But perhaps the more vital intertext is that of *King Lear,* where exalted fathers (Lear and Gloucester) are reduced to "coxcombs" and less.[41] Gloucester, indeed, is made into an "eyeless villain" in an act of political sadism (3.7.96), and no play of Shakespeare's evokes "bare life" (Giorgio Agamben) and blinding annihilation of Father-land like this one does:

> I' th' last night's storm I such a fellow saw,
> Which made me think a man a worm. (4.1.32–33)

Hegel's primary mention of Shakespeare in *Phenomenology* centers precisely on the question of "bare" (as opposed to significant) existence, and draws a sharper distinction between the two than Mandelstam would. The skull, says Hegel, has not

> the value even of a *sign.* Look and gesture, tone of voice, even a pillar or post erected on a desert island, directly proclaim that they mean something else than what they *simply are* at first sight. They at once profess to be signs, since they have in them a peculiarity which points to something else, by the fact that it does not properly belong to them. A variety of ideas may well occur to us in connection with a skull, like those of Hamlet over Yorick's skull; but the skull-bone just by itself is such an indifferent, natural thing that nothing else is to be directly seen in it, or fancied about it, than simply the bone itself. (*PS,* pp. 200–201)

Mandelstam follows Hamlet here rather than Hegel, and insists on permanent reading, on the convertibility of the dead artifact, on its inscriptive value as a passageway to significations—the plurality could include, perhaps, no signification at all. In the midst of the wreckage of "Verses," the eighteenth stanza stands as a weird oasis of panegyric, a memento of memento as such, indeed of memory itself. It pays a last, specifically modern homage to the interlocutive, mutual dependence of object and consciousness, in a space where inscription would seem irrelevant.[42]

But what, then, finally distinguishes the verses "about" the Unknown Soldier from any monument *to* the Unknown Soldier? Perhaps simply that, in the face of the apparent nothingness of the "grave of air," the verses-about still attempt to suppress any *single* memorializing content that might be poured into that vacuum. For at least that one stanza, the skull remains something other, to be confronted rather than coded or "ground into a beam": both traumatized silence and triumphal restitution meet with resistance. But other claims are still left unanswered by this stance. What of the honor that might be paid to the dead *as* dead—the other, corporeal resistance that would acknowledge the impossibility of any recovery operations in the depths of the "windowless ocean"? It might generally be said that Mandelstam, like many writing within the so-called Modernist phase of modernity, resists corporeality as such, allowing himself instead to be pulled inexorably into the vast battlefield of cultural struggle over meanings. Yet, as I suggested earlier, corporeality in Mandelstam is registered primarily on the phonic-scriptive level, where the material character of language plays the role of a palpable mnemonic container (a bottle or vessel) onto which meanings might adhere. As anxiety about destruction increases—and nowhere is it stronger than in "Verses"—the corporeality of sound-texture is intensified in an effort to fashion a medium that might persevere through all change. Moving through the thicket of sounds toward significance becomes more difficult, of course, and what we are left with, almost, is pure "bottle": the sound of the verse itself:

> Nepodkupnoe nebo okopnoe—
> Nebo krupnykh optovykh smertei,—

These sounds, it might be said, are the poem's testimony to the blanked-out "family of crutches," the "human stream" in "a bed of trenches."[43]

Yet "Verses" finally testifies only to a realm in which testimony itself becomes irrelevant. In his discussion of "the ethical order," Hegel had suggested that the motive for burial (a ritual the Family is charged with executing) lies in the refusal of humans to relinquish their dead fellows to the mindlessness of natural forces:

> The dead individual [. . .] is an empty singular, merely a passive being-for-another, at the mercy of every lower irrational individuality and the

> forces of abstract material elements, all of which are now more powerful than himself: the former on account of the life they possess, the latter on account of their negative nature. The Family keeps away from the dead this dishonoring of him by unconscious appetites and abstract entities, and puts its own action in their place, and weds the blood-relation to the bosom of the earth, to the elemental imperishable individuality. The Family thereby makes him a member of a community which prevails over and holds under control the forces of particular material elements and the lower forms of life, which sought to unloose themselves against him and to destroy him. (*PS*, p. 271)

Monuments to unknown soldiers are, on this account, the full insertion of state power into the place of both Family and dead individual. As we know from the great discussion in *Phenomenology* of the struggle between Antigone and Creon, Hegel thought that any attempt by the state to fully usurp "the sacred claims of the Family" would work an intolerable profanation of the state's own roots in common forms of faith, and thereby sabotage its legitimacy.[44] But *Antigone* is not one of the dramatic works alluded to in "Verses." For Mandelstam at this late stage, the "repressed" will return only as their own absence, that is, in the purely negative form of an impoverishment of the present. In the world of unknown soldiers, the making of monument, of art itself, is indeed no longer "based on ritual" but "on another practice—politics,"[45] and specifically a politics of the elimination of political alternatives. The "little family of wooden crutches" is not a Family.

And the skull-place of Absolute Spirit is no Hegelian Golgotha but rather a literal pile of skulls. Above and beyond it floats the New ("novoe"), the premature but effective technical resolution of all contradictions. Technology and the state have indeed wrought a bright new collectivity, with social effectivity and value (the "glittering news") separated absolutely from corporeality, now reduced to less than detritus: crutches, craters. Conversion is one-way, without dialectical circulation, and Mandelstam annihilates his own monument to memory in an astonishing image of near-Platonovan violence:

> I soznan'e svoe zatovarivaia
> Poluobmorochnym bytiem,
> Ia l' bez vybora p'iu eto varevo,
> Svoiu golovu em pod ognem?
>
> And, glutting my consciousness
> With half-unconscious being,
> Will I have no choice but to drink this swill,
> To eat my own head beneath the fire?

Here Baudelairean ennui reaches its apotheosis, as moribund consciousness loses any objects of nostalgic sentiment, and can only perceive the carcass of its own (now unrecognizable) history.

The last stanza juxtaposes dulled corporeal process with the abstract identity of enumerated birth, the residues of reprisals against psychological justification:

> Nalivaiutsia krov'iu aorty,
> I zvuchit po riadam shepotkom:
> —Ia rozhden v devianosto chetvertom,
> Ia rozhden v devianosto vtorom . . . —
> I v kulak zazhimaia istertyi
> God rozhden'ia—s gur'boi i gurtom
> Ia shepchu obeskrovlennym rtom:
> —Ia rozhden v noch' s vtorogo na tret'e
> Ianvaria v devianosto odnom
> Nenadezhnom godu—i stolet'ia
> Okruzhaiut menia ognem.
>
> Aortas are filled with blood,
> And it is heard through the ranks, in a whisper:
> "I was born in '94,
> I was born in '92 . . . —"
> And, clenching a worn-out birth tag
> In my fist, I murmur with bloodless lips
> Along with the crowd, en masse:
> "I was born during the night, between the second
> And third of January in the irresponsible year
> 1891[46]—and the centuries
> Surround me with fire."

The "centuries" that had surrounded the early Mandelstam with a wealth of latent creative projects have met their end in holocaust. The theatricality of that final image ("the centuries/Surround me with fire"), almost Blokian in feeling, should be read ironically as the seizure, for purposes of testimony, of a stage that clearly no longer exists. Those technological, cultural, and political instabilities that for earlier moderns (including Mandelstam) had offered pathways to imaginings of new audiences and new sensoria have fully hardened into legitimating orders; the corporeal for its part has been either banished through the hypertrophy of meaning-production (viz. the Unknown Soldier) or itself hypertrophied into a community of bones.

The poem's vision of modernity is itself hyperbolic, of course—although one is tempted to call it prophetic as well. Its relationship to the poetic work of one of the greatest interpreters of the post-1938

European catastrophes—Paul Celan, translator of Mandelstam, who would have understood only too well what "Verses" was getting at—deserves full exploration. Although history has assuredly not ended, the almost unimaginable failure that Mandelstam mourns did happen; his late work, by registering the broken *Aufhebung* of modernity, reminds us of why it is so hard today to recapture any of that earlier utopian hope in "significant stone."

Coda: In Descending Sizes

If we are to seek any pathways out of the "Verses," it should first be recalled that Mandelstam (like Benjamin) here presages a new critical attitude that would emerge post—World War II, the *Kulturkritik* that (in Rancière's terms) preserves Romantic aspirations through the negative procedures of disenchantment.[1] Needless to say, Mandelstam's poem should be taken to refer to far more than the Great War and Soviet forms of barbarism alone; his writings on the Caucasus and many of his poems show a pained consciousness of earlier enormities, although I would single out, for its special critical edge, his remarkable 1923 interview with Ho Chi Minh (then known as Nguyen Ai Quoc) focusing on resistance to French colonization:

> European civilization operates with bayonets and liquor, concealing them beneath the Catholic missionary's soutane. Nguyen Ai Quoc breathes culture, not European culture, but perhaps the culture of the future.[2]

The question remains, however, whether anything of the constructive aspiration of the modern inscription might be salvaged, apart from the vital critical imperative: can we only de-heroize unknown soldiers, shatter the Vendôme column, topple Ozymandias over and over again? Perhaps poetry is the wrong place to look for the inscription these days; perhaps this mode has migrated into conceptual or installation art, for instance, where the participation of a diverse public in the shaping of the "art object" is not only required but where (as in some of the recent work of Ilya and Emilia Kabakov) the old inscriptive poetic matrix is occasionally explicitly recalled.[3] And then there are all the vast areas of the globe left unexamined in this study: surely other responses to modernity and other kinds of inscription have taken and are taking shape there as well.

And then there is poetry. As a contrasting coda on monument, let me offer a brief reading of Elizabeth Bishop's very late-modern revision of Shelley's (and, indirectly, Mandelstam's) anti-monumental stand in her meta-inscriptive poem "The Monument."[4]

"Ozymandias," precursor of all later English monument poems—and surely another concealed meditation on the Napoleonic project—is short enough to cite a second time:

I met a traveller from an antique land,
Who said—"Two vast and trunkless legs of stone
Stand in the desart. . . . Near them, on the sand,
Half sunk a shattered visage lies, whose frown,
And wrinkled lip, and sneer of cold command,
Tell that its sculptor well those passions read
Which yet survive, stamped on these lifeless things,
The hand that mocked them, and the heart that fed;
And on the pedestal, these words appear:
My name is Ozymandias, King of Kings,
Look on my Works, ye Mighty, and despair!
Nothing beside remains. Round the decay
Of that colossal Wreck, boundless and bare
The lone and level sands stretch far away."[5]

Bishop's poem (like "Ozymandias" itself, most probably) is an ekphrasis, a meditation on the "mute surface" of a series of Max Ernst frottages entitled (with delicious irony) *Histoire Naturel.*[6] Thus the question of the function of cultural production in general can be taken as the poet's unspoken motivation. Like Shelley's sonnet, "The Monument" is set up as a visit of two voices—one a guide and apologist, the other her reluctant companion—back to the dry and "antique land," now a kind of stage set which is, like the monument itself, "wooden," "full of glistening splinters." This monument, an eroding "temple of crates" rather than a ruin, apparently lacks an inscription ("a sort of fleur-de-lys" is the most it can manage),[7] allowing for certain hypotheses of origin: the monument *might* be the work of an "artist-prince"—Ozymandias the sculptor?—who *might* "have wanted [. . .] to mark a tomb or boundary."

Yet "what can it prove," asks the companion, this tribute crumbling in obscurity? The apologist has the last word, through which we learn that her real companion is Shelley:

The crudest scroll-work says "commemorate,"
while once each day the light goes around it
like a prowling animal,
or the rain falls on it, or the wind blows into it.
It may be solid, may be hollow.
The bones of the artist-prince may be inside
or far away on even drier soil.

> But roughly but adequately it can shelter
> what is within (which after all
> cannot have been intended to be seen).
> It is the beginning of a painting,
> a piece of sculpture, or poem, or monument,
> and all of wood. Watch it closely.

The motive for monument is at least partially a fear of time and annihilation, and yet Bishop's theory of monument places something like a vacuum—perhaps it might be called a cave—in its very midst. The call to "commemorate" is that which shelters "what is within," which is most likely nothing; it is joined by an implied injunction not to show what "cannot have been intended to be seen," and together these two principles generate the "beginnings" to which the last three lines refer.

The monument is no more than a thin wall between commemoration and realization—or between commemoration and its official motivation ("the heart that fed"), such as a king—which memory keeps piling higher. Again, the monument seems to imply chains of impulses/responses: from king to sculptor to reader to traveler to Shelley to Bishop to . . ., in a structure resembling Bishop's monument itself,

> Built
> like several boxes in descending sizes
> one above the other.

The subjunctive caution of her language ("may be," "may be," "But roughly but adequately") suggests the fragility and potential exhaustion ("in *descending* sizes") of this ongoing commemorative building project, always threatened by real destruction or real positivity. Ozymandias's "Look on my Works" becomes "*Watch it closely,*" which I read as an urging of both imagination and vigilance vis-à-vis what is done with monument—where "monument" means no less than "documents of human culture" as such. Few poems about monuments are half as critical as "Ozymandias," and most are more inclined to put some king's bones (their authenticity attested) back inside, with a peephole for viewing—and so, Bishop warns, "*watch* it!" Where Shelley wants to work a ferocious, de-signifying counter-violence on Ozymandias, Bishop's poem argues for preserving that doubtful cavity of mystery within the most decrepit and discredited monuments, and inserting it into a wider circuit of (critical) response.

Of course, it can be countered that Bishop here is simply concerned to provoke the production of artworks—"a painting, a piece of sculpture, or poem, or monument"—regardless of any critical or transformative effect they might have. On such a reading, "The Monument" might be taken as the more stately "aestheticized" flipside of Rolf Dieter Brinkmann's "Hymne." Bishop's poem expresses the need for a protected (if impoverished) grotto ("a tomb or boundary") in which to house art production and reception: a space distanced, supposedly, from the logo-noise of the public square, but wherein the iterative dynamic of mass culture (yet another painting, another sculpture, another book about poetry) is replicated as another specialized if privileged consumer niche.[8] This critique is quite unanswerable given current conditions, and resonates with many familiar and, I believe, accurate accounts of our own postmodern cultural moment. A partial response would re-stress both Bishop's foregrounding of ironic dialogue (which determines the poem's very form) as the real "setting" that sustains or fails to sustain commemorations of any kind, and the monument's own splintery decrepitude as a reminder of the ultimately *made* character of those commemorations—no matter how thickly laminated by commodity logic they may be. Bishop's speaker still finds a way to pin some hope for a space both creative and social on the device of a monument: hovering between solemn memorial and Rube Goldberg machine, fertile in its hollowness and squalor, roughly adequate (perhaps) to our own place and the "eroded air" in which we must build.

Notes

Introduction

1. James Hutton, *The Greek Anthology in Italy to the Year 1800* (Ithaca: Cornell University Press, 1935), p. 55.

2. Geoffrey H. Hartman, "Wordsworth, Inscriptions and Romantic Nature Poetry," in *From Sensibility to Romanticism: Essays Presented to Frederick A. Pottle,* ed. Frederick W. Hilles and Harold Bloom (London: Oxford University Press, 1965), pp. 389–414; reprinted and cited here as "Inscriptions and Romantic Nature Poetry," in *The Unremarkable Wordsworth,* intro. Donald G. Marshall (Minneapolis: University of Minnesota Press, 1987), pp. 31–46. All further citations from this essay are from this edition, with page numbers cited in parentheses.

3. "Epitafiia barinu" (Epitaph on a nobleman [1818–20]), by M. A. Iakovlev (1798–1858), a poet, dramatist, journalist, translator, and student of French epigram; included in the excellent collection *Russkaia stikhotvornaia epitafiia,* ed. S. I. Nikolaev and T. S. Tsar'kova (St. Petersburg: Akademicheskii proekt, 1998), p. 243. My translation of Iakovlev's epigram doggerelizes the wittier original: "On barin byl i zhizn' po-barski provozhdal: / Poutru spal, el, pil; a noch'iu pil, el, spal."

4. See Reitzenstein, *Epigramm und Skolion: Ein Beitrag zur Geschichte der Alexandrinischen Dichtung* (Hildesheim: G. Olms, 1970); and Hutton, *The Greek Anthology.* The influence (relayed in part through Scaliger) of Martialian precepts like "Omne epigramma sit instar apis, sit aculeus illi, / Sint sua mella, sit & corporis exigui" (Let any epigram be like a bee: let it have its sting, / Its honey, and let it be of insignificant size) was, as Hutton shows, Europe-wide, influencing writers in Italy, France, Germany, England, and beyond; Petrarch, Boccaccio, Ariosto, Marot, Scève, and many others practiced it. Feofan Prokopovich (1681–1736), the archbishop of Pskov (and later of Novgorod) and a modernizing colleague of Peter I, wrote an important Scaliger-derived *De Arte Poetica* (1705) that transmitted the epigrammatic canons into Russia; chapters 4 to 7 of his "Liber III" (on non-epic, non-dramatic poetry) are devoted to epigram and include a discussion of its origins in inscription or "nadpis' " (see Feofan Prokopovich, *Sochineniia,* ed. I. P. Eremin [Moscow: Akademiia Nauk, 1961], pp. 317–30, 437–51). These principles were later themselves transmitted in verse, most famously by A.P. Sumarokov in his "Epistle on the Writing of Poetry" (1748); see *Russkaia epigramma (XVIII–XIX v.v.),* ed. V. Manuilov (Leningrad: Sovetskii pisatel', 1958), pp. 11–12.

5. From the important collection by Robert Bland et al., eds., *Collections from the Greek Anthology; and from the Pastoral, Elegiac and Dramatic Poets of Greece* (London: John Murray, 1813), p. 557. I have not identified the translator; the original was in Doric.

6. See Hartman, "Inscriptions and Romantic Nature Poetry," pp. 42–44; and idem, "Romantic Poetry and the Genius Loci," in *Beyond Formalism: Literary Essays 1958–1970* (New Haven: Yale University Press, 1970), pp. 311–36.

7. See Robert Arnold Aubin's fascinating survey *Topographical Poetry in XVIII-Century England* (New York: Modern Language Association of America, 1936).

8. For examples and discussion, see both ibid., and M. H. Abrams, "Structure and Style in the Greater Romantic Lyric," in idem, *The Correspondent Breeze: Essays on English Romanticism,* intro. Jack Stillinger (New York: W. W. Norton, 1984).

9. Of course, actually titled "Lines Composed a Few Miles above Tintern Abbey, on Revisiting the Banks of the Wye during a Tour. July 13, 1798."

10. See Abrams, "Structure and Style," esp. pp. 83–89, 103–108.

11. Hartman, "Inscriptions and Romantic Nature Poetry," p. 35.

12. Exemplary of the critical attitude I aspire to here is the one articulated by David Simpson in the chapter "Romanticism and Localism" in his *Academic Postmodern and the Rule of Literature: A Report on Half-Knowledge* (Chicago: University of Chicago Press, 1995), pp. 135–59.

13. See, especially, the section "Toward the Indescribable" in Alan Liu, *Wordsworth: The Sense of History* (Stanford: Stanford University Press, 1989), pp. 115–37. More generally, with the term "projection" I also hope to allude to the notion of "project" offered by Jean-Paul Sartre in *Search for a Method,* namely, "the subjective surpassing of objectivity toward objectivity, [. . .] stretched between the objective conditions of the environment and the objective structures of the field of possibles, represent[ing] *in itself* the moving unity of subjectivity and objectivity, those cardinal determinants of activity" (*Search for a Method,* trans. and intro. Hazel E. Barnes [New York: Vintage, 1963], p. 97). On the level of poetics, Charles Olson's notion of "projective verse" is pertinent here as well: "[T]he use of a man, by himself and thus by others, lies in how he conceives his relation to nature, that force to which he owes his somewhat small existence. [. . .] [T]he projective act, which is the artist's act in the larger field of objects, leads to dimensions larger than the man" ("Projective Verse" [1950], in Charles Olson, *Collected Prose,* ed. Donald Allen and Benjamin Friedlander, intro. Robert Creeley [Berkeley: University of California Press, 1997], p. 247).

14. Hartman, "Inscriptions and Romantic Nature Poetry," p. 32. See also Lessing's remarks in the *Zerstreute Anmerkungen über das Epigramm* (1771): "The true inscription is not to be thought of apart from that whereon it stands, or might stand. Both together make the whole from which arises the impression which, speaking generally, we ascribe to the inscription alone" (quoted in Hartman, "Inscriptions and Romantic Nature Poetry," p. 33).

15. Hartman, "Inscriptions and Romantic Nature Poetry," p. 24. For this reason, I prefer the "genius loci" concept to the more familiar trope of the poet's "Muse," inasmuch as the latter idea tends to imply the possibility of a purely private legitimation (at the expense, that is, of social intentionality) and therefore to frame the whole issue as purely a matter of the individual poet's choice, of "poetic personality" alone.

16. James Hutton, *The Greek Anthology in France to the Year 1800* (Ithaca: Cornell University Press, 1946), p. 70. It was through the verse of French writers like Chénier and Parny (whose *Poésies Erotiques* "may owe something to his conception of the style of the epigrams" [Hutton, ibid., p. 73]) that the revived "Greek" inscription exerted an influence on Russians like Pushkin and Baratynsky.

17. See, inter alia, William H. Sewell Jr., *A Rhetoric of Bourgeois Revolution: The Abbé Sieyès and "What Is the Third Estate?"* (Durham: University of North Carolina Press, 1994); and Ralph Gibson, *A Social History of French Catholicism: 1780–1914* (London: Routledge, 1989).

18. Hutton, *The Greek Anthology in France*, pp. 70, 74. Mediated by the French, the newly interpreted Anthology became powerfully influential in Russia as well; suffice it here to mention Batiushkov and Uvarov's 1820 essay "On the Greek Anthology." The new Hellenism coexists (in Russia and elsewhere) with incipient efforts to discover a specifically national purity, free of "the dust of antiquity and the rattling of foreign dialects" (quote from Aleksandr Bestuzhev-Marlinskii, "A Look at Old and New Writing in Russia" [1823] ["Vzgliad na staruiu i novuiu slovesnost' v Rossii," in *Dekabristy*, ed. Vladimir Orlov (Leningrad: Khudozhestvennaia literatura, 1975), 2:380–98; here p. 381]).

19. Hartman, "Inscriptions and Romantic Nature Poetry," p. 38.

20. Ibid. In turn, this "inverted" appellation may become a kind of norm or topos for later poets writing in elegiac modes. We find it, for example, in the locodescriptions "Homeland" ("Rodina" [1821]) and "Desolation" by Evgeny Baratynskii, a writer thoroughly familiar with Chénier and "anti-Classical classicism," and who might well have felt the Akensidean influence through intermediaries like Southey and Byron. The opening lines in question are (from "Homeland") "Ia vozvrashchusia k vam, polia moikh otsov" ("I shall return to you, fields of my fathers") and (from "Desolation") "Ia posetil tebia, plenitel'naia sen' " ("I visited you, fascinating canopy") (in E. A. Baratynskii, *Stikhotvoreniia i Poemy* [Moscow: Khudozhestvennaia literatura, 1982], pp. 48–50, 179–81).

21. Hartman, "Inscriptions and Romantic Nature Poetry," p. 38.

22. Here I am paraphrasing Hartman's comment that, in Wordsworth, "we are made to see the vital, if perverse, relationship of the solitary to his favorite spot" (ibid., p. 40).

23. Perry Anderson, "Marshall Berman: Modernity and Revolution," in idem, *A Zone of Engagement*, pp. 25–55 (London: Verso, 1992).

24. More recently Anderson has moved the "end of modernism" to a slightly later period, with the shift to "postmodernism" occurring through the 1950s and 1960s. Here I am more interested in using Anderson's shifting triangulation of conditions than in setting any hard-and-fast limits to period. See his *Origins of Postmodernity* (London: Verso, 1998).

25. Anderson, "Modernity and Revolution," p. 34.

26. Ibid., pp. 35–36.

27. See Fredric Jameson's remarks on anti-modernizing modernisms in his *Postmodernism, or, The Cultural Logic of Late Capitalism* (Durham: Duke University Press, 1991), pp. 302–13.

28. See, for example, Eric Hobsbawm, "From Feudalism to Capitalism," in idem, *The Transition from Feudalism to Capitalism*, intro. Rodney Hilton, pp. 159–64 (London: New Left Books, 1976); and Mike Davis, *Late Victorian Holocausts: El Niño Famines and the Making of the Third World* (London: Verso, 2001).

29. Certainly, I do not intend my use of "modernization" to invoke the progressivism of capitalist "modernization theory" or to reify the processes of historical change (and the conflicts that move them) as a kind of "force that rolls through all things," as Wordsworth might put it. The value of the term as a discursive shorthand is well articulated by Jonathan Crary: "Modernization becomes a useful notion when extracted from teleological and primarily economic determinations, and when it encompasses not only structural changes in political and economic formations but also the immense reorganization of knowledge, languages, networks of spaces and communications, and subjectivity itself.... Modernization is a process by which capitalism uproots and makes mobile that which is grounded, clears away or obliterates that which impedes circulation, and makes exchangeable what is singular. This applies as much to bodies, signs, images, languages, kinship relations, religious practices, and nationalities as it does to commodities, wealth, and labor power" (*Techniques of the Observer: On Vision and Modernity in the Nineteenth Century* [Cambridge, Mass.: MIT Press, 1990], p. 10).

30. Giovanni Arrighi, *The Long Twentieth Century: Money, Power, and the Origins of Our Times* (London: Verso, 1994).

31. Of course, literary history has long been attentive to the social roots of the great foundational shifts in representational modes during the Renaissance; to how, "in Rabelais, Cervantes, and Shakespeare, those vernacular giants, popular culture joins the learned muses. [. . . .] The 'vegetable gold' of great art is to bring Sancho Panza into relation with Don Quijote" (Geoffrey Hartman, "Toward Literary History," in idem, *Beyond Formalism*, pp. 377–78). I am also aware that the crisis of "modernity" I describe is plangently forecast in early modern rhetorical studies (and the "Logique du Port-Royal") as described by Franco Moretti: "The aim [of rhetoric] is not to ascertain an intersubjective truth but to enlist support for a *particular* system of values. In the seventeenth century—which witnessed the first great flowering of empirical science, and *at the same time* the collapse of all social 'organicity' in the fight to the death between opposing faiths and interest[s]—the perception of this contrast was extremely acute" (*Signs Taken for Wonders: Essays in the Sociology of Literary Forms*, trans. Susan Fischer, David Forgacs, and David Miller [London: Verso, 1997], p. 3).

32. This point is strongly made in Fredric Jameson's recent précis of Anderson's argument: "[Anderson's] proposition is not that the artists of the modern occupy the same space as these new social forces, nor even manifest any ideological sympathy for or existential knowledge of them; but rather that they feel that force of gravity at a distance, and that their own vocation for aesthetic change and new and more radical artistic practices finds itself powerfully reinforced and intensified by the dawning conviction that radical change is simultaneously at large in the social world outside" (quoted from *A Singular Modernity: Essay on the Ontology of the Present* [London: Verso, 2002], p. 134).

33. Fredric Jameson, *The Political Unconscious: Narrative as a Socially Symbolic Act* (Ithaca: Cornell, 1981), pp. 75–99.

34. Quoted in Fredric Jameson, "Reification and Utopia in Mass Culture," in idem, *Signatures of the Visible* (New York: Routledge, 1992).

35. For a lucid "ideologeme"-focused discussion of the conflicting "corporate and individualist idioms" that emerged out of this motto in the postrevolutionary period, see William H. Sewell Jr., *Work and Revolution in France: The Language*

of Labor from the Old Regime to 1848 (Cambridge: Cambridge University Press, 1980), pp. 279–81.

36. Jameson, *The Political Unconscious*, pp. 95–96.

37. Ibid., p. 98.

38. Quoted from Jürgen Habermas, "Excursus on Schiller's 'Letters on the Aesthetic Education of Man,' " in *The Philosophical Discourse of Modernity: Twelve Lectures*, trans. Frederick Lawrence (Cambridge, Mass.: MIT Press, 1990), p. 45. Schiller's *On the Aesthetic Education of Man in a Series of Letters* was first published in 1795. Cf. Moretti's contention that "the substantial function of literature is to *secure consent*. To make individuals feel 'at ease' in the world they happen to live in, to reconcile them in a pleasant and imperceptible way to its prevailing cultural norms" (*Signs Taken for Wonders*, p. 8).

39. Habermas, "Excursus on Schiller's 'Letters,' " p. 48.

40. Friedrich Schiller, *On the Aesthetic Education of Man in a Series of Letters*, ed., trans., and intro. Elizabeth M. Wilkinson and L. A. Willoughby (Oxford: Clarendon, 1967), esp. pp. 103–107.

41. Jacques Rancière, "The Aesthetic Revolution and Its Outcomes: Emplotments of Autonomy and Heteronomy," *New Left Review*, second series, 14 (March–April 2002): 133–51. Elsewhere Rancière has given an apt summary of the relationship in Schiller's thought between art and community formation within modernity: "It was [Schiller's *On the Aesthetic Education of Man*] that determined the notion that domination and servitude are above all ontological distributions (the activity of thought vs. the passivity of sensuous matter), and [which] defined a neutral state, a state of double negation wherein the activity of thought and sensible receptivity become a single reality, constituted as a new region of being [. . .] that makes thinkable the equality that the French Revolution, according to Schiller, showed to be impossible to materialize directly. It is this specific mode of habitation within the sensible world which must be developed by 'aesthetic education' in order to form humans capable of living in a free political community" (*Le Partage du Sensible: Esthétique et Politique* [Paris: La Fabrique, 2000], pp. 39–40).

42. T. J. Clark expresses this aspiration perfectly in his book on modernism in painting: "Modernism had two great wishes. It wanted its audience to be led toward a recognition of the social reality of the sign [. . .]; but equally it dreamed of turning the sign back to a bedrock of World / Nature / Sensation / Subjectivity which the to and fro of capitalism had all but destroyed. [. . .] [Modernism involves] a desperate, marvelous shuttling between a fantasy of cold artifice and an answering one of immediacy and being-in-the-world" (*Farewell to an Idea: Episodes from a History of Modernism* [New Haven: Yale University Press, 1999], pp. 9–10).

43. There are, of course, more direct modes of fashioning community—the conscious formation of groups or schools, seeking out patronage, the writing of criticism—in which poets participate; my readings will stress (by contrast) how the poems themselves allegorize their historical situation and social ambitions while also touching on the more direct interventions.

44. William Wordsworth, "Preface to *Lyrical Ballads, with Pastoral and Other Poems* [1802]," in idem, *The Poems*, ed. John O. Hayden, 2 vols. (London: Penguin Books, 1977), 1:867–96; here pp. 870–71.

45. Ibid., pp. 870, 873.

46. "The most effective of these causes are the great national events which are daily taking place, and the increasing accumulation of men in cities, where the uniformity of their occupations produces a craving for extraordinary incident, which the rapid communication of intelligence hourly gratifies" (ibid., pp. 872–73).

47. "The Man of Science seeks truth as a remote and unknown benefactor; he cherishes and loves it in his solitude: the Poet, singing a song in which all human beings join with him, rejoices in the presence of truth as our visible friend and hourly companion" (ibid., p. 881).

48. Eric Hobsbawm, *The Age of Extremes: A History of the World, 1914–1991* (New York: Vintage Books, 1994), pp. 21–222.

49. As Anderson writes: "After 1945, the old semi-aristocratic or agrarian order and its appurtenances were finished, in every [European] country. Bourgeois democracy was finally universalized. With that, certain critical links with a pre-capitalist past were snapped. At the same time, Fordism arrived in force. Mass production and consumption transformed the West European economies along North American lines. There could no longer be the smallest doubt as to what kind of society this technology would consolidate: an oppressively stable, monolithically industrial, capitalist civilization was now in place" ("Modernity and Revolution," p. 37). Anderson might have added a reference to the Soviet Union, where in the postwar years the Stalinism that had consumed aristocracy, bourgeoisie, intelligentsia, and peasantry alike in its statist and modernizing delirium could be seen to have left behind a structure and legacy of repressive conservatism that proved essentially indelible, despite all efforts at reform—this, even while Leninist ideas, petrified into dogma in the USSR itself, showed ongoing fertility in the de-colonizing "Third World." In the more recent *Origins of Postmodernity*, Anderson has moved the endpoint of modernism somewhere around twenty years later (taking into account central late modernisms like those of the Abstract Expressionists, the Situationists, and Godard) but retains the same general scheme of explanation.

50. Of course, the conceptions and period framings of postmodernism are diverse, although most do indeed regard the date "1945" as salient. For fuller treatments, see Simpson, *The Academic Postmodern and the Rule of Literature*, pp. 1–21; and Stephen Best and Douglas Kellner, eds., *Postmodern Theory: Critical Interrogations* (New York: Guilford, 1991).

51. Ben Jonson, "An Epitaph," in *The Complete Poetry of Ben Jonson*, ed. William B. Hunter Jr. (New York: W. W. Norton, 1968), p. 172. All further citations from Jonson's poetry are from this edition, with page numbers cited in parentheses.

52. These ideas of latency, and of unblossomed or limited existence and its commemoration in inscription, have already been linked to later developments in the lyric. Geoffrey Hartman speaks of the tendency of inscription to convey a "sense for a life (in nature) so hidden, retired, or anonymous that it is perceived only with difficulty. [. . . .] The lines [. . .] describe a person who has (1) lived unknown, in retirement, and (2) lived an unknown life. He resembles one of the 'unhonour'd Dead' whose 'artless tale' Gray begins to reveal in his 'Elegy.' The anonymity of nature and the anonymity of the common man join to produce an elegiac tenor of feeling" ("Inscriptions and Romantic Nature Poetry," p. 33).

53. This suggests, perhaps, another way of accounting for that notorious too-simple-to-analyze quality of the Jonsonian "plain style" (although not, of

course, of all his lyrics). Cf. Wesley Trimpi, *Ben Jonson's Poems: A Study of the Plain Style* (Stanford: Stanford University Press, 1962); and John Gordon Nichols, *The Poetry of Ben Jonson* (London: Routledge and Kegan Paul, 1969).

54. For a demonstration of the reliance of the Jonsonian epitaph on religious machinery, see Joshua Scodel, *The English Poetic Epitaph: Commemoration and Conflict from Jonson to Wordsworth* (Ithaca: Cornell University Press, 1991), esp. pp. 80–85.

55. My use of "epitaph" here to designate "inscription prior to being effectively de-linked from metaphysical authority" is also my own pragmatic inflection of the term, for the purposes of exposition. Other approaches to epitaph are readily available; see, for example, Paul Fry's superb discussion of epitaph as "the poetic search for burial" in the chapter "The Absent Dead: Wordsworth, Byron, and the Epitaph" in *A Defense of Poetry: Reflections on the Occasion of Writing* (Stanford: Stanford University Press, 1995), pp. 159–80; here p. 159.

56. "Michael: A Pastoral Poem" (1800), in William Wordsworth, *The Poems*, ed. John O. Hayden (London: Penguin Books, 1977), 1:455, ll. 1–2. All further references to "Michael" are to this edition, with line numbers indicated in parentheses.

57. Cf. Lotman, "The Poetics of Everyday Culture in Russian Eighteenth Century Culture," trans. N. F. C. Owen: "The trend towards fragmentation in Romantic texts has long been noted. However, it is vital to emphasize that this fragmentation was compensated for by plunging the text, once it had been fixed graphically (in print or manuscript), into the context of oral legend about the author's personality" (in Yu. M. Lotman and B. A. Uspenskij, *The Semiotics of Russian Culture*, ed. Ann Shukman [Ann Arbor: Michigan Slavic Contributions, 1984], p. 252).

58. Northrop Frye gives a succinct account of this inscriptive "stoppage effect," of the way it leads to a passage from object to story: "The private poem often takes off from something that blocks normal activity, something a poet has to write poetry about instead of carrying on with ordinary experience. This block has traditionally been frustrated love [. . . .] In another lyrical genre the block relates to the reader rather than the poet: this is what we find in the epitaph convention that we have had from Greek times on. Here the reader is assumed to be a traveler, pursuing his normal course through time and space, who is suddenly confronted with something he should stop and read. What he reads is the verbal essence of a life which has once had its own context in space and time but is now enclosed in a framework of words" ("Approaching the Lyric," in *Lyric Poetry: Beyond New Criticism*, ed. Chaviva Hosek and Patricia Parker [Ithaca: Cornell University Press, 1985], p. 32).

59. See David Simpson, *Wordsworth's Historical Imagination: The Poetry of Displacement* (New York: Methuen, 1987), pp. 145–46.

60. About "Michael," Wordsworth wrote in 1801, "I have attempted to give a picture of a man, of strong mind and lively sensibility, agitated by two of the most powerful affections of the human heart; the parental affection, and the love of property, landed property, including the feelings of inheritance, home, and personal and family independence" (letter to Thomas Poole of April 9, 1801; quoted in Wordsworth, *The Poems*, p. 969).

61. James K. Chandler, *Wordsworth's Second Nature: A Study of the Poetry and Politics* (Chicago and London: University of Chicago Press, 1984), p. 167. I certainly agree with Chandler that Wordsworth ultimately fears change (cf. p. 92);

however, the poet's sense (perhaps unconscious) of the inevitability of change forces him to imagine ideal, *new* continuities that try to hide their novelty.

62. Cf. David Bromwich's comments on "Michael" in his book on Wordsworth: "To interpret the symbolism of the covenant [between Michael and Luke] there has been much talk by critics about Abraham and Isaac. But God was in that story, and the prospect of a sacrifice of life itself. Michael's explanation with Luke, as he asks him to lay the stone, is an old man's speech to his son, in an assertion of human nature" (*Disowned by Memory: Wordsworth's Poetry of the 1790s* [Chicago: University of Chicago Press, 1998], p. 162).

63. " 'Preface' to *Lyrical Ballads,*" in Wordsworth, *The Poems,* p. 873.

64. "There is a suggestion of a man worn down in the grind of daily custom, but also of his sheer absorption in the scene, with pauses of thought or feeling: these utterly distinct possibilities are held in suspense—an ambiguity of life as much as poetry" (Bromwich, *Disowned by Memory,* p. 161).

65. In writing about "corporeality," I am strongly influenced by Fry's notion of "ostension" as articulated in his *Defense of Poetry*. Fry isolates two "non-signifying moments" in language—the "indicative" and the "phonic-scriptive"—which together constitute the field in which poetry (or, for Fry, literature as such) does its work. "Indication" is index, the mere "saying that something just is"; the "phonic-scriptive" is the raw "material character" of language, its status as sound and "uninterpreted trace"—think of rhyme, of echo, of the sheer physicality of the inscribed grapheme (p. 54). In literature, both these moments, while essential to the usual logical, associative, discursive, and, in my terms, projective functions of language, estrange themselves from all those "predicative" tasks, come into their own as realities of language, and thereby place a momentary block in the pathways of signification. This estrangement, Fry argues, "suspend[s] the instrumentality of language": "[This] structure [...] reduces the estranged, necessarily 'situated' utterance to sound and trace, and thus returns it to the unsignifying sphere of actuality, of things in themselves, from which history for its part is by nature forever estranged. Literature, then, is that mode of utterance which lays bare the irreducible distance between history and actuality from the *parti pris* of the latter" (p. 56). Fry's distinctive emphasis on the "communitarian" potential of this structure is of particular relevance to my discussion of inscription here: he writes tellingly (in a reading of Wordsworth's "Lucy" poems) of how poetry, in its indexical and inscriptive dimensions, turns our attention toward nothing less than "our mineral community" (p. 105), and later of Byron adapting "the language of commoners to a *lingua communis* that could express the community of our wide, bare existence" (p. 180). In the chapter "Disposing of the Body: The Common Sense of the Romantic Moment of Dying," Fry argues convincingly for a "romantic moment of death" that expresses what he calls genuine *common sense:* " 'Common': universal yet proletarian in an unenclosed [boundless] field [bounded]; 'sense': bodily experience of pleasure or pain which is also a coherence, a logic" (p. 185). Other similar and comparable (though less refined) indexes of "non-significance" in literary theory include Gerald Bruns's account of modern poetry as "nondiscourse" disclosing "the being of the world" (*Modern Poetry and the Idea of Language* [New Haven: Yale University Press, 1974], pp. 195–205), and the various Barthesian "grains" (of voice, of writing, of performing limb) (cf. Roland Barthes, "The Grain of the Voice," in *Image Music Text,* ed. and trans. Stephen Heath [New York: Hill and Wang, 1977], p. 188).

66. Here I have in mind the (probably now familiar) distinction between the "phenomenality" and "materiality" of signs, where the former term suggests the ability of signs concretely to intimate the non-signifying world in some way, and the latter the likelihood that, in T. J. Clark's words, signs "do *not* analogize or open onto 'sensations' or 'phenomena': that they posit a lack or failure of any such opening or analogy; and that they do so precisely in their material individuality as marks—their atomized facticity, their separateness" ("Phenomenality and Materiality in Cézanne," in *Material Events: Paul de Man and the Afterlife of Theory,* ed. Tom Cohen, Barbara Cohen, J. Hillis Miller, and Andrzej Warminski [Minneapolis: University of Minnesota Press, 2001], p. 102). I should add that I think Fry's notion of "ostension" manages to overcome this opposition in a way, by conceiving of "non-signification" as an effect emerging out of the structure of language itself. To argue this here, however, would get a bit involved.

67. Susan Stewart eloquently expresses the relation between inscription and the need (like Michael's) to create a significant world: "Speech leaves no mark in space; like gesture, it exists in its immediate context and can reappear only in another's voice, another's body, even if that other is the same speaker transformed by history. But writing contaminates; writing leaves its trace, a trace beyond the life of the body. Thus, while speech gains authenticity, writing promises immortality, or at least the immortality of the material world in contrast to the mortality of the body. Our terror of the unmarked grave is a terror of the insignificance of a world without writing. The metaphor of the unmarked grave is one which joins the mute and the ambivalent; without the mark there is no boundary, no point at which to begin the repetition. Writing gives us a device for inscribing space, for inscribing nature: the lovers' names carved in bark, the slogans on the bridge, and the strangely uniform and idiosyncratic hand that has tattooed the subways" (*On Longing: Narratives of the Miniature, the Gigantic, the Souvenir, the Collection* [Durham: Duke University Press, 1993], p. 31).

68. Nothing makes this clearer than the works of the greatest utopian, Fourier, who is continually finding in nature its own suggestions for ideal organization; see, for example, the section titled "The Passions" in *Harmonian Man: Selected Writings of Charles Fourier,* trans. Susan Hanson, ed. Mark Poster (Garden City, N.Y.: Anchor Books, 1971).

69. Cf. Jameson on Durkheim and Heidegger in *The Political Unconscious:* "Durkheim's view of religion [. . .] as a symbolic affirmation of human relationships, along with Heidegger's conception of the work of art as a symbolic enactment of the relationship of human beings to the nonhuman, to Nature and to Being, are in this society false and ideological; but they will know their truth and come into their own at the end of what Marx calls prehistory. At that moment, then, the problem of the opposition of the ideological to the Utopian, or the functional-instrumental to the collective, will have become a false one" (p. 293).

70. Hartman (writing about Wordsworth's "Resolution and Independence"), "Romantic Poetry and the Genius Loci," in idem, *Beyond Formalism,* p. 333. "Wordsworth would not be so centrally concerned with the character of his leading genius unless prompted by the hope that an enlightened poetry—the union of poetical genius with English spirit of place—was possible. The hope, this union, is the very 'consummation' for which his poetry aims to be the 'spousal verse' " (p. 329).

71. For two recent, probing sets of variations on this paradox, see Susan Buck-Morss, *Dreamworld and Catastrophe: The Passing of Mass Utopia in East and*

West (Cambridge, Mass.: MIT Press, 2000), pp. 2–39; and Moira Inés Fradinger, "Radical Evil: Literary Visions of Political Origins in Sophocles, Sade, and Vargas Llosa," Ph.D. dissertation, Yale University, 2003.

72. An analysis of the problems that real revolutions (specifically the Russian one) have in actually overcoming the local/international division is the burden of E. H. Carr's *Studies in Revolution* (New York: Grosset and Dunlap, 1964), esp. 134–227. For an incisive analysis of the dialectic of national and international from the eighteenth century to the present, see Perry Anderson, "Internationalism: A Breviary," *New Left Review,* second series, 14 (March–April 2002): 5–25.

73. "French Revolution as It Appeared to Enthusiasts at Its Commencement, Reprinted from 'The Friend,' " in Wordsworth, *The Poems,* pp. 636–37, ll. 5–17, 32–40; better known as lines 105–44 of *The Prelude,* bk. 11.

74. For an important effort to reinvent it for our time, see Michael Hardt and Antonio Negri, *Empire* (Cambridge, Mass.: Harvard University Press, 2000).

75. This is not to say, of course, that the effects of commercial signage on literature emerge exclusively after World War II. In *Advertising Fictions: Literature, Advertising, and Social Reading* (New York: Columbia University Press, 1988), Jennifer Wicke argues for an important dialectic between literature and advertising stretching back to the 1840s, and some of my reflections on Baudelaire (in this preface and in chapter 2) are influenced by her approach. Andrew Cowell has recently argued that medieval advertisement (the "boniment") actually "founds poetic textuality in the High Middle Ages" ("Advertising, Rhetoric, and Literature: A Medieval Response to Contemporary Theory," *Poetics Today* 22, no. 4 [winter 2001]: 765–94). My own comments here follow Anderson's suggestion that, in the post-sixties "spectacular" world, the main promulgator of culture has become the global market; on that speculative basis, I explore the kind of poetic textuality this change might imply (see Anderson, *The Origins of Postmodernity,* pp. 111–14). See also Fredric Jameson, *Marxism and Form* (Princeton, N.J.: Princeton University Press, 1971), pp. 104–105.

76. For an exploration of this commodifying function of signage—an exploration that might be used as the basis for a "poetics" of advertising—see Naomi Klein, *No Logo* (London: Flamingo, 2000).

77. *Advertisements,* on the other hand, are often at pains to invest product, store, and company names with historical resonance, although more nostalgic than elegiac; the archaizing (or "neoarchaizing," to use Edgar Morin's term) aspect of signage is generally limited to font style and background.

78. Perhaps the distinction between inscription and sign can add another dimension to Walter Benjamin's well-known observations on the role of architecture within a "culture of distraction" in "The Work of Art in the Age of Mechanical Reproduction," particularly if we think of the sign as a specific style of *access* to the built environment: "Buildings are appropriated in a twofold manner: by use and by perception—or rather, by touch and sight. Such appropriation cannot be understood in terms of the attentive concentration of a tourist before a famous building. On the tactile side there is no counterpart to contemplation on the visual side. Tactile appropriation is accomplished not so much by attention as by habit. As regards architecture, habit determines to a large extent even optical reception. The latter, too, occurs much less through rapt attention than by noticing the object in incidental fashion" (in *Illuminations,* ed. Hannah Arendt, trans. Harry Zohn [New York: Schocken Books, 1968], pp. 239–40.)

79. The relevant passage is in Jakobson's essay, "Futurism," in *Language and Literature,* ed. Krystyna Pomorska and Stephen Rudy (Cambridge, Mass.: Belknap Press of Harvard University Press, 1987), p. 32: "Perceptions, in multiplying, become mechanized; objects, not being perceived, are taken on faith. Painting battles against the automatization of perception; it signals the object. But, having become antiquated, artistic forms are also perceived on faith. Cubism and Futurism [therefore] widely use the device of impeded perception [....] A picture that gives itself with such reserve expects precisely that it will be questioned again and again."

80. Rolf Dieter Brinkmann, *Künstliches Licht,* ed. Genia Schulz (Stuttgart: Reclam, 1994), p. 111. Brinkmann's work, saturated with detail and pop-cultural references, is still not well known in this country but has generated great interest in Germany. Prolific as a visual artist and prose writer in addition to his lyrical work, he died in a car crash in 1975 in London at the age of thirty-five. See Rainer Kramer, *Auf der Suche nach dem verlorenen Augenblick: Rolf Dieter Brinkmanns innerer Krieg in Italien* (Bremen: Edition Temmen, 1999). The poem discussed here appeared in Brinkmann's finest collection, the posthumously published *Westwärts 1 & 2* (Reinbek: Rowohlt Verlag, 1975).

81. The title might be better translated as "written *on* an Italian square," as that English preposition manages to imply both location and (in the accusative) dedication (the dominant sense here of the German *auf*).

82. Cf. Franco Moretti on the use of ads in *Ulysses:* "To diffuse its essential content, advertising aims at a form of persuasion based on unawareness, rapid and deep because capable of circumventing all intellectual resistance. Advertising then becomes part of stream of consciousness to the point of dominating its mechanisms and organizing to its own advantage Cassirer's 'loss of self' and Eco's absence of boundaries between 'inside and outside.'... To be able to sell anything, that is, to spread out over the entire social universe; 'All kinds of places are good for ads' Bloom reflects..." (*Signs Taken for Wonders,* p. 196).

83. On Laforgue, see Christopher Prendergast, *Paris and the Nineteenth Century* (Oxford: Blackwell, 1992), pp. 193–200.

84. "On my first sonne," p. 20.

85. Quoted from Friedrich Hölderlin, *Gedichte,* ed. Jochen Schmidt (Frankfurt am Main: Insel, 1984).

86. Quoted from *Friedrich Hölderlin: Hymns and Fragments,* trans. and intro. Richard Sieburth (Princeton, N.J.: Princeton University Press, 1984).

87. "Apostrophe," in *The Pursuit of Signs: Semiotics, Literature, Deconstruction* (Ithaca: Cornell University Press, 1981), pp. 149–50.

88. *The Academic Postmodern and the Rule of Literature,* esp. pp. 96–98, 165–68.

89. To take one non-poetic but remarkable example: Jonathan Crary has discovered an extraordinary anticipation of Brinkmann's Piazza poem in a letter of Freud to his family from September 22, 1907, where Freud describes another Roman square, the Piazza Colonna, on which he finds a new environment of "magic lantern slides... cinematic projections, and the electrically lit advertisements" dissolve the previous "axial" and "monumental organization of the square." That Freud effectively ignores the grand column ("colonna") at the center of the square is taken by Crary as "a sign of the installation of a new temporality which subsists as a dehistoricized perpetual present, wavering between boredom and absorption, between self-extinguishing immersion in the crowd and unbearable social solitude" (*Suspensions of Perception: Attention, Spectacle and*

Modern Culture [Cambridge, Mass.: MIT Press, 1999], pp. 366, 369). Ascribing any direct reference to Freud's description within Brinkmann's "Hymn" would doubtless be going too far—tempting though that would be!

1. Lifeless Things

1. Samuel Johnson, "An Essay on Epitaphs" (1740), in *Selected Essays*, ed. and intro. David Womersley (London: Penguin Books, 2003), pp. 509–17; here p. 510 (italics in original). All further citations from Johnson's "Essay" are from this edition, with page numbers cited in parentheses.

2. A phrase used in Colin Jones's and Dror Wahrman's introduction (entitled "An Age of Cultural Revolutions?") to their edited collection *The Age of Cultural Revolutions: Britain and France, 1750–1820* (Berkeley: University of California Press, 2002), p. 13.

3. "Pope," *Lives of the English Poets*, ed. George Birkbeck Hill, 3 vols. (Hildesheim: Georg Olms, 1968 [reprint of Oxford 1905 edition]), 3:263–64. The phrase about "no character at all" evidently comes from Pope's *Moral Essays*, II.2, and actually reads: "Most women have no characters at all" (quoted in ibid., p. 263).

4. William Wordsworth, "Essay upon Epitaphs," in *The Prose Works of William Wordsworth*, ed. W. J. B. Owen and Jane Worthington Smyser (Oxford: Clarendon, 1974), 2:43–119; here p. 56. All further citations from Wordsworth's "Essay" are from this edition, with page numbers cited in parentheses.

5. "[I]f it be the *actions* of a man, or even some one conspicuous or beneficial act of local or general utility, which have distinguished him, and excited a desire that he should be remembered, then, of course, ought the attention to be directed chiefly to those actions or that act. . . ." (p. 61).

6. Cf. Paul Fry's comment to the effect that, in privileging poetry's non-signifying or "ostensive" aspects, "no assumption or production of special value need be involved, unless indeed the acknowledgement that calendar art, greeting card poetry, and the ambiance footage in films of every description are all privileged sites of the ostensive be taken for an endorsement of popular culture. As perhaps it should be: one has only to detach the aesthetics of form and the apparatus of literacy from the ostensive instinct to see that it is not a coterie emotion at all but a radically democratic one that is not historically (epochally or socially) determined" (*A Defense of Poetry*, p. 29). On cliché in Wordsworth and its role in undoing "the separation of literary (hieratic) and common speech," see Geoffrey H. Hartman, "The Unremarkable Poet," in idem, *The Unremarkable Wordsworth*, intro. Donald G. Marshall (Minneapolis: University of Minnesota Press, 1987), pp. 207–19; here p. 213.

7. Thomas W. Laqueur, "The Places of the Dead in Modernity," in Jones and Wahrman, *The Age of Cultural Revolutions*, pp. 17–32; here pp. 26, 29–30. Laqueur mordantly observes that the new cemeteries could attain their smooth, reified appearance only through macabre (and class-driven) cost cutting: "The dirty secret was that in fact the new cemeteries could survive economically only by egregious cheating on the one grave, one body program of the public health reformers. Whether in the *fosse commune* of the French cemetery or the British shaft graves that, with careful planning, could hold thirty or forty bodies, the poor

subsidized the middle classes. Unlike the churchyard imagined by [Thomas] Gray, the nineteenth-century cemetery could be 'read' by, and was readable for, them alone" (p. 30).

8. For an account of the "semiotic rectangle" and its functions, see Jameson, *The Political Unconscious,* pp. 46–49.

9. "The Pettichaps Nest," in John Clare, *Selected Poetry and Prose,* ed. Merryn Williams and Raymond Williams (London: Methuen, 1986), pp. 139–40.

10. See Marilyn Gaull, "Clare and the 'Dark System,' " in *John Clare in Context,* ed. Hugh Haughton, Adam Phillips, and Geoffrey Summerfield (Cambridge: Cambridge University Press, 1994), p. 291. Gaull writes elsewhere: "Largely because of its social implications, ornithology became the most popular scientific discipline. As ornaments or status symbols, birds had been bred, hunted, stuffed, and cooked; they had appeared caged in libraries and ornamental gardens, in poetry, heraldry, hats, porcelains, and textiles." Such works as White's *History,* "Thomas Bewick's *A History of British Birds* (1797–1803), and George Montague's *Comprehensive Ornithological Dictionary; or Alphabetical Synopsis of British Birds* (1802), along with inexpensive and widely distributed handbooks and periodicals, helped to educate a reading public in the procedures and pleasure of observing birds in their natural setting while encouraging the exchange of information" (Marilyn Gaull, *English Romanticism: The Human Context* [New York: W. W. Norton, 1988], p. 367).

11. Letter LVII of the *Natural History of Selborne* (addressed "to the Honourable Daines Barrington") contains White's own description of the pettichaps, a description Clare surely knew: "A rare, and I think a new little bird frequent my garden, which I have great reason to think is the pettichaps: it is common in some parts of the kingdom, and I have received formerly several dead specimens from Gibraltar. This bird much resembles the white-throat, but has a more white or rather silvery breast and belly; is restless and active, like the willow-wrens, and hops from bough to bough, examining every part for food; it also runs up the stems of the crown-imperials, and, putting its head into the bells of those flowers, sips the liquor which stands in the nectarium of each petal. Sometimes it feeds on the ground, like the hedge-sparrow, by hopping about on the grass-plots and mown walks" (Rev. Gilbert White, A.M., *The Natural History of Selborne, Observations on Various Parts of Nature; and The Naturalist's Calendar,* 3rd ed. [Edinburgh: Fraser, 1834], p. 259).

12. "[Clare's] conception of [his] correspondence . . . was such that he imaginatively placed himself at the center of a complex convivial network working together towards a vision of a new era of democratic art" (Alan D. Vardy, *John Clare, Politics and Poetry* [Houndmills: Palgrave Macmillan, 2003], p. 190).

13. This double alienation, always and necessarily pointed to in discussions of Clare, is perhaps best delineated by Merryn and Raymond Williams, who write of Clare's as "a class consciousness which is most sharply experienced as an alienated individual consciousness; the knowledge of a spectrum of deprivation which, as he directly experiences it, really does run from the more readily acknowledged and recorded facts of low wages and high prices, the humiliations of hirings, to the more painful and sometimes more immediate recognition of limited knowledge, limited interests, limited tolerance of other possible ways" (in their introduction to John Clare's *Selected Poetry and Prose,* p. 16).

14. Natural history had its own poetic tradition, of course, going at least as far back as Erasmus Darwin's *Loves of the Plants* (1789).

15. This impression is closely related to the illusion of painterly surface created by Clare's poems, which has been noted by readers from the beginning (see the introduction to Clare's first volume, *Poems Descriptive of Rural Life and Scenery* [1820] by his editor, John Taylor, as reprinted in *Clare: The Critical Heritage,* ed. Mark Storey [London: Routledge and Kegan Paul, 1973], pp. 47–50).

16. Fredric Jameson, "Baudelaire as Modernist and Postmodernist: The Dissolution of the Referent and the Artificial 'Sublime,' " in *Lyric Poetry: Beyond New Criticism,* ed. Chaviva Hosek and Patricia Parker (Ithaca and London: Cornell University Press, 1985), pp. 247–63; here p. 253.

17. The Enclosure Act for Clare's native Helpstone was promulgated in 1809. On Clare and enclosure, see John Barrell, *The Idea of Landscape and the Sense of Place: An Approach to the Poetry of John Clare* (Cambridge: Cambridge University Press, 1972).

18. For an excellent Bachelard-influenced discussion of the larger implications of "nest" and "nesting" in Clare's poetry, and of how the nest becomes for Clare "an image of the material imagination itself, a model of poetic form, an instance of how form itself is a model for being in the world," see Hugh Haughton, "Progress and Rhyme: 'The Nightingale's Nest' and Romantic Poetry," in Haughton, Phillips, and Summerfield, *John Clare in Context,* pp. 50–86; here p. 72.

19. Crary, *Techniques of the Observer,* p. 145.

20. Crary, *Suspensions of Perception,* p. 12.

21. James Thomson, "The Seasons" ("Spring" [1728]), in *The Complete Poetical Works of James Thomson,* ed. J. Logie Robertson (London: Henry Frowde for Oxford University Press, 1908), pp. 38–39, ll. 950–62. The passage is quoted in Barrell, *The Idea of Landscape and the Sense of Place,* p. 14.

22. On the relation of "prospect" poetry to mountain pilgrimage, see Marjorie Hope Nicolson, *Mountain Gloom and Mountain Glory: The Development of the Aesthetics of the Infinite* (New York: W. W. Norton, 1959), pp. 1–19, 289–358.

23. Barrell, *The Idea of Landscape and the Sense of Place,* pp. 21, 24. Common to Thomson's and the painter Claude Lorrain's attitude to landscape, argues Barrell, is an insistence that "it must keep its distance, and the features within it be kept in subjection to our sense of the general composition" (p. 24).

24. Ibid., p. 96.

25. As far as Clare reception in our own day is concerned, we might relate this predicament to the ongoing controversy about Clare's punctuation; his irregularities in this area (which Clare himself may well have wished to at least partially regularize) serve to sustain at once our (modernist) appreciation of the materiality of his verse and the "peasant poet" cliché. For a discussion of the punctuation debate, see Hugh Haughton's and Adam Phillips's "Introduction: Relocating John Clare," in Haughton, Phillips, and Summerfield, *John Clare in Context,* pp. 15–22.

26. Henri Lefebvre, *The Production of Space,* trans. Donald Nicholson-Smith (Oxford: Blackwell, 1991), p. 231.

27. "The effects of the division of labour, in the general business of society, will be more easily understood, by considering in what manner it operates in some particular manufactures. [. . .] in those trifling manufactures which are destined to supply the small wants of but a small number of people, the whole number of workmen must necessarily be small; and those employed in every different branch of the work can often be collected into the same workhouse, and placed

at once under the view of the spectator. In those great manufactures, on the contrary, which are destined to supply the great wants of the great body of the people, every different branch of the work employs so great a number of workmen, that it is impossible to collect them all into the same workhouse. We can seldom see more, at one time, than those employed in one single branch. Though in such manufactures, therefore, the work may really be divided into a much great number of parts, than in those of a more trifling nature, the division is not near so obvious, and has accordingly been much less observed" (from Adam Smith, *An Inquiry into the Nature and Causes of the Wealth of Nations,* ed. R. H. Campbell and A. S. Skinner, 2 vols. [Oxford: Clarendon, 1976], 1:14).

28. See the section in this chapter on monuments, below.

29. Certainly many have observed a tendency of this kind; for a discussion, see Fredric Jameson, "Ontology and Utopia," *L'Esprit Createur* 34, no. 4 (winter 1994): 47–48.

30. Cf. Harold Bloom's comments on the overtones of Wordsworthian unity in the poem (in *Shelley's Mythmaking* [Ithaca: Cornell University Press, 1959], p. 20); and Frances Ferguson, "Shelley's 'Mont Blanc': What the Mountain Said," in Michael O'Neill, ed., *Shelley,* intro. idem (London: Longman, 1993), p. 45.

31. The latter position is taken by John Rieder in one of the best readings the poem has received: "[...] 'Mont Blanc,' the enlightened local poem, needs to destroy the illusions of the ground if only that the poet may then find a ground for his illusions" ("Shelley's 'Mont Blanc': Landscape and the Ideology of the Sacred Text," *ELH: English Literary History* 48 [1981]: 778–98; here p. 796).

32. "Mont Blanc (Lines Written in the Vale of Chamouni)," in *Shelley's Poetry and Prose,* ed. Donald H. Reiman and Sharon B. Powers (New York: W. W. Norton, 1977), p. 90, l. 40. All quotes from "Mont Blanc" are from this edition, with line numbers cited in parentheses.

33. See Earl R. Wasserman, *Shelley: A Critical Reading* (Baltimore: Johns Hopkins University Press, 1971), pp. 230–35. "The symbolic scene that has given birth to the poem is splendidly equipped to represent the relation of the transcendent Power to the world of human experience: the gleaming and eternal snow of the mountain peak that symbolizes the inaccessible Power descends as glaciers, which melt into streams that become the river Arve in the ravine. [...] The glaciers, streams, and river, being successive transformations of the transcendent snow, are representations of the consecutiveness whereby the motionless Power manifests itself in the realm of mutability and supply sensory evidence of the Power's necessary and amoral law" (pp. 234–35).

34. Ibid., p. 225.

35. See Christian Metz, *The Imaginary Signifier: Psychoanalysis and the Cinema,* trans. Celia Britton et al. (Bloomington: Indiana University Press, 1982), pp. 42–57.

36. Paul H. Fry stresses this point in his reading of the poem: "Shelley's fantasy steadies him while he faces the 'Dizzy Ravine,' which in retrospect is no longer the valley of the Arve or even its Idea, but an absolute abyss. The 'human mind,' then, is *invented* in meditation to countervail the vertiginous magnetism of death" (*The Poet's Calling in the English Ode* [New Haven: Yale University Press, 1980], pp. 199–200).

37. Ferguson, "Shelley's 'Mont Blanc,'" pp. 45, 53.

38. "Believing that it was impossible for a geologist to consider either a creation or a consummation, Hutton replaced six thousand years of earth history

with a staggering tract of unaccountable time: 'We find no sign of a beginning—no prospect of an end.' For scientists and historians, he shifted the focus from origins to history, to the processes of nature and society, and participated in that secularization of nature and creativity that characterizes Romantic thought" (Gaull, *English Romanticism*, pp. 209–10). For a suggestive and highly informative if ultimately problematic reading of "Mont Blanc" in terms of the geological controversies of Shelley's time, see Nigel Leask, "Mont Blanc's Mysterious Voice: Shelley and Huttonian Earth Science," in *The Third Culture: Literature and Science*, ed. Elinor S. Shaffer, pp. 182–203 (Berlin: Walter de Gruyter, 1998).

39. Tilottama Rajan's phrase in her essay "Phenomenology and Romantic Theory: Hegel and the Subversion of Aesthetics," in *Questioning Romanticism*, ed. John Beer (Baltimore: Johns Hopkins University Press, 1995), p. 167.

40. In his "Essay on Christianity" Shelley wrote: "The universal Being . . . can only be described or defined by negatives, which deny his subjection to the laws of all inferior existences. Where indefiniteness ends idolatry and anthropomorphism begins" (quoted in Wasserman, *Shelley*, p. 233). See also Paul de Man's discussion of Marvell and "the pastoral convention" as "the eternal separation between the mind that distinguishes, negates, legislates, and the originary simplicity of the natural" in his "Dead-End of Formalist Criticism," in *Blindness and Insight: Essays in the Rhetoric of Contemporary Criticism*, intro. Wlad Godzich, 2nd ed. (Minneapolis: University of Minnesota Press, 1983), p. 239.

41. Jean-Joseph Goux, "Le temple d'Utopie" in *Les Iconoclastes* (Paris: Editions du Seuil, 1978), p. 47.

42. This is a crucial aspect of the approach taken by one of the most important recent studies of Shelley, namely, Jerrold E. Hogle's *Shelley's Process: Radical Transference and the Development of His Major Works* (New York: Oxford University Press, 1988). See also his essay "Shelley's Poetics: The Power as Metaphor": "[For Shelley] poetry must work to [. . .] brea[k] down the frames for thinking that users of signs have devised so skillfully. In fact, it should expand the possible range of metaphors beyond the present text of the usual public icons so that man, himself a production of metaphors in need of still others, can seek in 'unapprehended relations' for the means of self-extension alongside companions who would also surpass themselves" (from *Keats-Shelley Journal* 31 [1982]: 186).

43. On Shelley's "corporealizing" revision of Wordsworth, see Robert Brinkley, "Spaces between Words: Writing 'Mont Blanc,' " in *Romantic Revisions*, ed. idem and Keith Hanley (New York: Cambridge University Press, 1992), pp. 243–67.

44. Shelley's phrase in "A Defense of Poetry," in *Shelley's Poetry and Prose*, p. 505.

45. Although see also Fry, *The Poet's Calling in the English Ode*, pp. 202–203.

46. Rieder expresses the problem very well: "Although the sense of [Shelley's] message is, presumably, revolutionary and egalitarian, the structure of its revelation is priestly and aristocratic. [. . .] In this respect Shelley is thoroughly modern; he shares the uneasiness with an attempted aristocratic-egalitarian alliance which still, in the present day, afflicts much avant-garde artistry" ("Shelley's 'Mont Blanc,' " pp. 786, 788).

47. For an excellent and thoughtful tracing out of Shelley's uses of the cave topos, see Peter Butter, *Shelley's Idols of the Cave* (Edinburgh: Edinburgh University Press, 1954), pp. 55–66.

48. Tilottama Rajan, "Idealism and Skepticism in Shelley's Poetry ['The Triumph of Life' and 'Alastor']," in O'Neill, *Shelley*, p. 258.

49. Cf. Butter, *Shelley's Idols of the Cave*, p. 61: "Images [in the Shelleyan cave] are to be allowed to well up from the depths of the mind without too much conscious control." Butter's discussion of the varying significances of "cave" in Shelley is an important corrective to the interesting but overly binary reading offered by Nigel Leask, who sees a rather uncomplicated opposition in the poem between "an unflinching and reflective scrutiny" represented by the mountain and "the primitive, superstitious enclosure of the mind's cave" (Leask, "Mont Blanc's Mysterious Voice," p. 189). To assert this point, Leask is forced to distort Shelley's complex use of the cave topos, which in his poetry, more often than not, carries positive, visionary associations.

50. See William Keach, *Shelley's Style* (New York: Methuen, 1984), pp. 194–200.

51. Garrett Stewart, *Reading Voices: Literature and the Phonotext* (Berkeley: University of California Press, 1990), p. 162.

52. "At the very point of enjambment . . . in 'if to the human mind's imaginings / Silence and solitude were vacancy?' the pluralized subjectivity of 'imaginings,' figuring their variety without enumerating it, blurs over into—takes up or is taken up by—that existential 'silence' with whose signifier the previous plural will fuse and whose vacancy such multiplicity may infuse. The text itself is thus less 'silent' here than it seems, energizing the very gap at the end of a line with a sibilant ligature. The unsaid matrix of this whole interrogative image is blankness, with its suggestion of external void but also of emotional depletion. The constitutive textual blank itself, however—in this pivotal moment halfway between the portentous chimings of 'and Sea'/'-ancy' . . . —would defeat and repeal that implicit nullity, rendering it connective" (Stewart, *Reading Voices*, p. 163).

53. Here we might think of the long trail stretching from the pre-Romantics (especially the "Autumn" section of *The Seasons* and Collins's "Ode on the Popular Superstitions of the Highlands of Scotland, Considered as the Subject of Poetry") to E. M. Forster's Marabar Caves and no doubt beyond.

54. From Marcel Proust, *Remembrance of Things Past*, vol. 1, *Swann's Way* and *Within a Budding Grove*. trans. C. K. Scott-Moncrieff and Terence Kilmartin (New York: Random House, 1981), pp. 5–6.

55. A passage taken repeatedly, of course, throughout Proust's novel; see especially the late sections on concealment in the darkness of the Paris Métro during the World War I bombardments.

56. "Of two entrances, / one on the north allows descent of mortals, / but beings out of light alone, the undying, / can pass by the south slit; no men come there" (Homer, *The Odyssey*, trans. Robert Fitzgerald [New York: Anchor Books, 1963], pp. 232–33). For Porphyry, see *On the Cave of the Nymphs*, trans. and intro. Robert Lamberton (Barrytown, N.Y.: Station Hill, 1983).

57. Hans Blumenberg, *Höhlenausgänge* (Frankfurt am Main: Suhrkamp, 1996), pp. 27, 35.

58. See also the discussion of Benjaminian "aura" in chapter 2 of this volume.

59. See Peter Nicholls, *Modernisms: A Literary Guide* (Houndmills, Basingstoke: Macmillan, 1995), p. 13.

60. Mary Shelley, *Frankenstein; or, The Modern Prometheus*, intro. Harold Bloom (New York and Toronto: Signet, 1965), p. 53. For a fascinating account of the influence of theories of reanimation/rejuvenation (particularly those of Nikolai Fyodorov) on Russian writers, see Irene Masing-Delic, *Abolishing Death: A Salvation*

Myth of Russian Twentieth-Century Literature (Stanford: Stanford University Press, 1992).

61. Sylvia Scribner and Michael Cole, *The Psychology of Literacy* (Cambridge, Mass.: Harvard University Press, 1981), p. 38.

62. See, especially, the marvelous chapter "Reading as Poaching," in Michel de Certeau, *The Practice of Everyday Life,* trans. Steven Rendall, pp. 165–76 (Berkeley: University of California Press, 1984); and Göran Therborn, *The Ideology of Power and the Power of Ideology* (London: Verso, 1999), pp. 1–28 and passim.

63. G. W. Leibniz, *Selections,* ed. Philip P. Wiener (New York: Charles Scribner's, 1951), pp. 594–99. See my discussion of Khlebnikov's language in chapter 3 of this volume.

64. See the discussion of Blumenberg's notion of poetic language, below.

65. See Ulrich Ricken, *Leibniz, Wolff und einige sprachtheoretische Entwicklungen in der deutschen Aufklärung* (Berlin: Akademie-Verlag, 1989). The manifesto of this project is Leibniz's "Exhortation to the Germans to exercise their reason and language better, along with a proposal for a German Society" (1697): "Very few among our scholars have been pleased to write in German, partially because some of them believe that wisdom may be clothed only in Latin or Greek, or because of their fear that their secret ignorance, concealed within big words, will be discovered. But soundly learned people have nothing to fear; rather, they should accept it as a certainty that the more that wisdom and science make their rounds among the people, the more witnesses to their [i.e., those scholars'] excellence will be found—while those hiding among the truly learned and covered up with a coat of Latin or a Homeric fog will over time be discovered and exposed to shame" (Leibniz, *Unvorgreifliche Gedanken,* ed. Uwe Pörksen [Stuttgart: Reclam, 1983], p. 62).

66. Theodor W. Adorno, "On Lyric Poetry and Society," in *Notes to Literature,* ed. Rolf Tiedemann, trans. Shierry Weber Nicholson, 2 vols. (New York: Columbia University Press, 1991), 1:37–54; here p. 38. For a fascinating argument that attempts to show Adorno's "oscillation between a sociological and an ontological account" of art to be grounded in a false ascription of the "resistance" proper to natural objects (in the Kantian account) to art objects—while downplaying the properly historical, material context of Adorno's position, namely the reality of commodification in the cultural sphere—see Frances Ferguson, *Solitude and the Sublime: Romanticism and the Aesthetics of Individuation* (New York: Routledge, 1992), pp. 63–74.

67. Friedrich Bouterwek, "Lyrische Formen," in *Lyriktheorie: Texte vom Barock bis zur Gegenwart,* ed. Ludwig Völker (Stuttgart: Reclam, 1990), p. 158.

68. Friedrich Schiller, "Über Bürgers Gedichte," in Völker, *Lyriktheorie,* p. 115.

69. F. W. J. Schelling, "Konstruktion der einzelnen Dichtarten" (from *Philosophie der Kunst* [ca. 1802–1805], in Völker, *Lyriktheorie,* p. 156).

70. Friedrich von Hardenberg (Novalis), "Fragmente" (ca. 1800) in Völker, *Lyriktheorie,* p. 147.

71. Hegel, *Aesthetics: Lectures on Fine Art,* trans. T. M. Knox, 2 vols. (Oxford: Clarendon, 1974), 2:1111. All further references to the *Aesthetics* in English are from this edition, with page numbers cited in parentheses.

72. Hegel perhaps surpasses Kant in his aversion to any impression of "purposefulness" in poetry: "The relationship into which the parts are brought into connection should not be a mere teleological one. For in a teleological relationship, the end is the independently envisaged and willed universal which can bring

into conformity with itself the particulars through and in which it gains existence, but theses particulars it uses merely as means and it robs them of all independently free existence and therefore of every sort of life." (*Aesthetics*, p. 981)

73. Rancière, "The Aesthetic Revolution," p. 140. The contemporary critic who has most intently and brilliantly exposed the effects of truly microscopic (or electro-microscopic) attention-to-textual-detail upon interpretation is surely Garrett Stewart: see, especially, *Reading Voices;* and *Between Film and Screen: Modernism's Photo Synthesis* (Chicago: University of Chicago Press, 1999).

74. In a brilliant article Tilottama Rajan notes how the *Aesthetics,* although aspiring toward the abolition of art as such, in fact ends up reinscribing the *telos* of art—"the coming into being of the Idea"—into the phenomenological or *historical* narrative of aesthetic development through the doubt it casts upon the final adequacy of the one art wherein "the Idea" does find apparently adequate expression, namely, the *classical.* Thus the *Aesthetics* remains phenomenological rather than logical: "As the (im)possibility of the Idea, phenomenology is the haunting of Spirit by matter, an idealism that provides a philosophical cover for valorizing not the Idea but its displacement in material and phenomenal forms" ("Phenomenology and Romantic Theory: Hegel and the Subversion of Aesthetics," in *Questioning Romanticism,* ed. John Beer [Baltimore: Johns Hopkins University Press, 1995], pp. 155–78; here pp. 172–73).

75. In this respect, my treatment does not do full justice to Hegel, who discusses versification and "image" at some length. Questions of the general relation of the lyric mode to "language" as such, however, do not emerge in Hegel with the explicitness we find in Schleiermacher (see below).

76. In F. D. E. Schleiermacher, *Hermeneutik und Kritik,* ed. Manfred Frank (Frankfurt: Suhrkamp, 1977), p. 397. All quotations from Schleiermacher are from this edition, with page references cited in parentheses.

77. "For representation and conceptualizing on the broadest scale within the form of representation must stay at some particular level of generality or particularity, all of which concepts belong essentially together; each specific production has its truth insofar as it occupies a law-bound, determinate place [within the whole]—in other words, insofar as it is dependent upon this relationship [with the whole]. But to the extent that this relationship is provided to thought, it is the *science* of that which is" (*Hermeneutik und Kritik,* p. 396; my emphasis).

78. "We cannot maintain, at this point in our investigation, whether [to speak of] this 'truth of the content' is to say anymore than that logical truth is a necessary condition [of poetic language] in a broader sense. Without [logical truth], one would end up with a kind of music rather than language; and just as no work is poetic which does not strive for melodiousness, nor is it poetic when not directed towards this truth" (*Hermeneutik und Kritik,* p. 398).

79. Marshall Brown's succinct phrase in *Preromanticism* (Stanford: Stanford University Press, 1991), p. 353.

80. Cf. Rancière, "The Aesthetic Revolution": "Art is living so long as it expresses a thought unclear to itself in a matter that resists it. It lives inasmuch as it is something else than art, that is a belief and a way of life" (p. 141).

81. Hans Blumenberg, "Sprachsituation und immanente Poetik," in *Wirklichkeiten, in denen wir leben,* pp. 137–56 (Stuttgart: Reclam, 1981). Hereafter page numbers to this source are cited in parentheses.

82. "From a classificatory/typologizing point of view, it is not difficult to convert this very endangering [of meaning] into a norm, and to find the culmination

of language's poetic tendencies in pure nonsense, in Dada. But aesthetic appeal lies here as elsewhere in approaching [*Annäherung*] the point of sudden conversion into the impossible—I say in *approaching,* and not in identification with these extremes" (p. 147; Blumenberg's emphasis).

83. Cf. Blumenberg, "Wirklichkeitsbegriff und Wirkungspotential des Mythos": "Within the horizon of the reality principle ["Wirklichkeitsbegriff," not "Realitätsprinzip" (Freud)] of the modern age, the idea that gods might at some time appear is never again to be put into play. Whoever speaks of this—Hölderlin, say, or Hölderlin as interpreted by Heidegger—must hope as a consequence not merely for a occurrence relevant within the context of our reality, but for a radical change in the structure of reality itself. [. . .] Relative to the reality principle of immanent consistency, any such speculation, hope or historical metaphysics is necessarily eschatological" (in *Terror und Spiel* [Munich: Wilhelm Fink, 1971], p. 41).

84. Blumenberg, *Die Legitimität der Neuzeit* (Frankfurt: Suhrkamp, 1996), p. 14.

85. M. V. Lomonosov, "Nadpis' 1 k statue Petra Velikogo," in *M. V. Lomonosov: Izbrannye proizvedeniia,* ed. A. A. Morozov (Leningrad: Sovetskii pisatel', 1986), p. 207.

86. See Morozov's note in the edition cited above, p. 511.

87. Susan Stewart puts the point more sharply: "all public monuments of this type are monuments to death and the individual's prostration before history and authority . . . the abstract authority of the polis" (*On Longing,* p. 90).

88. In Thomson's "Winter," ll. 950–55.

89. Michael North, *The Final Sculpture: Public Monuments and Modern Poets* (Ithaca: Cornell University Press, 1985), p. 38.

90. Harsha Ram, "Russian Poetry and the Imperial Sublime," in *Russian Subjects: Empire, Nation, and the Culture of the Golden Age,* ed. Monika Greenleaf and Stephen Moeller-Sally (Evanston, Ill.: Northwestern University Press, 1998), p. 31.

91. Osip Mandelstam, "The Word and Culture," in *The Complete Critical Prose of Osip Mandelstam,* ed. Jane Gary Harris, trans. Jane Gary Harris and Constance Link (Ann Arbor: Ardis, 1997), p. 70. See also North, *The Final Sculpture,* pp. 18–20, 28.

92. *Shelley's Poetry and Prose,* p. 103.

93. Often the encounter with a monumental object triggers the poet's own meditation; in "Ozymandias," of course, the meditative element is compressed and mediated by reportage.

94. Thus, reflecting on the "unconsciously mimetic" impulses leading to poetry, Joseph Brodsky hit upon the idea of the vertical, giving it an anthropomorphic slant: "[. . .] a black, vertical clot of words in the midst of a white sheet of paper [. . .] reminds a person of his own position in the world, of the proportion which space bears to his body" ("Nobelevskaia lektsia" [Nobel Prize lecture], in *Forma vremeni* [Minsk: Eridan, 1992], 2:460).

95. On this, see Jacques Rancière, *The Ignorant Schoolmaster: Five Lessons in Intellectual Emancipation,* trans. and intro. Kristin Ross (Stanford: Stanford University Press, 1991), p. 37.

96. This is not to say, of course, that all kinds of aesthetic and other standards were not *felt* to be binding during this period, and indeed imposed in various ways (for the evidence, see Arno Mayer, *The Persistence of the Old Regime: Europe to the Great War* [New York: Pantheon Books, 1981]). Nor am I speaking of the

emergence of "philosophical relativism," which is, of course, just one position among others. The key point is again "conjunctural": the new field of possibilities forced "traditionalism" to emerge as one position (or reaction) within a proliferation of stances; thus attempts to impose standards must be read first as *anxieties*, and only secondarily as positions.

97. M. H. Abrams, "Structure and Style in the Greater Romantic Lyric," in *The Correspondent Breeze: Essays on English Romanticism* (New York: W. W. Norton, 1984), p. 83. See also my brief discussion of the poem at the beginning of chapter 2.

98. Friedrich Hölderlin, "Der Winkel von Hardt," in idem, *Gedichte*, ed. Jochen Schmidt (Frankfurt am Main: Insel, 1984), p. 134.

99. Friedrich Hölderlin, "The Shelter at Hahrdt" in idem, *Hymns and Fragments*, trans. and intro. Richard Sieburth (Princeton, N.J.: Princeton University Press, 1984), p. 49. Hereafter all citations in translation from Hölderlin's poetry are from this edition, with page numbers cited in parentheses.

100. The legend adds that Ulrich was saved by a spider that had spun a web across the shelter-entrance during the night. (This information comes from Jochen Schmidt's notes to the poem in Hölderlin, *Gedichte*, pp. 367–68.)

101. Mandelstam, "Conversation about Dante," in *The Complete Critical Prose*, p. 284.

102. "To Dasein's making room for itself belongs the self-directive discovery of something like a *region*. [...] The self-directive discovery of a region is grounded in an ecstatically retentive awaiting of the 'hither' and 'thither' that are possible. Making room for oneself is a directional awaiting of a region [....]" (Martin Heidegger, *Being and Time*, trans. John Macquarrie and Edward Robinson [New York: Harper and Row, 1962], p. 420).

103. Something like an under- or overlapping of growth and support is happening here. Coming from a more naturalistic interpretive angle (he sees the blossoming forest floor as soil covered with brilliant fall leaves), Wolfgang Binder noticed this circularity as well: "Two words within this depiction of autumn derive from the vocabulary of spring: 'buds' and 'blossoms up.' Autumn seems to have some of the characteristics of spring, which is a very Hölderlinian idea. [...] Autumn, opposed to spring within the cycle of the seasons, takes on its color as the sunset does that of the morning" (Binder, Wolfgang. " 'Der Winkel von Hardt,' 'Lebensalter,' 'Hälfte des Lebens,' " *Schweitzer Monatsheft* 6 [September 1965]: 584).

104. Richard Sieburth's sensitive translation registers this double resonance: "*For* Ulrich passed through / *These parts*...."

105. Both the Hölderlin and Bertaux quotes are from Bertaux, *Hölderlin und die Französische Revolution* (Frankfurt am Main: Suhrkamp, 1969), p. 125.

106. Wordsworth, *The Poems*, 1:737.

107. In the chapter "Wordsworth's Old Grey Stone," from Brown's indispensable *Preromanticism*, pp. 301–61.

108. Brown calls this "the asymptotic relationship of man and nature" in Wordsworth: "The spiraling course of a Wordsworthian meditation draws out the resources of the mind and penetrates the scene, discovering a wealth of active forces and factors that allow the apparently inert stone of the earth to be revealed as a suitable habitation for human beings" (*Preromanticism*, pp. 357, 356).

109. Ibid., p. 356.

110. On this dialectic, see Fry's reading of this sonnet and the "black rock" passage in Book 8 of *The Prelude* in *A Defense of Poetry*, pp. 97–107.

111. It is on this score that Brown's relation of Kant to Wordsworth's poem becomes interestingly problematic. He writes: "The trees surrounding the stone make an instance of what Kant, in the *Critique of Judgment,* called purposeless purpose, and they become a figure of mind by a structured interplay of parts rather than by an act of initiation or a mark of originary difference" (*Preromanticism,* p. 343). But if this is the case—if form, or "structured interplay of parts," is all that the poet/artist really requires—then the trees as *existent* "originators" or supports for imagination really are irrelevant. They can be replaced by "framed images," opening the imagination onto a nature-less textuality. Brown is certainly right, though, in thinking that this is not Wordsworth's own position.

112. The difference between the two poets can be related to the "split valorization" within Hegel's aesthetics "both of classical completion and of its undoing in the romantic": "For the classical fails because it limits the Idea to a concrete form, but the romantic also fails because it is unable to make the Idea concrete" (Tilottama Rajan, "Phenomenology and Romantic Theory," pp. 169–70).

2. Empty and Full

1. Walter Benjamin, *Illuminations,* trans. Harry Zohn (New York: Schocken Books, 1968), p. 108.

2. And as David Simpson and others have noted, it is not unimportant that Dorothy is Wordsworth's chosen tradition bearer: "the effort at localization goes with the effort at feminization" (*The Academic Postmodern and the Rule of Literature,* p. 156).

3. The most elaborate theoretical construct of this kind is possibly Walter Benjamin's notion of the "dialectical image"; for a thorough account, see Susan Buck-Morss, *The Dialectics of Seeing* (Cambridge, Mass.: MIT Press, 1989).

4. See "Signature Event Context" in Jacques Derrida, *Limited Inc.* (Evanston, Ill.: Northwestern University Press, 1988), pp. 1–23.

5. Cf. Jameson, *Marxism and Form,* p. 55: "[. . .] the practice of negative dialectics involves a constant movement away from the official content of an idea—as, for example, the "real" nature of freedom or of society as things in themselves—and toward the various determinate and contradictory forms which such ideas have taken, whose conceptual limits and inadequacies stand as immediate figures or symptoms of the concrete social situation itself. [. . .]" And p. 416: "The works of culture come to us as signs in an all-but-forgotten code, as symptoms of diseases no longer even recognized as such, as fragments of a totality we have long since lost the organs to see."

6. "A nexus of meaning can never be founded causally," as Benjamin pithily expressed it ("Fate and Character," in *Reflections,* ed. Peter Demetz, trans. Edmund Jephcott [New York: Schocken Books, 1978], p. 305).

7. A. R. Ammons, "Guide," in *The Selected Poems,* exp. ed. (New York: W. W. Norton, 1986), p. 23.

8. Walter Benjamin, "Some Motifs in Baudelaire," in idem, *Charles Baudelaire: A Lyric Poet in the Era of High Capitalism,* trans. Harry Zohn (London: Verso, 1983), p. 134. All further quotations from Benjamin's essays on Baudelaire are from this edition, hereafter abbreviated *CB;* the essay "The Paris of the Second Empire in Baudelaire" will be referred to as "Second Empire," the essay "Some Motifs in Baudelaire" as "Some Motifs." Page numbers are cited in parentheses.

9. Cf. Buck-Morss, *The Dialectics of Seeing,* p. 196: "Benjamin wanted to demonstrate 'with every possible emphasis' that Baudelaire's perception of modern temporality was not unique, that 'the idea of eternal recurrence pushes its way into the world of Baudelaire, Blanqui, and Nietzsche at approximately the same moment.' "

10. "The Storyteller," in Benjamin, *Illuminations,* p. 108.

11. Cf. Fredric Jameson's comments in *Marxism and Form*: "[. . .] [A] progressive work of art is one which utilizes the most advanced artistic techniques, one in which, therefore, the artist lives his activity as a technician, and through this technical work finds a unity of purpose with the industrial worker [. . . .] [T]here can be no doubt that Benjamin first came to a radical politics through his experience as a specialist: through his growing awareness, within the domain of his own literary activity, of the crucial influence exerted on the work of art by changes in the public and developments in technique, in short by history itself" (p. 81).

12. Priscilla Parkhurst Ferguson, *Paris as Revolution: Writing the Nineteenth-Century City* (Berkeley: University of California Press, 1994), p. 81.

13. See David Harvey, *Paris, Capital of Modernity* (New York: Routledge, 2003), esp. pp. 93–105, 141–71.

14. "Where there is experience in the strict sense of the word, certain contents of the individual past combine with material of the collective past" (Benjamin, "Some Motifs," p. 113).

15. See the chapter "Science and Sentiment, Modernity and Tradition," in Harvey, *Paris, Capital of Modernity,* pp. 253–66.

16. See Buck-Morss, *The Dialectics of Seeing,* pp. 68–70.

17. For example: "Punctuality, calculability, and exactness, which are required by the complications and extensiveness of metropolitan life are not only most intimately connected with its capitalistic and intellectualistic character but also color the content of life and are conducive to the exclusion of those irrational, instinctive, sovereign human traits and impulses which originally seek to determine the form of life from within instead of receiving it from the outside in a general, schematically precise form" (Georg Simmel, *On Individuality and Social Forms,* trans. and intro. Donald N. Levine [Chicago: University of Chicago Press, 1971], p. 328).

18. "For the crowd really is a spectacle of nature—if one may apply the term to social conditions. A street, a conflagration, or a traffic accident assemble people who are not defined along class lines. They present themselves as concrete gatherings, but socially they remain abstract—namely, in their isolated private interests" (*CB,* "Second Empire," p. 62).

19. Georg Lukács, "Reification and the Consciousness of the Proletariat," in idem, *History and Class Consciousness: Studies in Marxist Dialectics,* trans. Rodney Livingstone (Cambridge, Mass.: MIT Press, 1968), p. 128.

20. *The Satires of Juvenal,* trans. Rolfe Humphries (Bloomington: Indiana University Press, 1958), Satire III, p. 42, l. 232. In Juvenal's time, the streets of Rome were especially noisy at night because of an edict prohibiting traffic during the day in the city center.

21. Victor Hugo, *Poèmes,* ed. Jean Gaudon (Paris: Flammarion, 1985), p. 90.

22. Raymond Williams's phrase in his *The Country and the City* (New York: Oxford University Press, 1973), p. 1.

23. Italo Calvino, *Invisible Cities* (New York: Harcourt Brace, 1974), p. 18.

24. "L'Art Poétique," in Nicolas Boileau Despréaux, *Oeuvres complètes,* ed. Françoise Escal (Paris: Gallimard, 1966), Chant III, p. 178.

25. Ferguson, *Paris as Revolution,* p. 24

26. I allude here to the distinction between "exhibition" and "cult" value made in Benjamin's "Work of Art in the Age of Mechanical Reproduction" (in idem, *Illuminations,* p. 225).

27. The most immediate inspiration of Benjamin's concern with the distinction between the "unique" and "non-unique" object is probably Georg Simmel, particularly in his essay "Das Problem des Stiles": "The essence of the [manufactured] craft-object lies in its existing many times; its distribution is the quantitative expression of its efficacy, for it always serves some purpose shared by many people. The essence of the artwork is, by contrast, its uniqueness [. . .] through which a [particular] soul, following what is unique in itself, finds direct expression in one single object" (*Aufsätze und Abhandlungen 1901–1908,* in *Gesamtausgabe,* ed. Otthein Rammstedt et al. [Frankfurt am Main: Suhrkamp, 1993], 8:376–77.)

28. "The Work of Art in the Age of Mechanical Reproduction," p. 222.

29. E.g., *Poetics,* chap. 4, where Aristotle links the pleasure of mimesis to the fact that "we take pleasure in contemplating the most precise images of things whose sight in itself causes us pain [. . . .]" (*The Poetics of Aristotle,* trans. and commentary Stephen Halliwell [Chapel Hill: University of North Carolina Press, 1987], p. 34).

30. Schiller, *On the Aesthetic Education of Man,* p. clxvii; see introduction, n. 40.

31. Cf. ibid., p. clxviii: "[. . .] without [distance] we can never gain access to the import of the work as a whole, but remain content with the adventitious excitements of its subject-matter." See also Edward Bullough, " 'Psychical Distance' as a Factor in Art and an Aesthetic Principle" in his *Aesthetics: Lectures and Essays,* ed. Elizabeth M Wilkinson (Stanford: Stanford University Press, 1957), pp. 91–130.

32. "The Work of Art in the Age of Mechanical Reproduction," p. 223.

33. Lines 112 and 25–28 from Schiller's "Die Götter Griechenlands," in *Gedichte,* ed. Gerhard Fricke (Stuttgart: Reclam, 1980), pp. 132, 129.

34. From the article "Law," in John L. McKenzie, *Dictionary of the Bible* (New York: Macmillan, 1970), p. 499.

35. In a recent essay, Gyorgy Markus discusses this aspect of Benjaminian aura in a way that shows its affinity with Rancière's "aesthetic sensorium": "The auratic experience offers for a fleeting instance the purely subjective fulfillment of the promise of a 'nature' that no longer is the resistant object of our efforts at its utilization and exploitation, but encounters us in an unforced way with 'favor' [the Kantian *Gunst der Natur*]. In this experience the rigid division between subject and object is dissolved in a reciprocal, mimetic-communicative relation between human beings and their world, a world, the things of which became liberated from the compulsion to be useful. [. . . .] Thus the decay of the aura which Benjamin registers as an ongoing process is itself ambiguous: it designates an emancipatory possibility connected with the radical refunctioning of art and a danger, the disappearance not only of the privatized, empathic, autonomous, aesthetic experience, but also of the ability to imagine and experience fulfillment, the gift of happiness" (Gyorgy Markus, "Walter Benjamin or the Commodity as Phantasmagoria," *New German Critique* 83 [spring–summer 2001]: 32–33).

36. See Buck-Morss, *The Dialectics of Seeing,* pp. 110–20.

37. Theodor Adorno, *Aesthetic Theory,* ed. Gretel Adorno, Rolf Tiedemann, Robert Hullot-Kentor, trans. Robert Hullot-Kentor (Minneapolis: University of Minnesota Press, 1997), p. 79.

38. Benjamin expressed the historical relation of allegory to "recession" in the following way: "In the Baroque age [...] the commodity had not yet so deeply engraved its stigma—the proletarianization of the producers—on the process of production. Allegorical perception could thus constitute a style in the seventeenth century, in a way that it no longer could in the nineteenth. Baudelaire as allegorist was entirely isolated. He sought to recall the experience of the commodity to an allegorical experience. In this, he was doomed to founder, and it became clear that relentlessness of his initiative was exceeded by the relentlessness of reality. Hence a strain in his work that feels pathological or sadistic only because it missed out on reality—though just by a hair" (*The Arcades Project*, trans. Howard Eiland and Kevin McLaughlin [Cambridge, Mass.: Belknap Press of Harvard University Press, 1999], p. 347).

39. Sartre calls it "a social idea of sterility" and traces it back to "a personal reaction to the problem of the social position of the writer [. . . .] The aristocracy bestowed on [the writer] a little of its *mâna*. He shared its idleness and the fame which he hoped to win was a reflection of the immortality which its hereditary title confers on a royal family. When the nobility collapsed, the writer was completely bewildered by the fall of his protectors and had to look for some fresh form of justification. His connection with the sacred caste of priests and nobles really had made him into a *déclassé*" (Jean-Paul Sartre, *Baudelaire*, trans. Martin Turnell [New York: New Directions, 1950], pp. 146, 137).

40. "The treason of the petty bourgeois in 1848 discredited *politics* in the eyes of the exploited—all politics was bourgeois, even when practiced by politicians who claimed to be socialists" (Sartre, *Critique of Dialectical Reason*, trans. Alan Sheridan-Smith [London: New Left Books, 1976], 1:756).

41. In Charles Baudelaire, *Oeuvres complètes*, ed. Claude Roy and Michel Jamet (Paris: Robert Laffont, 1980), pp. 39–40. Unless otherwise indicated, all further citations from Baudelaire in the original are from this edition, with page numbers cited in parentheses.

42. "L'Invitation au Voyage," in Charles Baudelaire, *Selected Poems*, trans. and intro. Carol Clark (London: Penguin Books, 1995), p. 60.

43. Sartre, *Baudelaire*, p. 44.

44. Baudelaire, *Selected Poems*, pp. 74–75.

45. Cf. Benjamin on memory in "Zentralpark": "The souvenir [*Andenken*] is the secularized relic. [. . . .] During the 19th century allegory vacated the external world in order to settle within the internal world. The relic derives from the corpse, the souvenir from the deadened collective experience [*abgestorbene Erfahrung*] which euphemistically calls itself *lived* experience [*Erlebnis*]" (*Illuminationen*, ed. Siegfried Unseld [Frankfurt am Main: Suhrkamp, 1955], p. 259). My translation here is indebted to the one offered by Gyorgy Markus in his essay "The Commodity as Phantasmagoria" (p. 35); see note 35, above.

46. Sartre, *Baudelaire*, p. 69.

47. Rancière, "The Aesthetic Revolution," p. 142.

48. Ibid., pp. 144–45.

49. For an excellent account of (among other things) the posterity of Baudelairean influence, see Nicholls, *Modernisms*, pp. 2–83.

50. Saint-Beuve, *Les Consolations: Pensées d'août*, poems, part 2; quoted in Benjamin, *The Arcades Project*, p. 776.

51. For some varying viewpoints, see Benjamin, *The Arcades Project*, esp. pp. 745–77; Charles M. Lombard, *Lamartine* (New York: Twayne, 1973); Karl Marx,

"The Class Struggles in France, 1848 to 1850" in *Collected Works,* ed. Jack Cohen et al., 50 vols. (Moscow: Progress, 1978), 10:45–146; Roger Price, *A Concise History of France* (Cambridge: Cambridge University Press, 1993), pp. 170–79; and Peter N. Stearns, *The Revolutions of 1848* (London: Weidenfeld and Nicolson, 1974).

52. See Henri Guillemin, *Le Jocelyn de Lamartine: Etude Historique et Critique avec des Documents Inédits* (Paris: Boivin, 1937), pp. 123–26. In his well-known letter of 1856 to the Fourierist Alphonse Toussenel, Baudelaire calls de Maistre "the great genius of our times—a seer!" (in Charles Baudelaire, *Oeuvres complètes,* ed. Claude Pichois, vol. 2 [Paris: Gallimard, 1975–76], p. 337). See Pierre Glaudes, "Le dialogue avec De Maistre," *Magazine Littéraire* 418 (March 2003): 53–56.

53. Guillemin, *Le Jocelyn de Lamartine,* p. 97.

54. Lamartine, "Des Destinées de la poésie" (second preface to *Les Méditations*); quoted in Benjamin, *The Arcades Project,* p. 777.

55. Lamartine described the fall of the Republic in terms of the replacement of its central slogans—" 'Honor to God! Respect for the altars! Liberty to their ministers! Self-denial, harmony, protection to the weak, inviolability of property, assistance to the miserable!"—by the ideas of "abject Materialism . . . gross Socialism" and "besotted Communism": "It was not until after the cooling of this enthusiasm that the materialistic sects, who waited their opportunity afar off, and who now torment the People, dared to offer their sensual symbols, and to set up Capital and Interest, the organization of labor, the increase of wages, and equality of conditions in this human manger, as the sole Divinities,—dared to infuse envy against the happy, the breath of hatred as the only consolation to the hearts of the miserable, lightning vengeance against the wrongs of Providence, imprecations against society, blasphemies against the existence of God, the enjoyments and bestialities of the corporeal nature, purchased by complete forgetfulness of the moral nature, and enjoyed in a debauch of ideas, and in a deification of matter" (*Lamartine on Atheism. Atheism among the People* [Boston: Phillips, Sampson, 1850], pp. 55, 56, 69). See also his *Past, Present and Future of the Republic* (New York: Harper, 1850).

56. Giovanna Procacci, "To Survive the Revolution or to Anticipate It?: Governmental Strategies in the Course of the Crisis of 1848," in *Europe in 1848: Revolution and Reform,* ed. Dieter Dowe et al., trans. David Higgins (New York and Oxford: Berghahn Books, 2001), p. 518. Procacci is quoting Lamartine's *La France Parlementaire.*

57. Lamartine, "Utopie" (written 1837; in *Recueillements Poétiques*), in *Oeuvres poètiques,* ed. Marius-François Guyard (Paris: Gallimard, 1963), p. 1150. Unless otherwise noted, all references to Lamartine are to this edition; page numbers are cited in parentheses.

58. Ibid., p. 1157.

59. Cf. Frank E. Manuel and Fritzie P. Manuel on the Saint-Simonian assertion that "the natural was inequality": "Most of mankind, whose primary aptitude was the motor capacity, were destined to remain manual laborers, though a small elite of this class with essentially the same kind of talent would become the administrators of the temporal affairs of society—the men who organized states and directed public works and engineered vast projects for the exploitation of nature" (*Utopian Thought in the Western World* [Cambridge, Mass.: Belknap Press of Harvard University Press, 1979], p. 601).

60. From Sartre's analysis of Sade's "sadism" in *Search for a Method,* p. 114.

61. Cf. the following quotation (in Benjamin, *The Arcades Project,* p. 745) from Friedrich Szarvady on Lamartine: "It is as though Lamartine had made it

his mission to implement Plato's teaching on the necessity of banishing poets from the republic, and one cannot help smiling as one reads this author's account of the worker who was part of the large demonstration in front of the Hôtel de Ville, and who shouted to the speaker: 'You're nothing but a lyre! Go sing!' "

62. Alphonse de Lamartine, *Méditations Poétiques: Nouvelles Méditations Poétiques Suivies de Poésies Diverses,* ed. Marius-François Guyard (Paris: Gallimard, 1981).

63. In their discussion of the dynamics of "contamination" in the nineteenth-century city, Peter Stallybrass and Allon White note how "the body of the Other produced contradictory responses. Certainly, it was to be surveyed . . . from 'some high window' or superior position. . . . At the same time, new forms of propriety must penetrate and subjugate the recalcitrant body" (*The Politics and Poetics of Transgression* [Ithaca: Cornell University Press, 1986], p. 126).

64. Lamartine, *Jocelyn,* in *Oeuvres poètiques,* ed. Marius-François Guyard (Paris: Gallimard, 1963), p. 720. All further references to *Jocelyn* are to this edition, with page numbers cited in parentheses.

65. Cf. Jean Cassou, *Quarante-Huit:* "We discover in [Lamartine's 'democratic lyricism'] a secret thought: our possessions, along with all their train of spiritual delights, accompany us to the very threshold of immortality. [. . .] [Lamartine's] supreme desire [was] that of living on in a realm of physical immortality where every object preserves its perfect and savory reality" (quoted in Benjamin, *The Arcades Project,* p. 777). Guillemin quotes Lamartine's 1861 *Cours Familier de Littérature:* "THE PROPRIETOR-BEING: that is the most beautiful name of man" (*Le Jocelyn de Lamartine,* p. 122).

66. An intervention issuing from the "invisible current." On Lamartine and the "forces of order," see Benjamin, *The Arcades Project,* p. 767.

67. This is so, especially coming from a priest. The relevant verses are the following (2:7–8, Jerusalem Bible): "But he emptied himself, / taking the form of a slave, / becoming as human beings are; / and being in every way / like a human being, / he was humbler yet, / even to accepting death, / death on a cross."

68. This information and the citation come from Ernst Robert Curtius, *European Literature and the Latin Middle Ages,* trans. Willard R. Trask (Princeton, N.J.: Princeton University Press, 1990), p. 37: "It was in quattrocento Florence that artists awoke to self-consciousness. They no longer wished to be confused with artisans. [. . . .] The Italian 'meccanico' acquires the meaning 'uneducated, crude'; 'la turba meccanica' is 'the common herd.' " (Nigel Alderman also reminds me of the lowly "mechanics" in *A Midsummer Night's Dream.*) See William H. Sewell Jr.'s superb pages on shifts in attitudes toward the mechanical arts, in *Work and Revolution in France,* pp. 21, 23–25, 64–72, 138–42.

69. Simmel, *On Individuality and Social Forms,* p. 331.

70. Jean-Jacques Rousseau, *La Nouvelle Héloïse,* trans. Judith H. McDowell (University Park: Pennsylvania State University Press, 1968), p. 204.

71. Ibid., pp. 203–204.

72. See Guillemin, *Le Jocelyn de Lamartine,* p. 124.

73. Charles Baudelaire, "Crowds," in idem, *The Poems in Prose with La Fanfarlo,* trans. Francis Scarfe (London: Anvil, 1989), p. 59.

74. Sohn-Rethel formulated this term in his *Intellectual and Manual Labour: A Critique of Epistemology* (London: Macmillan, 1978): "the [real-abstract] form of exchangeability" emerges "out of the exchanging agents *practicing* their solipsism against each other" (p. 45; my emphasis).

75. Baudelaire, "Crowds," in idem, *The Parisian Prowler,* trans. Edward K. Kaplan (Athens and London: University of Georgia Press, 1997), p. 21; my emphasis.

76. Baudelaire, *The Parisian Prowler,* p. 38.

77. This last point is made superbly by Jacques Rancière: "[*Kulturkritik* is] a discourse which purports to speak the truth about art, about the illusions of aesthetics and their social underpinnings, about the dependency of art upon common culture and commodification. But the very procedures through which it tries to disclose what art and aesthetics truly are were first framed on the aesthetic stage. They are figures of the same poem. The critique of culture can be seen as the epistemological face of Romantic poetics, the rationalization of its way of exchanging the signs of art and the signs of life. *Kulturkritik* wants to cast on the productions of Romantic poetics the gaze of disenchanted reason. But that disenchantment itself is part of the Romantic re-enchantment that has widened *ad infinitum* the sensorium of art as the field of disused objects encrypting a culture, extending to infinity, too, the realm of fantasies to be deciphered and formatting the procedures of that decryption" ("The Aesthetic Revolution," pp. 146–47).

78. Charles Baudelaire, *Complete Verse,* ed., intro., and trans. Francis Scarfe (London: Anvil, 1986). 186. Further citations from this work are followed by page numbers in parentheses.

79. Cf. Geoffrey Hartman's statement that the aura "could [. . .] be regarded as a principle of psychic economy necessitated by the pressures of a real, capitalistic economy: a defense mechanism, that is, against shock, labor, and pure secularism" (*Criticism in the Wilderness* [New Haven: Yale University Press, 1980], p. 69).

80. " 'Fugitive beauté / Dont le regard m'a fait soudainement renaître" is indistinguishably gallant and religious in its diction, just as 'je buvais . . . / Dans son oeil, ciel livide" is a perversion of such diction that evokes the poet's desire to liquidate distance, to incorporate by a vampirelike act the source of the image, or the very organ that allows it to be caught at a distance" (Hartman, *Criticism in the Wilderness,* p. 68).

81. The relevant passage is from the end of Schiller's Fifteenth Letter: "[M]an only plays when he is in the fullest sense of the word a human being, and *he is only fully a human being when he plays.* [. . .] [This proposition will] prove capable of bearing the whole edifice of the art of the beautiful, and of the still more difficult art of living. [. . .] Guided by the truth of [the] same proposition, they banished from the brow of the blessed gods all the earnestness and effort which furrow the cheeks of mortals, no less than the empty pleasure which preserve the smoothness of a vacuous face; freed those ever-contented beings from the bonds inseparable from every purpose, every duty, every care, and made *idleness* and *indifferency* the enviable portion of divinity—merely a more human name for the freest, most sublime state of being. Both the material constraint of natural laws and the spiritual constraint of moral laws were resolved in their higher concept of Necessity, which embraced both worlds at once; and it was only out of the perfect union of those two necessities that for them true Freedom could proceed. [. . .] It is not Grace, nor is it yet Dignity, which speaks to us from the superb countenance of a Juno Ludovisi; it is neither the one nor the other because it is both at once. While the woman-god demands our veneration, the god-like woman kindles our love; but even as we abandon ourselves in ecstasy to her heavenly grace, her celestial self-sufficiency makes us recoil in terror. The whole

figure reposes and dwells in itself, a creation completely self-contained, and, as if existing beyond space, neither yielding nor resisting; here is no force to contend with force, no frailty where temporality might break in. Irresistibly moved and drawn by those former qualities, kept at a distance by these latter, we find ourselves at one and the same time in a state of utter repose and supreme agitation, and there results that wondrous stirring of the heart for which mind has no concept nor speech any name" (*On the Aesthetic Education of Man,* pp. 107, 109).

82. Rancière, "The Aesthetic Revolution," pp. 136–37.

83. Cf. *CB,* "Second Empire": "Far from eluding the erotic in the crowd, the apparition which fascinates [the poet] is brought to him by this very crowd. [. . .] The *never* marks the high point of the encounter, when the poet's passion seems to be frustrated but in reality bursts out of him like a flame. He burns in this flame, but no Phoenix arises from it" (p. 43).

84. Crary, *Suspensions of Perception,* pp. 172, 225.

85. Such an aspiration would entail a rereading of the "free appearance" as (in Rancière's words) "the product of a human mind which seeks to transform the surface of sensory appearances into a new sensorium that is the mirror of its own activity" ("The Aesthetic Revolution," p. 137). See the discussion of Charles Poncy, below.

86. Charles Baudelaire, "The Painter of Modern Life," in idem, *Selected Writings on Art and Literature,* trans. and intro. P. E. Charvet (London: Penguin Books, 1972), pp. 402–404.

87. Discussing the same essay, Paul de Man writes that "the paradox of the problem is potentially contained in the formula 'représentation du présent,' which combines a repetitive with an instantaneous pattern without apparent awareness of the incompatibility" ("Literary History and Literary Modernity," *Blindness and Insight: Essays in the Rhetoric of Contemporary Criticism,* 2nd ed., intro. Wlad Godzich [Minneapolis: University of Minnesota Press, 1983], p. 156).

88. Baudelaire, "The Painter of Modern Life," p. 401; my emphasis.

89. "The use-value of the impossible," trans. Liesl Ollman, in *Bataille: Writing the Sacred,* ed. Carolyn Bailey Gill (London: Routledge, 1995), pp. 133–53; here p. 147.

90. Ibid., p. 148.

91. Cf. Barbara Johnson's more Freudian discussion of Baudelairean fetishism in "Poetry and Its Double: Two 'Invitations au voyage,' " in *Charles Baudelaire,* ed. and intro. Harold Bloom (New York, New Haven, Philadelphia: Chelsea House, 1987), p. 61.

92. In Sewell, *Work and Revolution in France,* pp. 236–42. My discussion of Charles Poncy depends heavily on Sewell's work, while my general understanding of the literary expression of French workers derives from Rancière's *The Nights of Labor: The Worker's Dream in Nineteenth-Century France,* trans. John Drury, intro. Donald Read (Philadelphia: Temple University Press, 1989).

93. Sewell, *Work and Revolution in France,* p. 236.

94. Ibid.

95. Ibid., p. 238.

96. Ibid., p. 239.

97. Ibid., p. 238.

98. Ibid., pp. 239, 241.

99. From the famous passage on myth in the introduction to Karl Marx, *Grundrisse: Foundations of the Critique of Political Economy,* trans. and intro. Martin Nicolaus (New York: Vintage Books, 1973), p. 110.

100. Benjamin, *The Arcades Project,* p. 328.

101. The distinction is discussed brilliantly in Wollen's "Art in Revolution" in *Readings and Writings: Semiotic Counter-Strategies* (London: New Left Books, 1982), pp. 65–78.

102. Sewell, *Work and Revolution in France,* pp. 238–39.

3. Kernels of the Acropolis

1. "Poshlost' tainstvennaia" (mysterious vulgarity) is a phrase from Blok's "Tam damy shchegoliaiut modami" (There women parade in the latest styles), in Aleksandr Blok, *Sobranie sochinenii,* ed. V. Orlov and I. Isakovich, intro. M. Dudin, 6 vols. (Leningrad: Khudozhesvennaia literatura, 1980), 1:395. All further citations from Blok's poetry are from this edition, with page numbers cited in parentheses.

2. "His demonic portrayal of the urban landscape and of women, the presentation of the 'poet-hero engaged on a tragic quest' and his 'loathing and self-loathing' (P. France), the 'épiphanie du musical dans l'antiusicalité hideuse de la vie contemporaine' (G. Nivat), the comparison of sexual love with a surgical operation and the lugubrious vision of contemporary life as a *dance macabre* (R. Poggioli) are some of Blok's Baudelairean features highlighted by literary critics" (Adrian Wanner, *Baudelaire in Russia* [Gainesville: University Press of Florida, 1996], p. 192).

3. "Both Baudelaire and Blok were exceedingly close to their mothers throughout their lives, each lost his father at an early age, and their mothers both remarried military men. Both poets were dominated by sense of duty toward a wife-figure (Jeanne Duval, Lyubov Dmitrievna), who was working as an actress, yet both frequented prostitutes and contracted syphilis [. . .]" (ibid., p. 193).

4. Ibid.

5. Avril Pyman, *The Life of Aleksandr Blok,* vol. 1, *The Distant Thunder* (Oxford: Oxford University Press, 1979), p. 181.

6. Alexander Blok, *Selected Poems,* trans. Alex Miller (Moscow: Progress, 1981), pp. 107–108.

7. "By the turn of the century [problems such as alcoholism, disorder, illegitimacy, and insufficient housing] made the urban scene not just unhealthy but unsafe as well. Once rare, suicides were now an everyday response to seemingly hopeless situations. Crime increased. Arrests soared. Attempts at assassination were increasingly successful and already one tsar, Alexander II, had fallen victim. Some of the seething discontent was manifested during the upheaval of 1905, and in this case a massive popular demonstration was at least partly responsible for bringing about some measure of political and social reform [in the form of the Duma]. [. . . .] The organization of labour became more effective and the number of strikes grew. Within the city the inflationary spiral eroded workers' incomes and produced further dissatisfactions. Revolutionists and anarchists were quick to point out various easily recognized sores on the urban scene—probably 10 per cent of the population lived in an *ugol* [incredibly overcrowded and wretched habitations that were no more than "corners" of partitioned rooms], disease was endemic and the cost of living exorbitant. But all around was evidence of wealth and ostentation. The labouring population was not especially literate, but by word

of mouth if nothing else information about the conditions of life and labour in other European urban-industrial centres was filtering through. The hopes if not the expectations of an eight-hour working day compared with the statutory maximum of 11.5 hours in Russia did not require much kindling. Resentment rose" (in James H. Bater, *St. Petersburg: Industrialization and Change* [Montreal: McGill-Queen's University Press, 1976], p. 381). In the discussion that follows I rely heavily on Bater's account of the city, especially pp. 213–411.)

8. Ibid., p. 254.

9. Ibid., pp. 406–407.

10. Aleksandr Blok, *Sochineniia,* ed. V. Orlov, 2 vols. (Moscow: Khudozhestvennaia literatura, 1955), 2:30. All further citations from Blok's prose works are from this edition, with page numbers cited in parentheses.

11. See V. I. Semevskii, *Krest'ianskii vopros v Rossii v XVIII i pervoi polovine XIX veka* (St. Petersburg: Obshchestvennaia pol'za, 1888), 2:390–401.

12. See Jeffrey Brooks, *When Russia Learned to Read: Literacy and Popular Literature, 1861–1917* (Princeton, N.J.: Princeton University Press, 1985), pp. 296–340.

13. See the discussion of "culture vs. civilization," in R. D. Reeve, *Aleksandr Blok: Between Image and Idea* (New York and London: Columbia University Press, 1962), pp. 35–39. This dichotomy has familiar Romantic and (earlier) Vichian roots, but a possible immediate source for Blok's use of it (most explicitly in his essay, "The Decline of Humanism" [1919]), is a work by Oswald Spengler that appeared the previous year, *The Decline of the West,* ed. Helmut Werner and Arthur Helps, trans. Charles Francis Atkinson (New York: Oxford University Press, 1991), pp. 25–26. As we will see, Blok came to see the revolution as a sweeping out of "civilization" by a new mass "culture."

14. Cf. "The Decline of Humanism," where Blok speaks of the appearance "in the arena of European history" of a "new motive force—not the personality, but the mass" (p. 306), attributing the formation of this group to the capitalist organization (i.e., atomization and reconfiguration) of labor (pp. 310–17). He derived his ideas about the emergence of the masses at least in part from Johann Honegger (1825–1896), a virtually forgotten Swiss cultural historian and early commentator on Marx and on Russian literature (*Russische Literatur und Cultur* [Leipzig: J. J. Weber, 1880]); see, esp., *Grundsteine einer allgemeinen Culturgeschichte der neuesten Zeit,* vol. 5 (Leipzig: J. J. Weber, 1874), pp. 3–10, 144–89.

15. In his seminal essay, "Blok i narodnaia kul'tura goroda" (Blok and the folk culture of the city), in *Nasledie A. Bloka i Aktual'nye Problemy Poetiki (Blokovskii Sbornik IV)* (Tartu: Tartu State University, 1981), pp. 7–26: "If Blok's 'World Symbols' ignore everyday vulgarity and ordinariness in his first phase, during the second they shine through [that vulgarity and ordinariness]. [...] For Blok, the mass culture of the contemporary city has meaning; its vulgarity is mysteriously connected with meanings of profound importance, distinguishing it from the vulgarity of the 'cultured' world of the intelligentsia, which is bereft of meaning. The simple and primitive vulgarity of that world of restaurant music, *café chantant,* and street entertainments, is a form of life—but a life that is primitive, primordial and naive, and therefore carrying a secret meaning. The 'cultured' style of life is inwardly empty; its very lack of crudeness testifies to its lifelessness [...]" (pp. 12–13).

16. The "bakery-pretzel" refers to the pretzel-shaped sign typically hung outside on Russian bakeries in this period.

17. On the notion of the late imperial suburb as a liminal space of danger and instability, see Stephen Lowell, "Between Arcadia and Suburbia: Dachas in Late Imperial Russia," *Slavic Review* 61, no. 1 (spring 2002): 66–87, esp. 84.

18. M. Iu. Lermontov, *Sochineniia,* ed. I. S. Chistovaia, intro. I. L. Andronikov, 2 vols. (Moscow: Pravda, 1988), 1:184–85.

19. Cf. Katerina Clark, "The City versus the Countryside in Soviet Peasant Literature of the Twenties: A Duel of Utopias": "Scythianism viewed the Revolution—the 'proletarian' revolution—as the triumph of the Russian village over the urban way of life. It was able to do so because it found a role for the Revolution in a version of the old Slavophile lament about Russia's downfall under Peter the Great. During Peter's reign, the lament would have it, a new way of life, a way antithetical to Russian traditions, had been imported from Europe and imposed on the country. The Scythians rejoiced in the overthrow of the Old Order because it was, as Pilniak reminded his readers *ad nauseam,* the Old Order of Peter, Catherine, et al. which had taken a 'straight edge' to higgledy-piggledy old Russia [. . . .] In all the violent upheaval and chaos, the peasant had effectively dismantled the city and returned Russia, willy-nilly, to her natural anarchic state" (in *Bolshevik Culture,* ed. Abbott Gleason, Peter Kenez, and Richard Stites [Bloomington: Indiana University Press, 1985], pp. 175–89; here p. 178).

20. A stove-bench (*lezhanka*) is a shelf running along the side of the stove in a Russian peasant house, or *izba,* that one can sleep on.

21. Leon Trotsky, *Literature and Revolution,* trans. Rose Strunsky (Ann Arbor: University of Michigan Press, 1960), p. 66. I have altered the translation slightly.

22. These and other biographical details are taken from the introduction by S. I. Subbotin and I. A. Kostin to their edited volume of Nikolai Kliuev's poetry, *Pesnoslov* ([Petrozavodsk: Kareliia, 1990), here p. 23, and mainly from the best book to date on Kliuev's life and poetry, K. M. Azadovskii's *Nikolai Kliuev: Put' poeta* (Leningrad: Sovetskii pisatel', 1990), here p. 319.

23. Kliuev, *Pesnoslov,* p. 104.

24. Trotsky, *Literature and Revolution,* p. 63.

25. See K. M. Azadovskii, " 'Menia nazval kitezhankoi': Anna Akhmatova i Nikolai Kliuev," *Literaturnoe obozrenie* 5 (1989): 67.

26. Yuri Slezkine notes how doctrines about the essentially "counter-revolutionary" nature of the peasantry had been promulgated as early as 1921. "The 'peasant element' was aggressive, contagious and menacing. No one assumed that its brand of savagery would dialectically dissolve itself through further development because the stubbornly 'somnolent' Russian peasant was incapable of development *as a peasant* (his was a difference 'in content')" ("The USSR as a Communal Apartment; or, How a Socialist State Promoted Ethnic Particularism," in *Becoming National: A Reader,* ed. Geoff Eley and Ronald Grigor Suny [New York: Oxford University Press, 1996], pp. 203–38; here p. 210).

27. Kliuev, *Pesnoslov,* p. 104.

28. In an important recent article, Ronald Vroon argues: "the canonical and dogmatic aspects of Old Belief interested Kliuev much less than its aesthetic side. It is apparent that he regarded the Old Belief as a projection of an entire world of Russian peasant culture, containing within itself (if only potentially) Orthodox devotion, Old Belief in all its persuasions and groupings, and of course sectarianism. If Kliuev distinguished Old Belief from the other [Orthodox] confessions, this can be explained by reference to its ethnocultural particularities, an ethos that outgrew its dogmatic and ritual foundations. Indeed, by the beginning of the

20th century, Old Belief was generally regarded as an emblem of a specific social structure and corresponding worldview, as having gone beyond its initially defining canon and rituals" ("Staroobriadchestvo, sektanstvo i 'sakral'naia rech'" v poezii Nikolaia Kliueva," *Nikolai Kliuev: Issledovaniia i materialy,* ed. S. I. Subbotin [Moscow: Nasledie, 1997], pp. 54–67; here pp. 61–62).

29. This phrase is from "Prostit'sia s laptem-miliagoi" (To say farewell to the dear little bast shoe)—bast shoes are the traditional peasant footwear, and *miliaga* (dear) is ironic—of 1921, a poem particularly rich in Kliuevan globalism (*Pesnoslov,* p. 122).

30. It is unclear to what extent Kliuev is creating a wholly personal mythology here; his sectarian interests and family background may have introduced him to the writings of Coptic (Egyptian) or "Thomas" (Indian) Christian groups, and some "exotic" narratives were demonstrably known among the peasantry. One of his finest poems is entitled "White India" ("Belaia India"), a utopian vision of the village. The medieval "Skazanie ob Indiiskom tsarstve" (Tale of the Indian kingdom), first translated into Bulgarian in the thirteenth century, was widely circulated and retold from the fifteenth century on, entering peasant culture through *byliny* (folk epics) about the hero Diuk Stepanovich, who hails from, among other places, "rich India" (or "Indeiushka"). See *Byliny,* ed. B. N. Putilov (Moscow: Sovetskii pisatel', 1986), pp. 309, 529–30. Kliuev's mother, of a literate Old Believer family, may have been another source. He wrote in 1919 that she "knew the 'Swan and Rose' from the '[book of] Six Wings,' the 'New Margaret'—a translation from the language of black Christians—[. . .] the fiery letters of Avvakum, the Indian Gospel and much more that secretly salts the people's soul: word, dream, and prayer that salted me as well, down to the bones; to the nether depths of my spirit and song" (*Pesnoslov,* p. 6).

31. Kliuev, *Pesnoslov,* p. 104.

32. As is well known, the first exposure of the Russian intelligentsia to Kliuev came in Blok's article, "Stikhiia i kul'tura" ("Culture and the elements" [December 1908]), a follow-up to his famous "The People and the Intelligentsia" of a month earlier), where Blok anonymously cites a letter to him from Kliuev (designated only as a "peasant, describing the atmosphere in one of the northern provinces"), a letter filled with accounts of unrest and apocalyptic, "Scythian" foreboding: "Even just two or three sincere, blood-consecrated words of the revolutionaries [. . .] make their mysterious, untraceable way into the people's heart, and find ready soil, and send their roots deep. For example: 'the land is God's,' 'all the land is the property of all the people' " ("Stikhiia i kul'tura," in Blok, *Sochineniia,* ed. V. Orlov, 2:92–101; here p. 99). Further references to this article are indicated with parenthetical page references. Kliuev and Blok were in correspondence from 1907 until at least 1911.

33. See Kliuev, *Pesnoslov,* pp. 8–9; and Azadovskii, *Nikolai Kliuev,* p. 47. Some of Kliuev's comments at the meetings were apparently published, anonymously, in a local newspaper. Much later, in April 1920, he was ejected from the Communist Party.

34. I quote these lines from the first volume of *Nikolai Kliuev: Sochineniia,* ed. G. Struve and B. Fillipov (Germany [no city indicated]: A. Neimanis, 1969), p. 470.

35. Kliuev, *Pesnoslov,* p. 98.

36. "Kerzhenskii" refers to Kerzhenets, a northern settlement of Old Believer hermits active from the seventeenth to the nineteenth centuries;

Andrei Denisov's "Pomorskie otvety" ("Pomorski responses") comprise the central document of Old Believer apologetics.

37. The history of the connections between religious dissent and social-democratic and other "secular" activism is worthy of more investigation. I mention here only one intriguing link, which is also the partial subject of Laura Engelstein's study of the "self-castrators," *Castration and the Heavenly Kingdom: A Russian Folktale* (Ithaca: Cornell University Press, 1999). This is the major, seven-volume compilation of various materials (testimonies, letters, legal documents, songs, and poems) about the various sectarian groups and branches of Old Belief. It was initially published from 1908 to 1916 under the title "Materials pertaining to the history and study of Russian sectarianism and schismatics" (later changed to "[...] the history and study of religious-social movements in Russia") by Vladimir Bonch-Bruevich (1873–1955), a close associate of Lenin in the prerevolutionary period and a major publisher of social-democratic and Bolshevik tracts and propaganda. It is, of course, hard to verify that Kliuev knew these volumes. See Vladimir Bonch-Bruevich, ed., *Materialy k istorii i izucheniiu russkago sektanstva i raskola,* 7 vols. (St. Petersburg, 1908–16).

38. See also Clark, "The City versus the Countryside," pp. 177–78.

39. V. Zhivov notes how the poet moved from describing the bloodshed of the revolution as signaling "universal and cosmic renovation" in the work around 1917 to describing the Bolsheviks as an "expanding atrocity, committing outrages on the image of the Virgin" in his 1933 *Burned Ruins* (V. Zhivov, "Kosmologicheskie utopii v vospriatii bol'shevistskoi revoliutsii i antikosmologicheskie motivy v russkoj poezii 1920–1930-x godov ('Stikhi o neizvestnom soldate' O. Mandel'shtama)," in *Sbornik statej K70–letiiu Prof. Iu. M. Lotmana,* ed. A. Mal'ts and V. Stolovich [Tartu: Tartu State University, 1992], p. 414).

40. Iu. Lotman, in "Blok i narodnaia kul'tura goroda," discusses the interest among Blok's contemporaries in finding ways both to generate a participatory mass culture and to accommodate diversity; projects for "democratization" were marked by "the tendency to carry the principles of folk art into the more traditional spheres of ['high'] art, including efforts to draw audiences directly into a co-creative process" (p. 12).

41. According to Andrea Graziosi, in *The Great Soviet Peasant War: Bolsheviks and Peasants, 1917–1933* (Cambridge, Mass.: Harvard University Press [Ukrainian Research Institute, Harvard], 1996), p. 2: "Of these victims *grosso modo* a few hundreds of thousands died in the fighting and the repressions of 1918–22; 5 million in the 1921–22 famine; up to one million in the deportations and the repressions of the early 1930s; more than one million during the denomadization of Central Asia (where at least another million people had perished between 1917 and 1920); and close to seven million in the 1932–33 famine [. . . .]" Among the works of history and testimony to be consulted regarding collectivization is *Dokumenty svidetel'stvuiut: Iz istorii derevnii nakanune i v khode kollektivizatsii 1927–1932 gg.,* ed. V. P. Danilov and N. A. Ivnitskii (Moscow: Izdatel'stvo politicheskoi literatury, 1989). The death tolls involved in the "West's" central expansionist modernizations—colonialism and slavery—came earlier and are, alas, easily comparable; see, inter alia, Mike Davis, *Late Victorian Holocausts: El Niño Famines and the Making of the Third World* (London: Verso, 2001).

42. In this formulation I again borrow from Graziosi, who finds the specificity of the Soviet "solution" to the peasant problem in "the maximum repression

possible of the peasants' autonomous participation—*on their own terms*—in the process of modernization, i.e., in their own disappearance" (*Great Soviet Peasant War*, p. 75).

43. "[...] Trotsky identifies the use of standard, educated Russian with political progress [....] [He] and the Productionists ['a militantly utilitarian group'] both identified folkisms, grammatical infelicities, and most other forms of substandard speech as tendencies in language that impeded rational and efficient patterns of speech and thought and should therefore be banned. [...] Their linguistic reforms were conceived as part of a general program for overhauling patterns of daily life that included rationalized communal living" (Clark, *Petersburg*, pp. 208–209).

44. Ibid., p. 286: "Gorky mandated that all dialecticisms and substandard expressions be kept out of Soviet literature. Thanks to his policies, the "living speech" of the urban proletariat so idealized in the late 1920s by writers, linguists and reformers in the theater and opera was now expunged with particular zeal. [...] Gorky's emphasis was on avoiding the prosaic; his model was the language of epic, rhetoricized language."

45. Ibid.

46. See Paul de Man's essay, "The Epistemology of Metaphor," in *Aesthetic Ideology*, ed. and intro. Andrzej Warminski (Minneapolis: University of Minnesota Press, 1996).

47. See Frederick Winslow Taylor, *The Principles of Scientific Management* (New York: W. W. Norton, 1967), p. 123. See also Steven Roger Fischer, *A History of Language* (London: Reaktion Books, 1999), pp. 172–85.

48. Michel de Certeau, *The Writing of History*, trans. Tom Conley (New York: Columbia University Press, 1988), p. 223.

49. It should be noted that, within the Soviet context, strategies of normalization were crucially informed by vulgar misinterpretations of Engels's "call" for the abolition of "the antithesis between town and country" in *The Housing Question* (1872–73). In truth, Engels refused to formulate any program, not to speak of a proto-Stalinist one, for achieving this "abolition": "To be utopian [meant here negatively as authoritarian "utopian socialism"] does not mean to maintain that the emancipation of humanity from the chains which its historic past has forged will be complete only when the antithesis between town and country has been abolished; the utopia begins only when one ventures, 'from existing conditions,' to prescribe the *form* in which this or any other antithesis of present-day society is to be resolved" (*Collected Works*, ed. Eric Hobsbawm et al., vol. 23 [Moscow: Progress, 1988], pp. 384–85). For a good discussion of Engels's general ideas on urban development, see Carl E. Schorske, "The Idea of the City in European Thought: Voltaire to Spengler," in *The Historian and the City*, ed. Oscar Handlin and John Burchard (Cambridge, Mass.: Harvard University Press, 1963), pp. 105–107. For an account of the Soviet debates that implicated Engels's views, and of the fate of the Russian "garden-city" movement, see S. Frederick Starr, "The Revival and Schism of Urban Planning in Twentieth-Century Russia," in *The City in Russian History*, ed. Michael F. Hamm, pp. 230–40 (Lexington: University of Kentucky Press, 1976).

50. These remarks on language were written between 1914 and 1922; see Velimir Khlebnikov, *Collected Works*, trans. Paul Schmidt, ed. Charlotte Douglas (Cambridge, Mass.: Harvard University Press, 1987), pp. 400–405.

51. Trotsky, *Literature and Revolution*, p. 132.

52. The "enamel" and "painted branch" are allusions to the practice of icon painting; "Sirin" is a divine bird in Russian pagan mythology that enchants with her singing.

53. Lev Aleksandrovich Mei (1822–1862), a poet who used Russian folklore and history in his work, is most famous as the author of "Tsarskaia nevesta" (The tsar's bride), which was made into an opera by Rimsky-Korsakov. Ivan Savvich Nikitin (1824–1861) began as a conservative and religious poet, becoming more and more a poet of protest (partially under the influence of Chernyshevsky) in his descriptions of peasant life and poverty. Aleksei Vasil'evich Kol'tsov (1809–1842), a poet of nature and of peasant life and labor, hailed by Belinsky as a great populist artist. Monuments to both Nikitin and Kol'tsov were erected soon after the 1917 Revolution. "Veles" is a Russian pagan divinity.

54. The archpriest Avvakum (d. 1682 at the stake), one of the most fiery leaders of the first generation of Old Believers, was immortalized by his autobiography, which is among the most celebrated works of Russian prose.

55. Pustozersk is a remote northern place of exile where Avvakum was burned at the stake, along with three associates, in 1682.

56. The adjectives refer, of course, to Pushkin's dark skin and curly hair.

57. Thus Kliuev's poem is probably best classified as "iconic" in Jean Hagstrum's sense: a work that "strikingly illustrates the association of verbal and graphic art" where "the poet contemplates a real or imaginary work of art that he describes or responds to in some other way." Hagstrum finds the prototype of such writing in the description of Achilles shield in book 18 of the *Iliad* (Jean H. Hagstrum, *The Sister Arts: The Tradition of Literary Pictorialism and English Poetry from Dryden to Gray* [Chicago: University of Chicago Press, 1958], p. 18).

58. Mandelstam's longest mention of Kliuev emphasized a similar kind of "harmony," although he selected a different canonical master for comparison: "[Kliuev] came from the majestic Olonetsk region where Russian life and Russian peasant speech repose in Hellenic dignity and simplicity. [He] is a national poet because the iambic spirit of Baratynsky lives harmoniously in his verse along with the prophetic melody of the illiterate Olonetsk teller of tales" ("A Letter about Russian Poetry" [1922], in *The Complete Critical Prose*, p. 100). We should also note the resonance of Kliuev's use of the peasant-nanny figure with Friedrich A. Kittler's well-known argument about the way that "mother-tongues" were naturalized in the early nineteenth century through technologies of language learning that were made into the province of mothers and their surrogates, like nannies. After around 1800, "the system of equivalents Woman = Nature = Mother allowed acculturation to begin from an absolute origin. A culture established on this basis speaks differently about language, writes differently about writing. Briefly put, it has Poetry. For only when phonetics and the alphabet shortcircuit the official route from a natural source to those on the receiving end can a kind of speech arise that can be thought of as an ideal of Nature. This placing of mothers at the origin of discourse was the condition of production for Classical poetry, and the Mother was the first Other to be understood by poetical hermeneutics. . . . What is important are not biographical mothers with their comedies and tragedies, but the mothers and midwives of a completely new ABC book; not the transformation of dreams or desires but a new technique of transcription that determines writing" (*Discourse Networks, 1800/1900*, trans. Michael Metteer and Chris Cullens, intro. David E. Wellbery [Stanford: Stanford University Press, 1990],

p. 28). Kliuev's own poetic midwifery, it might be said, attempts both to preserve this naturalizing mechanism and to enlarge what it might "legitimately" yield.

59. Calling Kliuev a "ruralist decadent" does not seem inaccurate. Cf. Paul Bourget on the decadent preoccupation with the "rare word": "A decadent style is one where the unity of the book is broken down in favor of the independence of the page, where the page is broken down to allow the independence of the phrase, and [similarly] the phrase in favor of the word" (quoted in Nicholls, *Modernisms*, p. 59).

60. Cf. Fredric Jameson's comment on Northrop Frye's "identification of mythic patterns in modern texts" as "awakening a sense of the continuity between our psychic life and that of primitive peoples" (*The Political Unconscious*, p. 130).

61. We know too little about Kliuev's education; apart from his own travels, associations with the "khlysty," and contact with poets (including participation in the short-lived "Krasa" group [1915]), an attempt to unite "peasant" and "city" poets (including Ivanov and Remizov), it is hard to know the exact sources of his knowledge. The fact of his "book learning" is not in doubt, however, and his biographer, Azadovskii, argues: "Kliuev's 'Russianness' is for the most part of literary [*knizhnyi*] origin" (*Put' poeta*, p. 326). Of course, Kliuev would have had a huge body of nineteenth-century folkloristic work to draw upon, from Dal' and P. V. Kireevsky through the *byliny* collections of Rybnikov and Hilferding to the historical studies of V. F. Miller.

62. An "ethnographer-lexicographer," Dal' set purely oral variants alongside bookish ones; as an ardent nationalist, he also excluded foreign borrowings on the grounds of extraneousness or impurity. Indeed, he sometimes translated foreign words into his hypothetical "folk Russian" (among Viktor Vinogradov's examples: instead of *garmoniia* [harmony], *soglas*; for *sinonim* [synonym], *tozhdeslov*) when he could not find them there. Many of the missing foreign words were added in later editions. See V. V. Vinogradov, *Izbrannye trudy: Leksikologiia i leksikografiia* (Moscow: Nauka, 1977), pp. 223–30.

63. Kliuev, as is well known, provided his own glossary for readers of his *Burned Ruins*.

64. For a penetrating discussion of some of the French avant-garde subversions of the standardizing lexicon, see Denis Hollier, *Against Architecture: The Writings of Georges Bataille*, trans. Betsy Wing (Cambridge, Mass.: MIT Press, 1992), pp. 27–31.

65. The lexicon as discussed here should be related to Jacques Rancière's brilliant account of "the plot of the Museum, conceived not as a building and an institution but as a mode of rendering visible and intelligible the 'life of art.' [. . . .] Our museums [. . .] exhibit a time-space of art as so many moments of the incarnation of thought. [. . . .] [Within this time-space] the works of the past can be considered as forms for new contents or raw materials for new formations. They can be reviewed, re-framed, re-read, re-made. It is thus that museums exorcized the rigid plot of the 'spirit of forms' leading to the 'end of arts.' Artistic ruptures became possible, too, because the museum offered a multiplication of the temporalities of art, allowing for instance Manet to become a painter of modern life by re-painting Velásquez and Titian" ("The Aesthetic Revolution," pp. 141, 143).

66. Mandelstam, "On the Nature of the Word," in *The Complete Critical Prose*, pp. 77, 79

67. Vladimir Markov, *Russian Futurism: A History* (Berkeley: University of California Press, 1968), pp. 13, 93. For a useful and highly entertaining list of some of Khlebnikov's verbal creations, see V. P. Grigor'ev, *Budetlianin* (Moscow: Iazyki

russkoi kul'tury, 2000), pp. 371–76. Grigor'ev's book gives an encyclopedic account of the poet's linguistic practice.

68. "Simple Names of the Language" is the title of a famous essay by Khlebnikov that lists and explains some of his discoveries around the letters M, V, K, and S (in *Snake Train: Poetry and Prose,* ed. Gary Kern, trans. Gary Kern et al. [Ann Arbor: Ardis, 1976], pp. 201–206).

69. Velimir Khlebnikov, *Sobranie sochinenii,* ed. R. D. Duganov et al., 6 vols. (Moscow: IMLI RAN, "Nasledie," 2000), 1:209. Other "neologic" poems, including later ones like the marvelous "Angels" and "Steppe" (both from 1919) could have been selected for analysis here as well.

70. *Snake Train,* trans. Kern et al., p. 62.

71. Markov, *Russian Futurism,* p. 8.

72. Khlebnikov, "Slava tebe, koster chelovechestva" (1920), in *Sobranie sochinenii,* 2:77.

73. Harvey Goldblatt has reminded me of the similarity of Khlebnikov's experiment to the "word-weaving" characteristic of writing during the East Slavic Orthodox Revival, particularly in the "Life of St. Stefan of Perm'." On the relation of the poem to the "paregmenon" ("proizvozhdenie") of classical rhetoric, see Roman Jakobson, "Noveishaia russkaia poeziia," in *Mir Velimira Khebnikova: stat'i, issledovaniia 1911–1998,* ed. V. V. Ivanov et al. (Moscow: Iazyki russkoi kul'tury, 2000), p. 56.

74. Markov, *Russian Futurism,* p. 58.

75. Andrew Wachtel, "Translation, Imperialism, and National Self-Definition in Russia," in *Alternative Modernities,* ed. Dilip Parameshwar Gaonkar (Durham: Duke University Press, 2001), pp. 58–85; here pp. 74–75.

76. Rancière, "The Aesthetic Revolution," p. 143.

77. "To the Artists of the World," in *The King of Time,* trans. Paul Schmidt, ed. Charlotte Douglas (Cambridge, Mass.: Harvard University Press, 1985), p. 147 (my emphasis); quoted in Wachtel, "Translation, Imperialism, and National Self-Definition," p. 73.

78. Rancière, *The Ignorant Schoolmaster,* p. 38.

79. Mandelstam, "Some Notes on Poetry," in *The Complete Critical Prose,* pp. 104–105).

80. This distinguishes Khlebnikov from the Joycean project as well, for the latter still hopes to be *comprehensive,* to offer us a "book of the world."

81. On Khlebnikov and Lobachevskii, see H. Baran, "Poeticheskaia logika i poeticheskii alogizm Velimira Khlebnikova," in idem, *Mir Velimira Khlebnikova,* trans. Iu. A. Kleiner, ed., V. V. Ivanov et al. (Moscow: Iazyki russkoi kul'tury, 2000), pp. 550–67; here p. 567.

82. Cf. Jameson's discussion in *Postmodernism,* pp. 16–25; see introduction, n. 27.

83. Bill Readings, *The University in Ruins* (Cambridge, Mass.: Harvard University Press, 1996), pp. 110–11.

4. Unkind Weight

1. Osip Mandelstam, "Konets romana" (The end of the novel), in *Sochineniia,* ed. P. Nerler and A. Mikhailov, intro. S. Averintsev, 2 vols. (Moscow:

Khudozhestvennaia literatura, 1990), 2:203. Further references to this essay are cited in the text, with page numbers in parentheses.

2. Buck-Morss, *Dreamworld and Catastrophe,* p. 102. J. N. Findlay describes the relation of Napoleon's spirit to Spirit per se: "The Cunning of Reason 'lets passions forth, whereby that which is put into existence through these, pays the penalty and suffers loss.' This Cunning of Reason is shown at its highest in the careers of certain World-historical Individuals, men like Alexander, Caesar or Napoleon, who in aggrandizing themselves, or in defending themselves against rivals, make the transition to completely new levels in self-consciousness, generally destroying themselves in the process" (*Hegel: A Re-examination* [New York: Oxford University Press, 1958], p. 330).

3. Cf. Jameson's remarks in his *Marxism and Form,* pp. 42–43: "The dominant figure of Napoleon [. . .] is symbolic of the basic ambiguity of this [early nineteenth-century] moment which follows the collapse of the feudal order in Europe and precedes the definitive setting up of the new ethical, political and economic institutions of the middle classes which triumphed over it. He combines something of the fading values of feudality and sacred kingship with the frankly secular and propagandistic appeal of the charismatic political leaders of later middle-class society, yet at the same time can be assimilated neither to the bewigged absolute monarchs of the sixteenth and seventeenth centuries nor to the demagogues of the twentieth."

4. Christopher Winks, "Ruins and Foundation Stones: The Paris Commune and the Destruction of the Vendôme Column," in *Revolutionary Romanticism,* ed. Max Blechman (San Francisco: City Lights Books, 1999), pp. 101–24; here pp. 103, 110. See also David Harvey's account of the Commune and the ongoing history of its commemoration in *Paris, Capital of Modernity,* pp. 311–40.

5. Kristin Ross, *The Emergence of Social Space: Rimbaud and the Paris Commune,* intro. Terry Eagleton (Minneapolis: University of Minnesota Press, 1988), p. 4.

6. For one powerful recent account of this situation, see Peter Gatrell, *A Whole Empire Walking: Refugees in Russia during World War I* (Bloomington: Indiana University Press, 1999).

7. Mandelstam's dates are 1891 to 1938; a victim of the purges, he died in a labor camp on December 27, 1938. On the termination of utopian speculation in the USSR during the 1930s and Stalin's "intense hatred of revolutionary utopianism" and his "anti-utopian utopia," see Richard Stites, *Revolutionary Dreams: Utopian Vision and Experimental Life in the Russian Revolution* (New York: Oxford University Press, 1989), esp. pp. 242–53 (above quote at pp. 246–47). This is not to say, of course, that the Russia of 1905–17, or the USSR of 1918–28, were in any way "achieved utopias," harrowed as they were by famine, war, and state violence.

8. From the Sixth Letter in Schiller's *On the Aesthetic Education of Man in a Series of Letters,* ed., trans, and intro. Elizabeth M. Wilkinson and L. A. Willoughby (Oxford: Oxford University Press, 1967), p. 35. All further quotations from Schiller are from this edition.

9. These theories also influenced the development of Meyerhold's "biomechanics," and their strong effects are apparent in the film-theoretical writings of Kuleshov, Eisenstein, Pudovkin and Vertov. See Katerina Clark, *Petersburg, Crucible of Cultural Revolution* (Cambridge, Mass.: Harvard University Press, 1995), pp. 76, 86, 90–91, 105–260; and Susan Buck-Morss's discussion

of the mass reenactments of the October Revolution during the early years of the Soviet Union in her *Dreamworld and Catastrophe,* pp. 134–49.

10. Osip Mandelstam, "Government and Rhythm." This and other citations from Mandelstam's prose works are drawn, unless otherwise indicated, from Osip Mandelstam, *The Complete Critical Prose,* ed. Jane Gary Harris, trans. Jane Gary Harris and Constance Link (Ann Arbor: Ardis, 1997); here pp. 68–69. All further references to this volume are in parentheses in the main text, with essay title and page number indicated.

11. Jacques Rancière, "The Aesthetic Revolution," p. 136.

12. Ibid., pp. 139–40.

13. Ibid., p. 143. Citing the contemporary French theorist here is less arbitrary than it might seem, for Rancière has written brilliantly and in detail on Mandelstam's poetry elsewhere, and indeed it would seem that Mandelstam has had no small influence on Rancière's own ideas about culture. In a recent essay he focuses on Mandelstam's "poetic labor upon time: the sudden overturning of the black earth—the *chernozem*—of time which places all languages, arrangements of words and significant sedimentations of the past at the disposal of the poet. 'Classical poetry,' writes Mandelstam [in "The Word and Culture," p. 116] 'is the poetry of revolution.' [. . . .] But the plainly anti-futurist provocation of this proclamation in no way turns the culture of the past into an encyclopedia placed at the disposition of the young revolution. [. . . .] [The] words and verses [of the classical writers] remain unfulfilled promises, instruments whose greatest capabilities are still to be discovered" ("De Wordsworth à Mandelstam: Les Transports de la Liberté," in *La Chair des Mots: Politique de l'écriture* [Paris: Galilée, 1998], pp. 17–54; here pp. 46–47).

14. Cf. "Conversation about Dante," p. 420: "For Dante time is the content of history understood as a simply synchronic act; and vice-versa: the contents of history are the joint containing of time by its associates, competitors, and co-discoverers. Dante is an antimodernist. His contemporaneity is continuous, incalculable and inexhaustible. That is why Odysseus' speech, as convex as the lens of a magnifying glass, may be turned toward the war of the Greeks and Persians as well as toward Columbus' discovery of America, the bold experiments of Paracelsus, and the world empire of Charles V."

15. Immanuel Kant, *Critique of Judgment,* trans. and intro. J. H. Bernard (New York: Hafner, 1951), p. 200; my emphasis.

16. Hart Crane, "Modern Poetry," in *The Collected Poems of Hart Crane,* ed. Waldo Frank (New York: Liveright, 1946), pp. 175–79. Considered within the English-language tradition, Crane is continuing a line of thought here to which Wordsworth in the "Preface to *Lyrical Ballads*" gave the best-known articulation: "The remotest discoveries of the Chemist, the Botanist, or Mineralogist, will be as proper objects of the Poet's art as any upon which it can be employed, if the time should ever come when these things shall be familiar to us, and the relations under which they are contemplated by the followers of these respective Sciences shall be manifestly and palpably material to us as enjoying and suffering beings" (*The Poems,* 1:881).

17. As has been noticed, Mandelstam (like Benjamin) invokes Bergson as the contemporary philosopher who had done most to undo the grip of notions of mechanical causality upon thought. "[Bergson] is interested exclusively in the internal connection among phenomena. He liberates this connection from time and considers it independently. Phenomena thus connected to one another form,

as it were, a kind of fan whose folds can be opened up in time; however, this fan may also be closed up in a way intelligible to the human mind" ("On the Nature of the Word," p. 73). Hilary L. Fink has observed that the "organic noncausality" to which Mandelstam appeals is "in many ways the essence of duration" (*Bergson and Russian Modernism: 1900–1930* [Evanston, Ill.: Northwestern University Press, 1999], pp. 64–65). A common Bergsonian line also seems to link Mandelstam's ideas of poetry's poly-temporality with Gilles Deleuze's poly-temporal cinematic "time-image" (see *Cinema 2: The Time-Image,* trans. Hugh Tomlinson and Robert Galeta [Minneapolis: University of Minnesota Press, 1989], pp. 83–125).

18. Tilottama Rajan finely locates this dialectic for us within Hegel's own reflections on aesthetics: "[F]or Hegel there is no author in the sense of an origin. The author is merely the medium through which the conflicting voices of a given historical period speak, and the aporetic texts or systems of thought thus produced can be properly read only as they are unfolded toward their resolution in the historical process. [. . .] Try as he will to salvage an essentialist concept of meaning [. . .] Hegel cannot really disentangle a transcendental signified from the process of its own signification, which constantly makes and unmakes it" (*The Supplement of Reading: Figures of Understanding in Romantic Theory and Practice* [Ithaca: Cornell University Press, 1990], pp. 55–56).

19. Mandelstam's strongest statement on the relation between study, criticism, and creation is in his short article "The Slump" (pp. 126–28), where he calls for a specifically "poetic literacy" (p. 127).

20. Here, specifically, of Andrei Bely ("On the Nature of the Word," p. 76).

21. This is not the place to discuss Mandelstam's relationship to religious trends in the culture of his day; my own sense is that his theoretical work shows little trace of overt religious preoccupation after the early essays (written under the influence of Gippius and Ivanov) like "Pushkin and Scriabin." His profoundly secularized account of Dante in "Conversation," and his attack on the "cult of Dantean mysticism," seems far more representative of his mature attitude.

22. "The Storyteller," pp. 108–109. It would be interesting to know the extent to which Mandelstam's notion of historically cumulative verbal "events" might be influenced by or share common roots with Bakhtin's conception of event as "co-being" (*"so-bytie"*); for a lucid account of the latter idea, see Michael Holquist, *Dialogism: Bakhtin and His World* (London: Routledge, 1990), p. 25.

23. Mandelstam was undoubtedly familiar with Schiller and mentions him on several occasions (usually as part of his rather derisive accounts of his father's reading interests) in "The Noise of Time" (in *The Prose of Osip Mandelstam,* trans. and intro. Clarence Brown [Princeton, N.J.: Princeton University Press, 1965], pp. 63, 79, 82–83, 91, 120).

24. Schiller, *On the Aesthetic Education of Man,* pp. 19, 21.

25. See chap. 3 n. 58.

26. It should be added that the Baudelaire/Bataille fetish (discussed in chapter 2), or the fixations of "decadent" poetry, involve precisely *formless values,* in that they are "wanted" independently of any communicable standard.

27. David Quint, *Epic and Empire: Politics and Generic Form from Virgil to Milton* (Princeton, N.J.: Princeton University Press, 1993), p. 365.

28. In his poem "Ia—posviashchennyi ot naroda"; in Kliuev, *Pesnoslov,* p. 103.

29. Gregory Freidin, "The Whisper of History and the Noise of Time in the Writings of Osip Mandel'shtam," *Russian Review* 37, no. 4 (October 1978): 421–37; here p. 436.

30. Cf. Fredric Jameson in his chapter "Marcuse and Schiller," in *Marxism and Form:* "For hermeneutics, traditionally a technique whereby religions recuperated the texts and spiritual activities of cultures resistant to them, is also a political discipline, and provides the means for maintaining contact with the very sources of revolutionary energy during a stagnant time, of preserving the concept of freedom itself, underground, during geological ages of repression" (p. 84).

31. From Schiller's Ninth Letter in *On the Aesthetic Education of Man,* pp. 56–57.

32. Omry Ronen, *An Approach to Mandelstam* (Jerusalem: Magnes Press of Hebrew University, 1983), p. xii.

33. Catullus, "Poem 46," in *The Complete Poetry of Catullus,* trans. and ed. David Mulroy (Madison: University of Wisconsin Press, 2002), p. 36.

34. "Poets [. . .] can colour all that they combine with the evanescent hues of this ethereal world; a word, a trait in the representation of a scene or a passion, will touch the enchanted chord, and reanimate, in those who have ever experienced these emotions, the sleeping, the cold, the buried image of the past." ("A Defense of Poetry," in *Shelley's Poetry and Prose,* p. 505). See also Andrew Bennett, *Romantic Poets and the Culture of Posterity* (Cambridge: Cambridge University Press, 1999).

35. Cf. Paul Fry's argument (in his superb chapter, "The Absent Dead," in *A Defense of Poetry*) that much Romantic literature "understands what is vital and what is dead as the two faces of a single poetical character. For the Romantics, that is, life and death are not primarily a temporal sequence, but are equally potential in any single moment, depending on how that moment is affected by the imagination. Not just a funerary occasion but any occasion may then be marked as an epitaph" (p. 163).

36. Benjamin, "Some Motifs in Baudelaire," *Charles Baudelaire,* p. 140.

37. On the problem of comprehensibility in Mandelstam, see Rancière, "De Wordsworth à Mandelstam," pp. 49–54.

38. In fact, "construction" became a less important model for poetry after *Stone* (1913), when imagery of burial and retreat becomes more prominent. L. G. Kikhnei provides a succinct summary of the trajectory of Mandelstam's imagery of building and "domestication," in *Filosofsko-esteticheskie printsipy akmeizma i khudozhestvennaia praktika Osipa Mandel'shtama* (Moscow: Dialog-MGU, 1997), pp. 189–99; see also Ronen, *An Approach to Mandelstam.*

39. Susanne Langer, *Feeling and Form* (New York: Scribner's, 1953), pp. 98–99.

40. As usual, *Frankenstein* represents a limit point, in that the scientist there invents a process that could substitute for birth itself.

41. Langer, *Feeling and Form,* p. 99.

42. Cf. Nadezhda Mandelstam's dismissive account of Ivanov's cultural politics: "In his vision of the idyllic times to come, Ivanov dreamed of 'like-mindedness.' In the era of rampant Dionysianism, the individual spectator at tragedies and mysteries was to 'merge with the like-minded multitude.' Like-mindedness was indeed achieved; it was not, however, the work of the elite with its grand dreams, but of the revolutionary intelligentsia which, after its victory, knew very well how to curb freedom of thought and person" (*Hope Abandoned,* trans. Max Hayward [New York: Atheneum, 1974], p. 406). Her discussion implies that the early Mandelstam was indeed influenced by Ivanov's metaphors, with which he thereafter carried on a "hidden polemic" (p. 408).

43. Among the many excellent readings of this poem, the most helpful I have found are those by Clare Cavanagh (*Osip Mandelstam and the Modernist Creation of Tradition* [Princeton, N.J.: Princeton University Press, 1995], pp. 81–102); and Peter Steiner ("Poem as Manifesto: Mandel'shtam's 'Notre Dame,'" *Russian Literature* 3 [July 1977]: 239–56).

44. A line with a weight on it, used by builders to show vertical direction.

45. Steiner observes that "the selection of the word ["basilica"] by Mandel'shtam is quite intentional here, since a basilica was originally a hall of justice handed over by the Roman emperors and consecrated for religious use. Once again the cross-cultural link is being stressed" ("Poem as Manifesto," p. 244).

46. I. Gurvich, *Mandel'shtam: Problema chteniia i ponimaniia* (New York: Gnosis, 1994), p. 43; my emphasis.

47. No doubt Mandelstam wants the reference to a "joiner" to recall Peter the Great's unusual interest in and aptitude for carpentry (he worked as a shipwright in England and in Holland).

48. "How intelligently did Pushkin define the meaning of an all-powerful monarchy, and how generally intelligent he was in everything that he said in the last days of his life! 'Why is it necessary,' he said, 'that one of us be above all and even above the law? Because the law is unbending; a man feels in the law something cruel and unbrotherly. You do not get very far with only the literal fulfillment of the law; certainly none of us should transgress or violate it; for that a superior mercy is needed, to soften the law, a mercy which can be manifested among the people only by an all-powerful sovereign. A state without an all-powerful monarch is an automaton: it is already much if it achieves what the United States has achieved. And what is the United States? Carrion. A dead body. A man there is so empty spiritually that he is not worth an egg. A state without an absolute monarch is an orchestra without a conductor: all the musicians could be excellent, but if there is no one to control them with his baton, the concert will not take place. It seems that he does nothing himself, he plays no instrument, only gently waves his baton and looks at the musicians; but one look from him is sufficient to soften, in this or that place, a rough sound emitted by a fool of a drum or a clumsy trombone. Thanks to him, the first violin will not dare to break loose at the expense of the others; he will be concerned with the whole composition, he the animator of the whole, the supreme head of this supreme harmony!' How aptly Pushkin expressed it! How he understood the meaning of these great truths!" (Nikolai Gogol, *Selected Passages from Correspondence with Friends,* trans. Jesse Zeldin [Nashville: Vanderbilt University Press, 1969], pp. 53–54). This is apparently the only evidence we have of this particular Pushkinian observation, and serious doubt has been cast on its veracity, or at least on Gogol's peculiar "spin."

49. Certainly Mandelstam's is not the only way to look at the matter; for the story of the remarkably successful "conductor-less" orchestra Persimfans, see Stites, *Revolutionary Dreams,* pp. 135–40.

Conclusion

1. "Mole" here is a "gram molecule" (chem.).

2. I. M. Semenko, "Tvorcheskaia istoriia 'Stikhov o neizvestnom soldate,'" *Poetika pozdnego Mandel'shtama,* ed. S. Vasilenko, intro. L. Ginzburg (Moscow: Mandel'shamovskoe obshchestvo, 1997), p. 86.

3. L. F. Katsis, "Mandel'shtam i Bairon (k analizu 'Stikhov o neizvestnom soldate')," in *Slovo i sud'ba: Osip Mandel'shtam,* ed. Z. S. Papernyi (Moscow: Nauka, 1991), pp. 436–53.

4. O. Ronen, "K siuzhetu 'Stikhov o neizvestnom soldate,'" in Papernyi, *Slovo i sud'ba,* pp. 428–36.

5. Semenko, "Tvorcheskaia istoriia 'Stikhov o neizvestnom soldate,'" pp. 86–105. Semenko's fundamental study clears the ground for all further interpretive work on Mandelstam's "Verses."

6. Zhivov, "Kosmologicheskie utopii," pp. 411–34.

7. V. V. Ivanov, "'Stikhi o neizvestnom soldate' v kontekste mirovoi poezii," in *Zhizn' i tvorchestvo O. E. Mandel'shtama,* ed. S. Averintsev et al. (Voronezh: Izdatel'stvo Voronezhskogo Universiteta, 1990), pp. 356–66; here p. 362.

8. My discussion here will help, in general, to confirm Boris Gasparov's sense of Mandelstam's consciousness of affinity between his own time and that of the revolutionary Romantic period, and of the poet's vision of the 1930s as a renewed ossification of society into an "iron age." In an important essay on Mandelstam, Gasparov notes how Soviet writers in the 1920s began to assert similarities "between the contemporary era and the beginning of the nineteenth century, also a time of revolutions, European wars, and the stormy rise of Romantic and utopian idealism. This similarity prompted thoughts of a new beginning that would repeat, on the principle of a 'centennial return,' the revolutionary and Romantic upsurge of the era of Pushkin and Napoleon" ("The Iron Age of the 1930s: The Centennial Return in Mandelstam," in *Rereading Russian Poetry,* ed. Stephanie Sandler [New Haven: Yale University Press, 1999], pp. 78–103; here p. 80).

9. Benjamin, "The Storyteller," in idem, *Illuminations,* p. 84.

10. See Principle 7 of "The Principles of Philosophy, or, the Monadology" (1714): "There is [. . .] no way of explaining how a monad [or "a simple substance that enters into composites"] can be altered or changed internally by some other creature, since one cannot transpose anything in it, nor can one conceive of any internal motion that can be excited, directed, augmented, or diminished within it, as can be done in composites, where there can be change among the parts. The monads have no windows through which something can enter or leave. Accidents cannot be detached, nor can they go about outside of substances, as the sensible species of the Scholastics once did. Thus, neither substance nor accident can enter a monad from without" (G. W. Leibniz, *Philosophical Essays,* ed. and trans. Roger Ariew and Daniel Garber [Indianapolis: Hackett, 1989], pp. 213–14).

11. Ibid., p. 213.

12. *Molodaia Gvardiia* 8 (August 1933): 62. The poem is mentioned in the very useful endnotes in the Nerler edition, and contains, significantly, an epigraph from Lermontov.

13. Mikhail Iampolskii, "In the Shadow of Monuments," in *Soviet Hieroglyphics: Visual Culture in Late Twentieth-Century Russia* (Bloomington: Indiana University Press, 1995), pp. 93–112; here p. 106.

14. See Hartman, "Romantic Poetry and the Genius Loci," in idem, *Beyond Formalism,* pp. 311–36.

15. V. Zhivov, for example, argues that Lermontovian echoes—employed, as we recall, by Blok as well to set up a contrast between the subjectivities of

1840 and 1906—serve to recall an older Romantic individuality not subsumable into a collective identity ("Kosmologicheskie utopii," p. 423).

16. Napoleon.

17. *Byron's Poetry,* ed. Frank D. McConnell (New York: W. W. Norton, 1978), p. 53.

18. Francis Berry, "The Poet of Childe Harold," reprinted in *Byron's Poetry,* p. 381.

19. G. Wilson Knight, "An Essay on Byron," in idem, *The Burning Oracle: Studies in the Poetry of Action* (London: Oxford University Press, 1939), p. 210.

20. Quoted in Findlay, *Hegel: A Re-examination,* p. 32.

21. G. W. F. Hegel, *Phänomenologie des Geistes,* ed. Eva Moldenhauer and Karl Markus Michel (Frankfurt am Main: Suhrkamp, 1970), p. 591. All further references to the *Phenomenology* in the original are drawn from this edition (hereafter abbreviated *PG*); page numbers are cited in parentheses.

22. G. W. F. Hegel, *Phenomenology of Spirit,* trans. A. V. Miller, intro. J. N. Findlay (Oxford: Oxford University Press, 1977), p. 493. All further English citations from the *Phenomenology* are from this edition (hereafter abbreviated *PS*); page numbers are cited in parentheses.

23. Recognition of the similarities might be eased by displaying the Russian version; here, with the important sections in italics, is Gustav Shpet's translation of the same passage:

> Tsel', absoliutnoe znanie, ili dukh, *znaiushchii sebia v kachestve dukha,* dolzhen proiti put' vospominaniia o dukhakh, kak oni sushchestvuiut v nem samom i kak oni osushchestvliaiut organizatsiiu svoego tsarstva. Sokhranennie ikh [v pamiati], esli rassmatrivat' so storony ikh svobodnogo nalichnogo bytiia, iavliaiushchegosia v forme sluchainosti, est' istoriia, so storony zhe ikh organizatsii, postignutoi v poniatii,—nauka o iavliaiushchemsia znanii; obe storony vmeste—istoriia, postignutaia v poniatii,—*i sostavliaiut vospominanie absoliutnogo dukha i ego Golgofu* [*Schädelstätte,* skull-place], deistvitel'nost', istinu i dostovernost' ego prestola, bez kotorogo on byl by bezzhiznennym i odinokim; lish' —
>
> *Iz chashi etogo tsartstva dukhov*
> *Penitsia dlia nego ego bezkonechnost'.*
>
> (G. V. F. Gegel', *Sistema Nauk, Chast' Pervaia: Fenomenologiia Dukha,* trans. G. Shpet [St. Petersburg: Nauka, 1994], p. 434)

It is intriguing that Shpet was translating the *Phenomenology* (in forced Siberian exile) at the same time that Mandelstam was working on "Verses" (1937–38); however, I have been unable to track down any connections between the two men.

24. Friedrich Schiller, *Gedichte,* ed. Gerhard Fricke (Stuttgart: Reclam, 1980), p. 20.

25. Cf. Jürgen Habermas, *The Philosophical Discourse of Modernity: Twelve Lectures,* trans. Frederick Lawrence (Cambridge, Mass.,: MIT Press, 1987), pp. 34–50. "Hegel had [the reflective art of Romanticism] right before his eyes when he integrated Schiller's interpretation of modern art through the philosophy of history into his concept of the absolute spirit. In art in general the spirit is said to catch sight of itself as the simultaneous occurrence of self-externalization and return-to-self. [...] Hegel can displace that ideal of art which, according to

Schiller, modern art can only strive for but not attain, into a sphere beyond art where it can be realized as Idea" (pp. 34–35).

26. "The three Gospels which mention Golgotha [Matthew 27:33, Mark 15:22, John 19:17] [...] identify it by the [Greek] translation *kranion,* skull. [Luke] gives the name of the place as Kranion, but does not use the Aramaic word (23:33). Calvary comes into our language in the Rheims [New Testament] translation of the [Vulgate] *calvariae locus,* the [Latin] translation of [Greek] *kraniou topos,* place of the skull" (John L. McKenzie, "Golgotha," in idem, *Dictionary of the Bible* [New York: Macmillan, 1965], p. 319).

27. I am grateful to Katerina Clark for pointing this out to me.

28. Reported in Clarence Brown, *Mandelstam* (Cambridge: Cambridge University Press, 1973), p. 46. During the semester that Mandelstam attended Heidelberg University (1909–10), Windelband conducted the lecture courses "Introduction to Philosophy" and "History and System of the Theory of Knowledge" (see Pavel Nerler, *Osip Mandel'shtam v Geidel'berge* [Moscow: Art-Biznes Tsentr, 1994], p. 37). Although, according to Steinberg, Mandelstam found Windelband "dull," "[y]ears later, [...] still trying to pass his university exams in 1916 in Petersburg, [Mandelstam] would ask his mother to send him Windelband's history of ancient philosophy" (Brown, *Mandelstam,* p. 46).

29. Ibid. Steinberg added that Mandelstam found Lask's lectures "lively and even 'poetic.'" Lask is best known for his work on the theory of value and for his claim that a reconciliation of subjective and objective ways of interpreting the world was impossible; in a kind of modified return to the Platonic idea of "Forms," he argued that subjective experience, while constitutive of the subject, received its value from something outside simple subjectivity. Georg Lukács was another of Lask's students, and seems to have taken Lask's value-theory as exemplary of the kind of "contemplative" thinking he (Lukács) was trying to overcome. See Stephan Nachtsheim, *Emil Lasks Grundlehre* (Tübingen: J. C. B. Mohr, 1992); and Hartmut Rosshoff, *Emil Lask als Lehrer von Georg Lukács* (Bonn: Bouvier Verlag Herbert Grundmann, 1975).

30. Nerler, *Osip Mandel'shtam in Geidel'berge,* p. 37.

31. "Hegel in seinem Verhältnis zur Weltanschauung der Aufklärung," in *Gesammelte Schriften,* ed. Eugen Herrigel, vol. 1 (Tübingen: Mohr, 1923), pp. 344–45.

32. Following Marcuse, Jameson argues that "[Hegel's] defense of the Prussian state results from his inability, at his particular moment in history, to see clearly any form of genuine social change and reorganization which is not simply the explosion of the Terror" (*Marxism and Form,* p. 346).

33. Jean Hippolyte, *Genesis and Structure of Hegel's Phenomenology of Spirit,* trans. Samuel Cherniak and John Heckman (Evanston, Ill.: Northwestern University Press, 1974), p. 332.

34. I mention Popper only because of the enormous influence still wielded by his "totalitarian" caricature of Hegel in *The Open Society and Its Enemies* (Princeton, N.J.: Princeton University Press, 1966). The Hegelian notion of Contradiction, for example—the idea that any self-identity is necessarily mediated through an *other*—provokes from Popper the following outcry: "Science proceeds on the assumption that contradictions are impermissible and avoidable. [....] [The] Hegelian doctrine [...] must destroy all argument and progress. For if contradictions are unavoidable and desirable, there is no need to eliminate them, and so all progress must come to an end" (2:39). I leave it to my readers to decide which of the two thinkers is ultimately more "totalitarian." In truth, even the eternal accusation of "teleological thinking" proves grossly inadequate when confronted with

Hegel's actual philosophy. Many aspects of the old "totalitarian" line on Hegel have recently been consigned to the dustbin by Domenico Losurdo's grand philological study of the philosopher, which paints a far more nuanced picture of Hegel's politics than we have hitherto had. In particular, Losurdo shows how "Hegel's celebration of the State is born out of, and in support of, the antifeudal struggle, the struggle against the particularism, the privileges, the oppression, and the violence that typifies feudalism; its goal is to build a community of *citoyens*, since 'only within the State is freedom fully realized.' This celebration, however, is haunted by the reality of oppression, the 'negatively infinite judgment,' the violence perpetrated by economic and social relations against a class excluded from the reciprocal 'recognition' that serves as the basis for the community of *citoyens*" (Domenico Losurdo, *Hegel and the Freedom of Moderns*, trans. Marella Morris and Jon Morris [Durham and London: Duke University Press, 2004], p. 179).

35. *Hamlet*, 5.1.203–4. All citations from Shakespeare are from the editions in *The Riverside Shakespeare*, ed. G. Blakemore Evans et al. (Boston: Houghton Mifflin, 1974).

36. Buck-Morss, *The Dialectics of Seeing*, p. 161.

37. The two simultaneous meanings of the Hegelian master-term *Aufhebung*.

38. From J. N. Findlay's "Analysis" of paragraph 345 of the *Phenomenology* (p. 540).

39. Walter Kaufmann makes the superb point that "Hegel's *Geist* is closer to Schiller's *Spieltrieb* than it is to [Kantian] understanding" (*Hegel: A Reinterpretation* [Garden City, N.Y.: Anchor Books, 1966], p. 31).

40. Cf. Hippolyte's exegesis in *Genesis and Structure* (p. 270): " 'Spirit is a thing.' This infinite judgment is paradoxical in that it immediately connects two terms that have nothing in common. Yet it says something that we know, something that observing reason searched for unawares. That reason, or rather that instinct of reason, sought itself in being. It has now found itself. It sees itself as a thing, and moreover, as the most abstract thing, as the thing most lacking in signification. Thus, this judgment has a profound meaning, in contrast to its apparent absurdity. It sets forth the truth of idealism: the identity of thought and being. But this identity must be taken as a concept and not as a portrayal. The instinct of reason, which limits itself to representation, must move on from this infinite judgment to the judgment of reflection, and rise from immediateness to mediation."

41. See, especially, the wordplay with "crown" and "coxcomb" between Lear and the Fool in act 1, scene 4, lines 95–188.

42. Cf. Fry's comments on Wordsworth's "Essay on Epitaphs," and the Wordsworthian epitaphic mode in general: "The epitaph gets next to the living dead; it is written on the edge of time, and thus narrows, while it does not eliminate, the distance between the eternal and the temporal" (*A Defense of Poetry*, p. 167).

43. Benjamin, "The Work of Art in the Age of Mechanical Reproduction," p. 242.

44. "The outwardly actual [i.e., the government, Creon] which has taken away from the inner world its honor and power has in so doing consumed its own essence. The publicly manifest Spirit has the root of its power in the nether world. The self-certainty and self-assurance of a nation possesses the truth of its oath, which binds all into one, solely in the mute unconscious substance of all, in the waters of forgetfulness. Thus it is that the fulfillment of the Spirit of the upper world is transformed into its opposite, and it learns that its supreme right is a supreme wrong, that its victory is rather its own downfall. The dead, whose right

is denied, knows therefore how to find instruments of vengeance, which are equally effective and powerful as the power which has injured it. These powers are other communities whose altars dogs or birds defiled with the corpse, which is not raised into unconscious universality by being given back, as is its due, to the elemental individuality [the earth], but remains above ground in the realm of outer reality, and has now acquired as a force of divine law a self-conscious, real universality. They rise up in hostility and destroy the community which has dishonored and shattered its own power, the sacred claims of the Family" (*PS*, p. 287).

45. Benjamin, "The Work of Art in the Age of Mechanical Reproduction," p. 224.

46. Mandelstam's birth date.

Coda

1. Rancière, "The Aesthetic Revolution," pp. 146–47.

2. "Nguyen Ai Quoc (Ho Chi Minh): A Visit with a Comintern Member," p. 250.

3. I am thinking particularly of one installation in their brilliant *Palace of Projects* entitled "What Else Can Be Said about This?" The project is motivated (states the accompanying text) by a desire to restore the possibility, lost during the "iron XX century," of spontaneous expression in verse. "In beautiful corners of a park or at the intersection of busy streets, the following unusual 'sculpture' should be erected: attach to the ground an old woman's glove (of course, a plastic replica), and place around it in a semi-circle metal music stands holding texts written by invented personage who have seen this glove unexpectedly on the ground and express various associations that come into their heads as a result. These are the recollections of a woman who lost a glove just like it in her youth, of a man who recalls here a recent affair, there is a detective as well, and a lover of cleanliness... But what is very important is that each of these texts is expressed in poetic form, some of them are rhymed, some are 'blank' verses. The social meaning of such a sculpture composition can be guessed immediately: a passerby who approaches these stands and has read them one after another, will definitely say to himself: 'And what could I myself say about this? And shouldn't I try to say it in verse as well?' " (Ilya and Emilia Kabakov, *The Palace of Projects* [Essen: Kokerei Zollverein, 2001], 6.1).

4. Elizabeth Bishop, *The Complete Poems, 1927–1979* (New York: Farrar, Straus and Giroux, 1983), pp. 23–25. The poem first appeared in 1939 in *New Directions* and was republished in Bishop's collection *North & South* (1946).

5. *Shelley's Poetry and Prose*, p. 103.

6. See Anne Stevenson, *Elizabeth Bishop* (New Haven: Twayne, 1966), p. 68. "Shelley's poem may reflect recollection of a description and an illustration in Richard Pococke's *A Description of the East and Some Other Countries* (London, 1743)" (*Shelley's Poetry and Prose*, p. 103).

7. Although the lines "The monument is one-third set against / a sea; two-thirds against a sky," suggest that the whole scene is a kind of heraldric symbol.

8. See Andreas Huyssen, *After the Great Divide: Modernism, Mass Culture, Postmodernism* (Bloomington: Indiana University Press, 1986), pp. 209–21, and passim.

Works Cited and Consulted

Abrams, M. H. *The Correspondent Breeze: Essays on English Romanticism.* Intro. Jack Stillinger. New York: W. W. Norton, 1984.

Adorno, Theodor W. *Aesthetic Theory.* Ed. Gretel Adorno, Rolf Tiedemann, Robert Hullot-Kentor. Trans. Robert Hullot-Kentor. Minneapolis: University of Minnesota Press, 1997.

———. *Notes to Literature.* Ed. Rolf Tiedemann. Trans. Shierry Weber Nicholson. 2 vols. New York: Columbia University Press, 1991.

Ammons, A. R. *The Selected Poems.* Exp. ed. New York: W. W. Norton, 1986.

Anderson, Perry. "Internationalism: A Breviary." *New Left Review,* second series, 14 (March–April 2002): 5–25.

———. "Marshall Berman: Modernity and Revolution." In Perry Anderson, *A Zone of Engagement,* pp. 25–55. London: Verso, 1992.

———. *The Origins of Postmodernity.* London: Verso, 1998.

Aristotle. *The Poetics of Aristotle.* Ed. and trans. Stephen Halliwell. Chapel Hill: University of North Carolina Press, 1987.

Arrighi, Giovanni. *The Long Twentieth Century: Money, Power, and the Origins of Our Times.* London and New York: Verso, 1994.

Aubin, Robert Arnold. *Topographical Poetry in XVIII-Century England.* New York: Modern Language Association of America, 1936.

Azadovskii, K. M. "'Menia nazval kitezhankoi': Anna Akhmatova i Nikolai Kliuev." *Literaturnoe obozrenie* 5 (1989): 66–70.

———. *Nikolai Kliuev: Put' poeta.* Leningrad: Sovetskii pisatel', 1990.

Baran, H. "Poeticheskaia logika i poeticheskii alogizm Velimira Khlebnikova." Trans. Iu. A. Kleiner. In *Mir Velimira Khlebnikova,* ed. V. V. Ivanov et al., pp. 550–67. Moscow: Iazyki russkoi kul'tury, 2000.

Baratynskii, E. A. *Stikhotvoreniia i poemy.* Moscow: Khudozhestvennaia literatura, 1982.

Barrell, John. *The Idea of Landscape and the Sense of Place: An Approach to the Poetry of John Clare.* Cambridge: Cambridge University Press, 1972.

Barthes, Roland. *Image Music Text.* Ed. and trans. Stephen Heath. New York: Hill and Wang, 1977.

Bater, James H. *St. Petersburg: Industrialization and Change.* Montreal: McGill-Queen's University Press, 1976.

Baudelaire, Charles. *Complete Verse.* Ed., intro., and trans. Francis Scarfe. London: Anvil, 1986.

———. *Oeuvres complètes.* Ed. Claude Pichois. Vol. 2. Paris: Gallimard, 1976.

———. *Oeuvres complètes.* Ed. Claude Roy and Michel Jamet. Intro. Claude Roy. Paris: Robert Laffont, 1980.

———. *The Parisian Prowler.* Trans. Edward K. Kaplan. Athens and London: University of Georgia Press, 1997.

———. *The Poems in Prose with La Fanfarlo.* Trans. Francis Scarfe. London: Anvil, 1989.

———. *Selected Poems.* Trans. and intro. Carol Clark. London: Penguin Books, 1995.

———. *Selected Writings on Art and Literature.* Trans. and intro. P. E. Charvet. London: Penguin Books, 1972.

Beer, John, ed. *Questioning Romanticism.* Baltimore: Johns Hopkins University Press, 1995.

Benjamin, Walter. *The Arcades Project.* Trans. Howard Eiland and Kevin McLaughlin. Cambridge, Mass.: Belknap Press of Harvard University Press, 1999.

———. *Charles Baudelaire: A Lyric Poet in the Era of High Capitalism.* Trans. Harry Zohn. London: Verso, 1983.

———. *Illuminationen.* Ed. Siegfried Unseld. Frankfurt am Main: Suhrkamp, 1955.

———. *Illuminations.* Ed. Hannah Arendt. Trans. Harry Zohn. New York: Schocken Books, 1968.

———. *Reflections.* Ed. Peter Demetz. Trans. Edmund Jephcott. New York: Schocken Books, 1978.

Bennett, Andrew. *Romantic Poets and the Culture of Posterity.* Cambridge: Cambridge University Press, 1999.

Berman, Marshall. *All That Is Solid Melts into Air: The Experience of Modernity.* New York: Penguin Books, 1988.

Berry, Francis. "The Poet of *Childe Harold.*" In *Byron's Poetry,* ed. Frank D. McConnell. New York: W. W. Norton, 1978.

Bertaux, Pierre. *Hölderlin und die Französische Revolution.* Frankfurt am Main: Suhrkamp, 1969.

Best, Stephen, and Douglas Kellner, eds. *Postmodern Theory: Critical Interrogations.* New York: Guilford, 1991.

Bestuzhev-Marlinskii, Aleksandr. "Vzgliad na Staruiu i Novuiu Slovesnost' v Rossii." In *Dekabristy,* ed. V. Orlov, vol. 2, pp. 380–98. Leningrad: Khudozhestvennaia literatura, 1975.

Binder, Wolfgang. "Hölderlin: 'Der Winkel von Hardt,' 'Lebensalter,' 'Hälfte des Lebens.' " *Schweitzer Monatshefte* 45 (September 1965): 583–91.

Bishop, Elizabeth. *The Complete Poems, 1927–1979.* New York: Farrar, Straus and Giroux, 1983.

Bland, Robert, et al., eds. *Collections from the Greek Anthology; and from the Pastoral, Elegiac and Dramatic Poets of Greece.* London: John Murray, 1813.

Blok, Aleksandr. *Selected Poems.* Trans. Alex Miller. Moscow: Progress, 1981.

———. *Sobranie sochinenii.* Ed. V. Orlov and I. Isakovich. Intro. M. Dudin. 6 vols. Leningrad: Khudozhesvennaia literatura, 1980.

Bloom, Harold. *Shelley's Mythmaking.* Ithaca: Cornell University Press, 1959.

Blumenberg, Hans. *Höhlenausgänge.* Frankfurt am Main: Suhrkamp, 1996.

———. *Die Legitimität der Neuzeit.* Frankfurt: Suhrkamp, 1996.

———. "Sprachsituation und immanente Poetik." In *Wirklichkeiten, in denen wir leben,* pp. 137–56. Stuttgart: Reclam, 1981.

———. "Wirklichkeitsbegriff und Wirkungspotential des Mythos." In *Terror und Spiel,* ed. Manfred Fuhrmann, pp. 11–66. Munich: Wilhelm Fink, 1971.

Boileau Despréaux, Nicolas. "L'Art Poétique." In *Oeuvres completes,* ed. Françoise Escal, intro. Antoine Adam. Paris: Gallimard, 1966.

Bonch-Bruevich, Vladimir, ed. *Materialy k istorii i izucheniiu russkago sektanstva i raskola.* 7 vols. St. Petersburg, 1908–16.

Bouterwek, Friedrich. "Lyrische Formen." In *Lyriktheorie: Texte vom Barock bis zur Gegenwart,* ed. Ludwig Völker, pp. 158–60. Stuttgart: Reclam, 1990.

Brinkley, Robert. "Spaces between Words: Writing 'Mont Blanc.'" In *Romantic Revisions,* ed. Robert Brinkley and Keith Hanley, pp. 243–67. New York: Cambridge University Press, 1992.

Brinkmann, Rolf Dieter. *Künstliches Licht.* Ed. Genia Schulz. Stuttgart: Reclam, 1994.

Brodsky, Joseph. "Nobelevskaia lektsia." In *Forma vremeni,* vol. 2, pp. 450–62. Minsk: Eridan, 1992.

Bromwich, David. *Disowned by Memory: Wordsworth's Poetry of the 1790s.* Chicago: University of Chicago Press, 1998.

Brooks, Jeffrey. *When Russia Learned to Read: Literacy and Popular Literature, 1861–1917.* Princeton, N.J.: Princeton University Press, 1985.

Brown, Clarence. *Mandelstam.* Cambridge: Cambridge University Press, 1973.

Brown, Marshall. *Preromanticism* Stanford: Stanford University Press, 1991.

Bruns, Gerald. *Modern Poetry and the Idea of Language.* New Haven: Yale University Press, 1974.

Buck-Morss, Susan. *The Dialectics of Seeing.* Cambridge, Mass.: MIT Press, 1989.

———. *Dreamworld and Catastrophe: The Passing of Mass Utopia in East and West.* Cambridge, Mass.: MIT Press, 2000.

Bullough, Edward. "'Psychical Distance' as a Factor in Art and an Aesthetic Principle." In *Aesthetics: Lectures and Essays,* ed. Elizabeth M Wilkinson, pp. 91–130. Stanford: Stanford University Press, 1957.

Butter, Peter. *Shelley's Idols of the Cave.* Edinburgh: Edinburgh University Press, 1954.

Byron, George Gordon. *Byron's Poetry.* Ed. Frank D. McConnell. New York: W. W. Norton, 1978.

Calvino, Italo. *Invisible Cities.* New York: Harcourt Brace, 1974.

Carr, E. H. *Studies in Revolution.* New York: Grosset and Dunlap, 1964.

Catullus. "Poem 46." In *The Complete Poetry of Catullus,* trans. and ed. David Mulroy, p. 36. Madison: University of Wisconsin Press, 2002.

Cavanagh, Clare. *Osip Mandelstam and the Modernist Creation of Tradition.* Princeton, N.J.: Princeton University Press, 1995.

Certeau, Michel de. *The Practice of Everyday Life.* Trans. Steven Rendall. Berkeley: University of California Press, 1984.

———. *The Writing of History.* Trans. Tom Conley. New York: Columbia University Press, 1988.

Chandler, James K. *Wordsworth's Second Nature: A Study of the Poetry and Politics.* Chicago: University of Chicago Press, 1984.

Clare, John. *Selected Poetry and Prose.* Ed. Merryn Williams and Raymond Williams. London: Methuen, 1986.

Clark, Katerina. "The City versus the Countryside in Soviet Peasant Literature of the Twenties: A Duel of Utopias." In *Bolshevik Culture,* ed. Abbott Gleason, Peter Kenez, and Richard Stites, pp. 175–89. Bloomington: Indiana University Press, 1985.

———. *Petersburg, Crucible of Cultural Revolution.* Cambridge, Mass.: Harvard University Press, 1995.

Clark, T. J. *Farewell to an Idea: Episodes from a History of Modernism.* New Haven: Yale University Press, 1999.

———. "Phenomenality and Materiality in Cézanne." In *Material Events: Paul de Man and the Afterlife of Theory,* ed. Tom Cohen, Barbara Cohen, J. Hillis Miller, and Andrzej Warminski, pp. 93–113. Minneapolis: University of Minnesota Press, 2001.

Cowell, Andrew. "Advertising, Rhetoric, and Literature: A Medieval Response to Contemporary Theory." *Poetics Today* 22, no. 4 (winter 2001): 765–94.

Crane, Hart. "Modern Poetry." In *The Collected Poems of Hart Crane,* ed. Waldo Frank, pp. 175–79. New York: Liveright, 1946.

Crary, Jonathan. *Suspensions of Perception: Attention, Spectacle and Modern Culture* Cambridge, Mass.: MIT Press, 1999.

———. *Techniques of the Observer: On Vision and Modernity in the Nineteenth Century* Cambridge, Mass.: MIT Press, 1990.

Culler, Jonathan. *The Pursuit of Signs: Semiotics, Literature, Deconstruction.* Ithaca: Cornell University Press, 1981.

Curtius, Ernst Robert. *European Literature and the Latin Middle Ages.* Trans. Willard R. Trask. Intro. Peter Godman. Princeton, N.J.: Princeton University Press, 1990.

Danilov, V. P., and Ivnitskii, N. A., eds. *Dokumenty svidetel'stvuiut: Iz istorii derevnii nakanune i v khode kollektivizatsii 1927–1932 gg.* Moscow: Izdatel'stvo politicheskoi literaturoi, 1989.

Davis, Mike. *Late Victorian Holocausts: El Niño Famines and the Making of the Third World.* London: Verso, 2001.

Deleuze, Gilles. *Cinema 2: The Time-Image.* Trans. Hugh Tomlinson and Robert Galeta. Minneapolis: University of Minnesota Press, 1989.

De Man, Paul. *Aesthetic Ideology.* Ed. and intro. Andrzej Warminski. Minneapolis: University of Minnesota Press, 1996.

———. *Blindness and Insight: Essays in the Rhetoric of Contemporary Criticism.* Intro. Wlad Godzich. 2nd ed. Minneapolis: University of Minnesota Press, 1983.

Derrida, Jacques. "Signature Event Context." In Jacques Derrida, *Limited Inc.*, pp. 1–23. Evanston, Ill.: Northwestern University Press 1988.

Dowe, Dieter, et al., eds. *Europe in 1848: Revolution and Reform.* New York: Berghahn Books, 2001.

Engels, Friedrich. *The Housing Question.* In Karl Marx and Friedrich Engels, *Collected Works.* Ed. Eric Hobsbawm et al. Vol. 23. Moscow: Progress, 1988.

Engelstein, Laura. *Castration and the Heavenly Kingdom: A Russian Folktale.* Ithaca: Cornell University Press, 1999.

Ferguson, Frances. "Shelley's 'Mont Blanc': What the Mountain Said." In *Shelley,* ed. and intro. Michael O'Neill, pp. 43–55. London: Longman, 1993.

———. *Solitude and the Sublime: Romanticism and the Aesthetics of Individuation.* New York: Routledge, 1992.

Ferguson, Priscilla Parkhurst. *Paris as Revolution: Writing the Nineteenth-Century City.* Berkeley: University of California Press, 1994.

Findlay, J. N. *Hegel: A Re-examination.* New York: Oxford University Press, 1958.

Fink, Hilary L. *Bergson and Russian Modernism: 1900–1930.* Evanston, Ill.: Northwestern University Press, 1999.

Fischer, Stephen Roger. *A History of Language.* London: Reaktion Books, 1999.

Fourier, Charles. *Harmonian Man: Selected Writings of Charles Fourier.* Ed. Mark Poster. Trans. Susan Hanson. Garden City, N.Y.: Anchor Books, 1971.

Fradinger, Moira Inés. "Radical Evil: Literary Visions of Political Origins in Sophocles, Sade, and Vargas Llosa." Ph.D. dissertation, Yale University, 2003.

Freidin, Gregory. "The Whisper of History and the Noise of Time in the Writings of Osip Mandel'shtam." *Russian Review* 37, no. 4 (October 1978): 421–37.

Fry, Paul H. *A Defense of Poetry: Reflections on the Occasion of Writing.* Stanford: Stanford University Press, 1995.

———. *The Poet's Calling in the English Ode.* New Haven: Yale University Press, 1980.

Frye, Northrop. "Approaching the Lyric." In *Lyric Poetry: Beyond New Criticism,* ed. Chaviva Hoshek and Patricia Parker, pp. 31–37. Ithaca: Cornell University Press, 1985.

Gasparov, Boris. "The Iron Age of the 1930s: The Centennial Return in Mandelstam." In *Rereading Russian Poetry,* ed. Stephanie Sandler, pp. 78–103. New Haven: Yale University Press, 1999.

Gatrell, Peter. *A Whole Empire Walking: Refugees in Russia during World War I.* Bloomington: Indiana University Press, 1999.

Gaull, Marilyn. "Clare and the 'Dark System.'" In *John Clare in Context,* ed. Hugh Haughton, Adam Phillips, and Geoffrey Summerfield, pp. 279–94. Cambridge: Cambridge University Press, 1994.

———. *English Romanticism: The Human Context.* New York and London: W.W. Norton, 1988.

Gibson, Ralph. *A Social History of French Catholicism: 1780–1914.* London: Routledge, 1989.

Glaudes, Pierre. "Le dialogue avec De Maistre." *Magazine Littéraire* 418 (March 2003): 53–56.

Gogol, Nikolai. *Selected Passages from Correspondence with Friends.* Trans. Jesse Zeldin. Nashville: Vanderbilt University Press, 1969.

Goux, Jean-Joseph. *Les Iconoclastes.* Paris: Editions du Seuil, 1978.

Graziosi, Andrea. *The Great Soviet Peasant War: Bolsheviks and Peasants, 1917–1933.* Cambridge, Mass.: Harvard University Press (Ukrainian Research Institute, Harvard), 1996.

Grigor'ev, V. P. *Budetlianin.* Moscow: Iazyki russkoi kul'tury, 2000.

Guillemin, Henri. *Le Jocelyn de Lamartine: Etude historique et critique avec des documents inédits.* Paris: Boivin, 1937.

Gurvich, I. *Mandel'shtam: Problema chteniia i ponimaniia.* New York: Gnosis, 1994.

Habermas, Jürgen. *The Philosophical Discourse of Modernity: Twelve Lectures.* Trans. Frederick Lawrence. Cambridge, Mass.: MIT Press, 1990.

Hagstrum, Jean H. *The Sister Arts: The Tradition of Literary Pictorialism and English Poetry from Dryden to Gray.* Chicago: University of Chicago Press, 1958.

Hardt, Michael, and Antonio Negri. *Empire.* Cambridge, Mass.: Harvard University Press, 2000.

Hartman, Geoffrey H. *Beyond Formalism: Literary Essays, 1958–1970.* New Haven: Yale University Press, 1970.

———. *Criticism in the Wilderness.* New Haven: Yale University Press, 1980.

———. *The Unremarkable Wordsworth.* Intro. Donald G. Marshall. Minneapolis: University of Minnesota Press, 1987.

Harvey, David. *Paris, Capital of Modernity.* New York: Routledge, 2003.

Haughton, Hugh. "Progress and Rhyme: 'The Nightingale's Nest' and Romantic Poetry." In *John Clare in Context,* ed. Hugh Haughton, Adam Phillips, and Geoffrey Summerfield, pp. 51–86. Cambridge: Cambridge University Press, 1994.

Haughton, Hugh, and Adam Phillips. "Introduction: Relocating John Clare." In *John Clare in Context,* ed. Hugh Haughton, Adam Phillips, and Geoffrey Summerfield, pp. 1–27. Cambridge: Cambridge University Press, 1994.

Haughton, Hugh, Adam Phillips, and Geoffrey Summerfield, eds. *John Clare in Context.* Cambridge: Cambridge University Press, 1994.

Hegel, G. W. F. *Aesthetics: Lectures on Fine Art.* Trans. T. M. Knox. 2 vols. Oxford: Clarendon, 1974.

———. *Phänomenologie des Geistes.* Ed. Eva Moldenhauer and Karl Markus Michel. Frankfurt am Main: Suhrkamp, 1970.

———. *Phenomenology of Spirit.* Trans. A.V. Miller. Intro. J. N. Findlay. Oxford: Oxford University Press, 1977.

———. *Sistema nauk, chast' pervaia: Fenomenologiia dukha.* Trans. G. Shpet. St. Petersburg: Nauka, 1994.

Heidegger, Martin. *Being and Time.* Trans. John Macquarrie and Edward Robinson. New York: Harper and Row, 1962.

Hippolyte, Jean. *Genesis and Structure of Hegel's Phenomenology of Spirit.* Trans. Samuel Cherniak and John Heckman. Evanston, Ill.: Northwestern University Press, 1974.

Hobsbawm, Eric. *The Age of Extremes: A History of the World, 1914–1991.* New York: Vintage Books, 1994.

———. "From Feudalism to Capitalism." In Eric Hobsbawm, *The Transition from Feudalism to Capitalism,* pp. 159–64, intro. Rodney Hilton. London: New Left Books, 1976.

Hogle, Jerrold E. "Shelley's Poetics: The Power as Metaphor." *Keats-Shelley Journal* 31 (1982): 159–97.

———. *Shelley's Process: Radical Transference and the Development of his Major Works.* New York: Oxford University Press, 1988.

Hölderlin, Friedrich. *Gedichte.* Ed. Jochen Schmidt. Frankfurt am Main: Insel, 1984.

———. *Hymns and Fragments.* Trans. Richard Sieburth. Princeton, N.J.: Princeton University Press, 1984.

Hollier, Denis. *Against Architecture: The Writings of Georges Bataille.* Trans. Betsy Wing. Cambridge, Mass.: MIT Press, 1992.

———. "The Use-Value of the Impossible." In *Bataille: Writing the Sacred,* ed. Carolyn Bailey Gill, trans. Liesl Ollmann, pp. 133–53. London and New York: Routledge, 1995.

Holquist, Michael. *Dialogism: Bakhtin and His World.* London and New York: Routledge, 1990.

Homer. *The Odyssey.* Trans. Robert Fitzgerald. New York: Anchor Books, 1963.

Honegger, Johann. *Grundsteine einer allgemeinen Culturgeschichte der neuesten Zeit.* Leipzig: J. J. Weber, 1874.

———. *Russische Literatur und Cultur.* Leipzig: J. J. Weber, 1880.

Hugo, Victor. *Poèmes.* Ed. Jean Gaudon. Paris: Flammarion, 1985.

Hutton, James. *The Greek Anthology in France to the Year 1800.* Ithaca: Cornell University Press, 1946.

———. *The Greek Anthology in Italy to the Year 1800.* Ithaca: Cornell University Press, 1935.

Huyssen, Andreas. *After the Great Divide: Modernism, Mass Culture, Postmodernism.* Bloomington: Indiana University Press, 1986.

Iampolskii, Mikhail. "In the Shadow of Monuments." In *Soviet Hieroglyphics: Visual Culture in Late Twentieth-Century Russia,* ed. Nancy Condee, pp. 93–112. Bloomington: Indiana University Press, 1995.

Ivanov, V. V. "'Stikhi o neizvestnom soldate' v kontekste mirovoi poezii." In *Zhizn' i tvorchestvo O. E. Mandel'shtama,* ed. S. Averintsev et al., pp. 356–66. Voronezh: Izdatel'stvo Voronezhskogo Universiteta, 1990.

Ivanov, V. V., et al., eds. *Mir Velimira Khlebnikova: stat'i, issledovaniia 1911–1998.* Moscow: Iazyki russkoi kul'tury, 2000.

Jakobson, Roman. *Language and Literature.* Ed. Krystyna Pomorska and Stephen Rudy. Cambridge, Mass.: Belknap Press of Harvard University Press, 1987.

———. "Noveishaia russkaia poeziia." In *Mir Velimira Khlebnikova: stat'i, issledovaniia 1911–1998,* ed. V. V. Ivanov et al., pp. 20–77. Moscow: Iazyki russkoi kul'tury, 2000.

Jameson, Fredric. "Baudelaire as Modernist and Postmodernist: The Dissolution of the Referent and the Artificial 'Sublime.'" In *Lyric Poetry: Beyond New Criticism,* ed. Chaviva Hosek and Patricia Parker, pp. 247–63. Ithaca: Cornell University Press, 1985.

———. *Marxism and Form.* Princeton, N.J.: Princeton University Press, 1971.

———. "Ontology and Utopia." *L'Esprit Createur* 34, no. 4 (winter 1994): 46–64.

———. *The Political Unconscious: Narrative as a Socially Symbolic Act.* Ithaca: Cornell University Press, 1981.

———. *Postmodernism, or, The Cultural Logic of Late Capitalism.* Durham: Duke University Press, 1991.

———. "Reification and Utopia in Mass Culture." In Fredric Jameson, *Signatures of the Visible,* pp. 10–34. New York: Routledge, 1992.

———. *A Singular Modernity: Essay on the Ontology of the Present.* London: Verso, 2002.

Johnson, Barbara. "Poetry and Its Double: Two 'Invitations au voyage.'" In *Charles Baudelaire,* ed. and intro. Harold Bloom, pp. 35–62. New York: Chelsea House, 1987.

Johnson, Samuel. "An Essay on Epitaphs." In *Selected Essays,* ed. and intro. David Womersley, pp. 509–16. London: Penguin Books, 2003.

———. *Lives of the English Poets.* Ed. George Birkbeck Hill. 3 vols. Hildesheim: Georg Olms, 1968.

Jones, Colin, and Dror Wahrman, eds. *The Age of Cultural Revolutions: Britain and France, 1750–1820.* Berkeley: University of California Press, 2002.

Jonson, Ben. *The Complete Poetry of Ben Jonson,* Ed. William B. Hunter Jr. New York: W. W. Norton, 1968.

Juvenal. *The Satires of Juvenal.* Trans. Rolfe Humphries. Bloomington: Indiana University Press, 1958.

Kant, Immanuel. *Critique of Judgment,* Trans. and intro. J. H. Bernard. New York: Hafner, 1951.

Katsis, L. F. "Mandel'shtam i Bairon (k analizu 'Stikhov o neizvestnom soldate')." In *Slovo i sud'ba: Osip Mandel'shtam,* ed. Z. S. Papernyi, pp. 436–53. Moscow: Nauka, 1991.

Kaufmann, Walter. *Hegel: A Reinterpretation.* Garden City, N.Y.: Anchor Books, 1966.

Keach, William. *Shelley's Style.* New York: Methuen, 1984.

Khlebnikov, Velimir. *Collected Works.* Ed. Charlotte Douglas. Trans. Paul Schmidt. Cambridge, Mass.: Harvard University Press, 1987.

———. *Snake Train: Poetry and Prose.* Ed. Gary Kern. Trans. Gary Kern et al. Ann Arbor: Ardis, 1976.

———. *Sobranie sochinenii.* Ed. R. D. Duganov et al. 6 vols. Moscow: IMLI RAN, "Nasledie," 2000.

Kikhnei, L. G. *Filosofsko-esteticheskie printsipy akmeizma i khudozhestvennaia praktika Osipa Mandel'shtama.* Moscow: Dialog-MGU, 1997.

Kittler, Friedrich A. *Discourse Networks, 1800/1900.* Trans. Michael Metteer, with Chris Cullens. Intro. David E. Wellbery. Stanford: Stanford University Press, 1990.

Klein, Naomi. *No Logo.* London: Flamingo, 2000.

Kliuev, Nikolai. *Pesnoslov.* Ed. S. I. Subbotin and I. A. Kostin. Petrozavodsk: Kareliia, 1990.

———. *Sochineniia.* Ed. G. Struve and B. Fillipov, 2 vols. Munich: A. Neimanis, 1969.

Knight, G. Wilson. *The Burning Oracle: Studies in the Poetry of Action.* London: Oxford University Press, 1939.

Kramer, Rainer. *Auf der Suche nach dem verlorenen Augenblick: Rolf Dieter Brinkmanns innerer Krieg in Italien.* Bremen: Edition Temmen, 1999.

Lamartine, Alphonse de. *Lamartine on Atheism. Atheism among the People.* Boston: Phillips, Sampson, 1850.

———. *Méditations poétiques: Nouvelles méditations poétiques suivies de poésies diverses.* Ed. Marius-François Guyard. Paris: Gallimard, 1981.

———. *Oeuvres poètiques.* Ed. Marius-François Guyard. 2 vols. Paris: Gallimard, 1963.

———. *The Past, Present and Future of the Republic.* New York: Harper, 1850.

Langer, Susanne K. *Feeling and Form.* New York: Scribner's, 1953.

Laqueur, Thomas W. "The Places of the Dead in Modernity." In *The Age of Cultural Revolutions: Britain and France, 1750–1820,* ed. Colin Jones and Dror Wahrman, pp. 17–32. Berkeley: University of California Press, 2002.

Lask, Emil. *Gesammelte Schriften.* Ed. Eugen Herrigel. 2 Vols. Tübingen: Mohr, 1923.

Leask, Nigel. "Mont Blanc's Mysterious Voice: Shelley and Huttonian Earth Science." In *The Third Culture: Literature and Science,* ed. Elinor S. Shaffer, pp. 182–203. Berlin: Walter de Gruyter, 1998.

Lefebvre, Henri. *The Production of Space.* Trans. Donald Nicholson-Smith. Oxford: Blackwell, 1991.

Leibniz, G. W. *Philosophical Essays.* Ed. and trans. Roger Ariew and Daniel Garber. Indianapolis: Hackett, 1989.

———. *Selections.* Ed. Philip P. Wiener. New York: Scribner's, 1951.

———. *Unvorgreifliche Gedanken.* Ed. Uwe Pörksen. Stuttgart: Reclam, 1983.

Lermontov, M. Iu. *Sochineniia.* Ed. I. S. Chistovaia. Intro. I. L. Andronikov. 2 vols. Moscow: Pravda, 1988.

Liu, Alan. *Wordsworth: The Sense of History.* Stanford: Stanford University Press, 1989.

Lombard, Charles M. *Lamartine.* New York: Twayne, 1973.

Lomonosov, M. V. *Izbrannye proizvedeniia.* Ed. A. A. Morozov. Leningrad: Sovetskii pisatel', 1986.

Losurdo, Domenico. *Hegel and the Freedom of Moderns.* Trans. Marella Morris and Jon Morris. Durham: Duke University Press, 2004.

Lotman, Iu. M. "Blok i narodnaia kul'tura goroda." In *Nasledie A. Bloka i aktual'nye problemy poetiki (Blokovskii sbornik IV),* 7–26. Tartu: Tartu State University, 1981.

Lotman, Iu. M., and B. A. Uspenskij. *The Semiotics of Russian Culture.* Ed. Ann Shukman. Ann Arbor: Michigan Slavic Contributions, 1984.

Lowell, Stephen. "Between Arcadia and Suburbia: Dachas in Late Imperial Russia." *Slavic Review* 61, no. 1 (spring 2002): 66–87.

Lukács, Georg. *History and Class Consciousness: Studies in Marxist Dialectics.* Trans. Rodney Livingstone. Cambridge, Mass.: MIT Press, 1968.

MacDiarmid, Hugh. *Selected Poetry.* Ed. Alan Riach and Michael Grieve. Intro. Eliot Weinberger. New York: New Directions, 1993.

Mandelstam, Nadezhda. *Hope Abandoned.* Trans. Max Hayward. New York: Atheneum, 1974.

Mandelstam, Osip. *The Complete Critical Prose of Osip Mandelstam.* Ed. Jane Gary Harris. Trans. Jane Gary Harris and Constance Link. Ann Arbor: Ardis, 1997.

———. *The Prose of Osip Mandelstam.* Trans. and intro. Clarence Brown. Princeton, N.J.: Princeton University Press, 1965.

———. *Sochineniia.* Ed. P. Nerler and A. Mikhailov. Intro. S. Averintsev. 2 vols. Moscow: Khudozhestvennaia literatura, 1990.

Manuel, Frank E., and Fritzie P. *Utopian Thought in the Western World.* Cambridge, Mass.: Belknap Press of Harvard University Press, 1979.

Manuilov, V., ed. *Russkaia epigramma (XVIII–XIX v.v.).* Leningrad: Sovetskii pisatel', 1958.

Markov, Vladimir. *Russian Futurism: A History.* Berkeley: University of California Press, 1968.

Markus, Gyorgy. "Walter Benjamin or the Commodity as Phantasmagoria." *New German Critique* 83 (spring–summer 2001): 3–42.

Marx, Karl. "The Class Struggles in France, 1848 to 1850." In *Collected Works,* ed. Jack Cohen et al., vol. 10, pp. 45–146. Moscow: Progress, 1978.

———. *Grundrisse: Foundations of the Critique of Political Economy.* Trans. and intro. Martin Nicolaus. New York: Vintage Books, 1973.

Masing-Delic, Irene. *Abolishing Death: A Salvation Myth of Russian Twentieth-Century Literature.* Stanford: Stanford University Press, 1992.

Mayer, Arno. *The Persistence of the Old Regime: Europe to the Great War.* New York: Pantheon Books, 1981.

McKenzie, John L. *Dictionary of the Bible.* New York: Macmillan, 1970.

Metz, Christian. *The Imaginary Signifier: Psychoanalysis and the Cinema.* Trans. Celia Britton et al. Bloomington: Indiana University Press, 1982.

Moretti, Franco. *Signs Taken for Wonders: Essays in the Sociology of Literary Forms.* Trans. Susan Fischer, David Forgacs, and David Miller. London: Verso, 1997.

Nachtsheim, Stephan. *Emil Lasks Grundlehre.* Tübingen: J. C. B. Mohr, 1992.

Nerler, Pavel. *Osip Mandel'shtam v Geidel'berge.* Moscow: Art-Biznes Tsentr, 1994.

Nicholls, Peter. *Modernisms: A Literary Guide.* Houndmills, Basingstoke: Macmillan, 1995.

Nichols, John Gordon. *The Poetry of Ben Jonson.* London: Routledge and Kegan Paul, 1969.

Nicolson, Marjorie Hope. *Mountain Gloom and Mountain Glory: The Development of the Aesthetics of the Infinite.* New York: W.W. Norton, 1959.

Nikolaev, S. I., and T. S. Tsar'kova, eds. *Russkaia stikhotvornaia epitafiia.* St. Petersburg: Akademicheskii proekt, 1998.

North, Michael. *The Final Sculpture: Public Monuments and Modern Poets.* Ithaca: Cornell University Press, 1985.

Novalis (Friedrich von Hardenberg). "Fragmente." In *Lyriktheorie: Texte vom Barock bis zur Gegenwart,* ed. Ludwig Völker, p. 147. Stuttgart: Reclam, 1999.

Olson, Charles. *Collected Prose.* Ed. Donald Allen and Benjamin Friedlander. Intro. Robert Creeley. Berkeley: University of California Press, 1997.

O'Neill, Michael, ed. *Shelley.* Intro. Michael O'Neill. London: Longman, 1993.

Papernyi, Z. S., ed. *Slovo i sud'ba: Osip Mandel'shtam.* Moscow: Nauka, 1991.

Popper, Karl. *The Open Society and Its Enemies.* Princeton, N.J.: Princeton University Press, 1966.

Porphyry. *On the Cave of the Nymphs.* Trans. and intro. Robert Lamberton. Barrytown, N.Y.: Station Hill, 1983.

Prendergast, Christopher. *Paris and the Nineteenth Century.* Oxford: Blackwell, 1992.

Price, Roger. *A Concise History of France.* Cambridge: Cambridge University Press, 1993.

Procacci, Giovanna. "To Survive the Revolution or to Anticipate it? Governmental Strategies in the Course of the Crisis of 1848." In *Europe in 1848: Revolution and Reform,* ed. Dieter Dowe et al., trans. David Higgins, pp. 502–28. New York: Berghahn Books, 2001.

Prokopovich, Feofan. *Sochineniia.* Ed. I. P. Eremin. Moscow: Akademiia nauk, 1961.

Proust, Marcel. *Remembrance of Things Past.* Vol. 1, *Swann's Way* and *Within a Budding Grove.* Trans. C. K. Scott-Moncrieff and Terence Kilmartin. New York: Random House, 1981.

Putilov, B. N., ed. *Byliny.* Moscow: Sovetskii pisatel', 1986.

Pyman, Avril. *The Life of Aleksandr Blok.* 2 vols. Oxford: Oxford University Press, 1979.

Quint, David. *Epic and Empire: Politics and Generic Form from Virgil to Milton.* Princeton, N.J.: Princeton University Press, 1993.

Rajan, Tilottama. "Idealism and Skepticism in Shelley's Poetry ['The Triumph of Life' and 'Alastor']." In *Shelley,* ed. and intro. Michael O'Neill, pp. 241–63 (London: Longman, 1993).

———. "Phenomenology and Romantic Theory: Hegel and the Subversion of Aesthetics." In *Questioning Romanticism,* ed. John Beer, pp. 155–78, Baltimore: Johns Hopkins University Press, 1995.

———. *The Supplement of Reading: Figures of Understanding in Romantic Theory and Practice.* Ithaca: Cornell University Press, 1990.

Ram, Harsha. "Russian Poetry and the Imperial Sublime." In *Russian Subjects: Empire, Nation, and the Culture of the Golden Age,* ed. Monika Greenleaf and Stephen Moeller-Sally, pp. 21–49. Evanston, Ill.: Northwestern University Press, 1998.

Rancière, Jacques. "The Aesthetic Revolution and Its Outcomes: Emplotments of Autonomy and Heteronomy." *New Left Review,* second series, 14 (March–April 2002): 133–51.

———. *La Chair des Mots: Politique de l'écriture.* Paris: Galilée, 1998.

———. *The Ignorant Schoolmaster: Five Lessons in Intellectual Emancipation.* Trans. and intro. Kristin Ross. Stanford: Stanford University Press, 1991.

———. *The Nights of Labor: The Worker's Dream in Nineteenth-Century France.* Trans. John Drury. Intro. Donald Read. Philadelphia: Temple University Press, 1989.

———. *Le Partage du Sensible: Esthétique et Politique.* Paris: La Fabrique, 2000.

Readings, Bill. *The University in Ruins.* Cambridge, Mass.: Harvard University Press, 1996.

Reeve, F. D. *Aleksandr Blok: Between Image and Idea.* New York: Columbia University Press, 1962.

Reitzenstein, Richard. *Epigramm und Skolion: Ein Beitrag zur Geschichte der Alexandrinischen Dichtung.* Hildesheim: G. Olms, 1970.

Ricken, Ulrich. *Leibniz, Wolff und Einige Sprachtheoretische Entwicklungen in der Deutschen Aufklärung.* Berlin: Akademie-Verlag, 1989.

Rieder, John. "Shelley's 'Mont Blanc': Landscape and the Ideology of the Sacred Text." *English Literary History* 48 (1981): 778–98.

Ronen, Omry. *An Approach to Mandelstam.* Jerusalem: Magnes Press of Hebrew University, 1983.

———. "K siuzhetu 'Stikhov o neizvestnom soldate.'" In *Slovo i sud'ba: Osip Mandel'shtam,* ed. Z. S. Papernyi, pp. 428–36. Moscow: Nauka, 1991.

Ross, Kristin. *The Emergence of Social Space: Rimbaud and the Paris Commune.* Intro. Terry Eagleton. Minneapolis: University of Minnesota Press, 1988.

Rosshoff, Hartmut. *Emil Lask als Lehrer von Georg Lukács.* Bonn: Bouvier Verlag Herbert Grundmann, 1975.

Rousseau, Jean-Jacques. *La Nouvelle Héloïse.* Trans. Judith H. McDowell. University Park: Pennsylvania State University Press, 1968.

Sartre, Jean-Paul. *Baudelaire.* Trans. Martin Turnell. New York: New Directions, 1950.

———. *Critique of Dialectical Reason.* Trans. Alan Sheridan-Smith. London: New Left Books, 1976.

———. *Search for a Method.* Trans. and intro. Hazel E. Barnes. New York: Vintage, 1963.

Schelling, F. W. J. "Konstruktion der einzelnen Dichtarten." In *Lyriktheorie: Texte vom Barock bis zur Gegenwart,* ed. Ludwig Völker, pp. 155–57. Stuttgart: Reclam, 1990.

Schiller, Friedrich. *Gedichte.* Ed. Gerhard Fricke. Stuttgart: Reclam, 1980.

———. *On the Aesthetic Education of Man in a Series of Letters.* Ed., trans., and intro. Elizabeth M. Wilkinson and L. A. Willoughby. Oxford: Clarendon, 1967.

———. "Über Bürgers Gedichte." In *Lyriktheorie: Texte vom Barock bis zur Gegenwart,* ed. Ludwig Völker, pp. 114–18. Stuttgart: Reclam, 1990.

Schorske, Carl E. "The Idea of the City in European Thought: Voltaire to Spengler." In *The Historian and the City,* ed. Oscar Handlin and John Burchard, pp. 95–114. Boston: MIT Press, 1963.

Schleiermacher, F. D. E. *Hermeneutik und Kritik.* Ed. Manfred Frank. Frankfurt: Suhrkamp, 1977.

Scodel, Joshua. *The English Poetic Epitaph: Commemoration and Conflict from Jonson to Wordsworth.* Ithaca: Cornell University Press, 1991.

Scribner, Sylvia, and Michael Cole. *The Psychology of Literacy.* Cambridge, Mass.: Harvard University Press, 1981.

Semenko, I. M. *Poetika pozdnego Mandel'shtama.* Ed. S. Vasilenko. Intro. L. Ginzburg. Moscow: Mandel'shamovskoe obshchestvo, 1997.

Semevskii, V. I. *Krest'ianskii vopros v Rossii v XVIII i pervoi polovine XIX veka.* Vol. 2. St. Petersburg: Obshchestvennaia pol'za, 1888.

Sewell, William H., Jr. *A Rhetoric of Bourgeois Revolution: The Abbé Sieyès and "What Is the Third Estate?"* Durham: University of North Carolina Press, 1994.

———. *Work and Revolution in France: The Language of Labor from the Old Regime to 1848.* Cambridge: Cambridge University Press, 1980.

Shakespeare, William. *The Riverside Shakespeare.* Ed. G. Blakemore Evans et al. Boston: Houghton Mifflin, 1974.

Shelley, Mary. *Frankenstein; or, The Modern Prometheus.* Intro. Harold Bloom. New York: Signet, 1965.

Shelley, Percy Bysshe. *Shelley's Poetry and Prose.* Ed. Donald H. Reiman and Sharon B. Powers. New York: W. W. Norton, 1977.

Shteinberg, Arkadii. "Mogila neizvestnogo soldata." *Molodaia gvardiia* 8 (August 1933): 62.

Simmel, Georg. *Aufsätze und Abhandlungen 1901–1908.* Ed. Otthein Rammstedt et al. Frankfurt am Main: Suhrkamp, 1993.

———. *On Individuality and Social Forms.* Trans. and intro. Donald N. Levine. Chicago: University of Chicago Press, 1971.

Simpson, David. *The Academic Postmodern and the Rule of Literature: A Report on Half-Knowledge.* Chicago: University of Chicago Press, 1995.

———. *Wordsworth's Historical Imagination: The Poetry of Displacement.* New York: Methuen, 1987.

Slezkine, Yuri. "The USSR as a Communal Apartment; or, How a Socialist State Promoted Ethnic Particularism." In *Becoming National: A Reader,* ed. Geoff Eley and Ronald Grigor Suny, pp. 203–38. New York and Oxford: Oxford University Press, 1996.

Smith, Adam. *An Inquiry into the Nature and Causes of the Wealth of Nations.* Ed. R. H. Campbell and A. S. Skinner. 2 vols. Oxford: Clarendon, 1976.

Sohn-Rethel, Alfred. *Intellectual and Manual Labour: A Critique of Epistemology.* London: Macmillan, 1978.

Spengler, Oswald. *The Decline of the West.* Ed. Helmut Werner and Arthur Helps. Trans. Charles Francis Atkinson. New York: Oxford University Press, 1991.

Stallybrass, Peter, and Allon White. *The Politics and Poetics of Transgression.* Ithaca: Cornell University Press, 1986.

Starr, S. Frederick. "The Revival and Schism of Urban Planning in Twentieth-Century Russia." In *The City in Russian History,* ed. Michael F. Hamm, pp. 230–40. Lexington: University of Kentucky Press, 1976.

Stearns, Peter N. *The Revolutions of 1848.* London: Weidenfeld and Nicolson, 1974.

Steiner, Peter. "Poem as Manifesto: Mandel'shtam's 'Notre Dame.'" *Russian Literature* 3 (July 1977): 239–56.

Stevenson, Anne. *Elizabeth Bishop.* New Haven: Twayne, 1966.

Stewart, Garrett. *Between Film and Screen: Modernism's Photo Synthesis.* Chicago: University of Chicago Press, 1999.

———. *Reading Voices: Literature and the Phonotext.* Berkeley: University of California Press, 1990.

Stewart, Susan. *On Longing: Narratives of the Miniature, the Gigantic, the Souvenir, the Collection.* Durham: Duke University Press, 1993.

Stites, Richard. *Revolutionary Dreams: Utopian Vision and Experimental Life in the Russian Revolution.* New York: Oxford University Press, 1989.

Storey, Mark, ed. *Clare: The Critical Heritage.* London: Routledge and Kegan Paul, 1973.

Taylor, Frederick Winslow. *The Principles of Scientific Management.* New York: W. W. Norton, 1967.

Therborn, Göran. *The Ideology of Power and the Power of Ideology.* London: Verso, 1999.

Thomson, James. *The Complete Poetical Works of James Thomson.* Ed. J. Logie Robertson. London: Henry Frowde for Oxford University Press, 1908.

Trimpi, Wesley. *Ben Jonson's Poems: A Study of the Plain Style.* Stanford: Stanford University Press, 1962.

Trotsky, Leon. *Literature and Revolution.* Trans. Rose Strunsky. Ann Arbor: University of Michigan Press, 1960.

Trumpener, Katie. *Bardic Nationalism: The Romantic Novel and the British Empire.* Princeton, N.J.: Princeton University Press, 1997.

Vardy, Alan D. *John Clare, Politics and Poetry.* Houndmills and New York: Palgrave Macmillan, 2003.

Vinogradov, V. V. *Izbrannye trudy: Leksikologiia i leksikografiia.* Moscow: Nauka, 1977.

Völker, Ludwig, ed. *Lyriktheorie: Texte vom Barock bis zur Gegenwart.* Stuttgart: Reclam, 1990.

Vroon, Ronald. "Staroobriadchestvo, sektanstvo i 'sakral'naia rech" v poezii Nikolaia Kliueva." In *Nikolai Kliuev: Issledovaniia i materialy,* ed. S. I. Subbotin, pp. 54–67. Moscow: Nasledie, 1997.

Wachtel, Andrew. "Translation, Imperialism, and National Self-Definition in Russia." In *Alternative Modernities,* ed. Dilip Parameshwar Gaonkar, pp. 58–85. Durham: Duke University Press, 2001.

Wanner, Adrian. *Baudelaire in Russia.* Gainesville: University Press of Florida, 1996.

Wasserman, Earl R. *Shelley: A Critical Reading.* Baltimore: Johns Hopkins University Press, 1971.

White, Rev. Gilbert, A.M. *The Natural History of Selborne, Observations on Various Parts of Nature; and The Naturalist's Calendar.* 3rd ed. Edinburgh: Fraser, 1834.

Wicke, Jennifer. *Advertising Fictions: Literature, Advertising, and Social Reading.* New York: Columbia University Press, 1988.

Williams, Raymond. *The Country and the City.* New York: Oxford University Press, 1973.

Winks, Christopher. "Ruins and Foundation Stones: The Paris Commune and the Destruction of the Vendôme Column." In *Revolutionary Romanticism,* ed. Max Blechman, pp. 101–24. San Francisco: City Lights Books, 1999.

Wollen, Peter. *Readings and Writings: Semiotic Counter-Strategies.* London: New Left Books, 1982.

Wordsworth, William. "Essay upon Epitaphs." In *The Prose Works of William Wordsworth*, ed. W. J. B. Owen and Jane Worthington Smyser, vol. 2, 43–119. Oxford: Clarendon, 1974.

———. *The Poems*. 2 vols. Ed. John O. Hayden. London: Penguin Books, 1977.

Zhivov, V. "Kosmologicheskie utopii v vospriatii bol'shevistskoi revoliutsii i antikosmologicheskie motivy v russkoj poezii 1920–1930-x godov ('Stikhi o neizvestnom soldate' O. Mandel'shtama)." In *Sbornik statej K 70–letiiu Prof. Iu. M. Lotmana*, ed. A. Mal'ts and V. Stolovich, pp. 411–34. Tartu: Tartu State University, 1992.

Index

John MacKay is Associate Professor of Slavic Languages and Literatures at Yale University. He is author of essays on autobiography, on the writings of Russian serfs, and on Soviet film. His book on the life and work of Dziga Vertov is forthcoming from Indiana University Press.